Strategic Planning:
Models and
Analytical Techniques

Strategic Planning: Models and Analytical Techniques

Robert G. Dyson

University of Warwick

JOHN WILEY & SONS

Chichester · New York · Brisbane · Toronto · Singapore

Copyright © 1990 by John Wiley & Sons Ltd.
      Baffins Lane, Chichester
      West Sussex PO19 1UD, England

Other Wiley Editorial Offices

John Wiley & Sons, Inc., 605 Third Avenue,
New York, NY 10158-0012, USA

Jacaranda Wiley Ltd, G.P.O. Box 859, Brisbane,
Queensland 4001, Australia

John Wiley & Sons (Canada) Ltd, 22 Worcester Road,
Rexdale, Ontario M9W 1L1, Canada

John Wiley & Sons (SEA) Pte Ltd, 37 Jalan Pemimpin 05-04,
Block B, Union Industrial Building, Singapore 2057

Library of Congress Cataloging-in-Publication Data

Strategic planning : models and analytical techniques : [articles /
   selected by] Robert G. Dyson.
        p.   cm.
      Includes bibliographical references.
      ISBN 0 471 92491 1
        1. Strategic planning.   I. Dyson, Robert G.
HD30.28.S73445   1990
658.4′012—dc20   89-37612
                                                      CIP

British Library Cataloguing in Publication Data

Dyson, R. G. (Robert Graham, *1942–*)
   Strategic planning.
   1. Organisations. Management. Long-range planning
   I. Title
   658.4′012′0724

   ISBN 0 471 92491 1

Phototypeset by Dobbie Typesetting Limited, Plymouth, Devon
Printed in Great Britain by Courier International, Tiptree, Essex

Contents

Part I

Introduction

Strategic decisions can be characterized by the extent to which they have enduring effects, are broad in scope and are difficult to reverse. Such decisions can be taken with little forethought but in most organizations are facilitated by a strategic planning process. The purpose of this book is to introduce and explore the range of models and analytical techniques which are available to support the strategic planning process.

The book starts with a model of the strategic planning process itself which identifies the essential elements of a strategic planning process and is then used as an organizing framework for the models and analytical techniques. These methods are introduced through the vehicle of published papers. Some of these papers are very recent but for some methods it is necessary and appropriate to go back to the original classic paper.

In selecting the topics to be included, a range of literature has been searched covering the general business area, strategic management and planning, and management science and operational research. This results in a unique collection of articles covering techniques ranging from simple to complex and from soft to hard.

Finally, a summary chapter indicates how the different models and techniques can support different parts of the strategic planning process.

Chapter 1

Strategic Planning

Robert Dyson
University of Warwick

The aim of this book is to consider the use of models and analytical techniques to support a strategic planning process. In this chapter, a framework for a strategic planning process is presented and the framework is used to organize topics of the book.

The strategic planning process is a management process involving consultation, negotiation, and analysis which is aimed at ensuring effective strategic decision making. Decisions in organizations can range on a spectrum from operational and tactical through to strategic. There are, of course, no sharp divisions between different categories of decisions, but strategic decisions can perhaps be characterized by the extent to which they have enduring effects, are broad in scope, and are difficult to reverse. For a motor vehicle producer a strategic decision might be to launch a new model; for a food supermarket chain to diversify into the do-it-yourself business; for a university to set up a new academic department; and for an oil producing and refining company to enter the filling station business. Such decisions may involve new business ventures related to either acquisitions or new products. They may involve an extension of the degree of vertical integration and they may involve major changes in the organization of the company. Often they will involve major capital investments.

A key part of the strategic planning process is to ensure the generation and formulation of strategic options, and because a strategic option when implemented will have enduring effects and be difficult to reverse, the planning process must be concerned with evaluating options before action is taken and be concerned with the future impact of the proposed decisions. The framework for, or conceptual model of, a strategic planning process to be used in this book starts from the idea of a simple control system as shown in Figure 1 and is based on the model presented in Tomlinson and Dyson (1983). The example used here is that of controlling the temperature of a room by means of a heat source such as hot water or warm air. This tactical system embodies the basic characteristic of a control system: there is a target to be met and a set of procedures aimed at meeting that target. This basic idea can be translated to strategic decision making and control where the target is some desirable future state or states of the organization and strategic decisions are taken aimed at guiding the organization in that direction.

The control system consists of a room and the performance measure of interest is the temperature of the room. The temperature is likely to be varying throughout the

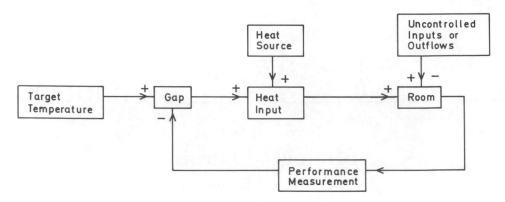

Figure 1. A simple control system

room but it is usually sufficient to record the temperature at a single point by a thermostat. The recorded temperature is the current level of performance of the system. The other level of performance of interest is the target temperature which is set exogenously to system. The temperature of the room is fed back and compared with the target temperature and the difference or gap is calculated. The gap increases for higher target temperatures and decreases for higher room temperatures. If the gap is positive the signal or command triggers the mechanism that calls on the heat source and inputs heat into the room. In addition to this controlled input the temperature will also be affected by uncontrolled factors such as heat losses through windows and doors, and through heat inputs from appliances, lights and occupants. If the gap is negative and air conditioning is installed then the inflow will be of cool air. The aggregate of the uncontrolled inputs may either increase or decrease the room temperature. The loop linking the room temperature back for comparison with the target is known as a feedback loop.

For such a system to work effectively it must have the following attributes:

– a target or standard;
– a measurement task;
– a feedback signal;
– a control procedure;
– an adequate resource source;
– a corrective action.

In this example the target is a target temperature which can be set exogenously to the system. The measurement task is carried out by a thermostat. The feedback signal is the electronic mechanism for transmitting the readings of the thermostat. The control procedure is a mechanism which compares the current temperature with the target temperature, calculates the gap and then transmits a command for corrective action. The resource is the heat source and the corrective action is the mechanism that inputs the heat into the room.

The temperature of a room can be controlled provided that all the listed attributes are present. If any one is missing then the system will fail. This is a good example of a tactical control system where action is taken only after the current performance is compared with the target. This is usually an adequate procedure as the consequences of missing the target are not usually too great, and any deviations can be corrected quickly.

A MODEL OF THE STRATEGIC DECISION MAKING PROCESS

If the same model is applied to the strategic decision making process of an organization the result is as shown in Figure 2. The organization requires a set of objectives against which the current performance can be compared through the procedure of gap analysis. If the gap is too great strategic options are formulated and appropriate ones selected. These must then be implemented thus affecting the state of organization. The implications of this model would be that only the current performance of the system is assessed, and if this is not satisfactory when compared to the current objectives then a strategic decision is taken. This model of decision making is inadequate because strategic decisions take time to affect the performance of an organization and by then a commercial organization may have gone into liquidation or a public sector organization into disrepute. Because of this time lag, and the potential severe consequences of deviating from the objectives, a reactive strategic decision making process is inadequate. Thus a strategic decision making process should measure not just the present performance, but also must predict possible future performances and take anticipatory action. It must be pro-active.

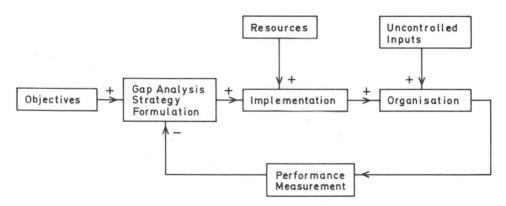

Figure 2. A reactive strategic decision making process

A pro-active strategic decision making process involves predicting possible future states of the organization, assessing the acceptability of these, formulating strategic options, and evaluating them through feasibility studies and an assessment of their impact on the future states of the organization. In short a strategic *planning* process is required. Figure 3 elaborates Figures 1 and 2 to accommodate strategic planning. The outer loop of the diagram is essentially the same as Figure 2 including an objective setting process, gap analysis and selection of strategies, the implementation process which calls on the necessary resources, the organization itself and the uncontrolled inputs, and a feedback loop which feeds back the current performance for comparison with the objectives.

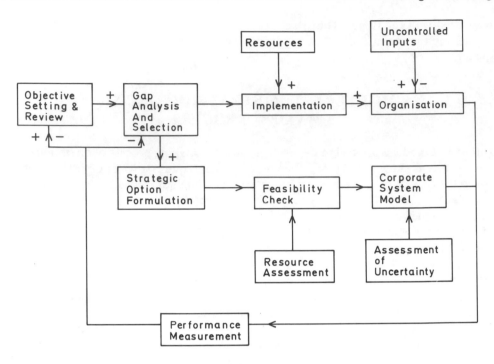

Figure 3. A pro-active decision making process

The model also includes a forward loop which involves strategic option formulation, feasibility study, resource assessment, a system model for predicting future states of the organization, and assessment of the uncontrolled inputs. The output from this forward loop, the prediction of future states of the organization, is also fed back and compared with objectives which of course must be objectives for the future. A system model of some kind, to predict future states of the organization, is essential as it is not possible to try out a range of strategies on the existing organization and see whether or not they work. Additionally, the organization itself will be changing due to previous strategic decisions irrespective of whether new strategies are adopted. Indeed, even if no previous strategies are having an impact and none has been adopted, the performance of the organization will still be changing due to changes in the uncontrolled inputs. These uncontrolled inputs include competitor actions, changes in exchange rates and the economic environment generally, customer preferences, and so on.

The form of the diagram suggests a highly systematic procedure, but this is not in reality the case. Some of the arrows are indeed representing a systematic input of resources or information, such as the arrow feeding the assessment of uncontrolled inputs into the system model. However, the arrow linking gap analysis and selection with strategic option formulation may be thought of more as an arrow in an influence diagram. Strategic option formulation may well go on irrespective of the extent to which an organization is on course to achieve its future objectives. However, this process will be influenced by any gap that is perceived, so that an organization which is clearly going off course is likely to set up new mechanisms to stimulate the search for additional strategies.

ELEMENTS OF THE STRATEGIC DECISION
MAKING PROCESS

The strategic decision making process as conceptualized in Figure 3 is considerably more complex than a tactical system as shown in Figure 1. This complexity is due both to the increase in the number of elements in the system and to the complexity of the elements. The tactical and strategic systems however do have one thing in common. For either of them to work effectively *every element must be present and working effectively*. For the strategic decision making process the following elements can be identified from Figure 3:

1. Objective setting and review.
2. Strategic option formulation.
3. Feasibility check.
4. Resource assessment.
5. Assessment of uncertainty.
6. Corporate system model.
7. Performance measurement.
8. Feedback signal.
9. Gap analysis and selection.
10. Implementation process.
11. Resources.

The first nine constitute the strategic planning process while the latter two are necessary to implement strategies. Although the implementation process here is separated from planning this is only in the final aspects of implementation. Much of the planning process itself is of course aimed at implementation. For example, feasibility studies and assessments of required resources are carried out to make implementation feasible. The planning process of most organizations will also include extensive consultation and negotiation to facilitate implementation. The recognition of planning as a political process is essential for the successful implementation of strategic decisions. The elements of the strategic decision making process listed above are also essential but may not necessarily be sufficient. The concern of this book, however, is with how models and analytical methods can best be deployed for effective strategic decision making by supporting the essential elements of the process. For an alternative set of elements or attributes of the strategic planning process see Dyson and Foster (1980, 1983).

The task of *setting and reviewing objectives* is of course an essential part of the strategic planning process. Future objectives are required and these are likely to involve financial objectives leading to financial performance targets, but may also include non-financial objectives such as technological leadership, service or quality objectives, and objectives associated with social responsibility and the ethos of the organization. The scope for modelling and analytical methods may be limited in this element of the planning process.

Gap analysis and selection involves comparing future possible states of the organization with the objectives and deciding whether existing strategies are acceptable or whether new strategies should be implemented. This element of the process will involve the calculation of financial measures through capital investment appraisal. It may also involve setting up matrices of options and consequences across a range of objectives. Assessment of the robustness or sensitivity of strategies to the uncertainty of the environment is also required. Models and analytical techniques have a key role to play in this part of the process and several papers are included in the book.

Successful organizations require a constant flow of *strategic options* so that the organization can adapt and change and a variety of techniques are available to aid this process. Situational analysis involving appraisals of the strengths and weaknesses of the organization, and threats and opportunities presented in the environment is a common form of analysis which can lead to new strategies being developed. Product portfolio techniques can aid organizations in assessing which businesses or parts of businesses should be supported. Statistical models relating return on investment with market share, quality, research and development and other factors may indicate appropriate strategies. Finally, conceptual models of the organization using cognitive maps or influence diagrams may support the strategic option formulation process. Clearly there is much scope in this part of the process for models and analytical techniques and again several papers are included in the book.

The *feasibility* of any proposed option must be thoroughly checked. For example, options requiring new facilities may require planning permission, and products requiring new processes may require development of new technology. There is perhaps little scope here for modelling so although this is an important element of the planning process it will not be focused on in the book.

New strategies typically involve *resources* such as finance, manpower, raw materials, and so on. The corporate system model of the organization, discussed later, will assess these requirements. Sometimes particular resource models such as manpower planning models are required but such specialist models are not included in this book.

The *assessment of uncertainty* associated with uncontrolled inputs to the organization is a key part of the strategic planning process. Consumer response, competitive reaction, exchange rates, cultural changes, economic trends, and so on can have a major impact on the future state of the organization but they are not under direct control and their future impact can be highly uncertain. The assessment of these factors may be attempted through risk analysis where uncertainty is modelled by probability density functions, and by cross-impact analysis where the effects of levels of one variable on another are assessed, but perhaps the current most effective and practical way of describing this phenomenon is through the use of scenarios. A number of papers and in particular two on scenarios are included.

In order to evaluate possible future states of the organization, which is the result of adopted strategies and the impact on the organization of uncontrolled inputs, some kind of *corporate system model* of the organization is required. Most organizations will use a corporate financial model to provide financial projections, and more broadly based corporate planning models may also be used. These models typically involve accounting relationships and rudimentary attempts at modelling the behaviour of the organization. In recent years there has been a growing interest in the development of behavioural simulation models using ideas of system dynamics. This is a part of the strategic planning process where models have an enormous potential to improve the effectiveness of planning where perhaps the potential has by no means been fully realized. Readings on the various aspects of corporate system modelling are included in the book.

Strategic information systems which record, store and *feed back* information in an appropriate manner are, of course, a key part of a successful strategic planning process but they are not a central concern of this book and readings have not been included.

Although all the elements of the process listed are essential for the process to be effective, many of the available models and analytical techniques may contribute to more than one element. For example, a corporate model whose basic purpose is evaluation may well through its use contribute to strategy formulation although a model aimed at formulation is likely to be much less detailed than one focusing on evaluation. Similarly, techniques of scenario development again have much in common with the situational analysis carried out as part of strategic option formulation. Also, although few techniques are aimed at objective setting, the use of models and techniques to aid in strategy formulation and evaluation may well call into question the existing objectives or suggest new ones.

The remainder of the book has been structured by groupings based on the list of essential elements of the strategic planning process. The groupings chosen are objective setting and review (element 1); strategic option formulation (element 2); assessment of uncertainty (element 5); corporate modelling (element 6); and finally performance measurement, gap analysis and selection (elements 7 and 9). The readings under these headings are introduced in the following parts. As described earlier in the chapter, many models and techniques can contribute to more than one element of the planning process. Each reading has been placed in the group where it seems to have the greatest impact on the planning process, but its impact on other parts of the process is also recognized.

OBJECTIVE SETTING AND REVIEW

A key part of the strategic planning process involves setting and reviewing objectives. This involves having overall mission statements for the organization and more specific objectives and goals, cascading down to specific quantitative and qualitative targets.

Objectives and goals need to be clearly stated if strategic options are going to be evaluated in any meaningful way. They also need to be reviewed as changes in the external environment, or the organization's own capability, may make objectives inappropriate. A major challenge facing organizations is reconciling the overall mission with objectives and goals for individuals and individual parts. Models and analytical procedures have so far had relatively little impact on this aspect of strategic planning, and in recognition of this no papers are included under this heading. However, the use of cognitive maps is a potential analytical tool here so the paper by Colin Eden, although appearing under Strategic Option Formulation (Part II) has relevance. Also, for organizations with many stakeholders, the paper by Michael Poulton, which appears in Part V, is relevant in that it illustrates how different interest groups may hold different competing objectives. The paper by Heinz Weihrich appearing in Part II can also contribute here by identifying relevant factors which may lead to the formulation of objectives. A recent paper by Molz (1987) discusses the objective setting process.

STRATEGIC OPTION FORMULATION

It might be thought that at first sight the formulation of strategic options is not an arena for the application of models or analytical techniques. The generation of ideas and options is surely an inspirational or creative process and individuals may generate options at any time under any circumstances, possibly while taking a leisurely bath. Alternatively, formal brainstorming sessions might be set up and such *ad hoc* processes may well be sufficient.

There is considerable evidence, however, that generating an adequate flow of options is by no means straightforward, particularly in large organizations. This was certainly a concern of the Shell Company some years ago, and appears to be true for GEC in the United Kingdom who do not seem to be able to find adequate use for large amounts of cash. In recent years a number of relevant models and analytical methods have been developed to ensure a sufficient flow of strategic options. A systematic structuring method involving an internal appraisal of the strengths and weaknesses of the organization, and an external appraisal aimed at identifying threats and opportunities in the environment is a well-established procedure, sometimes known as the TOWS matrix or SWOT analysis. The idea here is that carrying out the procedure can lead to ideas for strategies which may eliminate weaknesses, build on strengths, counter threats, and take advantage of opportunities. The paper by Weihrich gives an excellent exposition of this analytical tool. The TOWS matrix also contributes to performance measurement and objective setting through identifying factors of interest.

A simple analytical method, the experience curve, has proved valuable in supporting strategic option formulation. The basic lesson from the experience curve is that competitive advantage can be obtained by increasing the volume of production. The article by Arnoldo Hax and Nicholas Majluf (Chapter 3), one of three included in the book, excellently documents the analytical tool while also discussing the pitfalls arising from its use.

For large organizations having a portfolio of businesses, the technique perhaps having the greatest impact on strategy formulation in the 1970s was the Boston Consulting Group's growth–share matrix. This technique categorizes the businesses and helps identify where investments should be made and where profits should be taken or divestments made. This is the subject of a second paper by Hax and Majluf. Their third paper is concerned with the industry attractiveness–business strength matrix developed by General Electric which is an extension of the growth–share matrix. These approaches also make a rudimentary contribution to performance measurement, by identifying key measures such as market share.

Another approach of the 1970s is the PIMS study, which consists of a databank on business and a model which relates return on investment to various factors such as market share, quality, investment in R&D, and so on. This approach essentially compares a business unit with other similar units and can give indications as to what strategic variables should be changed to improve performance. This approach is documented in the paper by Sidney Schoeffler, Robert Buzzell and Donald Heany (Chapter 6). A critical appraisal of it appears in the paper by Anderson and Paine (1978). The approach clearly is an aid to strategic option formulation but can also aid in performance measurement and control and arguably could underpin the complete planning process in its own right.

More general approaches to modelling or structuring an organization in its environment can be a significant benefit to the option formulation process. In recent years models based mainly on concepts and their inter-relationships have been developed and may be generally termed 'qualitative models'. Such models include cognitive maps, and the influence diagrams of system dynamics. In Part II of the book the paper by Eden illustrates the use of cognitive maps to support the strategic option formulation process. Other models which may also be valuable in formulation have been included under

Corporate Modelling (Part IV), as they emphasize some of the detail necessary for the evaluation of the strategic options. The inclusion of cognitive mapping in Part II and other methods in Part IV, Corporate Modelling, is a matter of emphasis rather than a dichotomy between formulation and evaluation.

ASSESSMENT OF UNCERTAINTY

With strategic decisions having enduring effects and being difficult to reverse, a key issue in strategic planning and decision making is the uncertainty of the future. Organizations operate in an economic, political and social environment and aspects of this environment affect the performance of the organization, but the future state of the environment cannot be known when key decisions have to be taken.

For a major exporting company future values of the exchange rates will be the key factor influencing future profitability. For a tobacco company the social acceptance of smoking will be the driving cultural consideration. For a private service company providing catering, governmental views on whether catering in the National Health Service should be a public or private matter is crucial. For a components supplier in the automobile industry, the future health of the automobile manufacturing industry is a major concern.

The traditional way to assess uncertainties about the future was through the use of forecasting. The forecasting approach to planning would involve attempting to predict the future values of uncertain variables and then take decisions based on this most likely future. This is an approach that may have worked satisfactorily during the 1950s and 1960s but has proved to be of little value in the more turbulent 1970s and 1980s. The fault of the approach does not lie with the professional forecasters who, of course, embody uncertainty in their forecasts. The problem lies with the use of these forecasts where all but the most likely values of the forecast tend to be dissipated in the planning process so that the uncertainty disappears.

One of the first attempts to recognize this problem and relate uncertainty in the environment to decision making in an apt way was due to David Hertz in the 1960s. His concern was with capital investment decisions and strategic decisions often, if not invariably, involve large-scale capital investment. In a paper originally published in 1964 in *Harvard Business Review* and reprinted as a classic in 1979, Hertz proposed the use of risk analysis. This involves the explicit recognition of uncertainty and its modelling by probability density functions. The original paper by Hertz appears in the readings (Chapter 8). It could be reasonably argued by forecasters that the idea of modelling uncertainty by probability density functions is no more than what a professional forecaster would do. The importance of Hertz's work, however, is that the totality of uncertainty remained at the front of his approach whereas even today forecasts of the economic environment are still often presented as single shot views of the future. Risk analysis did not, however, resolve the problem of how to handle uncertainty in the strategic planning process. This was almost certainly because of the complexity associated with handling probability density functions, and the difficulty of presenting ideas about the future in those terms to senior management.

An alternative approach which has gained popularity in the 1970s and 1980s is the use of multiple scenarios to describe the future. The paper by Robert Linneman and

John Kennell (Chapter 9) presents a good prescription of how to build scenarios, while the paper by Steven Schnaars (Chapter 10) reviews the various approaches to scenario development. This paper also outlines the method of cross-impact analysis which attempts to assess the likely impact of the outcome of one uncertain variable on another. This method is also illustrated by Goldfarb and Huss (1988).

Scenarios have been widely used within the Royal Dutch Shell Company to support strategic planning and papers by Beck (1982) and Wack (1985a, 1985b) described the development of scenario planning. Scenarios can be used to model competitive behaviour but an alternative approach using catastrophe theory has been proposed by Olivia, Day, and MacMillan (1988).

In addition to assessing uncertainty the development of scenarios can also lead to the formulation of new strategies.

Although scenarios are at the fore of describing uncertainty with perhaps forecasting being in disrepute for strategic planning, it is merely the idea of a single forecast of the future that is inadequate. The model building technique of forecasters will be equally relevant to the production of scenarios as to the production of single line forecasts.

CORPORATE MODELLING

The requirement for a corporate model in strategic planning is in principle no different to the requirement for a model in any field of enquiry or decision. The purpose of the model is to act as a test-bed so that proposals for change can be tested and evaluated without imposing them on the real world. The history of corporate modelling goes back to the 1960s when a limited number of companies developed corporate simulation models, typically in the FORTRAN programming language. These were often cumbersome and ineffective.

The early models often had a very heavy financial orientation consisting mainly of accounting relationships. The paper by Thomas Naylor (Chapter 11) gives an account of the state of corporate simulation models in the early 1970s and also includes a conceptual framework for corporate modelling. This framework classifies the equations of corporate models into definitional relationships and behavioural relationships. Definitional relationships are mathematical or accounting definitions while behavioural relationships are hypotheses or theories which help to describe the behaviour of the organization.

From this dichotomy two streams of development of corporate modelling can be traced which are different in emphasis rather than in kind. One stream relies heavily on definitional relationships and has a financial orientation. There is evidence for this emphasis in the Naylor paper and modelling tools of this stream include spreadsheets and financial modelling systems. The development of this stream has been updated in a paper by Shim and McGlade (1984).

The second stream is concerned with models consisting mainly of behavioural relationships and the models in this stream may be termed behavioural simulation models. They differ both in the pre-eminence of behavioural relationships over definitional relationships, and in the computer tools. Behavioural simulation models are typically developed using system dynamics software. The paper by Roger Hall and William Menzies (Chapter 12) is one of the best illustrations of corporate behavioural simulation models, and the paper by John Morecroft (Chapter 13) discusses the role of such models for strategy support, and in particular for deducing the consequences of particular strategic proposals. Morecroft (1988) includes a more detailed review of system dynamics.

The difference between corporate financial models and behavioural models is one of emphasis, and perhaps so is the difference between the behavioural models of system dynamics and cognitive mapping as illustrated by Eden. Here the difference in emphasis is that cognitive mapping is seen primarily as supporting strategy formulation, while the use of behavioural simulation models puts a greater emphasis on consequence evaluation and performance measurement.

PERFORMANCE MEASUREMENT, GAP ANALYSIS AND SELECTION

The objectives of an organization should be supported by a set of quantitative and qualitative performance targets for both the near and the more distant future. These targets are necessary for deciding whether the organization is heading in the correct direction, and for deciding whether new strategies will be appropriate in the light of the targets. The targets themselves may depend to some extent on future states of the environment, and the projected performance of the organization under those future states is assessed through the use of the corporate modelling mechanism. The difference between the targets and the projected performance is known as the gap, and assessing this gap is known as gap analysis.

In commercial organizations financial performance measures and targets feature prominently, sometimes exclusively, and the financial appraisal of strategic options is a necessary part of the strategic planning process. The paper by Robert Dyson and Robert Berry (Chapter 14) reviews capital investment appraisal and includes material both from a manager's viewpoint as to what is an acceptable investment, and the shareholders' viewpoint through the capital asset pricing model. This latter topic is illustrated in a paper by Harrington (1983).

There have been concerns that orthodox capital investment appraisal mitigates against the adoption of strategies involving new technology, and this issue is addressed in the paper by Robert Ashford, Dyson, and Stewart Hodges (Chapter 15).

Given the uncertainty of the future it is often argued that it is important to adopt flexible strategies that can be adapted to changing circumstances. An analytical approach to this problem is robustness analysis and this is presented and its methodology discussed in the paper by Jonathan Rosenhead, Martin Elton, and Shiv Gupta (Chapter 16). The approach is updated by Rosenhead (1980) and Best, Parston and Rosenhead (1986).

The stakeholder view of organizations would argue that there are multiple interest groups with conflicting objectives and this issue needs to be formally addressed in planning. This aspect of planning is perhaps most to the fore in the public sector and the paper by Poulton (Chapter 17) has been included which squarely addresses the problem.

Finally, an analytical method developed by Thomas Saaty, known as the analytic hierarchy process, has been proposed as a way of assessing alternative courses of actions under a wide variety of situations. The method attempts to prioritize options taking account of the various scenarios, objectives and actors involved. The application of this approach to strategic planning has been documented in the paper by Jim Emshoff and Saaty (Chapter 18).

Although there appears to be a wide variety of approaches to performance assessment leading to the selection of strategic options, in fact they are mainly not incompatible. For example, the multiple interest group approach as illustrated by Poulton certainly does not exclude financial appraisal. In robustness analysis, and the analytical hierarchy process, financial measures can certainly be included, but the final measures of robustness scores and priorities of options can obscure the financial measures.

REFERENCES

Anderson, C. R., and Paine, E. T. (1978). PIMS: A re-examination, *Academy of Management Review*, **7**, 602–612.

Beck, P. W. (1982). Corporate planning for an uncertain future, *Long Range Planning*, **15**(4), 12–21.

Best, G., Parston, G., and Rosenhead, J. V. (1986). Robustness in practice—the regional planning of health services, *Journal of the Operational Research Society*, **37**, 463–478.

Dyson, R. G., and Foster, M. J. (1980). Effectiveness in strategic planning, *European Journal of Operational Research*, **5**(3), 163–170.

Dyson, R. G., and Foster, M. J. (1983). Effectiveness in strategic planning revisited, *European Journal of Operational Research*, **12**, 146–158.

Goldfarb, D. L., and Huss, W. R. (1988). Building scenarios for an electric utility, *Long Range Planning*, **21**(2), 78–85.

Harrington, D. R. (1983). Stock prices, beta, and strategic planning, *Harvard Business Review*, **61**(3), 157–165.

Molz, R. (1987). How leaders use goals, *Long Range Planning*, **20**(5), 91–101.

Morecroft, J. D. W. (1988). System dynamics and microworlds for policy makers, *European Journal of Operational Research*, **35**, 301–320.

Olivia, T. A., Day, D. L., and MacMillan, I. C. (1988). A generic model of competitive dynamics, *Academy of Management Review*, **13**, 374–389.

Rosenhead, J. V. (1980). Planning and uncertainty: II A methodology for robustness analysis, *Journal of the Operational Research Society*, **31**, 331–341.

Shim, J. K. and McGlade, R. (1984). The use of corporate planning models: past, present and future, *Journal of the Operational Research Society*, **35**, 885–894.

Tomlinson, R. C. and Dyson, R. G. (1983). Some systems aspects of strategic planning, *Journal of the Operational Research Society*, **34**, 765–778.

Wack, P. (1985a). Scenarios: shooting the rapids, *Harvard Business Review*, November–December, 139–150.

Wack, P. (1985b). Scenarios: unchartered waters ahead, *Harvard Business Review*, September–October, 73–89.

_____ Part II

Strategic Option Formulation

Chapter 2

The TOWS Matrix:
A Tool for Situational Analysis

Heinz Weihrich
Professor of Management, University of San Francisco

This article has two main purposes. One is to review general considerations in strategic planning and the second to introduce the TOWS Matrix for matching the environmental threats and opportunities with the company's weaknesses and especially its strengths. These factors *per se* are not new; what is new is systematically identifying relationships between these factors and basing strategies on them. There is little doubt that strategic planning will gain greater prominence in the future. Any organization — whether military, product-oriented, service-oriented or even governmental — to remain effective, must use a rational approach toward anticipating, responding to and even altering the future environment.

SITUATIONAL ANALYSIS: A NEW DIMENSION IN STRATEGIC PLANNING

Today most business enterprises engage in strategic planning, although the degrees of sophistication and formality vary considerably. Conceptually strategic planning is deceptively simple: analyze the current and expected future situation, determine the direction of the firm and develop means for achieving the mission. In reality, this is an extremely complex process which demands a systematic approach for identifying and analyzing factors external to the organization and matching them with the firm's capabilities.

The purpose of this article is twofold: first, the concept of strategy and a model showing the strategic process are introduced. This part not only provides an overview of strategic planning, but also alerts the reader to the various alternatives available for formulating a strategy. The second purpose of the article is to propose a conceptual framework for identifying and analyzing the threats (T) and opportunities (O) in the external environment and assessing the organization's weaknesses (W) and strengths (S). For convenience, the matrix that will be introduced is called TOWS, or situational analysis. Although the sets of variables in the matrix are not new, matching them in a systematic fashion is. Many writers on strategic planning suggest that a firm uses its strengths to take advantage of opportunities, but they ignore other important relationships, such as the challenge of overcoming weaknesses in the enterprise to exploit opportunities. After all, a weakness is the absence of strength and corporate development to overcome an existing weakness may become a distinct strategy for the company. Although efforts are now being made to gain greater insights into the way corporate strengths and weaknesses are defined, much remains to be done.[1]

The TOWS matrix, discussed later in detail, also serves as a conceptual framework for future research about the combination of external factors and those internal to the enterprise, and the strategies based on these variables. Equally important, the matrix 'forces' practicing managers to analyze the situation of their company and to develop strategies, tactics, and actions for the effective and efficient attainment of its organizational objectives and its mission.

STRATEGIC PLANNING

The term 'strategy' (which is derived from the Greek word 'strategos', meaning 'general') has been used in different ways. Authors differ in at least one major aspect. Some, such as Kenneth Andrews,[2] Alfred D. Chandler,[3] George A. Steiner/John B. Miner,[4] and Richard Vancil,[5] focus on both the end points (purpose, mission, goals, objectives) and the means of achieving them (policies and plans). But other writers such as Igor H. Ansoff[6] and Charles W. Hofer/Dan Schendel[7] emphasize the means to the ends in the strategic process rather than the ends *per se*. The great variety of meanings of the word 'strategies' is illustrated in the glossary of one book:

> [Strategies are] general programs of action and deployment of emphasis and resources to attain comprehensive objectives; the program of objectives of an organization and their changes, resources used to attain these objectives, and policies governing the acquisition, use, and disposition of these resources; the determination of the basic long-term objectives of an enterprise and the adoption of courses of action and allocation of resources necessary to achieve these goals.[8]

In this article, primarily because of space limitations, the narrow meaning will be used, that is, the ends will not be emphasized so that sufficient attention can be given to the analysis of the current situation. It is asumed that the purpose of the firm has already been established, yet is subject to change after an evaluation of the situation.

Although specific steps in the formulation of the strategy may vary, the process can be built, at least conceptually, around the following framework:

(1) Recognition of the various organizational inputs, especially the goal inputs of the claimants to the enterprise.
(2) Preparation of the enterprise profile.
(3) Identification of the present external environment.
(4) Preparation of a forecast with predictions of the future environment.

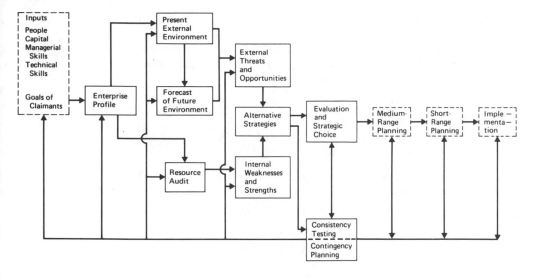

Figure 1. Strategic planning process

(5) Preparation of a resource audit with emphasis on the company's internal weaknesses and strengths.
(6) Development of alternative strategies, tactics and other actions.
(7) Evaluation and choice of strategies.
(8) Consistency testing.
(9) Preparation of contingency plans.

These steps—shown in Figure 1—then, serve as the framework for the discussion that follows.

Inputs for Strategic Planning

Strategic planning, to be effective, must carefully consider the inputs into the system. These inputs, de-emphasized in this discussion, are enclosed by broken lines, as shown in Figure 1. They include people, capital, managerial and technical knowledge and skills. In addition, various groups of people make demands on the enterprise. Unfortunately, many of the goals of these claimants are incongruent with each other and it is the manager's task to integrate these divergent needs and goals.

Employees, for example, want higher pay, more benefits and job security. *Consumers* demand safe and reliable products at a reasonable price. *Suppliers* want assurance that their products are purchased. *Stockholders* want not only a high return on their investment but also security of their money. Federal, state and local *governments* depend on taxes paid by the enterprise; they also expect the enterprise to comply with their laws. Similarly, the *community* demands that enterprises be 'good citizens', providing jobs and emit a minimum of pollutants. *Other claimants* to the enterprise may include financial institutions and labor unions; even competitors have a legitimate claim for fair play. It is clear that many of these claims are incongruent with each other, and it is management's job to integrate the legitimate objectives of the claimants.

The Enterprise Profile

The way an enterprise has operated in the past is usually a starting point to determine where it will go and where it should go. In other words, top executives wrestle with such fundamental questions as:

'What is our business?'
'Who are our customers?'
'What do our customers want?'
'What should our business be?'

These and similar questions should provide answers about the basic nature of the company, its products and services, geographic domain, its competitive position and its top management orientation and values. These topics demand elaboration.

Geographic orientation. A company must also answer questions such as:

'Where are our customers?'
'Where are those who should be our customers, but are not at present?'

Companies need to develop a profile of their geographic market. While some firms may restrict themselves to the eastern part of the United States, others view the whole country as their region of operations. Many large companies, of course, conduct their business on different continents.

Competitive situation. Business firms usually do not have an exclusive market, instead, they compete with other firms. But current market share is not necessarily a sufficient indicator of a firm's long-range potential. One must also consider other factors and competitive items such as price, quality, cost, service, product innovation, distribution systems, facilities and locations.

The assessment of the competitive situation involves several steps. First, key success factors must be identified. Then the relative importance of these key success factors needs to be estimated. Next, the firm's competitive position in respect to these key success factors must be evaluated and ranked. Thus, only a careful analysis of the current competitive position provides an indication of the company's future growth and profits.

The competitive analysis, especially for large firms, is done for individual business units, product lines or even specific products. Moreover, the competitive analysis focus is not only on the present situation, but also looks into the more distant future.[9] This analysis becomes intricate for firms that compete in the national and international markets.

Top management orientation. An enterprise profile is shaped by people, especially executives. They set the organizational climate, they influence the atmosphere in the organization and they determine the direction of the company. For example, management may not pursue opportunities in the liquor business because it conflicts with top management's values which are against the production and consumption of alcohol. Another example of the influence of values may be management's commitment to socially responsible actions, believing that these activities will benefit the enterprise in the long run.

An understanding of the past and the present postures of the enterprise and its policy as well as the values of managers are important factors in the development of the enterprise profile. *The next step in the strategic planning process is the analysis of threats, opportunities, weaknesses and strengths.*

The External Environment: Threats and Opportunities

In the analysis of the external environment, many diverse factors need to be considered. Today, the threats certainly would include the problems of inflation, energy, technological change and government actions. The diverse factors—which can be either threats or opportunities—can be grouped into the following categories: economic, social and political factors, products and technology, demographic factors, markets and competition, plus others.

Economic factors. The general state of the economy certainly affects strategy formulation. For example, the expansion phase of the business cycle in the 1960s created an abundance of business opportunities while the recession in the first half of the 1970s required many industries to change their strategy, and drastically reduce their business activities. The strategist, of course, takes other economic factors besides the business cycle into account, such as the level of employment, the availability of credit and the level of prices. Also, individual companies are affected differently by economic factors. What is a threat to one firm is an opportunity for another.

Social and political factors. Social developments also influence the business strategy. For instance, consumerism and consumer protection movements require the firm's attention to product safety and truth in packaging. Similarly, managers are confronted by a host of federal, state and local laws and regulations. The public's demand for clean air, clean water and a clean environment is often considered a threat to business. At the same time, these factors can become opportunities, as shown by the car emission test requirements in many states which presented opportunities for companies to develop, produce or operate such test equipment.

Products and technology. Products need to be adjusted to technological changes. For example, the astonishing success of the Volkswagen Beetle in the 1960s diminished in the 1970s. New customer demands for optional equipment, safety requirements and competition, along with new technology, gave rise to a new generation of VWs. It must be remembered that in almost all situations success is only temporary and product innovation is needed to ensure a competitive advantage for the firm. Of course, innovation is also costly and risky and the failure rate of new products is high; yet, a policy of no innovation at all may cause the demise of a company.

Demographic factors. Demographic changes significantly affect business. In the United States there are geographic shifts such as the movement of many people to the 'sun belt'. White-collar jobs tend to increase proportionally to blue-collar occupations. Income levels are expected to change, although the direction is less clear and may vary for different sectors of the labor market. The age composition will also change with elderly people making up an increasing proportion of the population. The strategist must take these and other factors into account because they influence the preferences for the kind of products and services demanded by consumers.

Markets and competition. In the United States, coping with competition in the marketplace is a corporate way of life. The following questions and the answers to them are crucial for formulating a strategy:

'Who are our competitors?'
'How does our company compare with the competition?'
'What are the strengths and weaknesses of our competitors?'
'What are their strategies?'
'How do we best compete?'

Other factors. There are, of course, many other factors that might be particularly important to a specific firm. The availability of raw materials, suppliers and the transportation system, are a few examples. The everchanging environment demands continuous scanning for opportunities and threats. A company that discovers customer needs and provides the products and services demanded, certainly has a better chance for success than an enterprise that ignores such changes.

Information gathering and forecast of the future. To collect data on the various factors is, to say the least, a tedious task. The study by Jerry Wall of 1211 executives, all readers of the *Harvard Business Review*, gives some insights on how companies collect information about their competitors. The sources used most frequently include: company sales persons, published sources, and personal and professional contacts with competitors and customers. Other less frequently used sources include: formal market research, brokers, wholesalers and other middlemen, analyses of processes and products of competitors, and suppliers. The least utilized sources include: employees of competitors, advertising agencies and consultants.[10]

Since there are many factors that need to be analyzed, the executives must be selective and concentrate on those factors which are critical for the success of the enterprise. Furthermore, it is not enough for the strategist to assess only the present environment. Planning for the future, and strategic planning in particular, is very much concerned with the more distant future. Thus, managers must anticipate the future and forecast changes in the environment that will crucially affect the enterprise.

The Internal Environment: Weaknesses and Strengths

The demands of the external environment on the organization must be matched with the resources of the firm. Internal strengths and weaknesses vary greatly for different enterprises; they may, however, conveniently be categorized into (1) management and organization, (2) operations, (3) finance and (4) other factors important for a particular organization.

Management and organization. This category includes not only managerial talent but also the labor force as a whole. It also encompasses labor relations; personnel policies; the appraisal, selection, training and development of employees; and the reward system. The planning and control system as well as the organization structure and climate are equally important for the success of the organization.

Operations. Operations must be carefully analyzed in terms of research and development capabilities, and the adequacy and productivity of the manufacturing facilities available to meet the expected growth and other objectives of the firm. Similarly, marketing must be assessed in terms of product distribution channels, brand name protection, competitive pricing, appropriate customer identification, service and company image.

Finance. A careful evaluation of the company's strengths and weaknesses also must be made in the areas of capital structure, financing, profitability, the tax situation, financial planning and the accounting system. Many financial ratios are available for making analyses. But financial management not only requires focusing on the past and the present situation, it also demands short- and long-term financial planning congruent with the firm's objectives and strategy.

Other factors. The focus here is on the obvious factors on which the strengths and weaknesses of the organization must be evaluated. Other factors, however, such as patents, inventions and the firm's image may be peculiar to an enterprise or may be prominent during a particular time period.

Strategic Alternatives

The foregoing analysis of environmental opportunities and threats and the company's strengths and weaknesses, encourages the creative process of developing alternatives. As any experienced manager knows, in almost all situations, alternative courses of action are available.

One strategy is to *specialize* or *concentrate*. Thus, a company may utilize its energy and strengths to pursue a single purpose or it may restrict its efforts to only a few aims. For example, American Motors for many years used its limited resources primarily for the production of small cars, rather than competing directly with General Motors, Ford or Chrysler who had a complete product line ranging from relatively small models to large, luxurious cars.

Other alternative strategies are backward and forward integration. In *backward integration* a company may acquire suppliers to ensure a steady flow of materials. In *forward integration* the attempt is to secure outlets for products or services and to reach toward the ultimate user of the product.

Another strategy focuses on *diversification* by moving into new and profitable markets. This may result in greater growth than would be possible without diversification.

Still another strategy would be to focus on *innovation* — new products and new services. Thus, a company, vulnerable to obsolescence, may look for new ideas whose time has arrived. Polaroid, a company known for innovation, developed through tremendous research and development efforts the successful SX70 instant picture camera, a truly innovative product. But, as exemplified by the same company, investing in innovation is also risky. Polaroid may have persisted too long and invested too much in promoting Polavision, the instant movie system.

A company may adopt a 'no change' strategy and decide to do nothing. Instead of innovation or expansion, a firm may continue to follow the tried and proven path, utilizing existing products and services and letting others make possible mistakes in innovation.

A company may also select an *international* strategy, repeating the approach which was successful in its home country and extending its operations from there to different parts of the world. Companies with global strategies include Unilever, Colgate-Palmolive, Singer, Nestlé and IBM, to mention a few.

Still another strategic alternative is for an enterprise to decide on *liquidation*, which may require terminating an unprofitable product line or service. If the company is a one-product firm, this may mean dissolving the company—an especially difficult strategic decision.

In some cases the extreme decision of liquidation may not be necessary. Instead, a *retrenchment* strategy may be more appropriate. To be sure, this is often only a temporary measure and may involve reducing operating expenses or restricting the scope of the operation. Still, such a strategy may be a viable alternative to liquidation.

Finally, there is the alternative of engaging in *joint ventures*, which may take different forms. For example, corporations may join with foreign firms to overcome political and cultural barriers. Another example of a joint venture is the Alaskan Pipeline which was a project even too big for one of the financially strong oil companies. Still another kind of joint venture occurs when two or more firms pool their resources and establish a new company, which then is jointly owned.

The strategies discussed above provide an overview of possible approaches. Within these categories, of course, many variations are possible. In reality, enterprises often pursue a *combination* of these strategies. What has become clear is that evaluating and choosing a strategy, the next topic of discussion, is not a simple task.

Evaluation and Choice of Strategies

The strategic manager has to evaluate a multiplicity of possible strategies. Clearly, such a manager has to take into consideration both external realities and internal capabilities. Unfortunately, environments are not static, but are *dynamic* and subject to constant change. Thus, the strategist has to make predictions of changes about the future.

In making strategic choices, opportunities must be evaluated in the light of *risks*. There may indeed be profit opportunities for a new product, but the company may not be able to afford the risks involved in the new venture. At other times, however, a firm cannot afford not taking a calculated risk.

Timing is another critical element in the strategic decision. Although early action may at times be desirable (e.g. to be the first in the market), a firm may not be able to take the risk associated with it. On the other hand, a company may have to enter a new field because its survival depends upon it.

Companies do not operate in a vacuum, of course. A new strategic action is usually met with a reaction from one or more *competitors*, this, in turn, requires counteractions.

Clearly, strategic choices are made in a dynamic environment and to cope with the many uncertainties demands executives with tolerance for ambiguity.

Consistency Testing

During all stages of strategy formulation, the steps have to be examined for consistency with the enterprise profile, the present and projected environment, and the resources of the firm. In addition, the goals of the claimants to the organization have to be considered since the choice of strategy is not only based on a rational analysis of the facts, but also on personal values and personal goals, especially those of the chief executive officer, an important claimant to the enterprise, as pointed out above.

Alternative strategies are then tested for congruency with other medium- and short-range plans which, in turn, may require adjustments of the master strategy. Similarly, the feasibility of implementing the plans also needs to be examined. For example, the organization structure as well as the availability and suitability of human resources should be considered before strategic choices are made. As shown in the model in Figure 1, consistency testing is necessary at the various steps in the strategic planning process.

Contingency Plans

Contingency plans will have to be prepared. Since the future cannot be predicted with great accuracy, plans need to be made with different premises. To be sure, not all possible contingencies can be taken into account, but those crucial to the survival and success of a firm—such as a cutoff or reduction of oil from foreign sources—should provide premises for alternative plans.

AN OPERATIONAL MODEL
FOR ANALYSIS OF THE SITUATION

As pointed out above, it has been common in the past to suggest that companies identify their strengths and weaknesses, and the opportunities and threats in the external environment. But what is often overlooked is that combining these factors may require distinct strategic choices. To systematize these choices, the TOWS Matrix is proposed in which 'T' stands for threats, 'O' for opportunities, 'W' for weaknesses and 'S' for strengths. Before describing this matrix, however, one should be aware of other 'tools' that have been used effectively in strategy formulation.

Today, strategy designers have been aided by a number of matrixes showing the relationships of critical variables. For example, the Boston Consulting Group developed the *Business Portfolio Matrix*, which essentially shows the linkages between the business growth rate and the relative competitive position of the enterprise (identified by the market share). However, this approach has been criticized as being too simplistic, and the growth rate criterion has been considered insufficient for the evaluation of the industry's attractiveness. Similarly, the market share as a yardstick for estimating the competitive position may be inadequate.

Another useful matrix for developing a firm's strategy is General Electric's *Business Screen*. Basically, the GE matrix consists of two sets of variables: business strengths

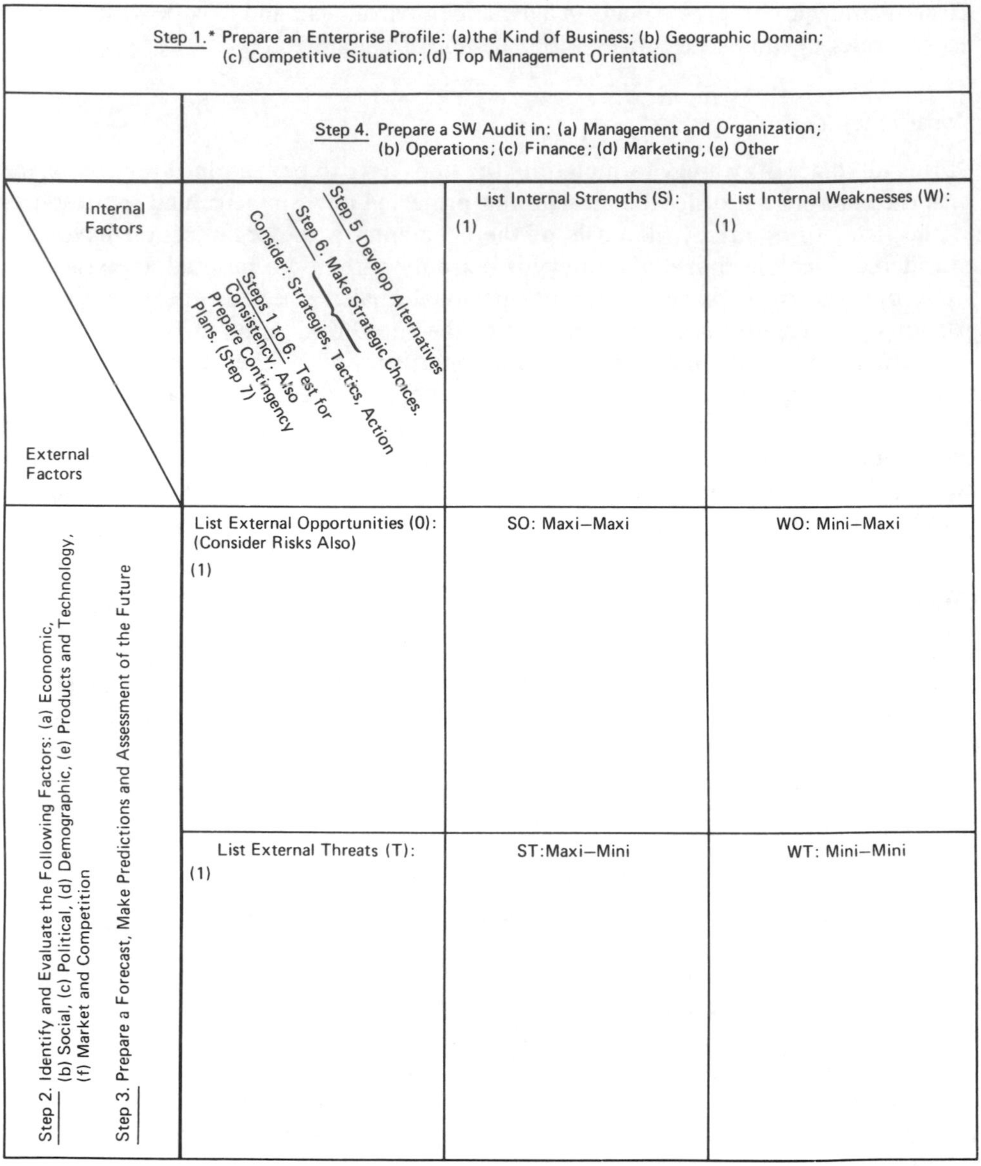

Step 1.* Prepare an Enterprise Profile: (a) the Kind of Business; (b) Geographic Domain; (c) Competitive Situation; (d) Top Management Orientation

Step 4. Prepare a SW Audit in: (a) Management and Organization; (b) Operations; (c) Finance; (d) Marketing; (e) Other

Internal Factors		List Internal Strengths (S): (1)	List Internal Weaknesses (W): (1)
External Factors	Step 5 Develop Alternatives. Step 6. Make Strategic Choices. Consider: Strategies, Tactics, Action Steps 1 to 6. Test for Consistency. Also Prepare Contingency Plans. (Step 7)		
List External Opportunities (0): (Consider Risks Also) (1)		SO: Maxi—Maxi	WO: Mini—Maxi
List External Threats (T): (1)		ST: Maxi—Mini	WT: Mini—Mini

Step 2. Identify and Evaluate the Following Factors: (a) Economic, (b) Social, (c) Political, (d) Demographic, (e) Products and Technology, (f) Market and Competition

Step 3. Prepare a Forecast, Make Predictions and Assessment of the Future

Figure 2. Process of corporate strategy and the TOWS analysis

and industry attractiveness. Each variable is divided into low, medium and high ratings, resulting in a nine-cell grid. Business strengths, for example, evaluates size, growth, share, position, profitability, margins and technology position, to mention a few of the items. Industry attractiveness, on the other hand, is judged in terms of size, market growth, market density, competitive structure, industry profitability and so on. But Charles W. Hofer and Dan Schendel suggest that the GE Business Screen does not give adequate attention to new industries that are beginning to grow. Consequently, they suggest a matrix in which the 'competitive position' and their 'stage of product/market evolution' are plotted.[11] Both matrixes, however, appear to give insufficient attention to the threats and constraints in the external environment.

The *TOWS Matrix*, described in this paper, has a wider scope and has different emphases than the ones mentioned above. This matrix does not replace either the Business Portfolio Matrix, the GE Business Screen, or the matrix by Hofer and Schendel, but it is proposed as a conceptual framework for a systematic analysis that facilitates matching the external threats and opportunities with the internal weaknesses and strengths of the organization.

The TOWS Matrix: A Conceptual Model

The process of strategy formulation, shown before in Figure 1, is now surrounding the TOWS Matrix in Figure 2. Preparation of the enterprise profile, Step 1, deals with some basic questions pertaining to the internal and external environments. Steps 2 and 3, on the other hand, concern primarily the present and future situation in respect to the external environment. Step 4, the audit of strengths and weaknesses, focuses on the internal resources of the enterprise. Steps 5 and 6 are the activities necessary to develop strategies, tactics and more specific actions in order to achieve the enterprise's purpose and overall objectives. During this process attention must be given to consistency of these decisions with the other steps in the strategy formulation process. Finally, since an organization operates in a dynamic environment, contingency plans must be prepared (Step 7).

There are different ways of analyzing the situation. One is to begin with the identification of important problems. A second approach is to start with determining the purpose and objectives of the firm. A third way is to focus on opportunities.[12] The question may be raised whether one should start with the analysis of the external environment or with the firm's internal resources. There is no single answer. Indeed, one may deal concurrently with the two sets of factors: the external and the internal environment. It is important, therefore, to remember that the process followed here is just one of several options.

The external environment. Within the suggested framework, the analysis starts with the external environment. Specifically, the listing of external threats (T) may be of immediate importance to the firm as some of these threats (such as the lack of available energy) may seriously threaten the operation of the firm. These threats should be listed in box 'T' in Figure 2. Similarly, opportunities should be shown in box 'O'.

Threats and opportunities may be found in different areas, but it is advisable to look carefully for the more common ones which may be categorized as economic, social, political and demographic factors, products and services, technology, markets and, of course, competition. As mentioned above, the analysis of these factors must not only pertain to the present but, even more important, the future environment.

The internal environment. The firm's internal environment is assessed for its strengths (S) and weaknesses (W), and then listed in the respective spaces in Figure 2. These factors may be found in management and organization, operations, finance, marketing and in other areas. Since they were previously discussed, they will not be repeated here.

Strategies, tactics and actions. The TOWS Matrix, Figure 2, indicates four conceptually distinct alternative strategies, tactics and actions. In practice, of course, some of the strategies overlap or they may be pursued concurrently and in concert. But for the purpose of discussion the focus is on the interactions of four sets of variables. The primary concern here is strategies, but this analysis could also be applied to the development of tactics necessary to implement the strategies, and to more specific actions supportive of tactics.

(1) The WT strategy (mini–mini). In general, the aim of the WT strategy is to minimize both weaknesses and threats. A company faced with external threats and internal weaknesses may indeed be in a precarious position. In fact, such a firm may have to fight for its survival or may even have to choose liquidation. But there are, of course, other choices. For example, such a firm may prefer a merger, or may cut back its operations, with the intent of either overcoming the weaknesses or hoping that the threat will diminish over time (too often wishful thinking). Whatever strategy is selected, the WT position is one that any firm will try to avoid.

(2) The WO strategy (mini–maxi). The second strategy attempts to minimize the weaknesses and to maximize the opportunities. A company may identify opportunities in the external environment but have organizational weaknesses which prevent the firm from taking advantage of market demands. For example, an auto accessory company with a great demand for electronic devices to control the amount and timing of fuel injection in a combustion engine, may lack the technology required for producing these micro-processors. One possible strategy would be to acquire this technology through cooperation with a firm having competency in this field. An alternative tactic would be to hire and train people with the required technical capabilities. Of course, the firm also has the choice of doing nothing, thus leaving the opportunity to competitors.

(3) The ST strategy (maxi–mini). This strategy is based on the strengths of the organization that can deal with threats in the environment. The aim is to maximize the former while minimizing the latter. This, however, does not mean that a strong company can meet threats in the external environment head-on, as General Motors (GM) realized. In the 1960s, mighty GM recognized the potential threat posed by Ralph Nader, who exposed the safety hazards of the Corvair automobile. As will be remembered, the direct confrontation with Mr. Nader caused GM more problems than expected. In retrospect, the initial GM response from strength was probably inappropriate. The lesson to be learned is that strengths must often be used with great restraint and discretion.

(4) The SO strategy (maxi–maxi). Any company would like to be in a position where it can maximize both strengths and opportunities. Such an enterprise can lead from strengths, utilizing resources to take advantage of the market for its products and services. For example, Mercedes Benz, with the technical know-how and the quality image, can take advantage of the external demand for luxury cars by an increasingly affluent public. Successful enterprises, even if they temporarily use one of the three previously mentioned strategies, will attempt to get into a situation where they can work from strengths to take advantage of opportunities. If they have weaknesses, they will strive to overcome

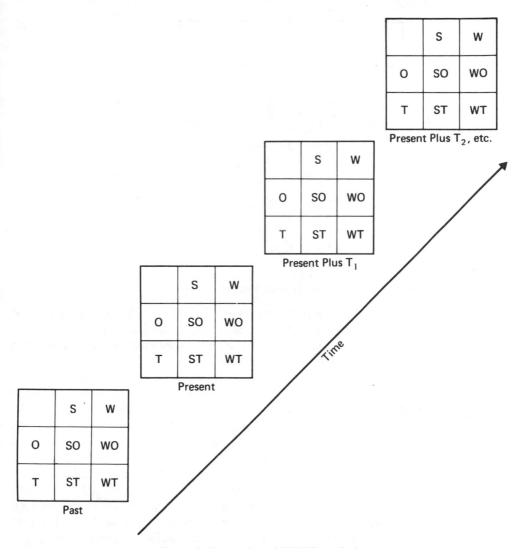

Figure 3. Dynamics of TOWS analysis

them, making them strengths. If they face threats, they will cope with them so that they can focus on opportunities.

Time Dimension and the TOWS Matrix

So far, the factors displayed in the TOWS Matrix pertain to analysis at a particular point in time. External and internal environments are dynamic; some factors change over time while others change very little. Because of the dynamics in the environment, the strategy designer must prepare several TOWS Matrixes at different points in time, as shown in Figure 3. Thus, one may start with a TOWS analysis of the past, continue with an analysis of the present, and, perhaps most important, focus on different time periods in the future.

	Strength									
Opportunity	1	2	3	4	5	6	7	8	9	10
1	+	0	+	0	0	+	+	0	0	0
2	+	0	0	+	0	0	0	+	0	0
3	0	0	0	+	0	0	0	0	0	+
4	+	+	+	0	+	+	0	+	+	+
5	+	0	+	0	0	0	+	0	0	0
6	+	0	0	0	+	0	0	0	+	+
7	+	+	0	+	+	0	+	+	+	+
8	0	0	0	0	0	+	0	0	+	0
9	+	0	0	+	0	0	0	+	0	0
10	+	+	0	0	+	0	0	0	0	0

Figure 4. Interaction matrix

Complexity of Interactions of Situational Factors

The conceptual model provides a good framework for identifying relationships, but it can become a complex process when many factors are being identified. The matrix, shown in Figure 4, is an example of one approach to identify combinations of relationships which, in turn, may become the basis for strategic choices.

In Figure 4, a ' + ' indicates a match between the strengths of the company and external opportunities, while an '0' indicates a weak or nonexistent relationship. Analysis of Figure 4 indicates that Strength No. 1 can be matched with several opportunities. Similarly, many strengths can be utilized to exploit Opportunity No. 7. Although this figure shows only the relationship between strengths and opportunities, similar tables can be used for analyzing the other three strategy boxes (WO, ST, WT) shown in Figure 2.

A word of caution is in order here. One cannot simply add up the number of pluses (although especially strong relationships could be indicated by two pluses such as ' + +') in each row and in each column to determine the best match between several strengths and opportunities. Clearly different relationships may have different weights in terms of their potential, so each should be carefully evaluated. Still, it is suggested that this matrix is a relatively simple way of recognizing promising strategies that use the company's strengths to take advantage of opportunities in the external environment.

APPLICATION OF THE TOWS MATRIX TO VOLKSWAGEN

The foregoing discussion of the conceptual framework for strategic planning can be illustrated by an example. Volkswagen (VW) was chosen because it demonstrates how a successful company experienced great difficulties in the early 1970s, but then developed a strategy that resulted in an excellent market position in the late 1970s. The TOWS Matrix shown in Figure 5 will focus on the crucial period from late 1973 to early 1975. The external threats and opportunities pertain mostly to the situation VW faced in the United States, but a similar situation prevailed in Europe at that time.

	Internal Strengths. (1) Strong R & D and Engineering (2) Strong Sales and Service Network (3) Efficient Production/Automation Capabilities	Internal Weaknesses: (1) Heavy Reliance on One Product (Although Several Less Successful Models were Introduced) (2) Rising Costs in Germany (3) No Experience With U.S. Labor Unions if Building Plant in U.S.
External Opportunities: (Consider Risks Also) (1) Growing Affluent Market Demands More Luxurious Cars with Many Options (2) Attractive Offers to Build an Assembly Plant in U.S. (3) Chrysler and American Motors Need Small Engines	SO (1) Develop and Produce Multiproduct Line with Many Options, in Different Price Classes (Dasher, Scirocco, Rabbit, Audi Line) $(O_1 \ S_1 S_2)$ (2) Build Assembly Plant Using R & D, Engineering, and Production/Automation Experience $(O_2 \ S_1 \ S_3)$ (3) Build Engines for Chrysler and AMC $(O_3 \ S_3)$	WO: (1) Develop Compatible Models for Different Price Levels (Ranging from Rabbit to Audi Line) $(O_1 \ W_1)$ (2) To Cope with Rising Costs in Germany, Built Plant in U.S., Hiring U.S. Managers with Experience in Dealing with U.S. Labor Unions $(O_2 W_2 \ W_3)$
External Threats: (1) Exchange Rate. Devaluation of Dollar in Relation to Deutshe Mark (DM) (2) Competition from Japanese and U.S. Automakers (3) Fuel Shortage and Price	ST: (1) Reduce Effect of Exchange Rate by Building a Plant in the U.S. $(T_1 \ T_2 \ S_1 \ S_3)$ (2) Meet Competition with Advanced Design Technology — e.g. Rabbit $(T_2 \ T_3 \ S_1 \ S_2)$ (3) Improve Fuel Consumption Through Fuel Injection and Develop Fuel Efficient Diesel Engines $(T_3 \ S_1)$	WT: A. Overcome Weaknesses by Making Them Strengths (Move Toward OS Strategy) (1) Reduce Threat of Competition by Developing Flexible Product Line $(T_2 \ W_1)$ B. Possible Options *not* Exercised by VW: (1) Engage in Joint Operation with Chrysler or AMC (2) Withdraw From U.S. Market

Figure 5. Application of the TOWS Matrix to Volkswagen. This illustrative analysis covers the period from late 1973 to early 1975

The External and Internal Environment

In a situational analysis as conceptualized above, one would first list and analyze the threats and opportunities in the external environment and the weaknesses and strengths of the enterprise before developing alternative strategies and tactics. However, in this illustration, to be concise, the situation and the related actions, shown in Figure 5, are combined.

Strategies and Tactics

Strategies, as discussed earlier, pertain to major courses of action for the achievement of the enterprise mission and comprehensive objectives. Tactics, on the other hand, refer to action plans by which strategies are executed. In practice, and even conceptually, these distinctions are often blurred.

Weaknesses and threats (WT). A company with great weaknesses often has to resort to a survival strategy. VW could have seriously considered the option of a joint operation with Chrysler or American Motors. Another alternative would have been to withdraw from the American market altogether. Although in difficulties, VW did *not* have to resort to a survival strategy because the company still had many strengths. Consequently, a more appropriate strategy was to attempt to overcome the weaknesses and develop them into strengths. In other words, the direction was toward the strength-opportunity position (SO) in the matrix shown as Figure 5. Specifically, the strategy was to reduce the competitive threat by developing a more flexible new product line that would accommodate the needs and desires of the car-buying public.

Weaknesses and opportunities (WO). The growing affluence of customers has resulted in 'trading up' to more luxurious cars. Yet, VW had essentially followed a one-model policy which presented a problem when the design of the Beetle became obsolete. A new model line had to be introduced to reach a wider spectrum of buyers. In order to minimize the additional costs of a multiproduct line, the building block principle was employed in the design of the new cars. This allowed using the same parts for different models that ranged from the relatively low-priced Rabbit to the higher priced Audi line.

Another weakness at VW was the rising costs in Germany. For example, in 1973 wages and salaries rose 19 per cent over the previous year. Similarly, increased fuel costs made the shipping of cars to the United States more costly. This situation favored setting up an assembly plant in the United States. However, this also created some problems for VW because it had no experience in dealing with American organized labor. To overcome this weakness, VW's tactic was to recruit managers from Detroit who were capable of establishing good union relations.

Strengths and threats (ST). One of the greatest threats to VW was the continuing appreciation of the Deutsche mark against the dollar. For example, between October 1972 and November 1973 the mark appreciated 35 per cent. This meant higher prices for the buyer. The result, of course, was a less competitive posture. Japanese and American automakers obtained an increasingly larger share of the small-car market. To reduce the threats of competition and the effects of the unfavorable exchange rate, VW was forced to build an assembly plant in the United States.

Another strategy for meeting competitive pressures was to build on VW's strengths by developing a car based on advanced-design technology. The result of this effort was the Rabbit, a model with features later adopted by many other car manufacturers.

The oil crisis in 1973–1974 not only caused a fuel shortage, but also price rises, a trend that has continued. To meet this threat, VW used its technological capabilities not only to improve its engines (through the use of fuel injection, for example), but also to develop the very fuel-efficient diesel engine. This tactic, which was congruent with its general strategy, helped improve the firm's market position.

Strengths and opportunities (SO). In general, successful firms build on their strengths to take advantage of opportunities. VW is no exception. Throughout this discussion VW's strengths in research, development, engineering, and its experience in production technology became evident. These strengths, under the leadership of Rudolf Leiding, enabled the company to develop a product line that met market demands for an economical car (the Rabbit, successor to the Beetle), as well as the tastes for more luxurious cars with many available options (Scirocco and the Audi line).

Eventually the same company's strengths enabled VW to plan and build the assembly facility in New Stanton, Pennsylvania. Thus, VW could benefit from substantial concessions granted by the state government to attract VW which, in turn, provided many employment opportunities.

In another tactical move, VW manufactured and sold small engines to Chrysler and American Motors. These companies urgently needed small engines for installation in their own cars and revenues from these sales improved the financial position of VW.

APPLICATION OF THE TOWS
MATRIX TO WINNEBAGO INDUSTRIES INC.

Winnebago, the largest manufacturer of recreational vehicles (RVs) produced a full line of such vehicles, but emphasized traditional motor homes. The company, located in Forest City, Iowa, operated a large, modern and efficient plant.[13]

The External and Internal Environment

The threats and opportunities in the external environment are condensed into the table shown as Figure 6. In the past, the company had prospered by the high demand for RVs. However, serious threats from competitors as well as the gasoline shortage could have a great impact on the firm.

While Winnebago has considerable strengths, heavy reliance on essentially one product makes the company vulnerable to the external threats.

Strategies and Tactics

Based on the analysis of the situation, several alternative strategies and tactics are available to Winnebago.

Weaknesses and threats (WT). The factors in the external environment, particularly the gasoline shortage, the high fuel prices, the slackening in demand for recreational vehicles, as well as the increased competition constitute serious threats to the enterprise. When these threats are seen in relation to the weaknesses, an alternative would be to sell the company. But this strategic choice would probably be unacceptable to the family-dominated management group.

	Strengths:	Weaknesses:
	(1) Identifiable Corporate Name With a Good Reputation (2) Good Service and Warranty (3) Established Dealer Network With Good Dealer Relations (4) Extensive Research and Development Capabilities (5) Automated, Economical Plant (6) Manufacturing of Most Parts for the Motor Home	(1) Vulnerability Because of One-product Company (2) Concentration on Higher Priced Units (3) Heavy Investment in Toolmaking will Raise Cost of Model Changes (4) One-plant Location (5) No Preparation for Transition from Family to Corporate Management
Opportunities: (1) Demand for Smaller RVs (2) Development of International Market (3) Demand for Low-cost Modular Housing (FHA Subsidy for Mortgage Loans)	SO: (1) Emphasize Smaller, More Efficient Motor Homes $(O_1 \ S_1 \ S_2 \ S_3 \ S_4 \ S_5 \ S_6)$ (2) Expand into Foreign Markets $(O_2 \ S_1 \ S_4)$ (3) Diversify into Modular Housing $(O_3 \ S_1 \ S_4 \ S_6)$	WO: (1) Develop and Produce Smaller RVs $(O_1 \ O_2 \ W_1 \ W_2)$ (2) Build Smaller Plants in Different Parts of the Country and Abroad $(O_1 \ O_2 \ W_4)$
Threats: (1) Gasoline Shortage and Higher Prices of Gasoline (2) Slackening Demand for RVs (3) 'Trade-up' Creates Secondary Market (4) Increased Competition (GM, Ford, International Harvester, VW, Toyota) (5) Impending Safety Regulations	ST: (1) Diversify into Farm Equipment, Railroad Cars $(T_1 \ T_2 \ T_3 \ S_1 \ S_3 \ S_4 \ S_5)$ (2) Consider Diesel Engines for Motor Homes $(T_1 \ S_4)$ (3) Make RVs Safer in Anticipation of Safety Regulations (e.g. Visibility, Flame Retardant, Crash Resistant, Brakes) $(T_5 \ T_4 \ S_6)$	WT: (1) Sell the Company $(T_1 \ T_2 \ T_4 \ W_1 \ W_4 \ W_5)$

Figure 6. Application of the TOWS matrix to Winnebago. This illustration covers the period of the early 1970s

Weaknesses and opportunities (WO). Customers in the United States and abroad demand smaller RVs. But one of the weaknesses of the firm was the heavy reliance on relatively larger and higher-priced units. Consequently, the development and manufacture of smaller vehicles could take advantage of the demand for small RVs in a market segment neglected in the past by the firm. Furthermore, smaller plants could be built in various parts of the country, thus alleviating the comparatively high transportation costs for the smaller RVs from the factory to the dealers.

Strengths and threats (ST). To cope with the threats in the external environment the company may use its strengths. Specifically, diversifying into farm equipment and railroad cars, using the firm's capabilities, can alleviate problems caused by the slackening demand for RVs due to the secondary market created by the custom of 'trading up'. Similarly, the use of diesel engines in motor homes can reduce fuel consumption of these vehicles. Impending safety regulations are expected to make more demands on RV manufacturers. Rather than reacting to these regulations, Winnebago can use its extensive research and development capabilities to develop safer vehicles.

Strengths and opportunities (SO). Winnebago needs to use its strengths to take advantage of the opportunities. The good reputation of the firm, its service network, its research and development as well as the manufacturing facilities, can be effectively used to produce smaller RVs. Similarly, most of these strengths facilitate the expansion into the international market. Finally, the firm's capabilities can be used to diversify into modular housing. But the company has little or no knowledge of the housing market and some difficulties can be anticipated.

So far, the focus has been on strategy formulation in two product-oriented businesses, Volkswagen and Winnebago, but does strategic planning also apply to other kinds of organizations?

WHO NEEDS STRATEGIC PLANNING?

For a long time strategic planning meant making plans in light of the actions or potential actions of an adversary. In fact, it is the *military* that has had long experience with strategic planning.

In the business world, strategic planning has been used extensively by *product-oriented* firms. The concern is about the deployment of resources to make the kind of product the customers want at a price they are willing to pay. Companies also have to decide whether they want to be a product leader or follow the lead of innovative competitors.

But to focus only on businesses that make a distinct product leaves out the important sector of the *service* industry. Examples of service businesses are consulting, law, computer service firms, airlines, banks and theaters. Dan R. E. Thomas drew attention to the fact that strategic management for such enterprises is significantly different from companies that make a physical product.[14]

Clearly, to describe services is abstract and more difficult than to show and demonstrate a product. There are two kinds of services: one is equipment-based (e.g. automatic car washes) while the other is people-based (e.g. consulting). A few illustrations of the latter will indicate some implications for strategic planning. It may be extremely difficult to evaluate the quality of services of a consulting firm. Consequently, a client tends to employ the services of large consulting firms with established reputations. Unfortunately, this makes it extremely difficult for a small consulting firm without such an image to enter the market. Another example pertains to pricing in the service industry. Product-oriented firms usually aim to reduce the cost and price of a product to increase their market share. In the service industry, however, a low price is often perceived as and associated with providing poorer quality of professional services.

Does Thomas suggest that strategic management does not apply to the service industry? Certainly not. What is needed, however, is a change in the thinking pattern away from product-oriented management to the application of techniques and language peculiar to service-oriented businesses.

Of all the different kinds of organizations, Western *governments* probably make the least use of strategic planning. For example, little systematic planning was done to prepare for the oil shortage. There is a tendency to respond to problems rather than to anticipate them and prepare contingency plans. Many large busineses now make a situational analysis and establish goals that give the enterprise direction. Why should not the same managerial concept be applied by our government?

REFERENCES

(1) See the exploratory study by Howard H. Stevenson, Defining corporate strengths and weaknesses, *Sloan Management Review*, Spring (1976).
(2) K. Andrews, E. Learned, C. R. Christensen and W. Guth, *Business Policy: Text and Cases*, Richard D. Irwin, Homewood, Illinois (1965).
(3) A. Chandler. *Strategy and Structure: Chapters in the History of American Industrial Enterprise*, MIT Press, Cambridge, Massachusetts (1962).
(4) G. A. Steiner and J. B. Miner, *Management Policy and Strategy*, Macmillan, New York (1977).
(5) R. Vancil, Strategy formulation in complex organizations, *Sloan Management Review*, in Peter Lorange and Richard F. Vancil, *Strategic Planning Systems*, Prentice-Hall, Englewood Cliffs, NJ (1977).
(6) H. I. Ansoff, *Corporate Strategy*, McGraw-Hill, New York (1965).
(7) C. W. Hofer and D. Schendel, *Strategy Formulation: Analytical Concepts*, West Publishing, St. Paul (1978).
(8) H. Koontz, C. O'Donnell and H. Weihrich, *Management*, 7th edn, McGraw-Hill, New York (1980), p. 847. For additional meanings, see Roger Evered, 'The Strategic Decision Process', in Don Hellriegel and John W. Slocum, Jr., eds., *Management in the World Today*, Addison Wesley, Reading, Massachusetts (1975).
(9) For an excellent discussion of the various approaches to forecasting, see Spyros Makridakis and Steven C. Wheelwright, Forecasting: issues and challenges for marketing management *Journal of Marketing*, October (1977) in Harold Koontz, Cyril O'Donnell and Heinz Weihrich, *Management: A Book of Readings*, 5th edn, McGraw-Hill, New York (1980).
(10) J. Wall, What the competition is doing: your need to know. *Harvard Business Review*, November–December (1974).
(11) Hofer and Schendel, *op. cit.*, Chapter 2.
(12) See, for example, the comparison of steps suggested by different authors in G. A. Steiner and J. B. Miner, *op. cit.*, Chapter 8.
(13) H. E. R. Uyterhoeven, R. W. Ackerman and J. W. Rosenblum, *Strategy and Organization*, Richard D. Irwin, Homewood, Illinois (1977).
(14) D. R. E. Thomas, Strategy is different in service businesses. *Harvard Business Review*, July–August (1978).

Chapter 3

Competitive Cost Dynamics: The Experience Curve

Arnoldo C. Hax

Alfred P. Sloan School of Management, Massachusetts Institute of Technology, 50 Memorial Drive, Cambridge, Massachusetts 02139, USA

Nicolas S. Majluf

Universidad Catolica de Chile, Escuela de Ingenieria, Casilla 114-D, Santiago, Chile

This, the first of our series of three tutorial articles, explains the use of the experience curve for understanding the cost dynamics of an industry and positioning a firm strategically within that industry.

The management of cost of manufactured products is fundamental to long-term profitability for any firm operating in a competitive market. To a great extent, the strength of a business rests on its ability to deliver products at costs lower than its competitors. The cost of a product should not be viewed as the simple accumulation of direct and allocated expenses for its manufacture and sale, but also as an indicator of the firm's ability to manage its resources.

The experience curve is a key tool to assist managers in formally addressing the question of the competitive cost structure. It provides an empirical relationship between changes in direct manufacturing cost and the accumulated volume of production. Although its origins go back to the beginning of this century, it was only in the late 1960s that the Boston Consulting Group began to emphasize the experience curve's role for strategic decision making [1972].

The experience curve shows that the cost of doing a repetitive task decreases by a fixed percentage each time the total accumulated volume of production (in units) doubles (Figure 1). For example, the total cost might drop from 100 when the total production was 10 units, to 85 ($= 100 \times 0.85$) when it increased to 20 units, and to 72.25 ($= 85 \times 0.85$) when it reached 40 units. This relationship between the accumulated volume of production and the deflated direct cost can be expressed in a log-log graph as a straight

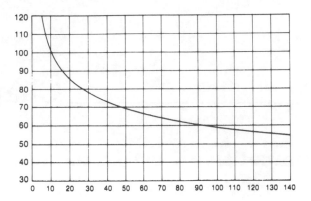

Figure 1. An 85% experience curve. The horizontal axis is the accumulated volume of production (in units), and the vertical axis the deflated direct cost per unit (the actual cost corrected for inflation). Every time the accumulated volume of production doubles, the cost per unit decreases to 85% of the previous level

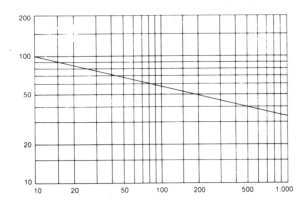

Figure 2. The relationship between the accumulated volume of production (horizontal axis) and the deflated direct cost (vertical axis) expressed in a log-log graph as a straight line, again an 85% experience curve

line, which is easier to work with (Figure 2). It should be emphasized that the accumulated volume of production represents the total number of units delivered since the very beginning of the production activity, and it should not be confused with the production rate, which corresponds to the number of units delivered in a stated period.

If nominal rather than deflated cost were to be used in plotting the experience curve, none of the previous effects could be observed. Most likely, instead of a decreasing cost curve, we would have obtained an increasing and unsystematic cost pattern.

The cost predicted by the experience curve effect can be obtained from a simple negative exponential relationship of the following type:

$$C_t = C_0 \left(\frac{P_t}{P_0} \right)^{-a}$$

where:

C_0, C_t = cost per unit (corrected for inflation) at times 0 and t, respectively;
P_0, P_t = accumulated volume of production at times 0 and t, respectively;
   a = constant, which reflects the elasticity of unit costs to accumulated volume.

In the 85% curve, the constant 'a' can be obtained by recognizing that doubling the production reduces the cost to 85% of its initial value. This corresponds to introducing the values.

$$C_t/C_0 = 0.85 \text{ and } P_t/P_0 = 2$$

in the expression:

$$\frac{C_t}{C_0} = \left(\frac{P_t}{P_0}\right)^{-a}$$

The resulting solution is $a = 0.234$.

Other values of this constant for different slopes of the exerience curve can be figured (Figure 3). The reduction that may be obtained by the experience effect is dependent on the industry. For example, the manufacturing of integrated circuits approaches a 70% slope, air conditioners show an 80% slope, and primary magnesium exhibits a 90% slope. Similar observations are obtained from other industries like cement manufacturing (70% slope), power tools (80% slope), and industrial trucks (90% slope).

The actual significance of the experience effects for a given industry depends not only on its inherent slope, but also on the speed at which experience accumulates, measured by the rate of growth in the market (Table 1).

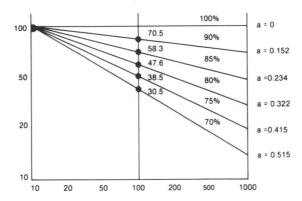

Figure 3. Experience curves for different relationships between accumulated production and deflated unit cost. For example, the 80% experience curve shows that the unit cost is reduced from 100 to 47.6 after a ten-fold increase in accumulated volume of production. The entire straight line corresponds to the negative ·xponential relationship

$$C_t = C_0 \left(\frac{P_t}{P_0}\right)^{-a}$$

the constant a being 0.322 in this case

Table 1. An estimate of the percentage of annual cost reductions for different combinations of experience-curve slope and annual market-growth rate. The potential of cost reduction is greatest in industries with strong experience effects and fast growing markets

Experience curve Slope	Annual Market-Growth Rate				
	2%	5%	10%	20%	30%
90%	0.3	0.7	1.4	2.7	3.9
80%	0.6	1.6	3.0	5.7	8.1
70%	1.0	2.5	4.8	9.0	12.6
60%	1.4	3.5	6.8	12.6	17.6

The potential for cost reduction is greatest in industries with strong experience effects and fast growing markets, like the semi-conductor and computer industries in recent years.

MANAGING THE EXPERIENCE EFFECT TO REDUCE COST

Although the impact of experience on lowering costs has been measured empirically in a wide spectrum of industries—ranging from broiler chickens to integrated circuits—its benefits can only be realized by careful management. The effects of the experience curve can be observed in every stage of the value-added chain. It affects each one of the value-added steps: research and development, procurement of raw materials, fabrication, assembly, marketing, sales, and distribution. The most important factors for a systematic decrease in cost with accumulated volume are:

(a) *Learning*. In repeating a task over and over, a person develops skills which allow him to do the work more efficiently. For this reason, the productivity per worker is expected to rise with increased dexterity [Hirschmann 1964].

(b) *Specialization and Redesign of Labor Tasks*. The increased volume leads to a division of labor that allows for specialization and standardization both contributing to improved productivity.

(c) *Product and Process Improvements*. As volume increases, many opportunities open up to improve the product and process and thereby achieve higher productivity and cost reductions. The kinds of changes that generate increases in productivity are modifications in the product, better utilization and substitution of materials, and rationalization of the product-mix; all of them dictated by the increased experience resulting from larger volume. Added opportunities for cost reduction arise from changes in the manufacturing process. Improved technologies, layout changes, better ways of handling and storing materials, parts, and products, adoption of more efficient maintenance methods, and better distribution of final products are some of the alternatives that can drive costs down. In general, the idea is to look for all improvements that can reduce costs.

(d) *Methods and Systems Rationalization*. Opportunities increase for improving the performance of a firm by introducing more up-to-date technology for handling operation. Also, adopting a policy of standardization allows coordination of different activities in the various steps of the value-added chain.

(e) *Economies of Scale*. The cost reduction observed in a historical series of real costs can be partly explained by the impact of accumulated volume of production and partly

by the changes of scale from increased throughput. The economies of scale correspond to the decline in unit costs as throughput increases. Economies of scale can affect nearly every function, and many technological factors combine to produce the downward trend of the cost-curve as volume increases. The dominant factors are:
—Improved technological processes for high volume production;
—The resources that can be profitably used together only in large operations;
—The possibility of integrating manufacturing processes for the various business activities of very large firms operating in stable environments;
—The sharing of resources, mainly those managed at the corporate level, that is possible for diversified firms with businesses in related product markets.

A typical scale effect can be seen in the use of the '.6–.8 rule' for estimating the investment required for a given plant capacity. The rule, which applies in many industrial settings, is that if capacity is doubled, the investment required increases only 2^a with the exponent varying between .6 and .8. This corresponds to an increase between 52% and 74% of investments for a 100% increase in capacity. Similarly, scale effects can be observed in distribution, sales, research and development, general administrative activities, and all stages of production.

Cost reductions with increased scale are another way for managers to improve their competitive cost position. When these factors are properly managed they can reduce the total cost of a product.

(f) *Organizational 'tune-up'*. A subtle result of experience is the 'tune-up' achieved by the organization after a long history of production, which is reflected in technological know-how and well developed formal systems that provide guidelines for smooth relationships among individuals responsible for different tasks in the production process. This organization tune-up is an asset that should be fostered and protected because it can give a competitive edge to a firm.

STRATEGIC IMPLICATIONS:
THE VALUE OF MARKET SHARE

Because a decline in unit costs accompanies an increase in production, market share is a primary variable in the strength of the strategic position of a business within an industry. Among those who advocate this view is the Boston Consulting Group, who state the following chain of causal relationships: high market share causes high accumulated volume of production causes low unit cost causes high profits. The association between market share and profitability has received empirical support in the work of project PIMS (Profitability Impact on Marketing Strategies) [Schoeffler, Buzzell, and Heany 1974; Buzzell, Gale, and Sultan 1975].

The implications of these relationships are clear when competing firms are positioned within a common experience curve; the firm with the largest volume has a commanding advantage over its competitors. The firm with the lowest volume struggles for its survival at the mercy of the strategic moves of the top firm and its own ability to sustain long-term losses (Figure 4). Under this approach, the only way for the low firm to improve its situation is to aggressively search for an increase in market share.

Bruce Henderson, the founder of the Boston Consulting Group, has been a leading

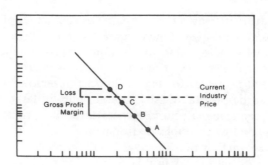

Figure 4. Four firms, A, B, C, and D positioned on a common experience curve clearly showing the advantage of large volume. Again the vertical axis is deflated cost per unit and the horizontal, accumulated volume of production

spokesman for this approach. In this book *On Corporate Strategy* [1979] he proposes the 'rule of three and four', which says that:

> A stable competitive market never has more than three significant competitors, the largest of which has no more than four times the market share of the smallest.

There are two primary reasons argued by Henderson to sustain this hypothesis:

> A ratio of two to one in market share between any two competitors seems to be the equilibrium point in which it is neither practical nor advantageous for either competitor to increase or decrease share.
>
> Any competitor with less than one quarter the share of the largest competitor cannot be an effective competitor.

The most important strategic implications suggested by Henderson are:

> If there are a large number of competitors, a shakeout is nearly inevitable in the absence of some external constraint or control on competition.
>
> All competitors wishing to survive will have to grow faster than the market in order to maintain their relative market shares with fewer competitors. The eventual losers will have increasingly large negative cash flows if they try to grow at all.
>
> All except the two largest share competitors either will be losers, and eventually be eliminated, or will be marginal cash traps reporting profits periodically and reinvesting forever.
>
> The quicker an investment is cashed out or a market position second only to the leader is gained, then the lower the risk and the higher the probable return on investment.
>
> Definition of the relevant market and its boundaries becomes a major strategy evaluation.

The validity of the rule of three and four is arguable. It is presented to illustrate the way a set of normative implications have been derived by interpreting the effects of the experience curve. What seems to be true is that industry concentration tends to be very high under stable conditions, and where this is not observed, perhaps the appropriate market is not defined correctly, or government regulations prevent the natural course of adjustments.

THE PRICE–COST RELATIONSHIP

Although cost has a fairly predictable trend along the experience curve, prices do not. Early in the introduction of a new product, the innovating firm makes a strategic decision

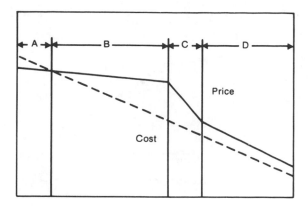

Figure 5. The relationship of price and cost (vertical axis) during the different stages in the life cycle of a product. Introduction (A), embryonic stage (B), shakeout period (C), and maturity (D), with the horizontal axis representing accumulated production

about price. The major question is whether to set a high price in the initial phases, when it is possible for the innovator to impose a monopolistic rent and enjoy an extraordinarily high profit, or to lower the prices at the same rate at which costs decline to discourage the entry of competing firms into the business. Usually in the introductory and embryonic stages prices tend to be fairly stable, providing a real bonanza or the innovative firm (Figure 5). This has been the case for electronic watches, video recorders, hand electronic calculators, and similar technology-intensive consumer products. As the embryonic phase ends, the entry of new competitors generates a turbulent shakeout in the industry with a rate of price reductions much faster than the cost decline. Quite often, a complete restructuring of the industry takes place at this stage, and even the original innovator may be forced out of business. That happened to Bowmar in electronic hand calculators.

At the end of the shakeout phase, only a few of the most efficient producers survive, and despite their small number, the profit margin should be consistent with a perfect market situation throughout the maturity stage of the product.

USING THE EXPERIENCE CURVE IN STRATEGIC PLANNING

The experience curve provides important insights for strategic planning, particularly in high-technology firms. However, according to Strategic Planning Associates, Inc., its use depends on some subtle guidelines. Not recognizing these guidelines can lead to misuse of the experience curve.

To determine the chronology of the experience curve, the starting point for the accumulation of experience must be detected. Also, occasionally, shifts in the experience curve take place over a long time span (Figure 6). Using an average slope will grossly underestimate the effects of recent technological advances or capacity expansions after major capital investments.

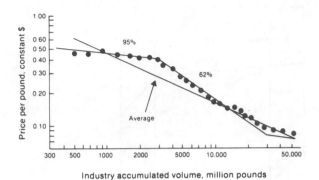

Figure 6. The accumulation of experience for Polyvinyl Chloride shifted from a 95% curve to a 63% curve after 2000 million pounds had been produced by the industry. Using an average slope would grossly underestimate the effects of recent technological advances or capacity expansions. (Source: Henderson and Zakon, 1980)

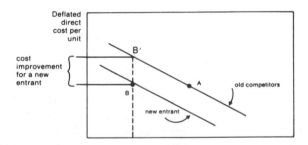

Figure 7. The experience curve of a new entrant whose business is supported by technology with a different experience curve than its competitors

ASSESSING THE STARTING POSITION OF A NEW ENTRANT

The strategic implications discussed so far require a common experience curve for every competitor in an industry. This assumption can be violated in two different situations.

First, a new entrant can support its business on a technology whose experience curve behaves differently (Figure 7). In spite of the larger accumulated volume of the established top firm compared to the new entrant, it may not have a cost advantage because of the different patterns of the two experience curves. The dominance of the Japanese in the US steel industry might be explained in this way.

A second way to explain an improved position of a new entrant, other than technological differences, is the quick transfer of technology and know-how as a new entrant follows the lead of the established firm. In today's industrial world of fast communications, it is often impossible to retain proprietorship of process and product technology. A new entrant with an experience curve of identical slope to that of the leader will have a better initial position than would have been predicted if no technological transfer had taken place (Figure 8).

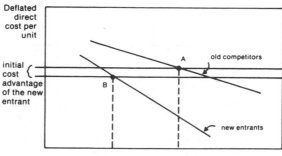

Accumulated volume of production (units)

Figure 8. The experience curve of a new entrant with smart followership and transfer of technology. The unit cost for a new entrant B is identical to that of an old firm A, despite the large difference in accumulated volume of production (horizontal axis), because of the quick transfer of technology and know-how as the new entrant follows the lead of the established firm. Without this transfer of technology, new firms would follow the experience curve of old competitors, and the unit cost for the new entrant would be at the level B′ instead of B

MARKET SHARE IS NOT THE ONLY GAME

There are some industries in which experience does not seem to play much part in cost reduction. In those industries, the strategic position of a business does not rely on cost advantages. This is the case with producers of specialty products. Commodity products have few opportunities for differentiation that can induce the consumer to pay a price premium. Specialty products, on the other hand, offer distinctive features valued by the consumer. The closer a product is to a commodity, the more its cost becomes crucial.

The classic example of this is Ford's loss of leadership in the automobile industry. In spite of the fact that Ford reduced its cost by 15% from 1908 to 1925 [Abernathy and Wayne 1974], it was overtaken by General Motors because of their creative strategy of segmentation of the market under the slogan 'A car for every purse and every purpose'. Ford was wrongly treating a car as a commodity ('I will give you any car provided it is a model T and it is black'), without realizing that the American public was ready to pay a price premium for a more distinctive product.

DON'T MEASURE ONLY AT THE END OF THE VALUE-ADDED CHAIN

A productive activity is composed of many different steps that can be ordered by stages of value-added. Among these stages are research and development, manufacture of parts, assembly, marketing, distribution, and retailing. Although experience will affect all these stages, seldom will it affect all of them equally, for instance, the 95% slope in retailing compared with the 70% slope in assembly indicates that experience in retailing is not as important as in assembly (Figure 9).

In addition to the different effects of experience because of the nature of the work, the impact of product mixes contributes to the accumulation of different amounts of

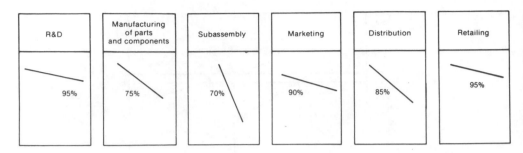

Figure 9. The effect of accumulated experience on the cost accrued in different stages of value-added. In this example, the productive activity is composed of six stages of value-added: research and development, manufacture of parts, assembly, marketing, distribution, and retailing. Experience is accumulated at different rates in each stage, represented by the slopes of the lines. For instance, the 95% slope for retailing indicates that experience in retailing is not as important as it is in assembly with a 70% slope

experience at each stage. This situation is observed in firms manufacturing many products that load with a different emphasis the various stages of the value-added chain. Experience will accrue more rapidly to those stages which are heavily loaded by the entire set of items produced.

Both of these effects must be recognized, and market share should not be measured just at the end of the productive chain.

To illustrate, in a business, the leader of the market is firm A with a market share four times that held by its competition, firm B. At first, it looks as if firm A has an insurmountable advantage, but this impression is tempered when the business is conceptualized in terms of two stages of value-added: manufacturing and distribution. In the manufacturing stage, firm A has a four to one advantage over firm B, but in the distribution stage, it is firm B which has an advantage of three to one because this business shares a system of distribution with many others. Assuming that experience in both stages has the same impact over cost, and that each stage contributes half the final value of the product, we could use a normalized market share to determine the relative standing of the two firms in the business.

$$= (4 \text{ to } 1 \text{ or } 4/5) (0.5) + (1 \text{ to } 3 \text{ or } 1/4)$$
$$(0.5)$$
$$= 0.525$$

Similarly, for firm B we obtain a market share of 0.475.

The relative market share of firm A over firm B in this weighted measure of experience is only $0.525/0.475 = 1.10$ times, which is far smaller than the four to one obtained by considering only the final product.

BEWARE OVEREMPHASIZING EXPERIENCE

Too much reliance on increasing scale and driving down costs might have undesirable effects. Too much emphasis on economies of scale might impair the firm's ability to respond to technological advance, environmental changes, and innovations taking place outside the firm. Also, it could prevent the firm's diversifying its products to capture a wider range of customers.

A successful firm might find itself chained to its existing business base, and prevented from adapting for long term and sustained profits. Success could be your worst enemy.

DIAGNOSIS OF THE INDUSTRY COST STRUCTURE

An assessment of the industry cost structure depends on determining the experience curve for each competitor in the industry. Where a single experience curve is common to everybody, the market share of each competitor is crucial to assessing their strength. When this is not the case, identifying the stages of value-added and the different technologies in use can provide insights for the strategic positioning of a business in that industry.

This might explain highly successful strategies such as the entry of Phillip Morris into the beer industry with Miller Light. Normally, entry into an aging industry is regarded as a highly unnatural and unproductive strategy. However, the success of Phillip Morris was based on a coherent set of strategies which included: heavy investment in new and efficient production facilities; introduction of an innovative product with a high potential market; and impressive marketing and distribution. This approach put Phillip Morris in a completely different experience curve than its competitors.

The entry of Procter and Gamble into the paper towel business against Scott Paper demonstrates the usefulness of identifying market share by stages of value-added. If market share, and therefore accumulated experience, were measured only by products sold, one would imagine that Procter and Gamble could do nothing in that business. However, the dominance of Procter and Gamble in marketing and distribution allowed them to start with a much stronger position than would otherwise be anticipated. It is this kind of strategic position that has permitted Procter and Gamble to enter late in many other consumer-product markets, without apparently having much of a disadvantage in its cost structure.

PROJECTING THE COST STRUCTURE

Very often firms in high technology areas, where experience plays a fundamental role, bid for contracts which, if obtained, would move them to the right of the experience curve and lower the cost of the units produced. It is essential to forecast such cost reductions so that the bids will incorporate them.

If the bid were to be accepted, the firm would need to use those projections, which were the basis for cost estimates, as controls. The actual cost realized would then be plotted in the experience curve charts against the estimates to detect any deviation. Management could then correct problems causing low productivity.

Events similar to those described took place in the aircraft division of a major firm. This firm simultaneously won bids from three government agencies. The combination pushed its production up by one order of magnitude. The bid cost per unit had been computed, passing the assumed cost reductions along to the client. Strict control of actual cost in each stage of production was necessary to make sure that the contracts would be profitable for the firm.

THE SELECTION OF A GENERIC STRATEGY

Michael Porter [1980] advocates three generic strategies to help a firm identify the position of a given business. The first strategy aims at *cost leadership* which depends on the firm having lower costs than its competitors. This strategy fully exploits experience curve effects.

The second generic strategy seeks for *differentiation*. Here the firm attempts to develop distinctive products in a given business to provide an advantage over the firm's competitors.

The third generic strategy consists of *targeting* a particular market segment where the firm can develop a distinctive strength.

Each strategy is designed to secure a long-term sustainable advantage in a competitive market, and each attempts to pursue that goal in quite distinctive ways. The justification for this positioning can be understood after recognizing the U-shape effect that is observed in the behavior of profitability of firms competing in some industrial sectors (Figure 10).

Firms with either large or small market share can get a high return on investment, while firms in an intermediate situation will have a depressed profitability. In fact, if a firm achieves a level of sales allowing the exploitation of the full benefits of the experience curve (a large market share), strategies that lead to cost leadership can truly pay off. If the firm cannot achieve a high level of sales, two alternatives are open.

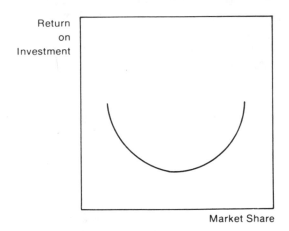

Figure 10. Firms with either large or small market share can get a high return on investment, while firms in an intermediate situation will have a depressed profitability. A large market share allows the exploitation of the full benefits of the experience curve, thus leading to high profitability. Small market share can only be viable in the long run with either a special product focused to a particular market or a unique item clearly differentiated from the competitors' products. In both cases the firm can enjoy a price-premium also leading to high profitability. The worst situation is in the lower part of the U-curve with no cost advantage and no distinctive product to offer

One is to choose unique differentiation, so the firm can enjoy a price-premium because of the special character of its products. The other is to redesign to target the output of the firm to a particular market. In both cases a small market share and a high profitability are obtained.

The worst situation is in the lower end of the U-curve with no cost advantage and no distinctive value to offer.

CONCLUSION

Although we have discussed the strategic implications of experience effects, it will not be a surprise to experienced managers that there are no simple answers to complex problems. The experience curve with its implicit message that benefits can be obtained by increasing the volume of production is valid and relevant. However, a blind and narrow pursuit of cost reductions by simply accumulating experience could lead to an unexpectedly poor position in the market place. Despite the series of warnings presented to make the best of the lessons of experience, the important message of the experience-curve methodology is that cost can and should be managed if firms want to insure a solid position in the marketplace.

REFERENCES

Abernathy, William J. 1978, *The Productivity Dilemma: Roadblock to Innovation in the Automobile Industry*, The Johns Hopkins Press, Baltimore.

Abernathy, William J. and Wayne, Kenneth 1974, 'Limits of the learning curve,' *Harvard Business Review*, Vol. 52, No. 5 (September–October), pp. 109–119.

Boston Consulting Group 1972, *Perspective on Experience*, Boston Consulting Group, Inc., Boston.

Buzzell, Robert D., Gale, Bradley T., and Sultan, Ralph G. M. 1975, 'Market share: a key to profitability,' *Harvard Business Review*, Vol. 53, No. 1 (January–February), pp. 97–106.

Fruhan, William E. 1972, 'Pyrrhic victories in fights for market share,' *Harvard Business Review*, Vol. 50, No. 5 (September–October), pp. 100–107.

Henderson, Bruce D. 1979, *Henderson on Corporate Strategy*, Abt Books, Cambridge, MA.

Henderson, Bruce D. and Zakon, Alan J. 1980, 'Pricing strategy: how to improve it (the experience curve),' *Handbook of Business Problem Solving*, edited by Kenneth J. Albert, McGraw-Hill, New York, pp. 3-51–3-68.

Hirschmann, Winfred B. 1964, 'Profit from the learning curve,' *Harvard Business Review*, Vol. 42, No. 1 (January–February), pp. 125–139.

Porter, Michael E. 1980, *Competitive strategy: techniques for analyzing industries and competitors*, Free Press, New York.

Schoeffler, Sidney, Buzzell, Robert D., and Heany, Donald F., 1974 'Impact of strategic planning on profit performance,' *Harvard Business Review* (March–April) Vol. 52, No. 2, pp. 137–145.

Chapter 4

The Use of the Growth-Share Matrix in Strategic Planning

Arnoldo C. Hax

Sloan School of Management, Massachusetts Institute of Technology, Cambridge, Massachusetts 02139, USA

Nicolas S. Majluf

Universidad Catolica de Chile, Escuela de Ingenieria, Casilla 114-D, Santiago, Chile

In the late 1960s the Boston Consulting Group (BCG) offered a new way to look at strategic planning activities [Henderson 1970, 1973]. In essence the BCG approach views the firm as a portfolio of businesses, each one offering a unique contribution to growth and profitability. These largely independent units have strategic directions which can be addressed separately.

In order to visualize the role played by each business unit, BCG developed the growth-share matrix, in which all the businesses in a firm are plotted on a four-quadrant grid (Figure 1). The horizontal axis corresponds to the market share enjoyed by a business relative to its major competitor, and is a way of characterizing the strength of the firm in that business. The vertical axis indicates the percent of growth in the market in the most recent year, or the attractiveness of the market for the business. Circles represent each business, with the area within them proportional to total sales.

The growth-share matrix is helpful in three ways. First, the graphic display offers a powerful and compact picture of the strengths of the businesses in the firm's portfolio. Second, it identifies the capacity of each business to generate cash and also reveals its requirements for cash; thus it assists in balancing the firm's cash-flow. And third, because it shows the distinct characteristics of each business unit, it can suggest strategic directions for each business. We will describe how to construct the matrix.

Reprinted by permission of A. C. Hax and N. S. Majluf, *Interfaces*, Volume 13, No. 1, January–February 1983, pp. 46–60, Copyright ©1983, The Institute of Management Sciences, 290 Westminster Street, Providence, Rhode Island 02903, USA.

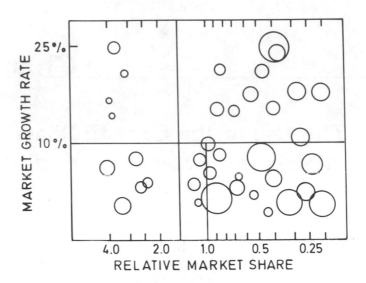

Figure 1. A typical product portfolio chart (growth-share matrix) of a comparatively weak and diversified company

MEASURING THE ATTRACTIVENESS OF THE MARKET

The market-growth rate, which is plotted in the vertical axis of the matrix, is used as a proxy for the attractiveness of the market for each of the firm's businesses. Based on data from the last year, this measure provides a static picture of the corporation at that time. For example, at the end of 1982 the market growth rate is measured as follows:

$$\text{Market Growth Rate 1982} = \frac{\left[\begin{array}{c}\text{Total Market} \\ 1982\end{array}\right] - \left[\begin{array}{c}\text{Total Market} \\ 1982\end{array}\right]}{\begin{array}{c}\text{Total Market} \\ 1981\end{array}} \times 100.$$

This indicator provides a measure of attractiveness for the total industry without regard for the position of a given firm. It is based on the business life-cycle concept, which postulates that a business follows a process of evolution with four stages: embryonic, growth, maturity, and aging (Figure 2). Factors other than market growth also determine where a given business is in its life-cycle. Nonetheless, the market growth rate is a key indicator to the attractiveness of that business.

The business life cycle concept has enormous implications for strategic planning. When the whole industry is growing fast, a firm can penetrate that industry aggressively and increase its market share significantly without necessarily eroding the sales of competitors.

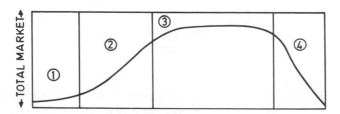

Figure 2. The business life-cycle: A business evolves through four stages: (1) embryonic, (2) growth, (3) maturity, (4) aging

Sales will continue to grow for the majority of the key competitors in the industry, but their share of the markets might be shrinking. However, in a mature or aging industry it is no longer possible for one business to increase its market share without decreasing the dollar sales of competitors. Arthur D. Little, Inc., has developed further implications of the life-cycle curve for strategic planning and has proposed its own portfolio matrix [Osell and Wright 1980].

To position a business in the growth-share portfolio matrix a cut-off point must be chosen to separate high growth from low growth businesses (Figure 1).

How is a cut-off point selected in practice? Whenever all the businesses of a firm belong to one industry, the decision is straightforward. The cut-off point is the average growth for that industry. Businesses above that level are in the embryonic or growth stage, and those below are in the maturity or aging stage. In highly diversified firms we could use a measurement of overall economic growth, such as growth of gross national product (if the businesses are all conducted within a given country). Otherwise, a weighted average of the growth rate of each individual business would be a logical selection. Occasionally, it might be legitimate and convenient to set up as a cut-off point a corporate growth target; this will separate businesses which contribute to realizing the target from those which detract from it.

Notice that if market-growth rate is expressed in deflated dollars, the cut-off point should measure the real growth of either the industry, the economy, or the corporate target. If nominal market-growth rates are used, the definition of the cut-off point should also use nominal values.

MEASURING THE INTERNAL STRENGTH OF THE BUSINESS

At first glance, market share seems a logical way to identify a business's strength in a competitive environment. But how would you describe a firm in a given business that controls a 10% share of the market? Is it strong or weak? The answer depends on how fragmented the industry is. In the pharmaceutical industry, the firm would probably have an extraordinary strong position; however, in the U.S. automobile industry, that firm would be near collapse. Following this reasoning relative market share is adopted as a measure of the internal strength of a given business. Going back to our 1982 example, relative market share is defined as follows:

$$\text{Relative Market} = \frac{\left[\begin{array}{c} \text{Business Sales} \\ 1982 \end{array}\right]}{\left[\begin{array}{c} \text{Leading Competitor's} \\ \text{Sales 1982} \end{array}\right]}.$$

Relative market share is not expressed as a percentage. It gives a ratio for the sales of a business against those of the most important competitor; for example, a relative market share of 2 means that the business's sales are two times larger than sales of the most important competitor, while a relative market share of 0.5 means that the business's sales are only half those of the leading competitor. The relative market share of each business is plotted in the growth-share matrix in a semi-log scale. The reason for doing this is that market share is linked to accumulated volume, and this in turn is relative to the experience curve. The decline of costs resulting from the experience curve effect can be plotted as a straight line in a semi-log scale.

The strategic implications of the experience curve were analyzed in the first of these three papers [Hax and Majluf 1982]. Briefly stated:

Higher Market Share	→	Higher Accumulated Volume	→	Lower Costs	→	Higher Profitability

The growth-share matrix requires that a cut-off point be established to separate business of high and low internal strength. BCG selected a relative market share of 1.0 as the cut-off point. The market leader (that is the business with relative market share greater than one), has significant strength. In our example the basic cut-off line is set at a relative market share of 1.5; at that level of competitive advantage, a business can truly dominate an industry (Figure 1).

MEASURING THE CONTRIBUTION OF EACH BUSINESS TO THE FIRM

Besides positioning its businesses in terms of industry attractiveness and competitive strength, a third parameter is used in the growth-share matrix to characterize the portfolio of the firm: the contribution of the business to the firm, measured in terms of sales. It is represented by the area within the circles in the matrix (Figure 1).

Sales is preferred as a measure of contribution, because it allows easy comparison with the portfolios of competitors, and it provides a good measure for comparing the strengths and weaknesses of all firms competing in an industry. Profitability measurements could be better, but those figures are difficult to obtain for the separate businesses of competitors. Moreover, even internally, using profits or return on investments to measure the contribution of a business for the firm might allow arbitrary allocation of overhead that would distort the real contribution of that business.

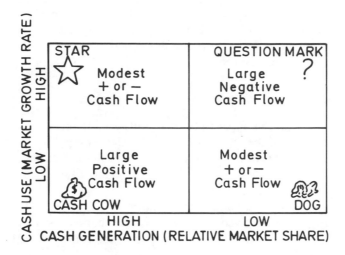

Figure 3. Cash-flow characteristics of business categories in the growth-share matrix

CASH-FLOW IMPLICATIONS OF THE GROWTH-SHARE MATRIX

A striking characteristic of the growth-share matrix is its simplicity. It tries to capture the complexities of a firm's portfolio in a graphical representation with only three indicators. Categorizing a firm's businesses this way has several implications; the most important concerns the transfer of cash among businesses. To visualize cash flow transactions the same growth-share matrix can be expressed in terms of cash-use and cash-generation (Figure 3).

In the previous section we divided the firm's business portfolio into four quadrants. The businesses in each quadrant also have distinctive qualities in regard to cash flow, and can be labelled with terms that have become popular jargon: 'stars,' 'cash cows,' 'question marks,' and 'dogs.'

The Stars

The Stars are the businesses in the upper-left corner of the matrix. They are highly attractive businesses (ones with high market growth), and they have strong competitive positions (high relative market share). They generate large amounts of cash because of their successful status but, at the same time, require significant cash resources to sustain their competitive strength in their rapidly growing markets. As a result, the amount of cash either contributed to or required from the firm is modest.

The Cash Cows

These businesses (in the lower left corner of the matrix) are sources of cash for the organization. Because of their extremely high competitive strength in declining markets, they generate more cash than they should reinvest in themselves. Therefore, they are sources of cash for developing other businesses within the firm. Ultimately, resource allocation in a firm has to be centralized at a managerial level. Otherwise, managers of cash cows will tend to reinvest the proceeds of their businesses in their own domains, sub-optimizing the use of resources.

The Question Marks

The Question Marks (in the upper right quadrant) are major untapped opportunities, very attractive because of the high market growth they enjoy. However, they have not achieved significant shares of their markets. Those businesses among them that can be successfully promoted to a leading position must be identified before committing the necessary large amounts of cash to them.

Alternatively, the firm might decide that it does not have the strength to advance the business, in spite of its attractiveness, because of the characteristics of its competitors. This calls for the toughest of decisions: that the best course of action would be to withdraw or liquidate.

The Dogs

These businesses (in the lower right quadrant) are clearly the great losers, unattractive and weak. They are 'cash traps', because what little cash they generate is needed to maintain their operations. If there is no legitimate reason to expect a turnaround in the near future, the logical strategy would be harvesting or divesting.

SUGGESTIONS FOR STRATEGIC POSITIONING

Before discussing suggestions to be extracted from the growth-share matrix for strategic positioning of each of the businesses within a firm, we will present the philosophy underlying it.

The primary objectives of corporations, implicit in the initial conceptualization of BCG, are growth and profitability [Henderson and Zakon 1980]. The fundamental advantage that a multibusiness organization possesses is the ability to transfer cash from businesses that are highly profitable but have limited potential for growth to others that offer expectations of sustained future growth and profitability.

This leads to an integrative management of the portfolio that will make the whole larger than the sum of its parts. To obtain this synergistic result, resource allocation must be centralized and designed to produce a balanced portfolio in terms of the generation and uses of cash.

The two dimensions used to position each business in the growth-share matrix are assumed to be related to its cash generation and cash requirement characteristics. In associating relative market share with the experience curve, it is implicit that those businesses holding stronger shares will also enjoy higher profitability and, consequently, higher cash generation. Conversely, businesses in industries with high growth rates require higher levels of cash for their future development.

Table 1. Implications for strategic positioning emerging from the growth-share matrix

Business Category	Market Share Thrust	Business Profitability	Investment Required	Net Cash Flow
Stars	Hold/Increase	High	High	Around zero or slightly negative
Cash Cows	Hold	High	Low	Highly positive
Question Marks	Increase	None or negative	Very High	Highly negative
	Harvest/Divest	Low or negative	Disinvest	Positive
Dogs	Harvest/Divest	Low or negative	Disinvest	Positive

Although it can be argued that firms have access to external sources of cash, primarily through debt and equity issuing, inherent in the BCG aproach is the belief that ultimately, any external debt will have to be matched by internal cash flow. Therefore, the balanced assignment of internal cash resources is vital to the proper development of a firm.

In addition to the balanced portfolio idea, BCG uses market share to express the strategic positioning desired for each business. They identify four major strategic thrusts in terms of market share:

to increase market share;
to hold market share,
to harvest, and
to withdraw or divest.

Although realizing these strategic thrusts would require spelling out complex programs for each business, expressed in terms of market share they convey a basic message for positioning a business in a competitive environment. Defining strategic thrust in terms of market share has been adapted and used by most of the alternative methodologies for portfolio analysis.

When we designate a strategic thrust, we summarize our basic intentions for the long term positioning of the business. Although normally a strategy is made up of a complex set of programs for action that affect all levels of the organization, the market share objective forcefully communicates the ultimate thrust of the strategy selected for that business.

Other methods of analyzing portfolios question the use of market share as an indicator of business strength, contending that many other factors should be considered in establishing the true competitive position of a business within an industry. Even so, most other approaches retain the four categories of market share thrust as a robust way of summarizing the direction of a business.

A summary of choices for strategic positioning emerging from the growth-share matrix, is presented in Table 1. Cash-flow is assigned primarily from the surplus cash resources of cash-cow businesses, to selected question-mark businesses that require large cash investment to increase their market share.

In using portfolio analysis for strategy for more than one period, we need some guidelines to judge the desirability of movements of businesses within the growth-share matrix. The ideal sequence is one where a question-mark business grows in size and strength to become a star in the first stage, and in the second stage inevitably declines

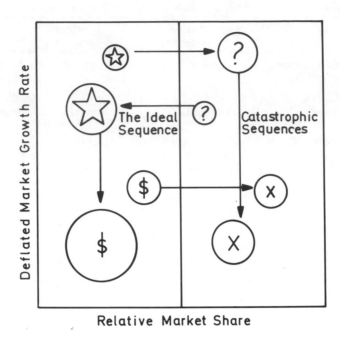

Figure 4. Conceptual sequences of business evolution

in growth rate but retains the competitive strength required to become a cash-cow. In undesirable sequences, which would lead to catastrophic losses for a firm, businesses evolve from strong to weak positions in the market despite sales increases (Figure 4).

MEASURING HISTORICAL EVOLUTION WITH GROWTH-SHARE POSITIONING

One could argue that the graphical representation of the growth-share matrix provides just a static snapshot of the business portfolio of a firm and ignores the historical trends of those businesses. We will now address this concern.

A very powerful tool used to understand the implicit or explicit strategies of a firm is the 'Share-Momentum Graph' [Lewis 1977] (Figure 5).

The graph is constructed by picking a relevant time-frame, say five years, and plotting the position of each business unit in terms of two dimensions: the total market growth for that period and the growth rate of sales for the same period, both defined either in nominal or real terms. As before, the area within the circles representing each business is proportional to total sales for the last year of the chosen period.

Those businesses that have grown at the same rate as the industry, and therefore hold their market share during the period of analysis, fall on the diagonal line. Below the diagonal line are businesses that have increased sales at a rate higher than their markets,

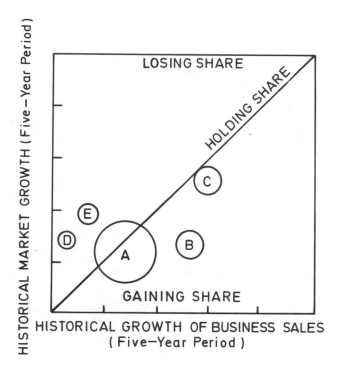

Figure 5. Example of a share-momentum graph

that is they have increased their market share. Falling above the diagonal, are businesses that decreased their share of the market (Figure 5).

The implications of this chart are straightforward but quite revealing. It is entirely possible for a business in a high growth industry to experience a gain in net sales while losing market share. If managers do not know this, they may feel proud of their performance and be ignorant of the grave consequences of their decline in competitive strength. The chart can serve as a diagnostic tool for detecting trends in the growth-share positioning of businesses, and for verifying whether the historical trend is consistent with intended strategic positioning of the business.

The share-momentum chart can be applied not only to one's own firm but also to key competitors. The information required to develop the chart for key competitors is the same information used to put together the original growth-share matrix; that is total market figures and competitors' sales information. By properly analyzing the share-momentum chart for each competitor, we can gain valuable intelligence regarding their strategies. This could reveal areas of vulnerability that could be advantageously exploited, or areas presenting insurmountable barriers to penetration. Figures 6 and 7 show how to apply this competitive analysis to the paper-related business of Boise-Cascade Corp.

Another approach for capturing the dynamic nature of a portfolio uses the original growth-share matrix to follow the historical movements of each business unit through

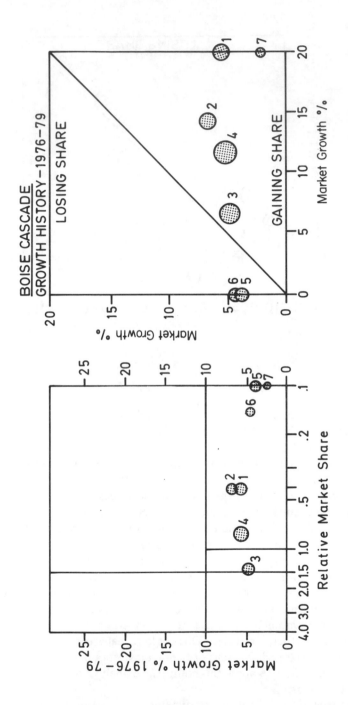

Figures 6 and 7 show the growth-share matrix and the share-momentum matrix for the paper-related business of Boise-Cascade in 1979. The information used to prepare these charts was publically available. The growth-share matrix (Figure 6) shows that the industry is plagued by slow growth, moreover Boise has a commanding strength only in business segment 3. Business segments 5 and 7 are so weak that Boise might be divesting them. However, Figure 7 shows that the firm is retiring only from business 5, while actively promoting business 7

a sequence of time periods. We have found this tool less effective than a share-momentum chart, because erratic variations observed on a yearly analysis make the resulting chart for a five-year time-frame clumsy. Also the cut-off point separating high from low market growths tends to change each year. Although this could be remedied by using an average growth rate for the five year period, such an average might hide important clues which are revealed by yearly data. An illustration of this approach is described in Hax and Majluf [1978].

MAXIMUM-SUSTAINABLE GROWTH

Maximum-sustainable growth is a critical dimension of the growth objective of the firm originally pointed out by Zakon [1976]. This concept represents the maximum growth that a firm can support using both its internal resources and its debt capabilities. Expressed in very simple terms, Zakon's formula for maximum-sustainable growth is:

$$g = p \cdot [ROA + \frac{D}{E}(ROA - i)]$$

where:
  g = maximum-sustainable growth, expressed as a yearly rate of increase of the equity base
  p = percentage of retained earnings
ROA = after-tax return on assets
  D = total debt outstanding
  E = total equity
  i = after-tax interest on debt.
This formula is derived through the following steps. Total assets are computed as total debt plus total equity:

$$A = D + E$$

Therefore, after-tax profits may be obtained as:

$$\pi = (D + E) \cdot ROA - D \cdot i$$

An equivalent expression is:

$$\pi = E \cdot ROA + D(ROA - i)$$

The growth of equity depends on the amount of retained earnings. Assuming that p is the retention ratio (equal to retained earnings over total earnings) and that g is the growth of equity, we can establish that:

$$g = \frac{p \cdot \pi}{E} = p \cdot [ROA + \frac{D}{E} \cdot (ROA - i)]$$

If we assume that the debt-equity ratio remains constant, and that the increment of equity will be followed by a similar increment of debt, we conclude that the above expression corresponds to the actual growth of total assets under the stated conditions.

The expression just derived represents a first cut and gross approximation of maximum-sustainable growth; it assumes a stable debt-equity ratio and dividend-payout policy, as well as a fixed overall rate of return on assets and cost of debt. Although a coarse approximation, it can provide guidance for corporate growth that should be taken into consideration at the corporate level.

There are many alternative expressions for maximum-sustainable growth. We have presented the simplest in order to stress the underlying concept that a firm faces an upper bound to its objectives for future growth unless the financing policy allows issuing new shares of stock

FURTHER APPLICATION OF THE
GROWTH-SHARE MATRIX

The growth-share matrix is primarily intended to analyze a portfolio from a corporate perspective. Only at that level is cash balance meaningful. However, a business may be segmented further using this diagnostic tool in order to understand the different positions of its individual product-lines or market segments.

For an example, we will depict the Norton Company portfolio at a time when the firm was confronted with a crucial strategic decision [Cushman 1979]. Norton's traditional business strength was in the abrasive industry, which was severely cyclical and had a low growth rate. Norton realized in the 1960s that it should use these profitable businesses to help it diversify into more attractive areas offering higher growth rates. The company used the growth-share matrix as the primary instrument for building its successful strategy of diversification away from the abrasive industry.

All Norton's business units were classified in terms of four categories for strategic implication. Although that conveyed a fairly meaningful message for the corporation as a whole, it was insufficient to guide the decisions of the individual managers of Norton businesses, who needed a finer segmentation of the unit under their jurisdiction. This was provided for the various market segments that are part of a business unit that may appear monolithic from the corporate level (Figure 8). The contributions of those market segments to the overall business unit can then be appreciated. Two markets are revealed as the most attractive ones for growth, but they have a very weak position. This suggests that a competitor is 'cherry-picking'; that is, concentrating a large amount of effort on those market segments. Moreover, two other markets are shown to be in such dismal positions that the only worthwhile strategy seems to be complete withdrawal. This ability to discriminate among components of a business unit, either product-lines or market segments, is a valuable application of the growth-share matrix at the business unit level.

Another important use of the tool which is crucial to multinational firms is to position business units across various countries. Normally, the most puzzling and difficult problem for a business manager in a multinational setting is to deal with the complexities posed by contradictory positions of a given business operating in various countries. Using the BCG terminology, a Star in the U.S. might be a Cash Cow in Colombia, a Dog in Germany, and a Question Mark in Saudi Arabia. It is difficult to establish a coherent international strategy in that situation (Figure 9).

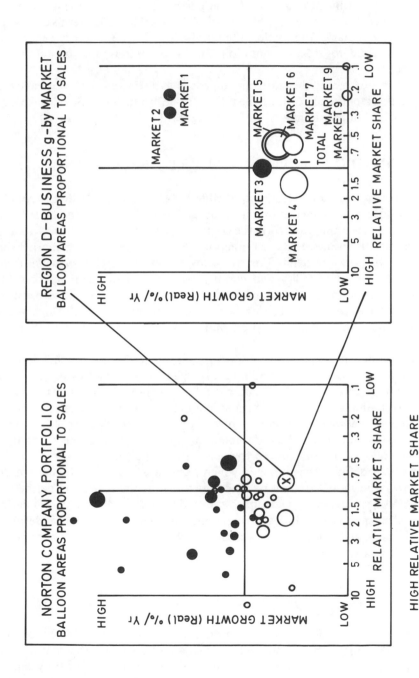

Figure 8. The figure on the left depicts corporate growth-share portfolio of the Norton Company and the one on the right depicts a finer analysis at the level of one business unit (source: Cushman, 'Norton's top-down, bottom-up planning process,' *Planning Review*, November 1979)

CRITICISM OF THE BCG APPROACH

The labels popularized by BCG to classify the positions of various businesses within the firm are often criticized. Recently, Andrews [1981] described these terms as a 'vulgar and destructive vocabulary.' In practice, the terminology has been widely accepted, in spite of its somewhat derogatory connotation. But, who would want to manage a Cash Cow or a Dog?

Mead Company, embraced this portfolio approach as a strategic tool, but gave more elegant designations to its matrix, using the terms: 'Bond' (cash cow), 'Savings Account' (star), 'Sweepstake' (question mark), and 'Mortgage' (dog) [Aguilar 1978].

THE RELIANCE ON MARKET DEFINITION

In the first paper in this series [Hax and Majluf 1982] we indicated that it could be a severe pitfall to use the achieved market share at the end of the value added chain to measure performance and, therefore, the competitive strength of the firm. Resources shared among various businesses at each functional level are ignored when market share is measured at the consumer end. For the growth-share matrix to provide a clear representation of the profitability and competitive strength of each business, it is mandatory that each business unit be portrayed as totally independent and autonomous. If in reality they are not autonomous we will be misled and be faced with Dogs in good health, Cash Cows with no milk, Question Marks without a question, and Stars that don't shine.

In a hilarious commentary published in *Fortune* magazine [1981], Kiechel described the BCG approach. 'A balanced portfolio, according to this scheme, consisted of a few stars shining away, getting ready to be cows; the bovinity throwing off cash and occasionally dwindling toward dogdom; and the promising question marks, in their pursuit of stardom, eating cash from the cows. Any money obtained from selling off the kennel should be employed to buy or finance question marks.' Obviously, managing a business portfolio cannot be reduced to such a simplistic formula.

Important also is defining the market in which a business competes. Relative market share compares a business' strength to its competitors. If the market is defined too narrowly the business invariably ends up as the leader of the segment; if it is defined too broadly the business is unrealistically represented as weak. Proper market definition is a very subtle issue, and unfortunately, this approach to business analysis rests heavily on this difficult matter.

VALID INDICATORS ARE NEEDED

The growth-share matrix relies on two indicators for positioning the different business units; their validity might be questioned. Is market share really the major factor determining profitability? Is industry growth really the only variable that fully explains growth opportunities? Certainly, these questions are subject to debate. A second but related objection to these indicators is that a good portfolio analysis should identify the competitive strengths and the industry attractiveness of each business unit.

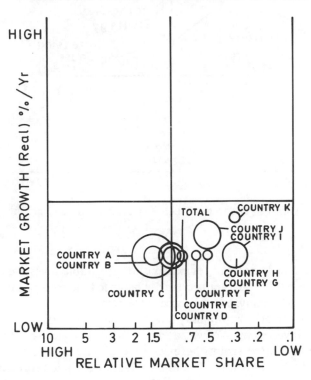

Figure 9. A finer analysis of a multinational business unit of the Norton Company (source: 'Norton's top-down, bottom-up planning process,' *Planning Review*, November 1979)

Alternatives to the growth-share matrix start by establishing that these two dimensions cannot be revealed by a single measurement, but require a wider set of critical factors for reliable positioning of the business units.

MARAKON'S VIEWS CHALLENGE THE BASIC PREMISES OF THE BCG APPROACH

Marakon, a management consulting company, has presented a theoretically better grounded approach to strategic investment planning which challenges the growth-share approach.

Marakon's views can be summarized as follows [1980]:

—Growth and profitability are not generally tightly linked. In fact they tend to compete or tradeoff.

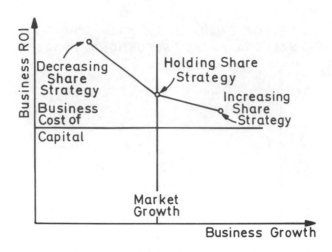

Figure 10. The tradeoff between profitability and growth

—Good planning should not call for passing up profitable investment opportunities.
—Ideal business portfolios are not necessarily balanced in terms of internal cash flows.
  We will now briefly analyze these three statements.

  The fact that growth and profitability tend to compete is easily demonstrated (Figure 10). Return on investment (*ROI*), a well-accepted measurement of short-term profitability, can be plotted against business growth to describe the investment options available to a given business unit. The horizontal cut-off line represents the business-unit cost of capital. Any investment option that falls above the line implies an attractive investment opportunity. The vertical cut-off line identifies the market growth rate for that business unit. A strategy that falls on that line corresponds to a holding market-share strategy; one to the left of the line implies a decreasing market-share strategy; one to the right of the line implies an increasing market-share strategy.

  A decreasing share strategy should be much more selective in the acceptance of its investment projects, in order to lead to a higher *ROI*. Conversely, an increasing share strategy would have to accept more marginal projects, and reduce the resulting *ROI*. This represents the profitability-growth tradeoff alluded to by Marakon.

  Sound financial principles suggest that a firm should accept all projects above its cost of capital. This favors the increasing share strategy (Figure 10), regardless of the position of the business in the growth-share matrix.

  The second statement of Marakon—that a firm should not pass up profitable investment opportunities—is directly linked to the previous argument. More formally, it is supported by the so-called *additivity principle* which states that every investment opportunity should be judged on its own merits and should be accepted or rejected depending on whether its projected return on investment falls above or below the cost of capital associated with that investment opportunity. In other words, there are no magic financial synergisms. The value of the firm is simply equal to the sum of the values of its components.

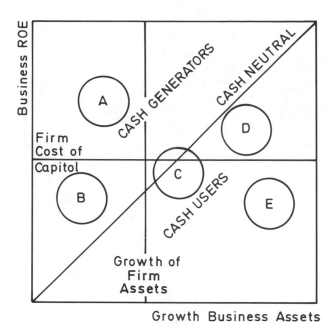

Figure 11. Cash generation and cash using characteristics of a business in terms of its growth and profitability

To explain the third statement of Marakon—that ideal portfolios are not necessarily balanced—it is useful to understand first the implications of cash generation and cash use in terms of the profitability and growth dimensions. Figure 11 provides a valuable insight into this question. The vertical axis corresponds to the *ROE* earned by a given business and the horizontal axis represents the corresponding business assets growth. A business placed in the diagonal is growing at the same rate as its *ROE*, and neither generates cash nor requires cash from the firm; it is a cash-neutral business. Similarly, businesses above the diagonal are cash generators and those below the diagonal are cash consumers.

To understand this line of reasoning, consider that the total equity investment in the business is E and the earnings generated are π. By the definition of return on equity (*ROE*), we can state that

$$\pi = E \cdot ROE$$

If we apply all earnings to the same business in order to tap new investment opportunities, the business growth as measured by the growth of the total investment is

$$G = \frac{\pi}{E}$$

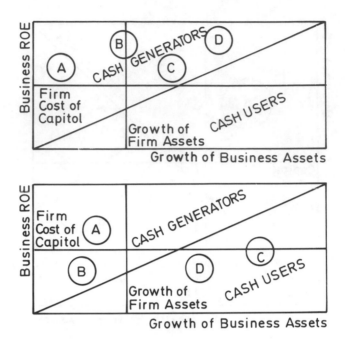

Figure 12. Examples of the relationship between the goodness of a portfolio and its cash-balance. The upper figure is an example of an excellent portfolio whichis not cash-balanced. The lower figure is an example of a balanced portfolio which is not necessarily profitable

This ratio is precisely the *ROE* of the business. Therefore, we can assert that a business growing at the same rate as its *ROE* is cash neutral from the corporate perspective. This is valid under stationary conditions for growth and profitability.

We can see that there can be good businesses (that is, businesses that earn more than the cost of capital) that generate cash (for example, business A) while others require cash (for example, business D). Similarly, some businesses (depicted as B and E) are examples of poor businesses that generate or require cash.

The final message is that a highly profitable portfolio may well be out of cash balance, while a rather poor portfolio may be perfectly balanced (Figure 12).

THE NEW BCG APPROACH:
A STRATEGY FOR THE EIGHTIES

In conclusion we will describe BCG's new matrix designed to avoid the misleading use of the growth-share matrix, as well as to respond to the changing nature of the competitive environment. Commenting on the 1981 BCG Annual Prospectus, Lockridge states:

In the 1970s, high inflation coupled with low growth, increased competition in the traditional fields, added regulation, and dramatic growth in international trade, again

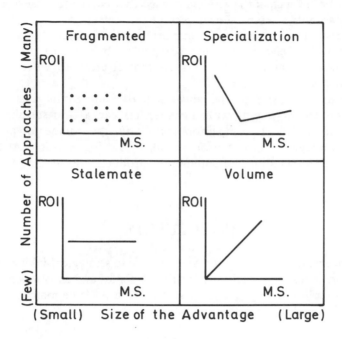

Figure 13. Underlying relationships between *ROI* and market share in the new BCG matrix

changed the rules of the game. Strategies in pursuit of market share and low-cost position alone met unexpected difficulties as segments specialists arose and multiple competitors reached economies of scale. The most successful companies achieved their success by anticipating market evolution and creating unique and defensible advantages over their competitors in the new environment.

To characterize this new environment, BCG proposes a matrix based on two different dimensions: the size of the competitive advantage, and the number of unique ways in which that advantage can be achieved. The resulting matrix and the new four-quadrant grid recognize four categories of businesses: 'Volume,' 'Stalemate,' 'Fragmented,' and 'Specialization.' The most appropriate strategy is different in each category and it depends on the relationship between return on investment and market share (Figure 13).

It is only in volume business that the strategies of market-share leadership and cost reduction are still meaningful. In this category, marketshare and profitability are closely associated.

A typical example of this kind of industry is the American automobile industry before foreign competitors emerged.

Stalemate businesses are those where profitability is low for all competitors regardless of size. There is small difference between the most profitable and the least profitable firm (Figure 13). The American steel industry is an example of this category.

The profitability of businesses in the fragmented category is not correlated with market share. Poor performers can be large or small, and good performers are also independent of size. They differ in which of the very many ways they choose to achieve a competitive advantage. Restaurants are typical examples of this category.

Finally, in the Specialty category the largest profitability is enjoyed by small businesses able to distinguish themselves among their competitors by pursuing a focused strategy. Japanese automobile manufacturers pursued that strategy to enter the American automobile industry.

With this matrix the size of the advantage (the horizontal axis) is definitely linked to barriers to entry; only with high barriers can a firm sustain a long-term defensible advantage over its competitors. Similarly, the number of approaches to achieving an advantage seem to be strongly linked to differentiation. At one extreme of the range of differentiation are commodity products and at the other, specialty products.

CONCLUSION

The growth-share matrix made a major contribution to strategic thinking and was used widely to support managerial decisions during the sixties and early seventies when the US economy was still growing. These days, a naive use of the matrix could produce inappropriate and misleading recommendations.

REFERENCES

Aguilar, Francis J. 1978, 'The Mead Corporation—strategic planning,' Harvard Business School, Case 9-379-070, Distributed by the Intercollegiate Case Clearing House, Soldiers Field, Boston, Massachusetts.

Andrews, Kenneth R. 1981, 'Replaying the board's role in formulating strategy,' *Harvard Business Review*, Vol. 59, No. 3 (May–June), pp. 18–19, 24–26.

Cushman, Robert 1979, 'Norton's top-down, bottom-up planning process,' *Planning Review*, Vol. 7, No. 6 (November), pp. 3–8, 48.

Hax, Arnoldo C. and Majluf, Nicolas S. 1978, 'A methodological approach for the development of strategic planning in diversified corporations,' in *Studies in Operations Management*, ed. Arnoldo C. Hax, North-Holland, Amsterdam, pp. 41–98.

Hax, Arnoldo C. and Majluf, Nicolas S. 1982, 'Competitive cost dynamics: The experience curve,' *Interfaces*, Vol. 12, No. 5 (October).

Henderson, Bruce D. 1970, 'The product portfolio,' The Boston Consulting Group, Perspectives No. 66, Boston, Massachusetts.

Henderson, Bruce D. 1973, 'The experience curve reviewed, IV. The growth share matrix of the product portfolio,' The Boston Consulting Group, Perspectives No. 135, Boston, Massachusetts.

Henderson, Bruce D. 1979, *Henderson on Corporate Strategy*, Abt Books, Cambridge, Massachusetts.

Henderson, Bruce D. and Zakon, Alan J. 1980, 'Corporate growth strategy: How to develop and implement it,' in *Handbook of Business Problem Solving*, ed. Kenneth J. Albert, McGraw-Hill, New York, Chapter 1, pp. 1.3–1.19.

Kiechel, Walter, III 'Oh where, oh where has my little dog gone? Or my cash cow? Or my star?' *Fortune*, Vol. 104, No. 9, November 2, 1981, pp. 148–154.

Lewis, W. Walker 1977, *Planning by Exception*, Strategic Planning Associates, Watergate 600, Washington, D.C.

Marakon Associates, 'Criteria for determining an optimal business portfolio,' presentation made at The Institute of Management Sciences, November 11, 1980.

Osell, Robert R. and Wright, Robert V. L. 1980, 'Allocating resources: How to do it in multi-industry corporations,' in *Handbook of Business Problem Solving*, ed. Kenneth J. Albert, McGraw-Hill, New York, Chapter 8, pp. 1.89–1.109.

Zakon, Alan J. 1976, 'Capital structure optimization,' in *The Treasurer's Handbook*, eds. J. F. Weston, and M. B. Goudzwaard, Dow Jones-Richard D. Irwin, Homewood, Illinois.

Chapter 5

The Use of the Industry Attractiveness-Business Strength Matrix in Strategic Planning

Arnoldo C. Hax

Alfred P. Sloan School of Management, Massachusetts Institute of Technology, 50 Memorial Drive, Cambridge, Massachusetts 02139, USA

Nicholas S. Majluf

Universidad Catolica de Chile, Escuela de Ingenieria, Casilla 114-D, Santiago, Chile

In the early seventies, General Electric became interested in the Boston Consulting Group's growth-share matrix approach. GE found appealing the visual display of the portfolio of businesses of a firm in terms of two dimensions: the attractiveness of the industry in which the business operates, and the internal strength of that business. As a multi-business organization, GE recognized that the tool was valuable for assigning priorities to each business and making rational investment and resource allocation decisions.

However, GE objected to the growth-share matrix's reliance upon single descriptors to characterize the two dimensions: total market growth rate for industry attractiveness, and relative market share for business strength. They thought that a wide variety of additional factors had to be identified and assessed to construct an appropriate representation of their portfolio of businesses. Accordingly, GE asked McKinsey and Company to develop what is now a highly popular and powerful portfolio approach: the industry attractiveness-business strength matrix (Figure 1). Prior to explaining in detail the necessary steps to implement this matrix, we will present an overview of its primary elements. First, the matrix requires the identification and assessment of both external and internal factors.

Critical external factors, which are not controllable by the firm, are used to determine the overall attractiveness of the industry in which the business belongs. Some external factors that have proved useful are market size, market growth rate, cyclicality,

Reprinted by permission of A. C. Hax and N. S. Majluf, *Interfaces*, Volume 13, No. 2, March–April 1983, pp. 54–71, Copyright ©1983, The Institute of Management Sciences, 290 Westminster Street, Providence, Rhode Island 02903, USA.

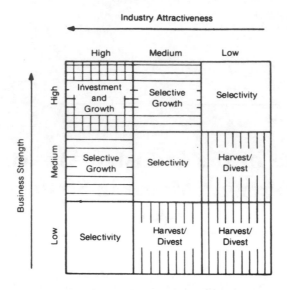

Figure 1. The position of the business in the industry attractiveness-business strength matrix suggests a priority for resource allocation. When both industry attractiveness and business strength are high, the natural strategy is to invest to grow. Whenever attractiveness and strength are both low, the strategy is harvest or divest. In intermediate positions resources should be concentrated in the most attractive segments or in segments where the firm has a unique competence. Business strength is determined by internal factors such as: market share, sales force, marketing, customer service, research and development, manufacturing, distribution, financial resources, image, breadth of product line, quality and reliability, and managerial competence. Industry attractiveness is measured by external factors such as: market size, market growth rate, cyclicality, competitive structure, barriers to entry, industry profitability, technology, inflation, regulation, manpower, availability, social issues, environmental issues, political issues, and legal issues

competitive structure, barriers to entry, industry profitability, technology, inflation, regulation, manpower availability, social issues, environmental issues, political issues, and legal issues.

In a similar way, critical internal factors, or *critical success factors*, which are largely controllable by the firm are identified: such as, market share, sales force, marketing, customer service, R&D, manufacturing, distribution, financial resources, image, breadth of product line, quality-reliability, and managerial competence. The position that a business achieves in these factors, compared to its key competitors, is a measure of the strength of the firm on the entire business being analyzed. Many of the factors (sales, marketing, R&D, customer services, manufacturing, distribution) are managerial functions. Ultimately, a strategy must be defined in terms of specific multifunctional programs for each business.

Once external and internal factors are identified and assessed each business is positioned in terms of overall industry attractiveness and business strength on a nine-cell grid (Figure 1). Three categories (high, medium, and low) are used to classify both attractiveness and strength.

Possible strategic actions are expressed in terms of basic thrusts:
—Invest to grow
—Selectivity to grow

—Selectivity
—Harvest or Divest

A METHODOLOGY FOR DEVELOPING AND USING THE ATTRACTIVENESS-STRENGTH MATRIX

In identifying the major steps for implementing this approach, a clear separation has to be made between the current state of internal and external factors and future projections for them. Positioning each business unit in the current state requires objective evaluation of overall industry attractiveness and business strength based on historical and current data. However, future positioning requires that trends for external factors be predicted to obtain a forecasted profile of industry attractiveness (Table 1). Once this information is on hand, we can develop a business strategy congruent with the goals for each business in the portfolio.

Table 1. Major steps for the implementation of the attractiveness-strength matrix

Analysis of current situation	Analysis of future situation
STEP 1 Definition of critical internal and external factors	
STEP 2 Assessment of external factors	STEP 5 Forecasting of trends for each external factor
STEP 3 Assessment of internal factors	STEP 6 Developing the desired position for each internal factor
STEP 4 Positioning of the business in the attractiveness-strength matrix	STEP 7 Desired positioning of each business in the attractiveness-strength matrix
	STEP 8 Formulation of strategies for each business

STEP 1: DEFINING CRITICAL INTERNAL AND EXTERNAL FACTORS

A traditional way to start the business planning process is to conduct an *environmental scan* to determine the opportunities and threats in the external environment and an *internal scrutiny* to identify the basic internal strengths and weaknesses of business.

The factors to be assessed can be separated into two groups. The critical external factors, that are *essentially uncontrollable* by the firm, are basic characteristics of the industry and competitive structure in which the business operates and a host of other factors, such as socio-political, economic, legislative, regulatory, and demographic factors. At best the firm could attempt to mildly influence those factors by negotiating, lobbying, and bargaining with the external agents that determine their behavior.

The internal factors are those which, to a large extent, are *controllable* by the firm. They are mainly the functional activities that can be deployed by business units to succeed against competition.

Selecting these factors is not a trivial matter. Normally, we start by immersing a group of key executives of the firm, including corporate, business and functional managers,

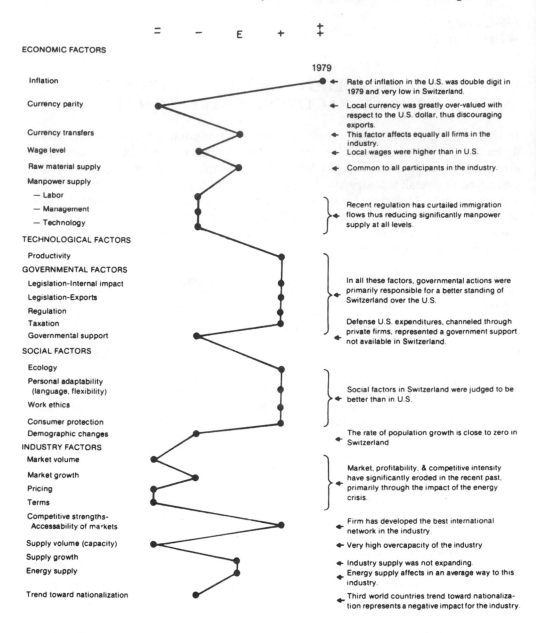

Figure 2. A profile chart showing the 1979 assessment of industry attractiveness for a business of a Swiss firm in a highly technological industry. The factors were identified by the managers participating in the evaluation. All the assessments of economic, technological, governmental, and social factors were made by comparing the influence of each factor in Switzerland and the US. The external factors under the heading Industry Factors, by and large, affect all firms in that industry in a similar way. The comments explain the classification of each factor. Because of the extraordinary impact of the quite adverse industry factors, the industry attractiveness was judged to be *low*

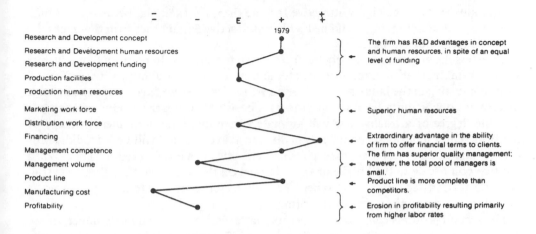

Figure 3. A profile chart assessing business strengths for the same Swiss firm shown in Figure 2, again using a five-point scale. The firm is revealed to have median composite business strength

in a collective effort to identify and assess those factors. This effort requires a great degree of intelligence, experience, and knowledge about the business and the industry.

It is unfortunate that the current state of knowledge in management precludes structuring this activity in a more precise way. We rely on an intuitive treatment because we lack a sounder and more solidly scientific method. We don't have a rich and comprehensive model of the firm to facilitate this task. In the absence of a sound theoretical foundation, at least we can submit the managers of the firm to an orderly process for extracting from them their vision of the firm and its environment.

One way to approach this descriptive task is to use standard lists of relevant external and internal factors. This is not advisable. An honest effort to produce meaningful lists of these factors can generate new and valuable insights, and engage managers in a totally fresh exercise as they probe to identify those issues that truly characterize the various businesses of the firm. We developed extensive lists of external and internal factors to analyze a specific business that we will use here to illustrate the implementation of the attractiveness-strength matrix (Figures 2 and 3).

STEP 2: ASSESSMENT OF EXTERNAL FACTORS

Once external uncontrollable factors are identified, we have to determine how much each contributes to the attractiveness of the industry to which the business belongs. We have found that 'profile charts,' provide helpful visual display of the complete assessment (Figure 2). Each factor is graded according to a five-point scale:

－ － Extremely unattractive
－ Mildly unattractive
E Even or neutral
＋ Mildly attractive
＋ ＋ Extremely attractive

An industry could be highly attractive for one firm, for example, because of its high technological standing, but could be highly unattractive for another firm that lacks the required technological base.

To assess the industry we classify the factors into two groups. In one group, are factors such as total market, market growth rate, and industry profitability, which affect all firms competing in the industry in similar ways. In this case, we favor using the average investment opportunity open to the firm as a basis for comparison. Our reasoning is that the degree of attractiveness will ultimately determine the investment strategy of the firm. Thus, a business ranked in a highly attractive position will be a candidate for a larger allocation of resources than a business classified in a less favored category. When the five point scale in the profile-chart is defined on this basis the 'Even' or 'Neutral' point identifies a degree of attractiveness for every factor equivalent to that of the average investment opportunity open to the firm.

The second group is composed of factors that affect the firm and its competitors in different ways. For example, external factors can affect multinational corporations quite differently when the parent firms are located in different countries, where currency parity, inflationary trends, demographic factors, and manpower supply are very different. To assess this group of factors, we resort to competitive evaluation, and the firm could use its most meaningful competitor as a basis of comparison. In this case, equal or neutral will mean that the factor being considered affects the firm and its most important competitor in a similar way.

The resulting assessment is heavily dependent upon judgment. This is not necessarily undesirable. A true understanding of a business invariably requires managerial insights. Assessing external factors is a systematic process that imposes order on the subjective judgments managers provide in an overall diagnosis of a business.

There are ways to enrich the information base needed for a thorough industry analysis. Surveys, market research efforts, and external data sources can be valuable. Such data may be acquired from external sources or by using the in-house staff. In either case, instead of launching a blind hunting expedition that might provide very little useful information at a great cost, it is better to conduct this highly judgmental exercise first to bring in the ideas of managers in an orderly fashion.

The last step is classifying the overall attractiveness of the industry in terms of the three categories of the matrix: high, medium, and low. One method assigns a weight to each factor (normalized to 100 percent), and a numerical grade from 1 to 5 (1 being very unattractive and 5 highly attractive). The final score of the industry attractiveness is determined as the weighted average of the numerical grades. This cardinal measurement will allow an exact positioning of the business unit within the matrix (Table 2).

This quantitative approach is highly questionable. Within its apparent objectivity, it hides the inherent complexities of quantifying very subtle issues. Rothschild [1976, p. 151] comments: 'I have found that weighting clouds the real issues and generates a reverence for numbers that may be unwarranted. In effect it tends to make a pseudo-science out of an art.'

A better, although more judgmental way to classify an industry, is for the managers conducting the analysis to examine carefully the impact of each factor. Once this review is completed, they should discuss their relative importance. In this process, factors can be ranked according to their influence over industry attractiveness, and participating managers can develop a feeling for the relative importance of each factor. The final step

Table 2. An example of an industry attractiveness assessment using the weighted score approach (Hofer and Schendel [1978]). Under weight some criteria may be of the GO/NOGO type. Ratings are on a scale of 1 (very unattractive) to 5 (highly attractive)

Attractiveness criterion	Weight	Rating	Weighted score
Size	.15	4	.60
Growth	.12	3	.36
Pricing	.05	3	.15
Market diversity	.05	2	.10
Competitive structure	.05	3	.15
Industry profitability	.20	3	.60
Technical role	.05	4	.20
Inflation vulnerability	.05	2	.10
Cyclicality	.05	2	.10
Customer financials	.10	5	.50
Energy impact	.08	4	.32
Social	GO	4	—
Environmental	GO	4	—
Legal	GO	4	—
Human	.05	4	.20
	1.00		3.38

is to produce by collective agreement a classification of the industry, expressed in terms of the high, medium, or low categories. The reason for advocating this approach is that the nine cells in the attractiveness-strength matrix give us sufficient resolution for assigning an appropriate investment strategy to each business.

STEP 3: ASSESSMENT OF INTERNAL FACTORS

Controllable success factors are normally evaluated by comparing them with those of the leading competitor in the business under consideration. The evaluation must be concentrated on a single competitive firm. If we would like to identify competitive strategies against more than one competitor, several evaluations should be conducted considering one firm at a time. It is important to avoid selecting a different firm, as a basis for comparison for each factor the firm that happens to excel in that dimension: the resulting profile would project an unrealistic disadvantage for the firm under evaluation. Again a five-point scale is used. Because the business strength evaluation has a clear competitor in mind its assessment is less ambiguous than that for industry attractiveness. Here, the five points of the scale correspond to:
- − Severe competitive disadvantage,
- − Mild competitive disadvantage,
 E Equal competitive standing,
 + Mild competitive advantage, and
+ + Great competitive advantage.

Most of these factors are managerial functions which are controllable and critical to success. A successful strategy for a business should put together a set of well integrated programs for R&D, production, marketing, finance, and distribution.

Table 3. An example of the business-strength assessment with the weighted score approach (from Hofer and Schendel [1978]). Under weight x indicates that the factor does not affect relative competitive position. Here, in rating the factors, 1 indicates a weak position, and 5 a very strong competitive position

Critical success factors	Weight	Rating	Weighted score
Market share	.10	5	.50
SBU growth rate	x	3	—
Breadth of product line	.05	4	.20
Sales distribution effectiveness	.20	4	.80
Proprietary and key account advantages	x	3	—
Price competitiveness	x	4	—
Advertising and promotion effectiveness	.05	4	.20
Facilities and location and newness	.05	5	.25
Capacity and productivity	x	3	—
Experience curve effects	.15	4	.60
Raw materials costs	.05	4	.20
Value added	x	4	—
Relative product quality	.15	4	.60
R&D advantages/position	.05	4	.20
Cash throw-off	.10	5	.50
Caliber of personnel	x	4	—
General image	.05	5	.25
	1.00		4.30

In the quantitative approach a weighted average is computed on the basis of assigned weights and ratings for each factor (Table 3).

The qualitative approach was used in the Swiss firm example in Figure 3. It was easy to conclude that the existing composite business strength was *medium*.

STEP 4: CURRENT POSITIONING OF THE BUSINESS IN THE ATTRACTIVENESS-STRENGTH MATRIX

Having made an overall assessment of industry attractiveness and business strength, it is simple to establish the current position of the business in one of the nine cells of the portfolio matrix (Figure 4).

In the growth-share matrix approach popularized by the Boston Consulting Group (BCG) a different procedure is used; there each individual business unit falls on a precise point, quantitatively determined by the value of the two coordinates (growth, and relative market share). In addition, the relative contribution of the business is indicated by the size of the area within its circle. We have reviewed the BCG approach in the second part of this tutorial series (Hax and Majluf [1983] and Chapter 4 of this book).

The weighted-score approach uses a quantifiable set of coordinate measurements with the attractiveness-strength matrix. For example Hofer and Schendel [1978] use a graphical display, similar to the one presented in Figure 5, in which the areas of the circles are proportional to the sizes of the various industries and the business's current market share in that industry is represented by a shaded pie-shaped wedge. Each circle is centered on the coordinates for that business unit (the scores for industry attractiveness and business strength.)

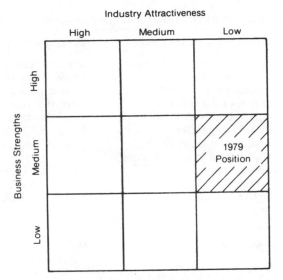

Figure 4. The 1979 positioning of the business of the Swiss firm in the attractiveness-strength matrix

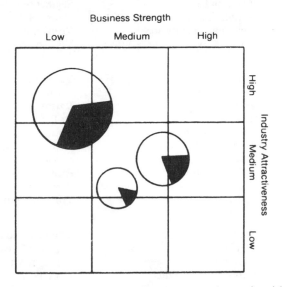

Figure 5. In positioning businesses in the attractiveness-strength matrix with the weighted score approach, each circle is centered on the coordinates for industry attractiveness and business strength. The area of the circle represents the size of the industry and the shaded wedge, the firm's current market share

One further application of the attractiveness-strength matrix deserves comment. William E. Rothschild [1976], a specialist in strategic planning at General Electric, suggests grouping factors into five major categories: market, competitive, financial and economic, technological, and sociopolitical (Table 4). Instead of identifying a list of uncontrollable factors to describe environmental characteristics and a set of controllable factors to assess internal strengths, he recommends using a unique generic list for assessing both industry attractiveness and competitive strength for the business. This procedure

Table 4. Determining industry-attractiveness and business-strength (Rothschild [1976])

	Attractiveness of your industry	Strength of your business

Market Factors	Size (dollar, units or both)
	Size of key segments
	Growth rate per year
	  for the total industry
	  for segments of the industry
	Diversity of market
	Sensitivity to price, service,
	  features, & external factors
	Cyclicality
	Seasonality
	Captive customers
		Share (in equivalent terms)
		Share of key segments
		Your annual growth rate
		  for the total firm
		  for the segments of the firm
		Your participation
		Your influence on the market
		
		Your sales lag or lead
		
		Extent to which your sales
		  are captive

Competitive Factors	Types of competitors Degrees of concentration Changes in type and mix Entries and exits Position changes in share Functional substitution Degrees & types of integration	Where you fit, how you compare Segments you have entered or left Your relative share change Your vulnerability Your own level of integration

Financial & Economic Factors	Profitability
	
	Ratios
	Dollars
	Contribution margins
	Leverage factors such as
	  economies of scale
	Barriers to entry or exit
	  (both financial & nonfinancial)
	Capacity utilization
		Your profitability per-
		  formance
		Ratios
		Dollars
		Your contributed value
		Any competitive advantage
		  you possess
		Problems you would have in
		  entering or exiting
		Your utilization

Technological Factors	Maturity & volatility Complexity Differentiation Patents & Copyrights Technology required Process of manufacturing	Ability to cope with change Depths of your skills Types of your skills Your position Your resources

Socio-Political Factors	Social attitudes & trends
	
	Laws & government agency
	  regulations
	Influence with pressure groups
	  & government
	  representatives
	Human factors such as
	  unionization & community
	  acceptance
		Your company's responsiveness
		  and flexibility
		Your company's ability to
		  cope
		Your company's aggressiveness
		
		Your company's relationships

may also lead to an acceptable positioning of the business in the matrix. However, it skips the discussion stage for generating and probing lists of factors, which is enriching and helpful for gaining a deeper and common understanding of a business.

STEP 5: FORECASTING THE TRENDS OF EACH EXTERNAL FACTOR

To assess what the future holds for the portfolio of the firm, first the trends that will take place for each of the external factors must be forecast. A composite of these trends indicates the future attractiveness of the industry. Forecasting trends is quite similar to assessing current external factors except that instead of making judgments based on past history we now rely on our ability to understand and predict future trends. This kind of forecasting is at the core of any strategic planning.

The main objective in this step is to understand the most likely environment the firm will face in the foreseeable future. By determining future trends for the critical external factors, the firm will be able to anticipate the competitive, economic, financial, sociopolitical, technological, and legislative assumptions on which to base strategic actions. Often, this step does not lead to a single most likely projection, but to a series of alternative scenarios. Then, contingency plans should be defined for alternative scenarios as well as for the most likely one.

The final aim in this effort is to predict whether the industry in which a business competes is going to maintain, increase, or decrease its current attractiveness within the planning horizon (normally a five-year span). Ultimately, detecting this final displacement of the attractiveness dimension is crucial because the success of the investment decision indicated by the attractiveness-strength matrix will depend on it (Figure 6).

STEP 6: DEVELOPING THE DESIRED POSITION FOR EACH INTERNAL FACTOR

Having resolved the future industry attractiveness for each business unit, the next step is to determine the strategic positioning for its future development. This means determining what moves need to be made within each controllable factor to result in the desired competitive position (Figure 7).

A strategy must be formulated in clear terms for multi-functional programs aimed at securing a long-term sustainable competitive advantage.

STEP 7: DESIRED POSITIONING OF EACH BUSINESS IN THE ATTRACTIVENESS-STRENGTH MATRIX

After forecasting industry attractiveness and the development of the business' strength, graphically representing the proper positioning of a business in the attractiveness-strength matrix may appear simple (see Figure 8).

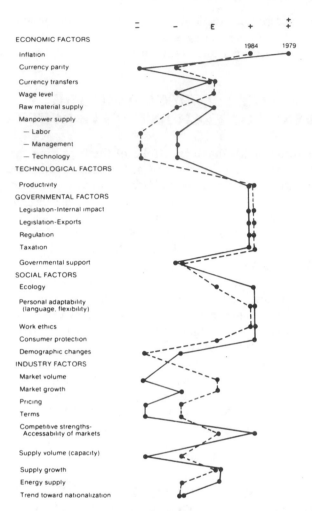

Figure 6. Assessment of the 1979 and future trends predicted for 1984 of industry attractiveness for the Swiss firm example. The industry factors are predicted to show a consistent improvement in the market volume, market growth, and profitability. Industry attractiveness would then move from low to medium in 1984

In practice, Steps 6 and 7 are carried out simultaneously. Having projected the future attractiveness for the industry, we decide on a global competitive strategy to achieve the desired business strength and we then identify the new positioning of each of the controllable success factors necessary for achieving that overall business strength. The global strategy chosen has to be fitted to the actual internal capabilities of the firm.

Rothschild [1976] suggests a slightly different and provocative approach for this step. He also starts by identifying the current positioning of the business in the matrix. Then he evaluates what the future position would be if our current strategy for that business were maintained unchanged (Figure 9). With this information on hand, the firm can then decide what strategy to follow to attain the desired future position of the business.

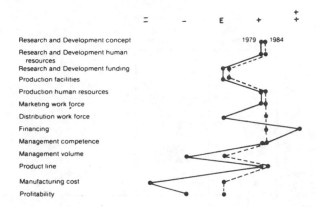

Figure 7. Assessment of business strengths for the Swiss firm example in 1979 and 1984 (predicted). An extraordinarily aggressive set of actions is proposed in order to reach a superior or at least equal standing with the leading competitor in all the critical controllable dimensions of the business. The resulting competitive strength would then take the business from a medium position in 1979 to a high position in 1984

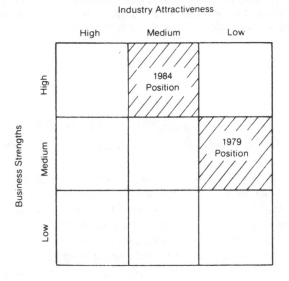

Figure 8. The 1979 and the future 1984 positioning of the business of the Swiss firm in the attractiveness-strength matrix

To summarize, formulating the base case and forecasting the trends in the external factors identify the most likely future scenario. Strategic action programs are then determined to achieve the desired position in each of the controllable internal factors. A subsequent sensitivity analysis can be used to construct meaningful alternative scenarios and to decide what programs the firm should follow for each of those scenarios. Contingency planning requires monitoring critical external factors to check whether the assumptions about the environment, on which the adopted plans are based, are still valid. Leading indicators and triggering mechanisms should signal significant departures

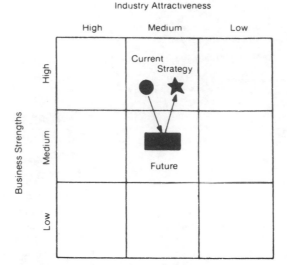

Figure 9. The current position of the business is here represented by a circle. Continuing current strategies would erode the firm's position to a medium position (rectangle), but committing increased resources should maintain its high position (star). (Source: Rothschild [1976])

from these basic assumptions and the appropriate alternative plan can be put into effect.

STEP 8: FORMULATION OF STRATEGIES FOR EACH BUSINESS

The analysis conducted so far has provided us with all the elements necessary for outlining the strategy to be pursued for developing each business. At the level of a business unit, *strategy* implies a set of broad *action programs* for achieving the long-term competitive strengths desired for that business unit and for managing the impact of external factors.

This basic strategy is directly distilled from the assessment of both internal and external factors. Thus, the strategy has two primary components:

—Broad programs of action for controllable success factors with the objectives of neutralizing the internal weaknesses and enhancing positions of strength.

—Broad programs for action based on the external factors, and designed to prevent the negative consequences of adverse trends and to take advantage of any beneficial environmental conditions.

Formulating programs for action based on internal analysis is straightforward because they involve only controllable factors. It is much more difficult to deal with uncontrollable external forces. In our opinion, understanding the essential message of external forces and adapting the firm to meet those challenges distinguishes the truly creative manager.

Analyzing external factors is significant in the beginning of the strategic process, when we are formulating broad statements of objectives and programs for action. After these objectives have been approved at the corporate level, the second planning cycle, strategic

Table 5. The strategy programs formulated for the Swiss firm example

I. Broad Action Programs Based on Controllable Internal Factors
  —Maintain R&D and Technical standing above leading competitor level.
  —Implement an automation program leading toward significant increases in labor productivity.
  —Improve the distribution network worldwide, developing a sense of priorities according to the attractiveness of each individual market.
  —Reduce manufacturing costs through proper rationalization in every stage of the production process.
  —Increase number of qualified managers via proper hiring, developing, and promotional procedures
  —Maintain market positioning by the allocation of financial and human resources compatible with competitive challenges.

II. Broad Action Programs to Deal with External Environmental Forces
  —Profit from a possibly temporarily favorable currency situation by taking advantage of a strong purchasing power, in terms of:
    —Switching from national to foreign suppliers
    —Engaging in an active acquisition of manufacturing facilities abroad.
  —Set up a task force to study the legal, financial, and sales implications of currency transfer.
  —Use local manufacturing, distribution, and marketing facilities whenever possible, seeking partnerships to neutralize trends toward nationalization.
  —Stockpile raw materials on critical items, and firm up long-term contracts for the procurement of those raw materials, taking advantage of the temporary strong currency situation.
  —Address the issue of manpower shortage by:
    —Internal development of qualified manpower at all levels
    —Seeking an increased government support.
  —Establish the base for a systematic information gathering conducive toward a better understanding of competitors and market opportunities.

programming can begin. At this stage, the broad strategic action programs are broken down into very specific tactical plans, suitable for implementation. Also, the impact of the overall strategies will be subjected to detailed financial analyses. Those analyses require a different kind of forecasting effort. For each of the meaningful scenarios identified in the previous steps, we will need numerical projections of parameters such as market volume, sales, prices, costs, interest rates, and tax rates in order to evaluate whether the plan is financially attractive during the relevant planning horizon.

Table 5 illustrates the broad action programs developed for the Swiss firm. Notice that a critical issue in this case is currency parity. An exchange rate which is a devastating disadvantage for an exporting firm is an extraordinary weapon from the point of view of purchasing strength. This is reflected in the proposed programs.

IMPLICATIONS FOR STRATEGIC POSITIONING

The attractiveness-strength matrix is important primarily for assigning priorities for investment in the various businesses of the firm, it is a guide for resource allocation. It does not deal with cash-flow balance, a fundamental concern of the growth-share matrix.

From the attractiveness-strength matrix a strategy can be designed for concentrating resources in those businesses that enjoy a higher degree of attractiveness and competitive

Industry Attractiveness

	High	Medium	Low
High	I	II	III
Medium	II	III	IV
Low	III	IV	IV

Business Strengths

Figure 10. Investment priorities can be set using the attractiveness-strength matrix. (Source: Rothschild [1979], and Wind and Mahajan [1981])

Industry Attractiveness

	High	Medium	Low
High	— Grow — Seek dominance — Maximize investment	— Identify growth segments — Invest strongly — Maintain position elsewhere	— Maintain overall position — Seek cash flow — Invest at maintenance level
Medium	— Evaluate potential for leadership via segmentation — Identify weaknesses — Build strengths	— Identify growth segments — Specialize — Invest selectively	— Prune lines — Minimize investment — Position to divest
Low	— Specialize — Seek niches — Consider acquisitions	— Specialize — Seek niches — Consider exit	— Trust leader s statesmanship — Sic on competitor's cash generators — Time exit and divest

Business Strengths

Figure 11. Implications for strategies are derived from the attractiveness-strength matrix by A. T. Kearney. (Source: Hofer and Davoust [1977])

strength, disengaging resources from businesses where the opposite is true, and deciding whether businesses in intermediate positions should receive greater or less attention (Figure 10). Specific guidance for strategies congruent with those investment priorities has been developed by A. T. Kearney (Figure 11).

The strategies suggested by these interpretations of the attractiveness-strength matrix are *natural strategies*, that is, logical and rational directions for the development of

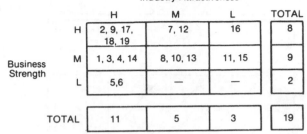

POSITIONING OF BUSINESSES

Industry Attractiveness

		H	M	L	TOTAL
Business Strength	H	2, 9, 17, 18, 19	7, 12	16	8
	M	1, 3, 4, 14	8, 10, 13	11, 15	9
	L	5,6	—	—	2
TOTAL		11	5	3	19

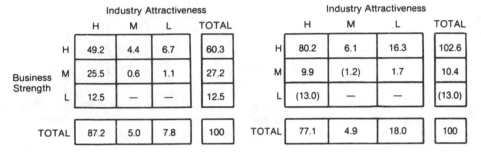

DISTRIBUTION OF CORPORATE SALES (%)

Industry Attractiveness

		H	M	L	TOTAL
Business Strength	H	49.2	4.4	6.7	60.3
	M	25.5	0.6	1.1	27.2
	L	12.5	—	—	12.5
TOTAL		87.2	5.0	7.8	100

DISTRIBUTION OF CORPORATE NET INCOMES (%)

Industry Attractiveness

		H	M	L	TOTAL
Business Strength	H	80.2	6.1	16.3	102.6
	M	9.9	(1.2)	1.7	10.4
	L	(13.0)	—	—	(13.0)
TOTAL		77.1	4.9	18.0	100

DISTRIBUTION OF CORPORATE ASSETS (%)

Industry Attractiveness

		H	M	L	TOTAL
Business Strength	H	42.1	3.4	5.7	51.2
	M	32.1	0.5	1.1	33.7
	L	15.1	—	—	15.1
TOTAL		89.3	3.9	6.8	100

RETURN ON NET ASSETS (%)

Industry Attractiveness

		H	M	L	TOTAL
Business Strength	H	12.8	12.2	19.1	13.5
	M	2.1	(19.5)	12.1	2.0
	L	(5.8)	—	—	(5.8)
TOTAL		5.8	8.7	17.8	6.7

Figure 12. A selected set of performance measurements to describe the whole portfolio of 19 businesses (numbered from 1 through 19) in the attractiveness-strength matrix

individual businesses consistent with their position externally and internally. Although they raise valid points, natural strategies should not be followed blindly.

It is also important to address the dynamics of business behavior. Definitive conclusions should not be drawn from static snapshots of the position of each business.

PORTFOLIO VISION IN THE ATTRACTIVENESS-STRENGTH MATRIX

All portfolio matrices can be used at different levels in the organization, to analyze units with different degrees of aggregation. So far, we have described the methodology for

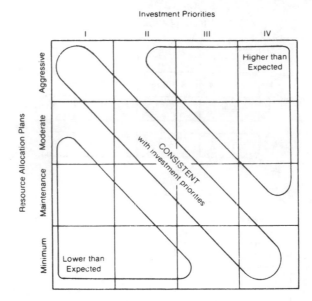

Figure 13. In a consistency check between investment priorities and resource allocation decisions, Rothschild [1980] compares historical expenditures to proposed expenditures to decide whether the proposed strategies are aggressive, moderate, maintenance, or minimum

using the attractiveness-strength matrix to analyze business units. An overall view of the corporate portfolio can be obtained when all the businesses of the firm are finally positioned in the matrix (Figure 12).

The matrix can also be used to produce a more detailed description of a single business unit, examining the performance of each of its product lines and helping to produce a strategy at the business level. The aim would be to identify those sub-segments that deserve either more or less support.

CONSISTENCY OF INVESTMENT STRATEGIES

Rothschild [1980], advocates a procedure for checking whether the proposal for allocating resources to each business is consistent with the investment priority for that business (Figure 13). He measures the level of expenditure during the last six years for: plant and equipment, marketing, engineering, working capital, and salaried employees. These figures are then compared with those proposed for the next three years both in terms of real dollars and as a percent of sales. Depending on the degree the future deviates from the past, the plans are classified as: aggressive, moderate, maintenance, or minimum. Those proposals that fall on the diagonal of the grid are judged to be consistent with investment priorities (Figure 13). Those falling above the diagonal command a higher than expected resource allocation, and those below it, a lower one. A position for the business outside the diagonal simply signals a discrepancy between the proposed strategy and a natural strategy; it deserves careful investigation. There are reasons why a business might adopt a more or less aggressive investment strategy than might seem natural.

In his book on strategic alternatives, Rothschild [1979] devotes a great deal of attention to linking overall investment strategies to natural functional strategies to support a specific investment thrust; he believes that successful management strategies tend to be driven by concentration on a particular function.

A CRITIQUE: THE AMBIGUITY OF A MULTIDIMENSIONAL MATRIX

Ironically, one of the problems with the attractiveness-strength matrix arises from one of its fundamental contributions. Historically, this matrix emerged as a response to criticisms of the growth-share matrix as too simplistic. The attractiveness-strength matrix requires searching for a multiplicity of factors that contribute to the strategic positioning of a business. By doing so, it offers a richer and more mature perspective for guiding strategic actions for business development. But, in doing so, it introduces the complexity of multidimensional indicators. We have criticized the weighted-score approach because of its pseudo-scientific character. However, when dealing with multiattributes, a weighting process is unavoidable whether done explicitly or implicitly.

Very often, when applying the attractiveness-strength matrix, managers do not agree and they may categorize a business as *medium* because they do not understand the issues involved and cannot reconcile diverging opinions.

Finally, it is hard to impose a uniform standard among businesses so that the final portfolio matrix will be consistent in terms of criteria used for classifying the businesses. Several firms try to bypass this difficulty by developing standard lists of external and internal factors to be used by all businesses in the firm. We find that this practice prevents the recognition of the idiosyncratic characteristics of each business, and presents obstacles to a rich diagnosis of its strengths and opportunities.

In contrast, the growth-share matrix is a much more precise and unambiguous tool. It can be easily applied to obtain comparisons of the portfolio strength of competing firms. Although conceptually nothing prevents applying the attractiveness-strength matrix to a competitor's firm as well as one's own, it is much more difficult to do. Therefore, we recommend the growth-share matrix as more useful for competitive analysis, and the attractiveness-strength matrix as a much more powerful tool for diagnosis and strategic guidance for one's own firm.

THE DIFFICULTY OF ASSESSING INDUSTRY ATTRACTIVENESS

Although ambiguity can be a problem in both dimensions of the attractiveness-strength matrix, industry attractiveness is most affected. In assessing business strength, we have a clear standard for comparison: the leading competitor. The evaluation of industry attractiveness is much more complex and subtle.

LEGITIMACY OF INVESTMENT PRIORITIES

A more technical criticism of the attractiveness-strength matrix is that priorities for investment are based on subjective judgment. One could argue that the only legitimate evaluation tool is the Net Present Value (NPV) of future cash-flows to be generated by a business, discounted at a proper cost of capital, which includes an adjustment for risk.

Those who want a broad basis for ranking priorities for investment (like the basis for the attractiveness-strength matrix) argue that the cash-flow projections required for NPV calculations ignore the qualitative merit of an investment. In the NPV game, it is always possible to show that an investment opportunity can meet the cost of capital hurdle. Therefore, before using NPV calculations, first consider the overall attractiveness of the industry and the strength of the business unit in order to understand the investment decision.

Both methods have value and have their own merits. Rather than being alternative procedures for analyzing investment proposals, they truly complement each other.

REFERENCES

Hax, Arnoldo C. and Majluf, Nicolas S. 1983, 'The use of the growth-share matrix in strategic planning,' *Interfaces*, Vol. 13, No. 1 (February), pp. 46–60

Hofer, Charles W. and Davoust, Merritt J. 1977, *Successful Strategic Management*, A. T. Kearney, Inc., Chicago.

Hofer, Charles W. and Schendel, Dan 1978, *Strategy Formulation: Analytical Concepts*, West Publishing Co., St. Paul, Minnesota.

Rothschild, William E. 1980, 'How to ensure the continued growth of strategic planning,' *The Journal of Business Strategy*, Vol. 1, No. 1 (Summer), pp. 11–18.

Rothschild, William E. 1976, *Putting It All Together: A Guide to Strategic Thinking*, Amacom, New York.

Rothschild, William E. 1979, *Stategic Alternatives: Selection, Development and Implementation*, Amacom, New York.

Wind, Yoram, and Mahajan, Vijay 1981, 'Designing product and business portfolios,' *Harvard Business Review*, Vol. 59, No. 1 (January–February), pp. 155–165.

Chapter 6

Impact of Strategic Planning on Profit Performance

Sidney Schoeffler, Robert D. Buzzell and Donald F. Heany
Harvard Business School

What rate of return on investment (ROI) is 'normal' in a given type of business, under given market and industry conditions? What factors explain differences in typical levels of ROI among various kinds of businesses?

How will ROI in a specific business be affected by a change in the strategy employed? By a change in competitive activity?

Many corporate presidents and planning directors wish they had more reliable answers to these kinds of questions, for they are at the heart of strategic planning in the modern corporation. Consider some of the ways in which these questions arise:

Forecasting profits. In a diversified company, the usual practice is for business plans to be prepared by each product division or other operating unit. These plans are then reviewed by corporate executives, often with the assistance of corporate staff specialists. Among the key elements of each unit's plan are, of course, estimates of investment requirements and profits for future periods.

Often these forecasts are simply projections of local experience. But when market conditions are expected to change, or when a change in strategy is contemplated, how reliable is the past as a guide to the future?

Allocating resources. A major purpose of reviewing divisional plans at the corporate level is to make effective allocations of capital, manpower, and other scarce resources among divisions. Often the capital appropriation requests of the divisions add up to more than headquarters can provide.

Author's note: We wish to acknowledge the contributions to this article of our associates on the PIMS Project Team. Ralph Sultan, who is now chief economist, Royal Bank of Canada, served as project director of Phase I of PIMS during 1972 and was responsible for much of the basic design of the study. Bradley Gale, Thomas Wilson, Bernard Catry, James Conlin, and Robert McDowell also participated in various stages of the research and offered valuable suggestions on this presentation of the latest results.

The problem, then, is one of emphasis: Which products and markets promise the greatest returns? Here, especially, the profit estimates supplied by divisional managers are likely to be of doubtful reliability, since each division is in the position of pleading its own case.

Measuring management performance. Closely related to the problem of forecasting profits is the need to evaluate actual profit results. Suppose Division A earns 30% on its investment (pretax), while Division B achieves an ROI of only 15%. Is A's management twice as effective as B's, and should it be rewarded accordingly.

Executives of Division B would no doubt object to this. They would attribute differences in ROI to differences in conditions such as market growth rate and strength of competition. Perhaps they are right. What corporate management would like, in this situation, is some way of determining what level of ROI is reasonable or 'normal' for different operating units under given circumstances.

Appraising new business proposals. Still another common problem in strategic planning is that of estimating ROI in a prospective new business which is being considered for either internal development or acquisition. When the business is new to the company, actual experience, by definition, cannot be consulted. Even when entry is proposed via acquisition, the current performance of the existing business may be of doubtful reliability as a guide to its future.

The common thread running through the four types of strategic planning situations just described is the need for some means of estimating return on investment in a given business, under given industry and market conditions, following a given strategy. Every experienced business executive and corporate planner knows that ROI varies enormously from one business to another and from year to year in an individual division or product line. How can these variations be explained and predicted?

Some answers to these questions are beginning to emerge from a unique research project called PIMS—a study of actual experiences of hundreds of businesses which is aimed at measuring the profit impact of market strategies. Building on work that has been under way at the General Electric Company for more than 10 years, the PIMS project is a sharing of experience among 57 major North American corporations.

PIMS was organized in early 1972 as a project of the Marketing Science Institute, a nonprofit research organization associated with the Harvard Business School. The project was established as a cooperative venture, with HBS faculty members and research assistants working alongside planning specialists from industry. (Industry personnel did not, of course, have access to any of the data supplied by other companies.) The project is now organizing its third yearlong phase.

This article is a progress report on Phases I and II of the PIMS project. In it, we shall describe how the study has been carried out and summarize some of the major findings of the first two years' work.

PIMS PROFIT MODELS

In Phase I of PIMS, 36 corporations supplied information on some 330 businesses. The information included descriptions of industry and market characteristics, as well as operating results and balance sheet figures for the years 1970 and 1971.

GE'S SEARCH FOR ANSWERS

The current effort to find better ways to explain and predict operating performance began back in 1960, as an internal project at the General Electric Company.

Fred J. Borch, then GE's vice president-marketing services, called in Jack McKitterick, his director of market research, and pointed out what today is generally accepted as an axiom: as the market share of a business goes up, so do operating economies. Borch asked McKitterick to survey any relevant published research and the experience of other businessmen with respect to this relationship. If the relationship were valid, executives might have an important clue as to how to improve operating results.

Equally important, Borch wanted to find a handle for GE's growing 'manageability' problem. Sales were already at the £4 billion level. By 1970, they were likely to be £8 billion to £9 billion. How could corporate officers like himself stay in touch with so many diverse businesses, ranging all the way from turbine generators to toasters?

After months of exploration, McKitterick became convinced that the best way to address the question was to do some basic pioneering work on the apparent causes of GE's own successes and failures. Borch agreed and authorized a major research project to probe for 'laws of the market place'. Project PROM (profitability optimization model) was organized under the direction of coauthor Sidney Schoeffler.

After five years of intensive research and testing, Project PROM produced a computer-based model that captured the major factors which explain a great deal of the variability in return on investment. Since this model reflects data from diverse markets and industries, it is often referred to as a 'cross-sectional' model—as contrasted to a time-series model based on data over a series of years for a single business.

With the help of this model, GE could estimate the 'average' level of profit or investment or cash flow that went with various combinations of the success determinants. The model did not and could not predict the 'precise' ROI of any one of GE's businesses in a given year.

When Borch became GE's chief executive officer in 1964, he found the PROM model to be (a) a tool for detecting high-risk strategic moves, (b) a rich source of questions for the review of strategies proposed by divisional managers, and (c) a means of computing the differential between the entire company's financial goals and the expected aggregate earnings of its components. (If the model predicted a shortfall, it could then be used to display the future implications of 'belt tightening' component by component.)

In addition to making extensive use of the model himself, Borch also encouraged his group executives and division managers to use it. He supported follow-on research to improve the coverage and predictive powers of the early models.

Today, cross-sectional models are standard elements of GE's corporate planning system.

(All financial data were submitted to PIMS in 'scaled' form—that is, actual dollar amounts were multiplied by a scaling factor, such as .5. This procedure served to ensure both the confidentiality of the original data and the relationships among the figures.)

The primary purpose of Phase I was to establish the feasibility of obtaining reasonably comparable data from a large number of diverse companies. Although differences in accounting systems and terminology did pose problems, the project was successful: profit results were explained and predicted with considerable accuracy. Moreover, the principal results of GE's earlier work were confirmed. By and large, the same factors that influenced ROI in GE business also showed up in the analysis of profitability among the 36 diverse corporations.

Thus, in late 1972, MSI agreed to sponsor a second, enlarged phase of the PIMS project. This time, 57 companies enlisted in the study and supplied more extensive information, covering the years 1970–1972, for 620 businesses. Analysis of this data base over the past several months has led to the current set of PIMS profit models. For the composition of our sample of businesses, see *Exhibit I*.

Exhibit I
PIMS sample of individual businesses

Number of companies	57
Number of businesses	620*
Type of company:	Percent of total:
Consumer product manufacturers	19.8%
Capital equipment manufacturers	15.6
Raw materials producers	11.9
Components manufacturers	24.1
Supplies manufacturers	16.5
Service and distribution	12.1
Total	100.0%

*The data presented in *Exhibits III-X* are based on analyses of 521 businesses. Since the time these analyses were made, information has been received on an additional 99 businesses.

Explaining ROI

The models we and our associates have developed are designed to answer two basic questions: What factors influence profitability in a business—and how much? How does ROI change in response to changes in strategy and in market conditions?

In building quantitative models to explain ROI and changes in ROI, we have drawn on economic theory and on the opinions and beliefs of experienced executives. Economic theory suggests, for example, that different 'market structures'—i.e. the number and relative size of competitors—will lead to different profit levels. Business experience indicates that product quality—a factor that has received little attention from economists—is also related to ROI.

Whatever economic theory or businessman's opinions may suggest, however, the ultimate test of whether and how a given factor is related to profitability is an empirical one. To make such a test, we have constructed an equation that explains more than 80% of the variation in profitability among the 620 businesses in the PIMS data base.

This profit level equation includes more than 60 terms composed of various combinations of 37 basic factors. As might be expected, profitability is related to many different factors. Some of the most important ones are listed and defined in *Exhibit II*.

The PIMS profit level equation and a separate equation which predicts changes in ROI have been used to construct separate reports for each business in the data pool. These reports 'diagnose' the factors influencing ROI in a business, given all of its specific characteristics such as its market, competitive position, capital intensity, and so on.

Because every business is, in some respects, unique, these diagnostic reports vary enormously. But by comparing businesses that are similar in terms of one or more basic profit-influencing factors with businesses that have different characteristics, we can identify some general patterns or relationships.

For example, we can determine an average relationship between market share and profitability by comparing average levels of ROI for groups of businesses with different market shares. This is the approach we have used in subsequent sections of this article.

Exhibit II
ROI and key profit influences

Return on investment (ROI):
The ratio of net, pretax operating income to average investment.
Operating income is what is available after deduction of
allocated corporate overhead expenses but before deduction
of any financial charges on assets employed. "Investment"
equals equity plus long-term debt, or, equivalently, total assets
employed minus current liabilities attributed to the business.

Market share:
The ratio of dollar sales by a business, in a given time period, to
total sales by all competitors in the same market. The "market"
includes all of the products or services, customer types, and
geographic areas that are directly related to the activities of the
business. For example, it includes all products and services
that are competitive with those sold by the business.

Product (service) quality:
The quality of each participating company's offerings, appraised
in the following terms: What was the percentage of sales of
products or services from each business in each year which
were superior to those of competitors? What was the percentage
of equivalent products? Inferior products? The measure used in
Exhibit IV and *Exhibit V* is the percentage "superior" minus the
percentage "inferior."

Marketing expenditures:
Total costs for sales force, advertising, sales promotion, marketing research, and marketing administration. The figures do not
include costs of physical distribution.

R&D expenditures:
Total costs of product development and process improvement,
including those costs incurred by corporate-level units which
can be directly attributed to the individual business.

Investment intensity:
Ratio of total investment to sales.

Corporate diversity:
An index which reflects (1) the number of different 4-digit
Standard Industrial Classification industries in which a corporation operates, (2) the percentage of total corporate employment
in each industry, and (3) the degree of similarity or difference
among the industries in which it participates.

PROFIT DETERMINANTS

As we mentioned a moment ago, our profit model includes 37 distinct factors which, in
various combinations, are significantly related to profitability. However, we shall limit our
discussion to just 3 major determinants of return on investment revealed by our analysis
of the PIMS data base—namely, market share, investment intensity, and company factors.

Market Share

Our analyses give strong support to the proposition that market share is indeed a major
influence on profitability. As shown in *Exhibit III*, ROI goes up steadily as market share

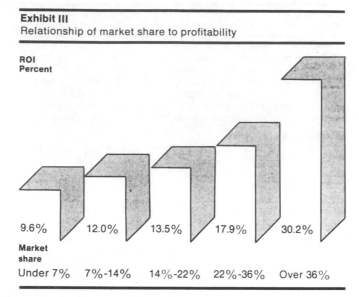

Exhibit III
Relationship of market share to profitability

ROI
Percent

| 9.6% | 12.0% | 13.5% | 17.9% | 30.2% |

Market
share

| Under 7% | 7%-14% | 14%-22% | 22%-36% | Over 36% |

increases. On the average, businesses with market shares above 36% earned more than three times as much, relative to investment, as businesses with less than 7% share of their respective markets. (Each of the five market share categories shown in this exhibit represents approximately one-fifth of the sample.)

The relationship between market share and profitability has been widely discussed since the inception of Project PROM at General Electric, when the idea was relatively novel. But how and why market share affects profitability is not fully understood as yet.

Our findings suggest that businesses with relatively large market shares tend to have above-average rates of investment turnover, particularly working capital. Also, the ratio of marketing expense to sales is generally lower for high-share businesses than for those with small market shares. These differences are indications of economies of scale that may go along with strong market positions.

However, much remains to be done, both in exploring the connection between market share and ROI and in determining how the relationship varies for different types of businesses or for different market conditions.

Whatever the reasons, the data in *Exhibit III* clearly show that it is very profitable to have a high share of market. Beyond this, the PIMS profit model sheds some light on how market share and other factors work together to influence ROI.

Consider, for example, the impact of both market share and product quality on ROI, as shown in *Exhibit IV*. In this exhibit, and in several others that follow, we have divided

Exhibit IV
Effect of market share and product quality on ROI

Market share	Product quality		
	Inferior	Average	Superior
Under 12%	4.5%	10.4%	17.4%
12%-26%	11.0	18.1	18.1
Over 26%	19.5	21.9	28.3

the PIMS sample of business into three approximately equal groups on the basis of each of two factors. The percentages for each of the nine subgroups shown include between 40 and 70 businesses.

The best of all possible worlds is to have both high market share and superior quality: businesses in this category averaged 28.3% return on investment. But even when quality was relatively inferior, average ROI for high-share businesses was a respectable 19.5%. On the other hand, superior-quality producers with weak market positions earned an average 17.4% on investment, which suggests that quality can partially offset low share.

It should be noted that product quality and market share usually, but by no means always, go together. The percent distribution of the three market share groups, in terms of quality levels, was as follows:

Percent of businesses with:	Market share		
	Under 12%	12%–26%	Over 26%
Inferior quality	47%	33%	20%
Average quality	30	36	30
Superior quality	23	31	50
Number of businesses	169	176	176

While it is not surprising that both market share and relative quality influence ROI, in the short term there may be relatively little that management can do to change these factors. Are some strategies more profitable than others, given the basic competitive position of a business? Analysis of the results achieved by the businesses in the PIMS sample suggests that some guidelines can, indeed, be formulated for businesses in different positions.

Consider, for example, the data in Part A of *Exhibit V*. Here, as in *Exhibit IV*, the sample has been divided into three roughly equal groups, this time in terms of (a) relative quality, and (b) the ratio of marketing expenditures to sales.

When quality is relatively low—exactly equivalent to competition or somewhat inferior—there is a strong negative relationship between marketing expenditures and RIO. In effect, these figures confirm the old adage that 'it doesn't pay to promote a poor product.'

ROI is somewhat diminished by a high level of marketing expenditure for business with 'average' or 'superior' relative product quality—but not nearly to the same extent as for competitors with lower-quality products. This might suggest, further, that sellers of higher-quality products or services could inflict severe short-term penalties on weaker competitors by escalating the level of marketing costs in an industry—and that lower-quality producers should avoid such confrontations like the plague.

Another clue to how profit influences vary, depending on competitive position, is given in Part B of *Exhibit V*. This shows, for businesses in the same market share categories as in *Exhibit IV*, the relationship of ROI to R&D spending levels. When market share is high, average ROI is highest when R&D spending is also high—above 3% of sales.

These figures do not, of course, show which is cause and which is effect; possibly businesses that are highly profitable—for whatever reason—are inclined to invest more of their earnings in research. Most likely, the positive relationship between ROI and

Exhibit V
Impact of expenditures on product quality and market share

A
High marketing expenditures damage profitability when quality is low

Product quality	Ratio of marketing expenditures to sales		
	Low Under 6%	Average 6%-11%	High Over 11%
Inferior	15.4%	14.8%	2.7%
Average	17.8	16.9	14.2
Superior	25.2	25.5	19.8

B
High R&D spending hurts profitability when market position is weak but increases ROI when market share is high

Market share	Ratio of R&D costs to sales		
	Low Under 1.4%	Average 1.4%-3.0%	High Over 3.0%
Under 12%	11.4%	9.8%	4.9%
12%-26%	13.8	16.7	17.0
Over 26%	22.3	23.1	26.3

R&D spending reflects both this kind of 'reverse causation' and a positive impact, in the other direction, of R&D on profits.

When market share is low, the relationship between R&D and profitability is exactly the reverse of that experienced by those with strong positions. The higher the level of R&D spending, the lower profits were, on the average. Here, there appears to be little doubt about cause and effect: low profits would be very unlikely to lead to high R&D spending.

We should emphasize, however, that these data represent short-term effects. Since the PIMS participants supplied information only for a three-year period, it may well be that Part B of *Exhibit V* reflects a 'transitional' cost of innovation. Some support can be given for this interpretation: among businesses with low market shares, ROI was higher (11.6%) when new products comprised a relatively high proportion of total sales than when new products represented only a small fraction of sales (average ROI, 5.3%).

Thus, when and if R&D spending is successfully converted into new products, it can pay off. But the most profitable course of all, for businesses with weak market positions, may be to seek new products without investing in research and development—via imitation, for instance.[1]

Investment Intensity

Apart from market share and product quality, the most important determinant of return on investment that was revealed by our analysis of the PIMS data

1. For further thoughts on this topic, see Theodore Levitt, 'Innovative Imitation,' HBR September–October 1966, p. 63.

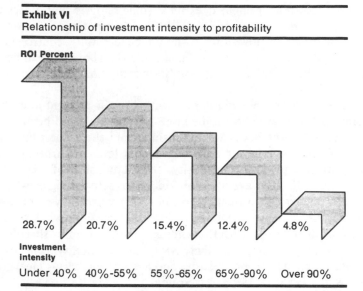

Exhibit VI
Relationship of investment intensity to profitability

ROI Percent

| 28.7% | 20.7% | 15.4% | 12.4% | 4.8% |

Investment
intensity

Under 40%   40%-55%   55%-65%   65%-90%   Over 90%

pool is investment intensity, which is simply the ratio of total investment to sales.

Exhibit VI shows the overall relationship between ROI and investment intensity: the higher the ratio of investment to sales, the lower ROI tends to be. Apparently businesses with high investment intensities are not able to achieve profit margins sufficient to offset the greater amounts of investment they require to sustain a given volume of sales. We suspect that a prime reason for this may be the heavy emphasis placed on achieving high volume, and thus high capacity utilization, in investment-intensive industries.

Since both market share and investment intensity are major determinants of profitability, it is not surprising that the combination of the two factors accounts for a substantial portion of total variation in ROI. As shown in *Exhibit VII*, average ROI for businesses that enjoyed both a high market share and a low degree of investment intensity was 34.6%—more than 17 times the average return earned by the unfortunate businesses with high investment intensity and small market share.

In most cases, the basic level of investment intensity required for a given business is probably not subject to much control by management. The amount of capital required to support a specified amount of sales is determined primarily by the technology of the business and by traditional terms of trade.

Exhibit VII
Low market share plus high investment intensity equals disaster

| Investment | Market share | | |
Intensity	Under 12%	12%-26%	Over 26%
Under 45%	21.2%	26.9%	34.6%
45%-71%	8.6	13.1	26.2
Over 71%	2.0	6.7	15.7

However, very often management does have some choices that affect investment intensity—such as the degree of mechanization or computer utilization. Our data indicate that these types of investments should be carefully controlled if market position is weak. Beyond this, what can managers do about investment intensity? Is a business that requires a high investment/sales ratio simply doomed to exist with low rates of return?

Comparison of various groups of businesses within the investment-intensive category shows that some strategies are likely to be more profitable than others. Consider, for example, the data in *Exhibit VIII*. Among businesses in the highest investment/sales group, ROI was strongly—and negatively—related to the level of marketing expenditures. For businesses with low investment intensity, the relationship of ROI to marketing expenditures was quite different: average profitability was actually higher when marketing expenditures were 'moderate' in relation to sales than when they were low.

Similar comparisons of subgroups within the PIMS sample show what when investment intensity is high (a) high levels of R&D spending depress earnings sharply, at least in the short run, and (b) high labor productivity is vital to profitability. (The average return for businesses with high investment intensity and low productivity—measured by sales per employee—was a negative 1% of investment.)

Company Factors

A third category of profit determinants revealed by the PIMS project consists of characteristics of the company that owns a business. Even when all of the characteristics of two businesses are identical, our analysis suggests that their profit results may vary if they belong to corporations that differ in terms of size, diversity, and other factors.

Exhibit IX shows average ROI levels for businesses belonging to companies that are in 'low', 'average', and 'high' sales categories, and that have different degrees of corporate diversity. The range of corporate size represented in the PIMS sample, is, of course, limited: 'small' companies are those with annual sales volume under $750 million. Within this range, ROI at the business level was highest for the largest companies and lowest for those in the 'average' group.

The explanation for this, we believe, is that the large corporations benefit from economies of scale, while the smaller companies gain some advantages from greater flexibility. Those in the middle are neither fish nor fowl, and consequently they earn the lowest rates of return.

The relationship between business-level ROI and corporate diversity is similar to that based on company size. On the average, ROI was practically identical for businesses belonging to highly diversified corporations and for those operated by nondiversified

Exhibit VIII
High marketing expenditures damage ROI in investment-intensive businesses

Investment intensity	Ratio of marketing expenditures to sales		
	Under 6%	6%-11%	Over 11%
Under 45%	29.3%	31.7%	22.0%
45%-71%	17.6	13.2	18.3
Over 71%	10.9	10.1	3.9

Exhibit X
Large companies benefit most from strong market positions

Company sales (in millions)	Market share		
	Under 12%	12%-26%	Over 26%
Under $750	14.5%	13.7%	19.6%
$750-$1,500	6.8	15.0	25.0
Over $1,500	12.0	17.8	29.4

companies. Presumably, the diversified corporations achieve good results through effectiveness as 'generalists'.

At the other extreme, profitability reflects the advantages of corporate specialization. The lowest levels of ROI are for the middle group, which benefits from neither. (These and other observed relationships between ROI and company characteristics are tentative findings, of course, because of the limited number of companies included in our sample.)

Our final example of a relationship between ROI and a combination of factors serves to illustrate further how company characteristics affect profitability. In *Exhibit X*, we show average levels of ROI for businesses that have different market shares and that belong to different company size groups.

As in earlier exhibits, the positive impact of a high market share is apparent. But, in addition, the data indicate that larger companies derive greater advantages from strong market positions than smaller companies do. This probably reflects the ability of larger companies to provide adequate support for strong positions, in terms of management personnel and funds for marketing or R&D.

On the other hand, smaller companies do slightly better than large ones in businesses with low market shares. This lends support to the belief that the relatively small companies derive some advantages from flexibility.

APPLYING THE FINDINGS

The corporate applications of the PIMS findings are many and varied. These include aid in profit forecasting for individual business units, measuring management performance, and appraising new business opportunities.

As part of the PIMS project, reports are prepared for each business, showing how its expected level of ROI is influenced by each of the 37 distinct factors included in the profit model. The result of this kind of analysis is what we call a 'PAR' return on

Exhibit IX
ROI varies with size and diversity of parent company

	Total company sales (in millions)		
	Low Under $750	Average $750-$1,500	High Over $1,500
Average ROI	15.8%	12.5%	21.7%
	Degree of diversity		
	Low	Average	High
Average ROI	16.1%	12.9%	22.1%

investment for a business, given its market and industry environment, its competitive position, its capital structure, and so on.

Some of the participating companies are beginning to put the findings to work by using the PAR reports as a standard of performance for individual divisions. For example, if actual ROI is substantially above the PAR level, this is an indication that divisional management is performing well. The excess of actual over PAR reflects gains made by current tactical superiority, since the factors considered in calculating PAR are largely aspects of the strategic position of the business.

Apart from management performance, special circumstances may cause actual ROI to fall above or below PAR. For instance, the effects of patents and trade secrets are not reflected in the profit model. Subject to this qualification, we believe that PAR or expected profit levels derived from the PIMS model—or from a similar analysis of actual experiences under different conditions—can serve as a meaningful standard for evaluating actual results. Certainly, this kind of standard is preferable to the simple interdivisional comparisons used to judge divisional profits in many large companies today.

Potentially, the most valuable application of the PIMS findings will come from using them to estimate the effects of strategic changes. Each participating corporation has recently received a second set of reports which show how ROI in a given business could be expected to change, both in the short and long term, if modifications were made in its strategic position.

It is too soon to tell how accurate those estimates will be. But it is clear already that many of the managers and planners have obtained valuable insights into the reasons for past performance and the most fruitful directions for change.

SUMMING UP

The PIMS project has demonstrated the feasibility and the benefits to be realized when companies pool their experiences. Information on strategic actions, market and industry situations, and results achieved can be organized into a multipurpose data base, and analysis of this data base has yielded useful general findings. Executives of the participating companies are beginning to utilize these results in the development and appraisal of strategic plans for individual business units.

Beyond the current benefits, we can also speculate on the broader impact that the approach represented by PIMS may have on the functioning of the private enterprise economy.

Competition is at the heart of our economic system. Will the process of competition become more effective or less effective if PIMS-type information becomes increasingly available? Is the answer the same if we judge effectiveness by some index of 'social benefit', rather than by the health and profitability of individual businesses?

It seems entirely probable that the answers are: *more effective* and *yes*.

While compensation has been one of the mainsprings for the dynamic growth of the U.S. economy, the great wastage of competition is increasingly retarding our national productivity. Can we maintain the benefits while reducing the drag of the wastage?

Research on multicompany data may enable us to accomplish just that by helping individual competitors to lessen the frequency and scale of their competitive mistakes.

The pooled record of business successes and failures, analyzed in PIMS-type fashion, can identify the courses of action that simply have no plausible promise at all, whether for the company or the customer or anyone else. It can also identify the other courses of action that have a good probability of yielding viable results. Competitors can therefore concentrate their energies on the higher-yield actions, and not dissipate their resources on quixotic ventures and forlorn causes.

Business is not a zero-sum game, where one man's gain is inevitably another man's loss. Sometimes most everyone wins, and sometimes most everyone loses. The systematic comparative study of ongoing experience can help maximize the frequency of the first outcome and minimize the second.

Chapter 7

Cognitive Maps as a Visionary Tool: Strategy Embedded in Issue Management

Colin Eden
Strategic Decision Support Research Unit,
University of Strathclyde, Scotland

INTRODUCTION

Making strategy work remains a relatively intractable problem for most organizations. Denning made this quite clear in his report on the 1983 Paris conference on Making Strategy Work. 'There was little guidance or clarification on the conference theme of making strategy work. Few of the papers which I heard threw much light on the question with which most executives are concerned: how to get something to happen. Strategic change still appears to happen largely as a result of crisis or from the impact of a key individual' (Denning 1984).

Developing strategy has, for the most part, been seen as an analytical activity which is devoid of urgency, fun, emotion, or passion. The focus of attention has usually been outside the organization where the environment and market have been seen as major determinants of strategy. In this paper I shall argue that the focus should be that of the embedded vision of the key powerful actors in the organization.

Four years ago Ansoff questioned some of the assumptions that underlay his original statements about how to develop a corporate plan. For my purposes the most important of these assumptions was that strategy formulation and strategy implementation are sequential and independent activities (Ansoff 1984). This paper argues that countering this assumption is important. Further I shall argue that the technique of 'cognitive mapping' is a powerful way of facilitating the linking of implementation and formulation. Indeed I shall argue that these tasks are hardly separable, rather that real managers cannot *think* about the future of their organization without thinking about action and implementation.

Within the context of Operational Research, I have argued that the definition of a situation regarded as problematic by the definer could not be construed without reference to possible courses of action (Eden, 1987). In other words encouraging people to define

To be published in *Long Range Planning*, Volume 24, Copyright ©1990, Pergamon Press PLC.

their world in 'idealised' forms is unnatural and relatively unhelpful. Thus problem solving methods that demand the construction of an idealised scenario do not relate to the natural process of working problems. This view of problem construction is largely influence by Kelly (1955) in as much as he argues, from the standpoint of a cognitive psychologist, that man attempts to make sense of his world in a practical way. Man seeks to predict and control—that is he construes his world in terms of *managing* it. In the same manner thinking about strategy is *seeing the future as something to be controlled and managed, not to be forecast.*

Because strategic management has been seen as planning rather than managing, it has been predominantly the business of 'staff officers' rather than the business of those with the power to act. However as Child and others argue '. . . power holders within organizations decide upon courses of strategic action . . . this "strategic choice" typically includes not only the *establishment of structural norms but also the manipulation of environmental features and the choice of relevant performance standards*' [my emphasis] (Child 1972).

The establishment of norms, performance standards both explicit and implicit, and control systems are the embedded ways in which an organization is self-fulfilling and potentially degenerative (Mitroff and Emshoff 1979). It is also the most powerful expression of strategy in action. The establishment of norms and cultures comes from those with power and not from those prosecuting an analytical staff role. It comes from what Pettigrew has called the 'management of meaning' (Pettigrew 1977). In other words the implementation of strategy depends upon subtle shifts and incrementalism (Quinn 1980) in the way in which powerful people *make sense of their world.*

All these assertions add up to the central thesis that those who have the power to act must be integrally involved in developing a strategy. They must be offered a way of working that captures their attention and their time. The method must be intrinsically relevant (in their terms), and must allow for continuous incrementalism rather than analysis and conclusion. And yet senior managers are no different from other humans in their demands for instant gratification, for a sense of concrete achievement, for a sense of vision/faith/magic (Raimond 1986).

Analytical techniques that focus on numbers and not on ideas will rarely meet these requirements—they are inherently unexciting and distanced from the experience and wisdom of managers as they think and picture futures.

Thus if we are to retain ownership and gain commitment from all the key power holders we must attend to their individual vision and yet negotiate a consensual vision.

Given all these practicalities how do we capture the involvement of these people? If we recognize an inclination to gain rewards from 'firefighting' and from the solving of important *problems* then maybe we should build strategic thinking out of the embedded theories that lie within the solving of strategic *issues*.

THE AIMS OF COGNITIVE MAPPING FOR STRATEGY DEVELOPMENT

Cognitive mapping as a technique set within an overriding methodology (Strategic Options Development and Analysis—SODA) has been used extensively for helping project teams work on messy strategic issues. The use of the technique, as it has been developed in the UK, has been well documented (Huxham and Bennett (1985), Smithin (1981), Eden et al (1983), Eden (1985)) as an Operational Research tool. However, it is only in the last few years that it has been used as a deliberate part of strategy development.

The reasons for expecting cognitive mapping and SODA to play a role in successful strategy development and implementation are implied from the aims of the method. The aims have been set down elsewhere (Eden 1989) but are, in brief, to provide:

— an instrument to help *negotiation* towards best solution;
— a way of *'hearing several people at once'* by setting the views of one person in the context of the ideas of others;
— a method for *providing structure* to multiple and conflicting aspects of argumentation;
— a method which is designed to *suggest ACTION* to resolve issues;
— a method for developing a consensus about a *SYSTEM of goals*;
— a method that does not violate the natural role of discussion;
— an efficient way of avoiding 'group-think' and 'bounded vision';
— a designed scheme for attending to both the *content* of issues and to the need for a recognition that *people* change organizations;
— a *designed environment* for ensuring effective decision making.

Given this list of aims it is not surprising that a team of senior managers who experience these aims being met within the context of working on a major strategic issue *of immediate and urgent concern* would see benefits in developing strategy in a similar fashion. As the introduction identified, senior managers have become increasingly disillusioned with the relevance and impact of corporate planners on their organization.

It was in the light of requests from 'real' clients that a coherence between the 'typical' SODA exercise and the felt inadequacies of strategic planning began to realize an approach to strategy development that was founded in *issue related* strategy workshops.

In order to describe meaningfully the link between strategy development and issue related projects we should consider the typical use of cognitive mapping within the context of messy strategic issues.

A TYPICAL SODA PROGRAMME

A SODA programme involves a 'SODA facilitator' in capturing the views, knowledge, and expertise surrounding the issue to be addressed. This might involve: interviews with key individuals who are involved in the resolution of the issue; and/or the analysis of background papers; and/or interviews with experts on the topic area. Often, where possible, it becomes important to include interviews with those who could sabotage the outcome or those who are integrally involved in implementation.

The interviews are conducted in a relatively open-ended manner (Eden and Wheaton 1980) where the prompt for focussing discussion is simply, and only, the 'label' given to the issue—for example in a product development project the prompt might be 'in your own view, how do you see things unfolding in the next few years if the product were to remain as it is now?' and/or 'what is your own personal image of the new product and its place in the market?' Each of these questions is used depending on the facilitator's view of the 'problem solving personality' (Eden et al 1983) of the interviewee—does

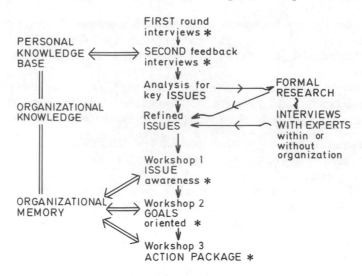

(Ideally max time between events marked * should be one
'psychological week' – Monday of first week to Friday
of the next week)

Figure 1. A typical SODA project

the person tend to see problems in terms of 'I'd like to be over there but am not sure how to get there' (the second prompt) or in terms of 'I know I'm not in the right place now but I'm not sure where I want to be' (the first prompt).

The interview is conducted so that further questions are built on the 'grounded data' generated during the interview and recorded as a cognitive map. Thus the cognitive map is used interactively during the interview to guide the interview (see Eden 1988, 1989 for examples).

After the interview the facilitator(s) constructs a COPE model of the knowledge and arguments he discovers, merging the various views so that 'synergy' and creativity become possible. The overall map that is produced by this procedure will highlight the goals, the supporting assumptions, the key issues, and the options available to the decision making team. Through careful analysis of the COPE model an agenda for an action oriented workshop will be generated. Ideally the SODA workshop will involve a large number of those who were originally interviewed. The model is then used to focus discussion, develop consensus, resolve conflict, promote creativity, and decide an action plan. Sometimes such workshops last for half a day and sometimes they run over several one-day events. The typical project follows the pattern illustrated by Figure 1.

The outcomes of a firefighting SODA project obviously depend upon the purpose for which SODA was used; however they usually include:

— a clear statement of *goals and strategic direction*;
— a management team with a *common understanding* and *commitment to action* to deliver selected policies;
— a *focus or specification for research* into new areas of business, or key assumptions revealed through COPE;

— a *comprehensive business model* which can be used as a decision support tool by members of the management team;
— an *action package* with time scales and responsibilities identified.

FROM ISSUES TO STRATEGY

Using cognitive mapping as the core technique in work on major issues undoubtedly produces high levels of ownership of the model constructed and of the agreed actions. This is largely because cognitive maps, by their very nature, are intended to relate to the way in which a person 'makes sense of' and explains the world around about him. If cognitive mapping, in the form we have been developing it, is a moderately successful translation of Personal Construct Theory (Kelly, 1955) into the world of problem solving, and Kelly's theory is sensible *and useful* in its own right, and the facilitator is skilled in interviewing and the construction of cognitive maps, then it follows that ownership will occur.

As people talk about their views on a particular problem they are drawing upon general theories they have about the organization, the market place, and the strengths and weaknesses of different courses of action. This occurs naturally, and can be understood and modelled by the facilitator, without recourse to SWOT analysis questions. These theories are often expressed in highly specific terms but nevertheless imply the translation of experience into assertions about the way in which the future may unfold. This is no more than we might expect if we follow the implications of a Kellyian model of man as someone who is continually striving to make sense of his world.

Thus, for example, the following arguments that have occurred in discussion about product development translate into clear concepts on a cognitive map:

'there are too many old timers involved who are far too set in their ways . . . an imaginative new concept like that would never fly . . . we need some young turks'

gives—

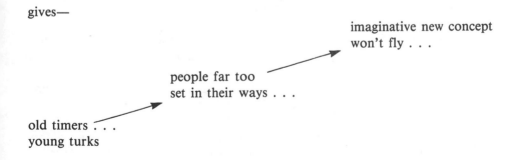

'we must keep up our direct role in maintenance because it means we can continually develop our relationship with customers, and so stand a greater chance of locking them in to our products . . . if we subcontract we won't get to know what our customers are thinking'

gives—

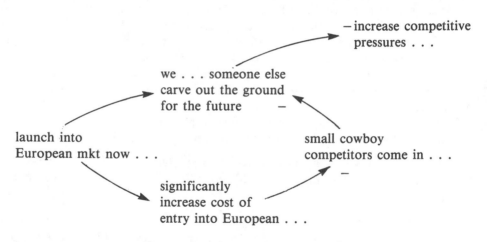

greater chance of locking
customers in to our products . . .

continually develop
relationship with customer . . .
won't get to know what our
customers are thinking

keep direct role in
maintenance . . . subcontract
maintenance

'competitive pressures are increasing and we must be prepared to launch into the
European market now or else someone else will carve out the ground for the
future . . . and unless we significantly increase the cost of entry into Europe all sorts
of small cowboy competitors will come in'

gives—

− increase competitive
pressures . . .

we . . . someone else
carve out the ground
for the future   −

launch into
European mkt now . . .

small cowboy
competitors come in . . .

−

significantly
increase cost of
entry into European . . .

All of these segments of a cognitive map were constructed for a team to work on a
strategic issue of considerable urgency, they were not statements made to consider a
future strategy of the organization. And yet they are all examples of how thinking about
the *implementation* of possible actions has strategic implications and also contains
embedded theories of general strategic intent. Thus while the first example suggests action
of 'hiring young turks', there is also the more generalizable and strategic theory that
imaginative concepts won't work if people are set in their ways. If we were to take this
theory seriously within strategy development then it draws attention to the possible
strategic organizational goal of creating imaginative products and the subordinate
strategic thrust of creating a culture that 'increases flexible attitudes' rather than 'people
set in their ways'. Similarly, and more obviously, in the other two examples we see
possible strategic goals *emerging* of 'reducing competitor pressures' and 'locking
people in'.

The point is not that these issue oriented goals should necessarily be strategic goals of the organization but rather that they have emerged *from the owners of the problem* as implied goals. Goals such as these, that are expressed in embedded ways of thinking about dealing with live issues, *will* be the strategic direction of the organization by default 'if men define situations as real, they are real in their consequences' (Thomas and Thomas 1928). By surfacing these goals, and possible strategic thrusts aimed at achieving them, it is possible to consider their coherence one with another and facilitate the team in reflecting upon the desirability of them. Because they have been surfaced during a firefighting episode and because they have ownership, it is more likely that a senior management team can be pursuaded to devote *their* time to strategic thinking, because the thinking will be *based upon their wisdom*.

I am arguing here that the strategic future of the organization depends as much on the theories of feasible action (or 'world-taken-for-granted') embedded in the thinking of the senior management team as the environment of the organization. Thus the role of strategic thinking by these managers must be to reflect upon these worlds taken for granted *in order that there is a real shift in the power balance between the impact of the environment and the impact of the organization on its future (Hrebeniak and Joyce 1985)*. A shift from reactive management dependent on implicit and potentially incoherent theories of control, to interactive management (see Ackoff 1974 for an interesting view of the difference between inactive, reactive, proactive and interactive) that is designed to *manage rather than forecast the future*.

THE ANALYSIS OF COGNITIVE MAPS FOR STRATEGIC THINKING

In a SODA project it is imperative that the ownership of an action portfolio is increased by the use of *cognitive* maps during the early stages of the project. As the project unfolds the maps are aggregated into a single 'group map' which will not belong to any member of the group; it has now become a device for facilitating negotiation, synergy, and creativity. The 'group map' will contain the concepts of each member of the group but they will have been set in the context of the view of all other members. Thus there will be ownership of a portion of the group map but not ownership of the overall map.

With the intention of persuading a management team to take seriously their own strategic ideas, sections of each of several 'firefighting group maps' will have been merged into one 'strategic map'. The process is bound to reduce further the ownership with respect to original 'cognitive maps'. The extent to which this reduced ownership matters will depend upon the ultimate ownership of the issue related group map prior to the implementation of the issue related actions.

If strategy development is deliberately built 'on the back' of a *number* of urgent issues then the strategic map will usually be large (our experience suggests 600–1000 concepts). The analysis of a strategic map takes a different form to that for issue related projects. Whereas in an issue related project the goals tend to be more clear cut and self-evident, this is not the case (nor ought it to be the case) for strategy development. A significant element of the time spent in strategy development will relate to the establishing of a coherent goal *system*. This task has traditionally been treated as the development of a 'mission statement' combined with a number of 'motherhood and apple pie' statements

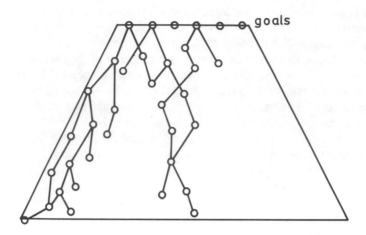

Figure 2. Pyramidal structure

for public consumption. However, our experience with several multinational organizations suggests that it is easy to engage the attention of senior managers when the issues derive directly from their own thinking, and from a clear portrayal of the implications and ramifications of this data for the future of the organization.

Thus analysis focusses mostly on the superordinate elements of the model by:

 (i) identifying potential goals and their interaction with one-another.
 (ii) identifying 'not-goals'—that is 'heads' of the model (concepts with no further consequences) that do not express a positive outcome that is likely to be desired but rather a ramification that is not wanted.
(iii) identifying potential strategic thrusts.
(iv) identifying potential options to form part of a strategic action portfolio.

The first two of these activities recognize a particularly important outcome of developing strategy in this manner. Most approaches to strategy development take an 'idealized' vision of the future as the starting point; in some instances this becomes the core of a dialectical approach (for example Ackoff 1970, Checkland 1981, and (by implication) Mason and Mitroff 1981). By doing so, it is highly likely that strategy becomes too tidy and so unrealistic. In mapping terms, the shape of the map developed through idealized planning approaches is pyramidal (Figure 2). By following an issue related procedure the strategic map that arises follows a 'wheatsheaf' shape (Figure 3) where the 'not-goals' outside the pyramid are important ramifications that need to be fully recognized in thinking about possible strategic thrusts.

When models are larger than 70 concepts we find it useful to use the computer software (COPE) to help analyze the present maps. In addition the computer support enables strategy workshops to be run using a fully developed 'Group Decision Support System' (Ackermann 1987, Eden 1988). The computer is able to undertake a variety of analyses of the strategic map to help in the identification of the above three sorts of data.

The simplest analysis is the location of 'heads', that is concepts that must be either category (i) or (ii). These are colour coded according to whether they are positively

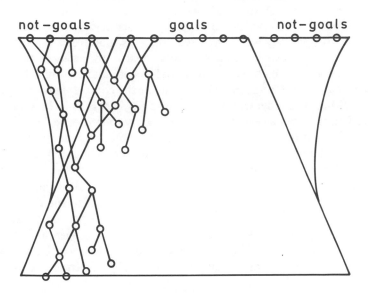

Figure 3. 'Wheatsheaf' structure

expressed goals, or outcomes that are not desired ('not-goals'); 'red' is used to colour goals and 'white' for not-goals. Many of the concepts immediately subordinate to 'heads' will also be goals and will give meaning to related goals as well as being integral to a possible goal *system*.

However, the next step is to identify potential strategic thrusts (strategic options). The software will analyze every concept and calculate the number of paths of argument giving support to the concept, the number of consequential paths, the number of goals that can be reached from the concept, the number of not-goals that can be reached, the number of concepts used to elaborate supporting arguments, the number of concepts that elaborate consequences, and the mean path length of supporting and consequential arguments. Using all these data a statistic is generated that gives an *indication* of the significance of the concept within the whole map relative to other concepts. The most significant concepts are likely to be *potential* strategic options and coloured 'magenta' to indicate the high relative centrality of the concept. It is at this stage that each of these potential options is evaluated as to whether they might be goals. If they look more like a desired outcome that is likely to be seen as 'a good thing in its own right' then it will be recorded in 'red' as a goal.

When working with a large map it is usually helpful to check the analysis for strategic options by establishing the overall structure of the map. If we take seriously the notion that the complexity of a large strategic issue can be helpfully managed by breaking it down into a system of interacting problems or strategic arenas then we may expect these arenas to broadly correlate with potential strategic thrusts. Indeed it seems sensible to argue that they must be conceptually related. Thus, the concepts identified as strategic options using the analysis of paths of argument should match that undertaken by an analysis of interconnected clusters of concepts.

COPE provided the user with the opportunity to identify clusters of concepts, where a cluster is a set of relatively well connected concepts that are relatively disconnected to other clusters. Each cluster will have pseudo 'heads' and pseudo 'tails' and can be seen as a strategic arena which has its own goal system and options. The goal system of each cluster may be seen as a strategic option for the complete model. There are two clustering algorithms available within COPE: the first treats links between concepts as direction-less and thus builds the matrix of similarity (based on calculating a form of the Jaccard coefficient (Everitt 1974)) without attention to hierarchy; the second form of analysis treats the map as a directed graph (Harary et al 1965). In either case the clustering is mathematically dependent upon the 'root' concept that starts the analysis, and so the user is given the option of specifying the root or allowing the algorithm to select a concept at random. In addition the user can constrain the cluster size (a particularly useful facility when clustering is used to produce printed maps). The output of the selected cluster analysis is compared with the list of 'magenta' concepts already identified and the facilitator will add further strategic options and delete some already identified based upon this comparison, *and* based upon attention to the content of concepts.

The concepts that lie between strategic options and goals may also be a part of the goal system or may simply be argumentation that describes the linkage. COPE will allow the user to inspect these lines of argument so that a proposed goal system can be formulated.

Given a 600–1000 concept model it is usual for about 50–60 concepts to make up a *potential* goal system that the group can evaluate. Many of these concepts will be a more detailed elaboration of other concepts, and so it is expected that the final approved goal system will be 30–40 concepts refined from the proposed goal system. In addition it is common for there to be about the same number of 'white' not-goals that will act as warning devices (indeed not-goals become an important part of the definition of 'performance criteria' or 'critical success factors' for the monitoring of the strategy).

The final stage of analysis for a strategy workshop is to tentatively identify the potential options that might provide the action portfolios to support potential strategic thrusts. Analytically, the first stage of identification is to check the 'tails' (concepts with no explanations). These concepts are usually either simply historical explanation, 'matters of fact', or alternatively are potential options. If they look as if they may be actionable then they are coloured 'cyan' (if they become agreed actions they are turned 'green'). Analyzing for 'tails' will not identify all options (indeed I have argued elsewhere that, in principle, all concepts are potential options (Eden and Huxham 1988), but it provides an encouraging starting point for action oriented strategy development.

It is likely that some options and strategic options are '*dilemmas*'. That is they are potential action points or strategic thrusts that evidently lead to a number of both positive and negative outcomes. After having identified options and strategic options, COPE will identify 'cyan' or 'magenta' concepts that lead to several goals or not-goals (red and white) with both positive and negative consequences (in order to do so the coding must have identified positive outcomes and actions as the first pole of the concept).

In the same way as dilemmas are important options to identify prior to a strategy workshop, it is also important to identify those potential options that have consequences for many 'heads' (that is goals and not-goals). COPE identifies these concepts by simply tracing back from all 'heads' and putting all concepts that are 'met' into a 'group' which is identified with respect to the 'head' which started the analysis. Any concept which appears in 'n' groups has consequences for 'n' 'heads'. If 'n' is large then it is likely that the concept is a significant strategic option or option and should be identified as such.

THE STRATEGY WORKSHOP

The analyses discussed above are designed to identify the 'agenda' for strategy workshops. The workshop is designed to bring together key members of the management team and allow them to work effectively and efficiently on strategic content which is appropriate and *action oriented*.

The format for a workshop is contingent upon facilities available and the style of strategic thinking to which the group are accustomed. In some instances it is appropriate to use mapping and associated analyses as the basic material for a 'traditional' report which is built around sections based upon each of the identified clusters within the map. Thus, for example, each section contains (i) discussion of the holistic nature and emergent properties of the cluster, including commentary about the relationship of the cluster to other clusters, (ii) description of the goals that drive the cluster, (iii) discussion of the key strategic options, and (iv) the action portfolio relating to the cluster, including commentary about dilemmas and options with a high number of ramifications. COPE is able to print to a file output that is in the above format, but without the linking text which communicates the drama and adds style and readability to the document. The file produced by COPE is the basic content set out in a format that is amenable to word processing.

In other instances the workshop can be built around enlarged pictures of the maps of each cluster within the model. These maps are produced by COPE onto 11×8 inch paper and then photocopied to 44×32 inch. The key concepts are highlighted in colour to match their role as goals, strategic options, or options. These 'pictures' are hung around the conference room and are each, in turn, used as an agenda item. As the discussion proceeds modifications to the maps can be written directly onto the pictures and the model updated in the computer.

However, when possible the most effective workshop is likely to occur when the full power of the SODA process is used by running the workshop in a designed Group Decision Support environment (Huber 1982, Ackermann 1987, Eden 1988). COPE running on a fast IBM PC AT clone with a 'slave' monitor and large screen facilities enables the facilitator to rebuild and re-present the model in 'real-time'.

CONCLUDING REMARKS

This paper has discussed the use of cognitive mapping as an aid to developing strategy. The procedure is based on paying attention to the *ownership* of data that are used as the basic material for debate about strategy. Designing 'strategy workshops' based on owned material that emerges from work on major strategic issues, of a 'firefighting' nature, is aimed at encouraging the direct involvement of senior managers in strategy development. By so doing strategy evolves from a human and emotional *process* rather than it being only the sterile evaluation of economic and market data.

Promoting a series of focussed strategy workshops can ensure coherence in strategy and also create 'logical incrementalism'. Coherence is not based on a plan but rather on providing managers with a way of constructing the events that pass them by. Construal will be opportunistic and yet in concert with that of colleagues, it will enable managers to pounce on some opportunities and ignore others with confidence.

REFERENCES

Ackermann, F. (1987). 'The role of computer support in decision management', paper presented to the Intl. Symposium on New Directions in Decision Management, Sept, Toronto.

Ackoff, R. L. (1970). *A Concept of Corporate Planning.* Wiley: New York.

Ackoff, R. L. (1974). *Redesigning the Future.* Wiley: New York.

Ansoff, I. (1984). *Implanting Strategic Management*, Prentice Hall: New York.

Checkland, P. (1981). *Systems Thinking, Systems Practice.* Wiley: Chichester.

Child, J. (1972). 'Organizational Structure, Environment and Performance: the role strategic choice'. *Sociology*, **6**, 1–22.

Denning, B. (1984). Report on the Paris Conference on 'Making Strategy Work'. *Society for Long Range Planning Newsletter.* January.

Eden, C. (1985). 'Perish the thought!' *Jnl. of the Operational Research Society*, **36**, 809–819.

Eden, C. (1987). 'Problem-solving or problem-finishing?' In Jackson, M. C. and Keys, P. (eds). *New Directions in Management Science*, Gower: Aldershot, Hants.

Eden, C. (1988) 'Cognitive mapping', *European Journal of Operational Research*, **36**, 1–13

Eden C. (1989), 'Using Cognitive Mapping for Strategic Options Development and Analysis', in Rosenhead, J. (ed). *Rational Analysis for a Problematic World*, Wiley: Chichester.

Eden, C., Jones, S., and Sims, D. (1983). *Messing about in problems.* Pergamon: Oxford.

Eden C. and Huxham, C. (1988) 'Action oriented strategic planning', *Jnl. of the Opnl. Res. Soc.*, **39**(10), 889–900.

Eden, C., and Wheaton, G. (1980). *In favour of structure.* Centre for the Study of Organizational Change and Development: University of Bath.

Everitt, B. (1974). *Cluster Analysis*, New York: Wiley.

Harary, F., Norman, R., and Cartwright, D. (1965). *Structural Models: an introduction to the theory of directed graphs.* Wiley: New York.

Hrebiniak, L. G., and Joyce, W. F. (1985). 'Organizational Adaptation: strategic choice and environmental determinism'. *Administrative Science Quarterly*, **30**, 336–349.

Huber, G. P. (1982). 'Group Decision Support Systems as aids in the use of structured group management techniques', *DSS-82 Transactions, 2nd Intl. Conference on Decision Support Systems.* June, 96–108.

Huxham, C. S., and Bennett, P. G. (1985). 'Floating ideas—an experiment in enhancing hypergames with maps', *Omega*, **13**, 331–347.

Kelly, G. A. (1955). *The Psychology of Personal Constructs: a theory of personality.* Norton: New York.

Mason, J., and Mitroff, I. (1981). *Challenging Strategic Planning Assumptions: theory, cases and techniques.* Wiley: New York.

Mitroff, I., and Emshoff, J. R. (1979). 'On strategic assumption making: a dialectical approach to policy and planning', *Academy of Management Review*, **4**, 1–12.

Pettigrew, A. M. (1977). 'Strategy formulation as a political process', *International Studies of Management and Organisation*, Summer 1977, volume VII, No. 2.

Quinn, J. B. (1980). *Strategies for Change: logical incrementalism.* Richard D. Irwin: Homewood, Illinois.

Raimond, P. (1986). *Using the Strategic Planning Process for Organizational Change.* PhD thesis, University of Bath.

Smithin, T. (1981). 'Stranger in a strange land: a working guide to cognitive mapping', *Jnl. of Management Development*, 1, 34–43.

Thomas, W. I., and Thomas, D. S. (1928). *The Child in America: behaviour problems and progress.* Knopf: New York.

_____ Part III

Assessment of Uncertainty

Chapter 8

Risk Analysis in Capital Investment

David B. Hertz
McKinsey & Company

Of all the decisions that business executives must make, none is more challenging — and none has received more attention — than choosing among alternative capital investment opportunities. What makes this kind of decision so demanding, of course, is not the problem of projecting return on investment under any given set of assumptions. The difficulty is in the assumptions and in their impact. Each assumption involves its own degree — often a high degree — of uncertainty; and, taken together, these combined uncertainties can multiply into a total uncertainty of critical proportions. This is where the element of risk enters, and it is in the evaluation of risk that the executive has been able to get little help from currently available tools and techniques.

There is a way to help the executive sharpen key capital investment decisions by providing him or her with a realistic measurement of the risks involved. Armed with this gauge, which evaluates the risk at each possible level of return, he or she is then in a position to measure more knowledgeably alternative courses of action against corporate objectives.

NEED FOR NEW CONCEPT

The evaluation of a capital investment project starts with the principle that the productivity of capital is measured by the rate of return we expect to receive over some future period. A dollar received next year is worth less to us than a dollar in hand today.

Expenditures three years hence are less costly than expenditures of equal magnitude two years from now. For this reason we cannot calculate the rate of return realistically unless we take into account (a) when the sums involved in an investment are spent and (b) when the returns are received.

Comparing alternative investments is thus complicated by the fact that they usually differ not only in size but also in the length of time over which expenditures will have to be made and benefits returned.

These facts of investment life long ago made apparent the shortcomings of approaches that simply averaged expenditures and benefits, or lumped them, as in the number-of-years-to-pay-out method. These shortcomings stimulated students of decision making to explore more precise methods for determining whether one investment would leave a company better off in the long run than would another course of action.

It is not surprising, then, that much effort has been applied to the development of ways to improve our ability to discriminate among investment alternatives. The focus of all of these investigations has been to sharpen the definition of the value of capital investments to the company. The controversy and furor that once came out in the business press over the most appropriate way of calculating these values have largely been resolved in favor of the discounted cash flow method as a reasonable means of measuring the rate of return that can be expected in the future from an investment made today.

Thus we have methods which are more or less elaborate mathematical formulas for comparing the outcomes of various investments and the combinations of the variables that will affect the investments. As these techniques have progressed, the mathematics involved has become more and more precise, so that we can now calculate discounted returns to a fraction of a percent.

But the sophisticated executive knows that behind these precise calculations are data which are not that precise. At best, the rate-of-return information he is provided with is based on an average of different opinions with varying reliabilities and different ranges of probability. When the expected returns on two investments are close, he is likely to be influenced by intangibles—a precarious pursuit at best. Even when the figures for two investments are quite far apart, and the choice seems clear, there lurk memories of the Edsel and other ill-fated ventures.

In short, the decision maker realizes that there is something more he ought to know, something in addition to the expected rate of return. What is missing has to do with the nature of the data on which the expected rate of return is calculated and with the way those data are processed. It involves uncertainty, with possibilities and probabilities extending across a wide range of rewards and risks. (For a summary of the new approach, see the ruled insert.)

The Achilles Heel

The fatal weakness of past approaches thus has nothing to do with the mathematics of rate-of-return calculation. We have pushed along this path so far that the precision of our calculation is, if anything, somewhat illusory. The fact is that, no matter what mathematics is used, each of the variables entering into the calculation of rate of return is subject to a high level of uncertainty.

For example, the useful life of a new piece of capital equipment is rarely known in advance with any degree of certainty. It may be affected by variations in obsolescence or deterioration, and relatively small changes in use life can lead to large changes in return. Yet an expected value for the life of the equipment—based on a great deal of data from which a single best possible forecast has been developed—is entered into the rate-of-return calculation. The same is done for the other factors that have a significant bearing on the decision at hand.

Let us look at how this works out in a simple case—one in which the odds appear to be all in favor of a particular decision. The executives of a food company must decide

After examining present methods of comparing alternative investments, the author reports on his firm's experience in applying a new approach to the problem. Using this approach, management takes the various levels of possible cash flow, return on investment, and other results of a proposed outlay and gets an estimate of the odds for each potential outcome.

Currently, many facilities decisions are based on discounted cash flow calculations. Management is told, for example, that Investment X has an expected internal rate of return of 9.2%, while for Investment Y a 10.3% return can be expected.

By contrast, the new approach would put in front of the executive a schedule that gives him the most likely return from X, but also tells him that X has 1 chance in 20 of being a total loss, 1 in 10 of earning from 4% to 5%, 2 in 10 of paying from 8% to 10%, and 1 chance in 50 of attaining a 30% rate of return. From another schedule he learns what the most likely rate of return is from Y, but also that Y has 1 chance in 10 of earning from 3% to 5% return, 2 in 10 of paying between 9% and 11%, and 1 chance in 100 of a 30% rate of return.

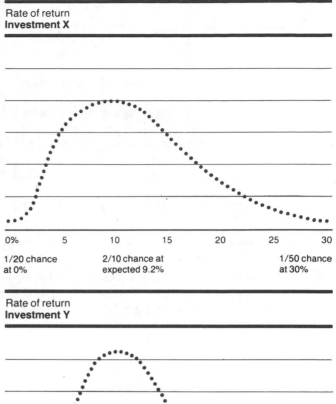

Rate of return
Investment X

| 0% | 5 | 10 | 15 | 20 | 25 | 30 |

1/20 chance
at 0%   2/10 chance at
expected 9.2%   1/50 chance
at 30%

Rate of return
Investment Y

| 0% | 5 | 10 | 15 | 20 | 25 | 30 |

1/10 chance
at 0%   2/10 chance at
expected 10.3%   1/100 chance
at 30%

In this instance, the estimates of the rates of return provided by the two approaches would not be substantially different. However, to the decision maker with the added information, Investment Y no longer looks like the clearly better choice, since with X the chances of substantial gain are higher and the risks of loss lower.

Two things have made this approach appealing to managers who have used it:

1. Certainly in every case it is a more descriptive statement of the two opportunities. And in some cases it might well reverse the decision, in line with particular corporate objectives.

2. This is not a difficult technique to use, since much of the information needed is already available — or readily accessible — and the validity of the principles involved has, for the most part, already been proved in other applications.

The enthusiasm with which managements exposed to this approach have received it suggests that it may have wide application. It has particular relevance, for example, in such knotty problems as investments relating to acquisitions or new products and in decisions that might involve excess capacity.

Exhibit I
Describing uncertainty—a throw of the dice

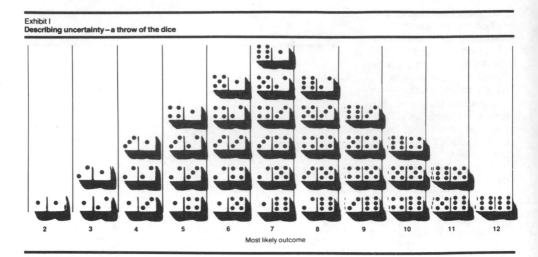

Most likely outcome

whether to launch a new packaged cereal. They have come to the conclusion that five factors are the determining variables: advertising and promotion expense, total cereal market, share of market for this product, operating costs, and new capital investment.

On the basis of the 'most likely' estimate for each of these variables, the picture looks very bright — a healthy 30% return. This future, however, depends on whether each of these estimates actually comes true. If each of these educated guesses has, for example, a 60% chance of being correct, there is only an 8% chance that all five will be correct ($.60 \times .60 \times .60 \times .60 \times .60$). So the 'expected' return actually depends on a rather unlikely coincidence. The decision maker needs to know a great deal more about the other values used to make each of the five estimates and about what he stands to gain or lose from various combinations of these values.

This simple example illustrates that the rate of return actually depends on a specific combination of values of a great many different variables. But only the expected levels of ranges (worst, average, best; or pessimistic, most likely, optimistic) of these variables are used in formal mathematical ways to provide the figures given to management. Thus predicting a single most likely rate of return gives precise numbers that do not tell the whole story.

The expected rate of return represents only a few points on a continuous curve of possible combinations of future happenings. It is a bit like trying to predict the outcome in a dice game by saying that the most likely outcome is a 7. The description is incomplete because it does not tell us about all the other things that could happen. In *Exhibit I*, for instance, we see the odds on throws of only two dice having 6 sides. Now suppose that each of eight dice has 100 sides. This is a situation more comparable to business investment, where the company's market share might become any 1 of 100 different sizes and where there are eight factors (pricing, promotion, and so on) that can affect the outcome.

Nor is this the only trouble. Our willingness to bet on a role of the dice depends not only on the odds but also on the stakes. Since the probability of rolling a 7 is 1 in 6, we might be quite willing to risk a few dollars on that outcome at suitable odds. But would we be equally willing to wager $10 000 or $100 000 at those same odds, or even at better odds? In short, risk is influenced both by the odds on various events occurring and by the magnitude of the rewards or penalties that are involved when they do occur.

To illustrate again, suppose that a company is considering an investment of $1 million. The best estimate of the probable return is $200 000 a year. It could well be that this estimate is the average of three possible returns—a 1-in-3 chance of getting no return at all, a 1-in-3 chance of getting $200 000 per year, a 1-in-3 chance of getting $400 000 per year. Suppose that getting no return at all would put the company out of business. Then, by accepting this proposal, management is taking a 1-in-3 chance of going bankrupt.

If only the best-estimate analysis is used, however, management might go ahead, unaware that it is taking a big chance. If all of the available information were examined, management might prefer an alternative proposal with a smaller, but more certain (that is, less variable) expectation.

Such considerations have led almost all advocates of the use of modern capital-investment-index calculations to plead for a recognition of the elements of uncertainty. Perhaps Ross G. Walker summed up current thinking when he spoke of 'the almost impenetrable mists of any forecast'.[1]

How can executives penetrate the mists of uncertainty surrounding the choices among alternatives?

Limited Improvements

A number of efforts to cope with uncertainty have been successful up to a point, but all seem to fall short of the mark in one way or another:

1. *More accurate forecasts*—Reducing the error in estimates is a worthy objective. But no matter how many estimates of the future go into a capital investment decision, when all is said and done, the future is still the future. Therefore, however well we forecast, we are still left with the certain knowledge that we cannot eliminate all uncertainty.

2. *Empirical adjustments*—Adjusting the factors influencing the outcome of a decision is subject to serious difficulties. We would like to adjust them so as to cut down the likelihood that we will make a 'bad' investment, but how can we do that without at the same time spoiling our chances to make a 'good' one? And in any case, what is the basis for adjustment? We adjust, not for uncertainty, but for bias.

For example, construction estimates are often exceeded. If a company's history of construction costs is that 90% of its estimates have been exceeded by 15%, then in a capital estimate there is every justification for increasing the value of this factor by 15%. This is a matter of improving the accuracy of the estimate.

But suppose that new-product sales estimates have been exceeded by more than 75% in one-fourth of all historical cases and have not reached 50% of the estimate in one-sixth of all such cases? Penalties for such overestimating are very real, and so management is apt to reduce the sales estimate to 'cover' the one case in six—thereby reducing the calculated rate of return. In so doing, it is possibly missing some of its best opportunities.

3. *Revising cutoff rates*—Selecting higher cutoff rates for protecting against uncertainty is attempting much the same thing. Management would like to have a

1. 'The Judgment Factor in Investment Decisions,' *HBR* March–April 1961, p. 99.

possibility of return in proportion to the risk it takes. Where there is much uncertainty involved in the various estimates of sales, costs, prices, and so on, a high calculated return from the investment provides some incentive for taking the risk. This is, in fact, a perfectly sound position. The trouble is that the decision maker still needs to know explicitly what risks he is taking—and what the odds are on achieving the expected return.

4. *Three-level estimates*—A start at spelling out risks is sometimes made by taking the high, medium, and low values of the estimated factors and calculating rates of return based on various combinations of the pessimistic, average, and optimistic estimates. These calculations give a picture of the range of possible results but do not tell the executive whether the pessimistic result is more likely than the optimistic one—or, in fact, whether the average result is much more likely to occur than either of the extremes. So, although this is a step in the right direction, it still does not give a clear enough picture for comparing alternatives.

5. *Selected probabilities*—Various methods have been used to include the probabilities of specific factors in the return calculation. L. C. Grant discussed a program for forecasting discounted cash flow rates of return where the service life is subject to obsolescence and deterioration. He calculated the odds that the investment will terminate at any time after it is made depending on the probability distribution of the service-life factor. After having calculated these factors for each year through maximum service life, he determined an overall expected rate of return.[2]

Edward G. Bennion suggested the use of game theory to take into account alternative market growth rates as they would determine rate of return for various options. He used the estimated probabilities that specific growth rates would occur to develop optimum strategies. Bennion point out:

'Forecasting can result in a negative contribution to capital budget decisions unless it goes further than merely providing a single most probable prediction. . . . [with] an estimated probability coefficient for the forecast, plus knowledge of the payoffs for the company's alternative investments and calculation of indifference probabilities . . . the margin of error may be substantially reduced, and the businessman can tell just how far off his forecast may be before it leads him to a wrong decision.'[3]

Note that both of these methods yield an expected return, each based on only one uncertain input factor—service life in the first case, market growth in the second. Both are helpful, and both tend to improve the clarity with which the executive can view investment alternatives. But neither sharpens up the range of 'risk taken' or 'return hoped for' sufficiently to help very much in the complex decisions of capital planning.

SHARPENING THE PICTURE

Since every one of the many factors that enter into the evaluation of a decision is subject to some uncertainty, the executive needs a helpful portrayal of the effects that the uncertainty surrounding each of the significant factors has on the returns he is likely to achieve. Therefore, I use a method combining the variabilities inherent in all the relevant factors under consideration. The objective is to give a clear picture of the

2. 'Monitoring Capital Investments,' *Financial Executive*, April 1963, p. 19.
3. 'Capital Budgeting and Game Theory,' *HBR* November–December 1956, p. 123.

relative risk and the probable odds of coming out ahead or behind in light of uncertain foreknowledge.

A simulation of the way these factors may combine as the future unfolds is the key to extracting the maximum information from the available forecasts. In fact, the approach is very simple, using a computer to do the necessary arithmetic. To carry out the analysis, a company must follow three steps:

1. Estimate the range of values for each of the factors (for example, range of selling price and sales growth rate) and within that range the likelihood of occurrence of each value.

2. Select at random one value from the distribution of values for each factor. Then combine the values for all of the factors and compute the rate of return (or present value) from that combination. For instance, the lowest in the range of prices might be combined with the highest in the range of growth rate and other factors. (The fact that the elements are dependent should be taken into account, as we shall see later.)

3. Do this over and over again to define and evaluate the odds of the occurrence of each possible rate of return. Since there are literally millions of possible combinations of values, we need to test the likelihood that various returns on the investment will occur. This is like finding out by recording the results of a great many throws what percent of 7s or other combinations we may expect in tossing dice. The result will be a listing of the rates of return we might achieve, ranging from a loss (if the factors go against us) to whatever maximum gain is possible with the estimates that have been made.

For each of these rates we can determine the chances that it may occur. (Note that a specific return can usually be achieved through more than one combination of events. The more combinations for a given rate, the higher the chances of achieving it—as with 7s in tossing dice.) The average expectation is the average of the values of all outcomes weighted by the chances of each occurring.

We can also determine the variability of outcome values from the average. This is important since, all other factors being equal, management would presumably prefer lower variability for the same return if given the choice. This concept has already been applied to investment portfolios.

When the expected return and variability of each of a series of investments have been determined, the same techniques may be used to examine the effectiveness of various combinations of them in meeting management objectives.

PRACTICAL TEST

To see how this new approach works in practice, let us take the experience of a management that has already analyzed a specific investment proposal by conventional techniques. Taking the same investment schedule and the same expected values actually used, we can find what results the new method would produce and compare them with the results obtained by conventional methods. As we shall see, the new picture of risks and returns is different from the old one. Yet the differences are attributable in no way to changes in the basic data—only to the increased sensitivity of the method to management's uncertainties about the key factors.

Investment Proposal

In this case, a medium-size industrial chemical producer is considering a $10 million extension to its processing plant. The estimated service life of the facility is ten years; the engineers expect to use 250 000 tons of processed material worth $510 per ton at an average processing cost of $435 per ton. Is this investment a good bet? In fact, what is the return that the company may expect? What are the risks? We need to make the best and fullest use of all the market research and financial analyses that have been developed, so as to give management a clear picture of this project in an uncertain world.

The key input factors management has decided to use are market size, selling prices, market growth rate, share of market (which results in physical sales volume), investment required, residual value of investment, operating costs, fixed costs, and useful life of facilities. These factors are typical of those in many company projects that must be analyzed and combined to obtain a measure of the attractiveness of a proposed capital facilities investment.

Obtaining Estimates

How do we make the recommended type of analysis of this proposal? Our aim is to develop for each of the nine factors listed a frequency distribution or probability curve. The information we need includes the possible range of values for each factor, the average, and some idea as to the likelihood that the various possible values will be reached.

It has been my experience that for major capital proposals managements usually make a significant investment in time and funds to pinpoint information about each of the relevant factors. An objective analysis of the values to be assigned to each can, with little additional effort, yield a subjective probability distribution.

Specifically, it is necessary to probe and question each of the experts involved—to find out, for example, whether the estimated cost of production really can be said to be exactly a certain value or whether, as is more likely, it should be estimated to lie within a certain range of values. Management usually ignores that range in its analysis. The range is relatively easy to determine; if a guess has to be made—as it often does— it is easier to guess with some accuracy a range rather than one specific value. I have found from experience that a series of meetings with management personnel to discuss such distributions are most helpful in getting at realistic answers to the *a priori* questions. (The term *realistic answers* implies all the information management does not have as well as all that it does have.)

The ranges are directly related to the degree of confidence that the estimator has in the estimate. Thus certain estimates may be known to be quite accurate. They would be represented by probability distributions stating, for instance, that there is only 1 chance in 10 that the actual value will be different from the best estimate by more than 10%. Others may have as much as 100% ranges above and below the best estimate.

Thus we treat the factor of selling price for the finished product by asking executives who are responsible for the original estimates these questions:

> Given that $510 is the expected sales price, what is the probability that the price will exceed $550?

> Is there any chance that the price will exceed $650?

> How likely is it that the price will drop below $475?

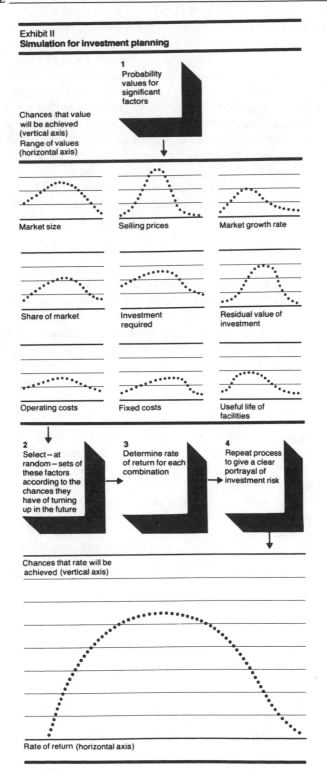

Exhibit II
Simulation for investment planning

1
Probability values for significant factors

Chances that value will be achieved (vertical axis)
Range of values (horizontal axis)

Market size

Selling prices

Market growth rate

Share of market

Investment required

Residual value of investment

Operating costs

Fixed costs

Useful life of facilities

2
Select – at random – sets of these factors according to the chances they have of turning up in the future

3
Determine rate of return for each combination

4
Repeat process to give a clear portrayal of investment risk

Chances that rate will be achieved (vertical axis)

Rate of return (horizontal axis)

Managements must ask similar questions for all of the other factors until they can construct a curve for each. Experience shows that this is not as difficult as it sounds. Often information on the degree of variation in factors is easy to obtain. For instance, historical information on variations in the price of a commodity is readily available. Similarly, managements can estimate the variability of sales from industry sales records. Even for factors that have no history, such as operating costs for a new product, those who make the average estimates must have some idea of the degree of confidence they have in their predictions, and therefore they are usually only too glad to express their feelings. Likewise, the less confidence they have in their estimates, the greater will be the range of possible values that the variable will assume.

This last point is likely to trouble businessmen. Does it really make sense to seek estimates of variations? It cannot be emphasized too strongly that the less certainty there is in an average estimate, the more important it is to consider the possible variation in that estimate.

Further, an estimate of the variation possible in a factor, no matter how judgmental it may be, is always better than a simple average estimate, since it includes more information about what is known and what is not known. This very lack of knowledge may distinguish one investment possibility from another, so that for rational decision making it must be taken into account.

This lack of knowledge is in itself important information about the proposed investment. To throw any information away simply because it is highly uncertain is a serious error in analysis that the new approach is designed to correct.

Computer Runs

The next step in the proposed approach is to determine the returns that will result from random combinations of the factors involved. This requires realistic restrictions, such as not allowing the total market to vary more than some reasonable amount from year to year. Of course, any suitable method of rating the return may be used at this point. In the actual case, management preferred discounted cash flow for the reasons cited earlier, so that method is followed here.

A computer can be used to carry out the trials for the simulation method in very little time and at very little expense. Thus for one trial 3600 discounted cash flow calculations, each based on a selection of the nine input factors, were run in two minutes at a cost of $15 for computer time. The resulting rate-of-return probabilities were read out immediately and graphed. The process is shown schematically in *Exhibit II*.

Data Comparisons

The nine input factors described earlier fall into three categories:

1. *Market analyses*—Included are market size, market growth rate, the company's share of the market, and selling prices. For a given combination of these factors sales revenue may be determined for a particular business.

2. *Investment cost analyses*—Being tied to the kinds of service-life and operating-cost characteristics expected, these are subject to various kinds of error and uncertainty; for instance, automation progress makes service life uncertain.

3. *Operating and fixed costs*—These also are subject to uncertainty but are perhaps the easiest to estimate.

These categories are not independent, and for realistic results my approach allows the various factors to be tied together. Thus if price determines the total market, we first select from a probability distribution the price for the specific computer run and then use for the total market a probability distribution that is logically related to the price selected.

We are now ready to compare the values obtained under the new approach with those obtained by the old. This comparison is shown in *Exhibit III*.

Valuable Results

How do the results under the new and old approaches compare? In this case, management had been informed, on the basis of the one-best-estimate approach, that the expected return was 25.2% before taxes. When we run the new set of data through the computer program, however, we get an expected return of only 14.6% before taxes. This surprising difference results not only from the range of values under the new approach but also from the weighing of each value in the range by the chances of its occurrence.

Our new analysis thus may help management to avoid an unwise investment. In fact, the general result of carefully weighing the information and lack of information in the manner I have suggested is to indicate the true nature of seemingly satisfactory investment proposals. If this practice were followed managements might avoid much overcapacity.

The computer program developed to carry out the simulation allows for easy insertion of new variables. But most programs do not allow for dependence relationships among the various input factors. Further, the program used here permits the choice of a value for price from one distribution, which value determines a particular probability distribution (from among several) that will be used to determine the values for sales volume. The following scenario shows how this important technique works:

Suppose we have a wheel, as in roulette, with the numbers from 0 to 15 representing one price for the product or material, the numbers 16 to 30 representing a second price, the numbers 31 to 45 a third price, and so on. For each of these segments we would have a different range of expected market volumes—for example, $150 000–$200 000 for the first, $100 000–$150 000 for the second, $75 000–$100 000 for the third. Now suppose we spin the wheel and the ball falls in 37. This means that we pick a sales volume in the $75 000–$100 000 range. If the ball goes in 11, we have a different price, and we turn to the $150 000–$200 000 range for a sales volume.

Most significant, perhaps, is the fact that the program allows management to ascertain the sensitivity of the results to each or all of the input factors. Simply by running the program with changes in the distribution of an input factor, it is possible to determine the effect of added or changed information (or lack of information). It may turn out that fairly large changes in some factors do not significantly affect the outcomes. In this case, as a matter of fact, management was particularly concerned about the difficulty in estimating market growth. Running the program with variations in this factor quickly demonstrated that for average annual growth rates from 3% to 5% there was no significant difference in the expected outcome.

In addition, let us see what the implications are of the detailed knowledge the simulation method gives us. Under the method using single expected values, management

Exhibit III
Comparison of expected values under old and new approaches

	Conventional "best estimate" approach	New approach
Market analyses		
1. Market size		
Expected value (in tons)	250,000	250,000
Range	–	100,000-340,000
2. Selling prices		
Expected value (in dollars/ton)	$510	$510
Range	–	$385-$575
3. Market growth rate		
Expected value	3%	3%
Range	–	0-6%
4. Eventual share of market		
Expected value	12%	12%
Range	–	3%-17%
Investment cost analyses		
5. Total investment required		
Expected value (in $ millions)	$9.5	$9.5
Range	–	$7.0-$10.5
6. Useful life of facilities		
Expected value (in years)	10	10
Range	–	5-15
7. Residual value (at 10 years)		
Expected value (in $ millions)	$4.5	$4.5
Range	–	$3.5-$5.0
Other costs		
8. Operating costs		
Expected value (in dollars/ton)	$435	$435
Range	–	$370-$545
9. Fixed costs		
Expected value (in $ thousands)	$300	$300
Range	–	$250-$375

Note: Range figures in right-hand column represent approximately 1% to 99% probabilities. That is, there is only a 1-in-100 chance that the value actually achieved will be respectively greater or less than the range.

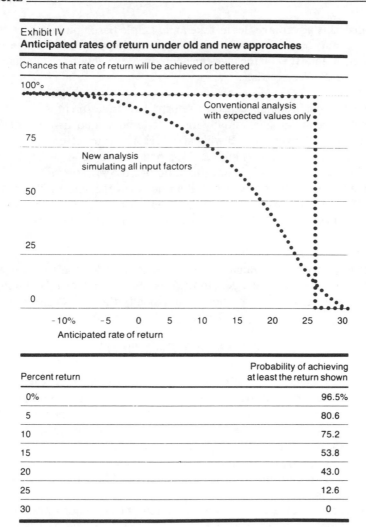

Exhibit IV
Anticipated rates of return under old and new approaches

Chances that rate of return will be achieved or bettered

Percent return	Probability of achieving at least the return shown
0%	96.5%
5	80.6
10	75.2
15	53.8
20	43.0
25	12.6
30	0

arrives only at a hoped-for expectation of 25.2% after taxes (which, as we have seen, is wrong unless there is no variability in the many input factors—a highly unlikely event).

With the proposed method, however, the uncertainties are clearly portrayed, as shown in *Exhibit IV*. Note the contrast with the profile obtained under the conventional approach. This concept has been used also for evaluation of product introductions, acquisition of businesses, and plant modernization.

Comparing Opportunities

From a decision-making point of view one of the most significant advantages of the new method of determining rate of return is that it allows management to discriminate among measures of (1) expected return based on weighted probabilities of all possible returns, (2) variability of return, and (3) risks.

To visualize this advantage, let us take an example based on another actual case but simplified for purposes of explanation. The example involves two investments under consideration, A and B. With the investment analysis, we obtain the tabulated and plotted data in *Exhibit V*. We see that:

1. Investment B has a higher expected return than Investment A.
2. Investment B also has substantially more variability than Investment A. There is a good chance that Investment B will earn a return quite different from the expected return of 6.8% — possibly as high as 15% or as low as a loss of 5%. Investment A is not likely to vary greatly from the anticipated 5% return.
3. Investment B involves far more risk than does Investment A. There is virtually no chance of incurring a loss on Investment A. However, there is 1 chance in 10 of losing money on Investment B. If such a loss occurs, its expected size is approximately $200 000.

Clearly, the new method of evaluating investments provides management with far more information on which to base a decision. Investment decisions made only on the basis of maximum expected return are not unequivocally the best decisions.

CONCLUDING NOTE

The question management faces in selecting capital investments is first and foremost: What information is needed to clarify the key differences among various alternatives? There is agreement as to the basic factors that should be considered — markets, prices, costs, and so on. And the way the future return on the investment should be calculated, if not agreed on, is at least limited to a few methods, any of which can be consistently used in a given company. If the input variables turn out as estimated, any of the methods customarily used to rate investments should provide satisfactory (if not necessarily maximum) returns.

In actual practice, however, the conventional methods do not work out satisfactorily. Why? The reason, as we have seen earlier in this article and as every executive and economist knows, is that the estimates used in making the advance calculations are just that — estimates. More accurate estimates would be helpful, but at best the residual uncertainty can easily make a mockery of corporate hopes. Nevertheless, there is a solution. To collect realistic estimates for the key factors means to find out a great deal about them. Hence the kind of uncertainty that is involved in each estimate can be evaluated ahead of time. Using this knowledge of uncertainty, executives can maximize the value of the information for decision making.

The value of computer programs in developing clear portrayals of the uncertainty and risk surrounding alternative investments has been proved. Such programs can produce valuable information about the sensitivity of the possible outcomes to the variability of input factors and to the likelihood of achieving various possible rates of return. This information can be extremely important as a backup to management judgment. To have calculations of the odds on all possible outcomes lends some assurance to the decision makers that the available information has been used with maximum efficiency.

Exhibit V
Comparison of two investment opportunities

Selected statistics	Investment A	Investment B
Amount of investment	$10,000,000	$10,000,000
Life of investment (in years)	10	10
Expected annual net cash inflow	$ 1,300,000	$ 1,400,000
Variability of cash inflow		
1 chance in 50 of being *greater than*	$ 1,700,000	$ 3,400,000
1 chance in 50 of being *less than**	$ 900,000	($ 600,000)
Expected return on investment	5.0%	6.8%
Variability of return on investment		
1 chance in 50 of being *greater than*	7.0%	15.5%
1 chance in 50 of being *less than**	3.0%	(4.0%)
Risk of investment		
Chances of a loss	Negligible	1 in 10
Expected size of loss	Negligible	$200,000

*In the case of negative figures (indicated by parentheses) *less than* means *worse than*.

Chances that rate of return will be achieved or bettered

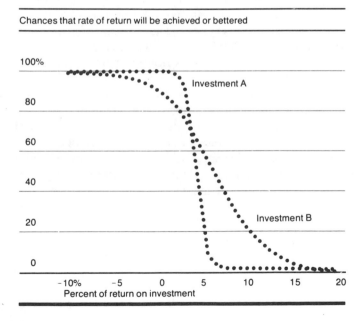

This simulation approach has the inherent advantage of simplicity. It requires only an extension of the input estimates (to the best of our ability) in terms of probabilities. No projection should be pinpointed unless we are certain of it.

The discipline of thinking through the uncertainties of the problem will in itself help to ensure improvement in making investment choices. For to understand uncertainty and risk is to understand the key business problem—and the key business opportunity. Since the new approach can be applied on a continuing basis to each capital alternative as it comes up for consideration and progresses toward fruition, gradᵗ al progress may be expected in improving the estimation of the probabilities of variation.

Lastly, the courage to act boldly in the face of apparent uncertainty can be greatly bolstered by the clarity of portrayal of the risks and possible rewards. To achieve these lasting results requires only a slight effort beyond what most companies already exert in studying capital investments.

RETROSPECTIVE COMMENTARY

When this article was published 15 years ago, there were two recurrent themes in the responses of the management community to it: (1) how the uncertainties surrounding each key element of an investment decision were to be determined, and (2) what criteria were to be used to decide to proceed with an investment once the uncertainties were quantified and displayed.

I answered the latter question in an HBR sequel, 'Investment Policies That Pay Off', describing the relationships of risks and stakes to longer term investment criteria. This article, published in 1968, showed how risk analyses can provide bases for developing policies to choose among a variety of investment alternatives. Similar approaches were subsequently developed for investment fund portfolio management.

The analysis of uncertainty in describing complex decision-making situations is now an integral part of business and government. The elements of an investment decision—private or public—are subject to all the uncertainties of an unknown future. As the 1964 article showed, an estimated probability distribution paints the clearest picture of all possible outcomes. Such a description contains considerably more information than simplistic combinations of subjective best estimates of input factors. Best estimates are point estimates (there may be more than one—high, medium, low) of the value of an element of the investment analysis used for determining an outcome decision criterion, such as internal rate of return or present value of the investment.

Thus even where the conventional approach was used for the best estimate in a single-point determination for the statistically estimated expected values from a distribution of an element, the single-point approach was shown to be exceedingly misleading. In *Exhibit III*, a single-point best-estimate analysis gave an internal rate of return of 25.2%. And a risk analysis employing estimated frequency distributions of the elements showed that an average of possible outcomes, weighted by the relative frequency of their occurrences at 14.6%, was more realistic as well as significantly different. It presented a truer picture of the actual average expectation of the result of this investment (if it could be repeated over and over again).

The case was thus made, and the point of this result—that risk and uncertainty were more accurately defined by a simulation of input variables—was little questioned thereafter. Managements began to adopt some form of this procedure to examine some, if not all, significant investments where doubt existed about the risk levels involved. My sequel article attempted to demonstrate that if enough investments were chosen consistently on the basis of criteria related to these kinds of risk portrayals, the overall outcomes would stabilize around the desired expected value or best estimate of the criterion.

All this now seems simple and straightforward. Earlier it was falsely thought that risk analysis was aimed at *eliminating* uncertainty, which was not worth doing at all since the future is so desperately uncertain. Thus in 1970 the *Financial Times* (of London) published an article intended to show the futility of risk analysis. It concerned a baker of geriatric biscuits who made an investment only to go bankrupt when his nursing home market precipitately disappeared with the death of its founder. The author cited as a moral, 'Don't put all your dough in one biscuit'.

It took a while for the points to diffuse through executive circles that (1) exactly such an analysis would have been just as bad, or worse, done via single-point subjective estimates, and (2) no one analytical technique could control future events, even with sensitive inputs and requirements for follow-up control to improve the odds as projected by the original risk analyses. But in the end, judgment would be required in both input estimation and decision.

I did not intend the article to be an argument in methodology but rather a cautionary note to examine the data surrounding an investment proposal in light of all the pervasive uncertainties in the world, of which business is simply one part. The years since 1964 have made it clear to me that this message should have been amplified and more emphatically insisted on in the article.

Had this point been clearer, the issue whether to take the risk and proceed with an investment might have been less troublesome. Had I been able to look with more prescience, I might have seen that the area of risk analysis would become routine in business and virtually universally adopted in public cost-benefit issues.

Cost-benefit analysis for public decisions is, of course, only a special form of investment analysis. Government issues that require decisions involving significant uncertainty are too numerous to catalog fully—energy, from both fossil and nuclear sources; chemical, drug, and food carcinogen hazards; DNA manipulation and its progeny of gene splicing.

The Three Mile Island nuclear accident brought home the fallibility of stating a risk analysis conclusion in simplistic terms. The well-known Rasmussen report on nuclear reactor safety, commissioned by the Nuclear Regulatory Commission, undertook what amounted to a risk analysis that was intended to provide a basis for investment decisions relating to future nuclear energy production. The Nuclear Regulatory Commission, in January 1979, disclaimed the risk estimates of that report; new studies to estimate risk are now underway. But there is also a school of thought saying we face too many risks each day to worry about one more.

A commonly stated estimate of the risk of a major nuclear power plant accident is 1 chance in 1 000 000 years. In the 1964 article, I portrayed the image of risk with a chart of the throws of two dice that would be required to give various outcomes—from two 1s to two 6s, each of these having a 1-in-36 chance of occurring. There should be no problem in visualizing or testing the meaning and the chances of any of the events pictured by these dice. And, although 1 in 1 000 000 is somehow presented as 'mind boggling' compared with 1 in 36, and so unlikely to occur as to be beyond our ken, I suggest that it is just as simply visualized.

We simply need to use eight dice at once. If we chart all the possible outcomes for eight dice, as we did for the two, we find that the sum of 8 (or 48) can occur just one way—via all 1s (or all 6s). The odds of this occurring are roughly 1 in 1 680 000. Thus the visualization of such odds, and more important, the lesson we must learn about risk—which incidents like Three Mile Island should teach us—is that *what can happen will happen if we just keep at it long enough*. Any of us can simulate a statistical picture of the estimated risks or even the complexities of the Rasmussen analysis with enough patient and enough dice (or a computer).

Incidentally, to make the eight dice act more like the odds of 1 in 1 000 000, simply mark any two 'non-1' sides with a felt pen and count them as 1s if they turn up; the odds of getting all 1s become a little less than 1 in 1 000 000. And the chances of human error can be included by similarly marking other dice in the set. The difficulty is not in constructing such a simulation to portray the odds but in determining events that may lead to these odds and estimating the frequencies of their occurrence.

Risk analysis has become one with public policy. Without it, any important choice that leads to uncertain outcomes is uninformed; with it, properly applied and understood, the decision maker—business executive, government administrator, scientist, legislator— is better able to decide why one course of action might be more desirable than another.

THE FEAR OF RISK-TAKING

To try to eliminate risk in business enterprise is futile. Risk is inherent in the commitment of present resources to future expectations. Indeed, economic progress can be defined as the ability to take greater risks. The attempt to eliminate risks, even the attempt to minimize them, can only make them irrational and unbearable. It can only result in that greatest risk of all: rigidity.

The main goal of a management science must be to enable business to take the right risk. Indeed, it must be to enable business to take *greater* risks—by providing knowledge and understanding of alternative risks and alternative expectations: by identifying the resources and efforts needed for desired results; by mobilizing energies for contribution; and by measuring results against expectations, thereby providing means for early correction of wrong or inadequate decisions.

All this may sound like mere quibbling over terms. Yet the terminology of risk minimization does induce a decided animus against risk-taking and risk-making—that is, against business enterprise—in the literature of the management sciences. Much of it echoes the tone of the technocrats of a generation ago. For it wants to subordinate business to technique, and it seems to see economic activity as a sphere of physical determination rather than as an affirmation and exercise of responsible freedom and decision.

This is worse than being wrong. This is lack of respect for one's subject matter—the one thing no science can afford and no scientist can survive. Even the best and most serious work of good and serious people—and there is no lack of them in the mangement sciences—is bound to be vitiated by it.

Chapter 9

Shirt-sleeve Approach to Long-range Plans

Robert E. Linneman and John D. Kennell
Templeton University and Sun Company Inc.

Forecasting and making long-range plans that are based on forecasts are inevitable. And while the importance of forecasting is recognized, so is its main limitation: too many key variables are just too unpredictable. Listen to the laments in 1974 after two humbling years for forecasters:

Roderick G. Dederick, chief economist for Chicago's Northern Trust Co.: 'We did not provide advance warning to our managements of the distressing situation into which the U.S. economy has drifted over the past several years.'

Milton W. Hudson, economist for Morgan Guaranty Trust Co.: 'We've decided that economic forecasting is so deficient that we're not going to perpetuate any more confusion. There is something misleading about giving people what purport to be accurate numbers when they are really no such thing.'

Perhaps Paul Samuelson isolated a major problem: 'I think that the greatest error in forecasting is not realizing how important are the probabilities of events other than those everyone is agreeing upon.'[1]

Planners usually choose one 'most probable' future environment as the basis of their thinking. They estimate uncontrollable variables as best they can, and a strategy is then developed to achieve the company's objectives. But what recourse does a company have when, because of faulty forecasting, the assumed values of key variables are wrong and its chosen strategy is inappropriate? Even tactical contingency plans may fail to compensate for a faulty strategy.

As a consequence, many companies now consider a range of plans that cover several possible environments rather than plans with only one outlook for the future. A partial listing of these companies includes: Dow Chemical, Exxon Corporation, Ford Motor Company, Hewlett-Packard, Marine Midland Bank, Olin Corporation, Sun Company,

---

1. 'Two Poor Years for the Forecasters,' *Business Week*, December 21, 1974, p. 51.

Exhibit I
Steps in multiple-scenario analysis

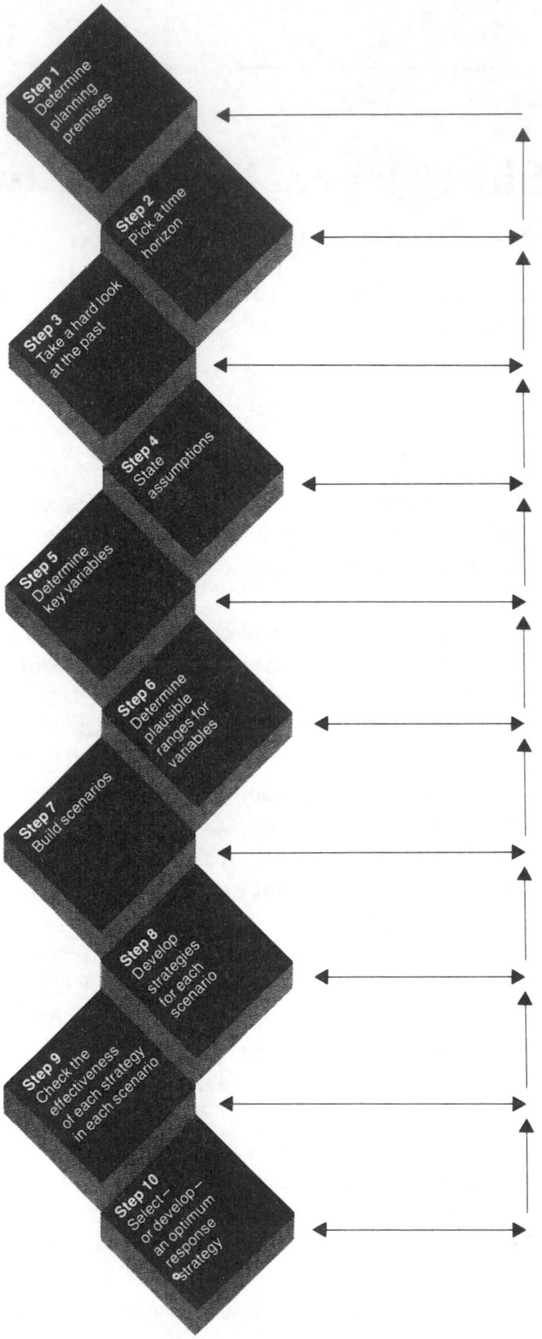

Step 1
Determine
planning
premises

Step 2
Pick a time
horizon

Step 3
Take a hard look
at the past

Step 4
State
assumptions

Step 5
Determine
key variables

Step 6
Determine
plausible
ranges for
variables

Step 7
Build scenarios

Step 8
Develop
strategies
for each
scenario

Step 9
Check the
effectiveness
of each strategy
in each scenario

Step 10
Select —
or develop —
an optimum
response
strategy

Uniroyal, and Weyerhaeuser. How-to-do-it literature is scanty, however, and the approaches described usually require a large planning staff, a highly structured long-range planning process, and sometimes even computerized routines.

Perhaps the greatest benefits can be gained from a highly sophisticated approach, but we contend that even a 'shirt-sleeve' method improves appreciation of the possibilities of the future. Consequently, smaller companies—or even larger companies without extensive planning resources—can devise a more adaptive strategy by using a simplified approach in considering several possible environments.[2]

Our purpose in this article is to give a simplified, ten-step approach to developing flexible strategies through what we call multiple-scenario analysis (MSA). *Exhibit I* illustrates the ten steps in MSA. (Although the process is presented in a step-by-step manner, the loop arrows indicate that it is not necessarily sequential. Multiple-scenario analysis involves many experiments that usually necessitate back-tracking.)

SIMPLIFIED ANALYSIS

This ten-step procedure assumes that a person, or perhaps a committee, can devote only part of his (or its) time to long-range planning. After describing each step, we shall use a case example of corporate-level planning at a hypothetical company named 'Quik-Serv' to show how the step would be carried out.

Step One

Identify and make explicit your company's mission, basic objectives, and policies.

At least on the first attempt, assume that your company's mission, objectives, and policies won't change. In order to establish a base for the following steps, you need to state these explicitly.

Mission. What is your company's basic reason for being in business? Probably because of existing strengths and commitments, the mission is unlikely to change over the next several years. Consequently, only after present business potential has been carefully examined and found wanting should other possibilities be examined.

Basic objectives. Does your company have long-term objectives for such factors as return on investment, earnings per share, or size? If explicit minimum acceptable standards have not been set, what are common-sense minimums?

Policies. Are there certain limitations, either explicit or implicit, such as 'will not expand overseas,' or 'must provide jobs for existing employees'?

2. Some of the most helpful literature follows: René D. Zentner, 'Scenarios: A New Tool for Corporate Planners,' *Chemical and Engineering News*, Industrial Edition, October 6, 1975, p. 22; Ian H. Wilson, 'Futures Forecasting for Strategic Planning at General Electric,' *Long Range Planning*, June 1973, p. 39; Frank L. Moreland, 'Dialectic Methods in Forecasting,' *The Futurist*, August 1971, p. 169; Peter F. Chapman, 'A Method of Exploring the Future,' *Long Range Planning*, February 1976, p. 2; and M. J. Creton and Audrey Clayton, 'Social Forecasting: A Practical Approach,' in *The Next 25 Years: Crisis and Opportunity*, ed. Andrew A. Spekke (Washington, D.C.: World Future Society, 1975), p. 267.

Explicit Planning Premises

Quik-Serv, our hypothetical company, is a small private-brand gasoline marketer. The company retails gasoline under its own brand name through a network of company- and dealer-operated outlets. Quik-Serv is nonintegrated, buying its products from major refiners.

Quik-Serv's mission is to serve consumer needs for automotive fuels. Its objectives are to remain competitive in the marketplace of the future, and to increase aftertax return on stockholders' equity to 12% by 1982. It has two policies: (1) the company's behavior will be both legal and ethical, and (2) new lines of business must be related to the company's mission and support its objectives.

Step Two

Determine how far into the future you wish to plan.

Your current planning horizon is probably one, two, or perhaps as many as five years. Time and planning facility limitations may prevent you from extending this horizon. The purpose of MSA is *not* to enable you to improve detail and precision in planning farther into the future. Rather, it is to give you an improved appreciation of the possible variations in future environments in which you must operate and, subsequently, the long-range implications of today's decisions.

For example, short-range forecasting might indicate a sales decline in the next three years. Given this forecast, one might follow a strategy of across-the-board cutbacks. On the other hand, because of discontinuities, certain scenarios might depict considerably higher sales in ten years (see *Exhibit II*). Such long-range forecasts also would probably call for retrenchment, but on a more selective basis to maintain a growth posture. In this respect, consideration of several scenarios makes the implications of present decisions more apparent.

The time length for scenarios is arbitrary, but generally it should be at least five years. The acid test is, of course, 'How far in the future are you committing your resources?'

Quik-Serv's planning horizon is 5 years. While management has little confidence in its ability to plan this far in advance, in some respects a 5-year planning horizon is too short. Quik-Serv's evaluation and depreciation of capital investments, for instance, is based on a 20-year economic life. Therefore, management decides to develop a set of scenarios with a 15- to 20-year horizon.

Step Three

Develop a good understanding of your company's points of leverage and vulnerability.

First, take a look at your industry. What was it like a decade or two ago? What is it like today? What are the causes for the changes?

Next, examine your own company. Look back over the same time span that you did for your industry. Then, take a look at your company today. Given conditions in the industry, what are the similarities and/or differences between your industry and your company? What are your points of leverage and vulnerability?

Although these analyses should be in writing, they need not be detailed. You are only seeking basic understandings.

Be careful of myths. In any business enterprise there is an abundance of information

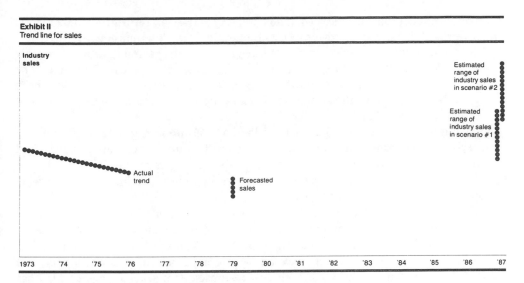

Exhibit II
Trend line for sales

Industry sales

Estimated range of industry sales in scenario #2

Estimated range of industry sales in scenario #1

Actual trend

Forecasted sales

1973   '74   '75   '76   '77   '78   '79   '80   '81   '82   '83   '84   '85   '86   '87

and opinion; unfortunately, much of it is false. From the history of Sears, Roebuck and Co., Peter Drucker came to the following conclusion:

'The right answers are always obvious in retrospect. The basic lesson of the Sears story is that the right answers are likely to be anything but obvious *before* they have proven themselves. 'Everybody knew' around 1900 that to promise 'satisfaction guaranteed or your money back' could only bring financial disaster to a retailer. 'Everybody knew' around 1925 that the American market was sharply segmented into distinct income groups. . . . 'Everybody knew'—as late as 1950—that the American consumer wanted to shop downtown, and so on.'[3]

Test for myths. Get data. Summarize past trends. Do they reinforce or oppose what you thought you knew?

Look at Past and Present

A decade ago in Quik-Serv's industry, fuel was cheap and abundant, and demand was growing steadily at approximately 4% a year. The major brand full-service station was the most prevalent type of outlet, and the number was increasing. Volume, not profitability, was the industry-wide criterion of success. Also, a pump-price spread of several cents existed between major and independent brands.

Today, the situation is almost exactly the opposite. Fuel is considerably more expensive, and demand is leveling off, with only a 2% near-term annual growth rate projected. The full-service outlet is still the most prevalent type but is losing ground to gasoline-only and self-service outlets. With profitability as the criterion of success, the outlet population is shrinking as companies close unprofitable units and withdraw from entire geographical areas. Finally, the pump-price spread between majors and independents is becoming blurred as majors increasingly offer self-service islands and gasoline-only outlets.

As for the company itself, ten years ago Quik-Serv was a small regional marketer with just over 100 outlets. Competing on a price basis, Quik-Serv enjoyed a 5% to 6%

3. Peter F. Drucker, *Management: Tasks, Responsibilities, Practices* (New York: Harper & Row, 1974), p. 57.

share of each local market it served. The company's aftertax return on stockholders' equity during this period of severe price competition and low margins averaged 6% to 7%. Quik-Serv's aggressive pricing strategy caused its gasoline volume to grow at about 6% per year, a rate some 50% higher than the industry average. The company's 100-odd outlets were of the gasoline-only type, some having been converted from acquired full-service outlets and others of newer construction without service bays.

After ten years of growth, Quik-Serv today has 165 modern gasoline-only outlets. Industry-wide conditions of a more stable pricing structure and wider margins have raised return on equity to just over 9%. Rapid inflation and a high cost of capital have significantly slowed Quik-Serv's expansion program. Volume at existing outlets is growing at about the same rate as the market.

Quik-Serv's management believes the comany has two major competitive advantages: a lean organization with capable, motivated management, and a chain of modern, efficient outlets in good markets and good locations. Management has also identified two points of vulnerability: dependence on other companies for product supply, and the fact that the company serves a highly price-conscious market segment which has little brand loyalty.

Step Four

Determine factors that you think will definitely occur within your planning time frame.

Some assumptions might stem from certain factors that can be forecasted with almost complete certainty (in Quik-Serv's case, for example, the number of licensed drivers in 1997), and you might consider some information, such as calculated natural resources, accurate and conclusive. Other projects, such as rate of economic growth, are unpredictable and should be classified as variables.

Assumptions must be accurate and conclusive, not merely variables with a high probability of occurrence. A test: if a 'prudent man' could doubt its value, consider it a variable.

Quik-Serv made the following assumptions: (a) by 1997 there will be a 9% increase in licensed drivers; (b) gasoline will remain the major fuel for automobiles; (c) government policies will be protective of small independent companies; (d) there will be less gasoline brand loyalty; (e) mass merchandisers will continue to increase in importance in tires, batteries, accessories (TBA), and repairs, and (f) improved technology will produce autos and TBA requiring less maintenance and repairs, and better gas mileage.

Step Five

Make a list of key variables that will have make-or-break consequences for your company.

Your main consideration at this step is to identify, without going into a lot of detail, the variables that have been crucial to your company in the past and those that will be important to it in the future. Try to use key variables that are commonly predicted and monitored, such as GNP and the rate of inflation. Easily identifiable vital signs facilitate forecasting and simplify control.

If time and resources permit, you may wish to broaden your viewpoint by scanning future-oriented periodicals, such as *Futures* and *The Futurist*, in addition to your normal fare of busines and general periodicals. Of course, there are also a number of proprietary services available, such as the Arthur D. Little Impact Service, the National Planning Association Economic Projections Series, Predicasts, the Futures Group Scout Service, and the Stanford Research Institute Business Intelligence Program.

You can keep the planning task on a 'shirt-sleeve' basis by limiting key variables to no more than four or five by using the following guidelines:

1. Delete variables having a low probability of occurrence and a low potential impact. On the other hand, include those with low probabilities but high impact and all those with high probabilities regardless of their impact.
2. Consider the timeliness of the variable. Because the future is so unpredictable, it is more important to include an event that is likely to happen or have an impact in the next few years than one that may not happen or be insignificant until near the end of the planning horizon.
3. Delete disaster events. Events that would cause total disaster—such as a major nuclear war—should not be considered seriously.
4. Aggregate when possible. For example, the factors responsible for economic growth include, to name a few, expenditures on consumer, investment and government goods. If only the economic growth rate is relevant, just use it as the representative variable for your analysis.
5. Separate dependent from independent variables. Check for interdependence. Is the value of one variable based upon the value of another? If so, then remove the dependent variable. Keep a separate list of dependent variables for use in building and enriching scenarios.

Exhibit III
Variable value matrix

Variable	Value (15 to 20 years in the future)		
	Extreme	Middle	Extreme
Inflation rate	10% to 20%	—	5% to 9%
Price and availability of gasoline	Same as present	—	Tight supply high prices
Growth in GNP	More than 4%	1.5% to 4%	Less than 1.5%

Quik-Serv thinks that the rate of inflation, GNP (as an indicator of car sales and usage), and gasoline price and availability are the variables that will have the greatest impact on its operations. The company's list of dependent variables is: availability of capital (as affected by rate of inflation and growth rate of GNP), government taxation (taxes to curtail consumption), government restriction (rationing), and the rate of technological change (as affected by growth rate of GNP).

Step Six

Assign reasonable values to each key variable.

Now you need to pick a reasonable range over which each variable may vary, and divide the range into two or three sets of values—a 'middle ground' and the extremes. Reasonability, of course, can only be determined by common sense. However, two helpful principles are: (1) reject values so extreme that they seem absurd; and (2) if a value lies between the marginal and the absurd, use it. Although it is generally recommended that three sets of values be estimated, in some instances two may suffice for all practical purposes.

To maintain objectivity, you may want to seek the opinions of fellow executives, trade association officials and staff, or, if relationships permit, customers and suppliers. The ranges of values for the key variables that Quik-Serv picked are shown in *Exhibit III*.

Step Seven

Build scenarios in which your company may operate.

Scenarios describe possible future operating environments for your organization. A scenario is built by (1) selecting a value for each key variable; (2) estimating the resulting interactions between key variables, dependent variables, and assumptions; and (3) developing a narration describing the future under this set of conditions.

When building scenarios, the following suggestions may be helpful.

1. Develop at least three, but no more than four, scenarios. Experience has shown that two are too few; the scenarios tend to be classified as good and bad. On the other hand, even four scenarios may be too many unless they have markedly different characteristics.[4] One of the scenarios should be for the most probable case.
2. Select values of key variables so that each scenario is distinct from the others. Scenarios with small variations have little value since strategies for these scenarios would be almost identical. In fact, it might be wise to look at a 'deadly enemy' scenario.[5]
3. Keep the scenarios plausible. This is partially accomplished by including only the values that are deemed realistic. But make sure that the combined variable mix in each scenario also makes sense, that it is feasible. For example, low double-digit inflation, rapid economic growth, and severe oil shortage by themselves might seem plausible but their joint occurrence does not. To keep from overlooking plausible combinations of key variables, examine all possibilities.
4. In writing a scenario, first state variables and assumptions in an abbreviated form. Then include the dependent variables and develop the scenario with more description. Write from the viewpoint of someone standing in the future (at the end of your time frame) describing conditions at that time and how they developed. The completed scenario should transmit an appreciation of this hypothesized environment.
5. Limit the length of each scenario to one or two paragraphs, keeping the length of each scenario the same, and using common language and classifications to allow for point-by-point comparison.

4. Rene S. Zentner, 'Scenarios: A New Tool'.
5. Frank L. Moreland, 'Dialectical Methods'.

6. Keep the themes of each scenario neutral. Although you may have scenarios for the 'worst', 'most probable,' and 'best' circumstances, avoid labeling them as such to prevent more consideration being given to the 'most probable' or 'best' scenarios.

Quik-Serv's Scenarios

Exhibit IV shows the matrix Quik-Serv constructed to test the plausibility of the combined variables. The 12 scenarios listed represent all possible combinations of the three key variables. The company rejected Scenarios 2, 4, 8, and 10 because of inconsistencies among the major variables. Scenarios 3, 6, 9, and 11 were selected for further development. Number 9 was thought to represent the middle of the variables' possible ranges, while numbers 3, 6, and 11 were chosen to represent more extreme possibilities. Scenarios 1, 5, 7, and 12 were not chosen because they were thought to be merely variations or extreme cases of the general themes of Scenarios 3, 6, 9, and 11 respectively. (For the sake of brevity, we shall only consider Scenarios 3 and 11 further.)

Scenario 3. Advances in technology and design have made the automobile of the early 1990s safer, more reliable, and nearly service-free. From the viewpoint of the gasoline retailer, however, the most significant change in the automobile has been the tremendous increase in fuel efficiency over the past two decades. Better mileage has offset the effects of increases in the number of cars on the road. Overall market demand has grown at an average of only 1% to 1.5% per year.

Because of a low rate of market growth and a high cost of capital, the number of retail gasoline outlets has increased only slightly since the late 1970s. Rapidly escalating labor costs and the 'service-free' automobile have been responsible for the demise of the full-service gasoline outlet. The high rate of inflation has made price-conscious consumers extremely receptive to the economies of self-service stations. The prize competition between majors and independents is head-on, so there is no pump-price spread.

Exhibit IV
Matrix for testing plausibility

Possible scenario	Variables			
	Inflation	Gas price and availability	GNP	Comments
1	10% to 20%	Present	More than 4%	Plausible
2	10 to 20	Tight supply, high prices	More than 4	Not plausible
3	10 to 20	Present	1.5 to 4	Plausible
4	10 to 20	Tight supply, high prices	1.5 to 4	Not plausible
5	10 to 20	Present	Less than 1.5	Plausible
6	10 to 20	Tight supply, high prices	Less than 1.5	Plausible
7	5 to 9	Present	More than 4	Plausible
8	5 to 9	Tight supply, high prices	More than 4	Not plausible
9	5 to 9	Present	1.5 to 4	Plausible
10	5 to 9	Tight supply, high prices	1.5 to 4	Not plausible
11	5 to 9	Present	Less than 1.5	Plausible
12	5 to 9	Tight supply, high prices	Less than 1.5	Plausible

Scenario 11. The gasoline-powered automobile is still the dominant mode of transportation. Yet, gasoline demand, which peaked in the late 1980s, has been declining slightly each year during this period of prolonged economic stagnation. Gasoline outlets have been decreasing in number since the early 1980s as retailers attempt to cover rising fixed costs in the face of static demand and strong consumer resistance to price increases. Low levels of profitability no longer justify the use of new capital in the retail gasoline business.

One important countertrend has been the growth of the full-service outlet as hard-pressed consumers increasingly choose to repair rather than replace their automobiles. Marketers in a position to do so strive to retain brand identification by building consumer loyalty through the service and repair portions of their operations. The economics of the full service outlet benefit from the general availability and the relatively low cost of labor. The federal government, concerned with the survival of the small companies in these difficult times, is especially watchful for anticompetitive practices by the larger companies.

Step Eight

Develop a strategy for each scenario that will most likely result in achieving your company's objectives.

The procedure for generating strategies is similar to traditional strategy development. Because of the 'unpredictable future', however, a greater emphasis should be placed on flexible strategies that have relatively high payoffs in short and intermediate time spans.

Your 'final' strategies, within their respective scenarios, should enable your company to come reasonably close to its objectives. Because of the imprecision inherent in long-term forecasting, avoid the 'numbers game'. Instead, make common-sense, intuitive judgments.

Constrained Opportunity . . .

The overall theme of Quik-Serv's Scenario 3 is one of constrained opportunity. That is, there is some opportunity for growth in the market segment in which Quik-Serv believes it has competitive advantages (gasoline-only), but this opportunity is constrained by the rather low rate of market growth, the high rate of inflation, the cost of capital, the high cost of labor, and head-on price competition from the majors. With this long-term view of the future, Quik-Serv's management formulates the following selective growth strategy:

Ownership of outlets. Strive for ownership of outlets and real estate on a leveraged basis as a hedge against inflation.

Increased debt posture. Increase debt/equity ratio as necessary to facilitate buying and building now instead of later during the inflationary period.

Selective expansion. Maintain share of market growth through highly selective and carefully timed expansion with new gasoline-only outlets, giving careful consideration to profitability criteria and market supply–demand balances.

Dealer-operated units. Minimize the effect of escalating labor costs by increasing emphasis on dealer-operated outlets and decreasing operation of outlets by direct company employees.

Automated self-service. Further minimize the effect of escalating labor costs at remaining company-operated outlets by making a shift to automated self-service.

. . . vs. Recessionary Outlook

The message emerging from Scenario 11 is threefold: a decline in the demand for gasoline, consumer resistance to price increases, and a decreasing number of service stations. Quik-Serv's management decides that under this set of conditions, the following strategy is the most feasible course of action:

Restricted ownership of outlets: Reduce ownership of low and negative profit outlets where real estate is usable as gasoline outlet only. Increase ownership of properties which have attractive alternatives for commercial usage.

Minimize debt. Avoid new debt and use excess cash to retire existing high-interest obligations.

Selective divestment. Identify and divest outlets which make zero or negative contribution to profit and for which turnaround would require large amounts of new capital.

Company-operated outlets. Increase profitability by stressing company operations, thus absorbing dealer margins during this period of readily available and relatively low-cost labor.

Exhibit V
Flexibility of strategies

Strategies	Fit in Scenario 3	Fit in Scenario 11
Scenario 3		
Ownership of outlets	—	Poor
Increase debt posture	—	Poor
Selective expansion	—	Poor
Dealer-operated outlets	—	Fair
Automated self-service	—	Fair
Scenario 11		
Restricted ownership	Fair	—
Minimize debt	Poor	—
Selective divestment	Fair	—
Company-operated outlets	Fair	—
Increase labor	Poor	—

Increase labor. Utilize inexpensive labor rather than automated self-service equipment which is relatively costly.

Step Nine

Check the flexibility of each strategy in each scenario by testing its effectiveness in the other scenarios.

Is each strategy adaptable to your other scenarios, or does its effectiveness depend on the values of key variables in the particular scenario for which it was originally developed? The construction of a matrix and subsequent ratings, as shown in *Exhibit V* for Quik-Serv, will help you to visualize each strategy's adaptability.

Step Ten

Select—or develop—an 'optimum response' strategy.

Now that you have developed a strategy for each scenario, you must choose one of them or form a 'compromise' strategy from among them. Because of personal and company attitudes toward risk, there can be no hard-and-fast rules to apply as you make this choice. However, in general, the final strategy should:

1. Provide maximum adaptability to the conditions of the several scenarios, or conversely, require only a short reaction time for adjustment to the demands of different environments.
2. Have favorable consequences in scenarios with relatively high probabilities of occurrence.
3. Be particularly attractive in the near future since the distant future is less predictable.
4. Provide for maximum delay of expenditures, taking the impact of possible inflationary price rises into consideration.

Quik-Serv's management believed a future environment similar to Scenario 3 was highly probable, especially over the next 5 to 7 years. It did not totally discount the harsher possibilities of Scenario 11, but felt that if such a condition did materialize it would not be until the latter part of the 15- to 20-year period. Accordingly, it decided to pursue the strategy outlined for Scenario 3; with three modifications to improve its flexibility:

Go slow on shift to dealer operations, since, if necessary, it would be easier to shift operations from the company to dealers rather than to shift from dealers back to the company.

Increase debt/equity ratio slowly by implementing a more selective expansion program.

Prepare for a selective divestment strategy by identifying a list of candidates.

Multiple-scenario analysis gave Quik-Serv management a better appreciation of the long-term outlook, thus providing an improved foundation for its strategic five-year planning.

PITFALLS AND BENEFITS

Of course, there may be a gap between your objectives and common-sense estimates of what you can hope to achieve with the 'optimum response' strategy. If so, you should first try to shrink the gap to tolerable limits by developing a better strategy. Perhaps in the planning process some factors have been overlooked or over- or underemphasized. Consider bringing in other viewpoints. Only afterwards should new ventures be investigated to supplement, or possibly replace, the basic mission.

To analyze new ventures, first list potential candidates. Seek those highly compatible with the basic mission. Fast screening of this list is necessary because, as a rule, new ventures will require separate sets of scenarios since some of their key variables will be different from those of the basic mission. Identify and eliminate weak candidates by working through, for each potential new venture, steps four to ten on a cursory basis. Then, perform a more detailed analysis for each of the more plausible ventures.

Although some of the make-or-break variables for venture candidates may be different from those of the basic mission, some will probably be the same (for example, the rate of inflation). Use, when possible, identical values for the same key variables in building scenarios. Then, in selecting the final strategy (for both the basic mission and the new ventures), make sure comparable scenarios are used.

Taking Corrective Action

A major concern is 'Will the actual environment, as it unfolds, provide a favorable climate for the implemented strategy?' Consequently, there must be an environmental monitoring system. To develop such a procedure, in general, first establish short-term standards for key variables that will tend to validate the long-range estimates. Although favorable long-range values have been estimated, short-term guidelines are needed to indicate if the scenario is unfolding as hoped. Next, set up criteria to decide when the strategy must be changed. Of course your decision will depend on the magnitude or the trend (or both) of the deviations.

If the optimum strategy was developed for environmental conditions different from those that actually are occurring, then examine how effective the strategy was judged to be in a scenario closer to the actual conditions, and determine necessary adaptions. In this manner your analysis of different scenarios also can be used to respond to 'unforecasted' situations as they develop.

Common Sense

Multiple-scenario analysis does improve the appreciation of the future, and so should enable management to develop strategies with better cognizance of potential risks. At first, however, the procedure may appear to 'muddy the water', since it calls for the development of more than one possible environment, and more than one strategy.

Also, you need to be aware of problems that might be caused by misusing MSA. At the beginning of the planning process, for instance, you must carefully avoid favoring what may seem to be *the* right scenario or *the* right strategy. Such prejudice minimizes the value of the process, as it would any type of planning model. Also, be careful of adopting a strategy simply because it fits more scenarios than does any alternative. It might not be the strategy most likely to lead to success.

Finally, in spite of your best laid plans, you may have missed developing a scenario that portrays an environment close to the one that actually occurs. Hence, it is necessary to adopt a systematic method of monitoring the environment and to consider long-range planning as a continuous process.

If you are aware of these pitfalls, the process can help you to focus on the assumptions underlying the scenarios, not on just whether to approve a plan or not. Actually, MSA is simply a matter of common sense. It is essentially a part of a decision-making procedure that we all use daily, although on a highly informal basis. By formalizing the process, however, you facilitate communication, thus improving multiparty participation and comprehension. And there is an important side benefit: a structured approach leads to more rigorous thinking. As a result, multiple-scenario analysis can be a valuable tool in helping to make today's decisions flexible enough for the uncertain future.

Chapter 10

How to Develop and Use Scenarios

Steven P. Schnaars

Associate Professor of Marketing, Baruch College, City University of New York

For many years, it was widely believed that the greatest potential for obtaining accurate forecasts lay in the development of complex, quantitative models. It was thought that with just a little more time, a few more equations and a lot more dollars, these models would be able to provide forecasts that were much more accurate than those produced by more mundane methods. This has not turned out to be the case. A multitude of comparative forecasting studies has clearly shown that such models are usually no more accurate than much simpler approaches.[1,2] As a result, many users of forecasts have become disillusioned with forecasting models that, under the guise of scientific analysis, attempt to predict the future from fancy mathematical manipulations of historical data. This as much as anything has fostered a growth market for scenario analysis.

Scenario analysis is not a new technique. Herman Kahn was writing scenarios as far back as the 1950s.[3] What is new is that the remarkably poor record of forecasters, even those armed with impressive credentials and gigantic computers, has become more obvious. If it ever was possible to predict accurately the future, it is surely a hazardous task today. Consequently, planners have recognized the importance of considering a number of plausible future environments that their firm may face, rather than relying on a single forecast that, in hindsight, may be grossly mistaken. This too has fostered a growth market for scenario analysis.

Oddly, this new-found interest in the use of scenarios has not fostered a great deal of interest in researching the approach itself. The topic has been largely ignored by business researchers. In the words of one study, 'Practice seems to be leading the literature.'[4]

Most of what is known about scenario analysis comes from three rather distinct sources. The first and smallest body of research consists of empirical studies that have focused on related topics that offer some evidence as to the value of scenarois as a forecasting tool. This research is not tied to any one academic discipline, and is widely dispersed in the literature.

A second group of articles consists of description of how scenario analysis is conducted at large firms. Most of these articles are written by corporate planners who have first-hand experience in the construction and use of scenarios. They offer many valuable heuristics regarding the construction of scenarios that are based on practical business opinions.

The final group of studies comes from the 'futures research' literature. It offers a plethora of methods for constructing scenarios, some of which are reasonable, many of which are arcane and impractical, most of which have never been fairly tested. Many of these studies deal with cross-impact analysis, a scenario-generating technique that has received a great deal of attention over the past 15 years.

This paper reviews the literature on scenario analysis. It summarizes what is currently known about the method, as well as what people think they know about it. In addition, it offers some guidelines regarding the construction and use of scenarios as a forecasting tool. It also evaluates some of the myriad techniques that have been offered to generate scenarios, and suggests which are worth while, and which are not.

This paper does not attempt to chronicle all of the applications of scenario analysis (there are too many). Nor does it spend a great deal of time on the technical aspects of the more complex quantitative methodologies that have been proffered (since there are serious problems with the basic premise of these approaches). Overall, the goal of this paper is to find out where we are now, so that we can move forward in the future.

WHAT IS SCENARIO ANALYSIS?

Scenario analysis differs from most other approaches to forecasting in two important ways. First, it usually provides a more qualitative and contextual description of how the present will evolve into the future, rather than one that seeks numerical precision. Second, scenario analysis usually tries to identify a set of possible futures, each of whose occurrence is plausible, but not assured. This combination of offering more than one forecast, and offering it in the form of a narrative, is deemed by advocates to be a more reasonable approach than trying to predict (to four significant decimal places) what *will* happen in *the* future.

Not everyone incorporates both aspects of this definition into their scenarios. Some adopt the narrative format, but offer only a single forecast. Others offer multiple forecasts, based on differing assumptions regarding the future environment, but do not present the results in the form of a stylized narrative. Both groups refer to the results of their efforts as scenarios.

Herman Kahn, the famous futurist, credits himself with coining the term 'scenario'. His brand of scenario analysis embraces the stylized narrative, and is usually referred to as 'scenario writing'.[5]

> As near as I can tell, the term scenario was first used in this sense in a group I worked with at the Rand Corporation. We deliberately chose the word to deglamorize the concept. In writing the scenarios for various situations we kept saying 'Remember, it's only a scenario', the kind of thing that is produced by Hollywood writers both hacks and geniuses. (p. 112).

Scenario writing is a highly qualitative procedure. It proceeds more from the gut than from the computer, although it may incorporate the results of quantitative models. Scenario writing is based on the assumption that the future is not merely some mathematical manipulation of the past, but the confluence of many forces, past, present and future that can best be understood by simply thinking about the problem.

As narratives, scenarios can either trace the evolution of the present into the future, or merely describe what the future will look like.[6,7] That is, they can be longitudinal or cross-sectional. The most widely quoted definition of scenarios, proposed by Kahn and Weiner,[8] focuses on longitudinal scenario analysis. They define scenarios as 'A hypothetical sequence of events constructed for the purpose of focusing attention on causal processes and decision points' (p. 6).

Many researchers also use the term 'scenarios' to describe any set of multiple forecasts. For example, Carlson and Umble[9] generate multiple forecasts of automobile sales from an econometric model using different assumptions regarding the future values of predictor variables. Such procedures are essentially quantitative and mechanistic, but still termed 'scenario analysis' since more than one forecast is provided.

The idea of providing multiple forecasts has become a cornerstone of scenario analysis. It is an explicit recognition of the frailty of forecasting, and the importance of underlying assumptions. It suggests that a forecast is only as accurate as its underlying assumptions, and that it makes more sense to consider a number of plausible assumptions, rather than a single one which may later turn out to be incorrect.

There is some strong empirical evidence to support this claim. A massive study by Ascher[10] reviewed past forecasts and concluded that the most frequent reason for errors was that they were predicated on erroneous underlying assumptions. He also found that the methodology used to construct the forecast was of trivial importance. This suggests that less attention should be paid to methodological issues, and more to the assumptions underlying a forecast; a point on which scenario analysis scores high.

Other reviews of historical forecast accuracy offer additional support. For example, Schnaars,[11] in a review of growth market forecasts published in the business press between 1960 and 1979, found that most of the technological forecasts of the late 1960s that foresaw fantastic innovations permeating nearly every aspect of life were predicated on the mistaken assumption that surging economic conditions, and massive funding of the space program would continue unabated. Similar mistaken assumptions, at other times (e.g. a continued dramatic rise in the price of oil), have caused the failure of other growth market forecasts.

THE USE OF SCENARIOS BY BUSINESS

Most of the evidence regarding the use of scenarios by U.S. industrial firms comes from a survey conducted by Linneman and Klein.[4] They inferred that about 22 per cent of the 'Fortune 1000' were using scenario analysis in the 1970s. Roughly three-quarters of these firms had adopted the approach after the oil embargo sent corporate strategies sailing into oblivion. Meristo,[12] reports that a survey of 1100 European firms showed that many of these firms also adopted scenarios after the oil crisis.

In an earlier study, McHale and McHale[13] found scenario analysis to be a popular forecasting tool among organizations in the United States.

Armstrong[2] notes that an earlier, unpublished study by McHale found scenarios to be the most popular 'futures research' tool among the 356 'organizations, institutional units, and individuals' that were polled.

In a follow-up study, Linneman and Klein[14] found that between 1977 and 1981 the use of scenario analysis as a business forecasting tool has grown even further.

Clearly, the growing popularity of scenario analysis can be directly attributed to the 'random shocks' of the 1970s. Less clear is whether the 1980s will be beset by similar disturbances, and if so, whether scenario analysis will prove superior to other forecasting approaches.

THE RELATIVE ACCURACY OF SCENARIO FORECASTS

The key question in scenario analysis is whether it works any better than alternative approaches. Schnaars[15] compared two unconditional forecasts prepared using scenario writing (optimistic and pessimistic) with two generated from a simple econometric model. The application was for one-quarter ahead forecasts of six types of U.S. auto sales (e.g. subcompacts, full-sized) in early 1983, a highly uncertain time since the economy was believed to be moving from recession to recovery. The scenario writing approach showed a slight advantage over the simple demand function. This advantage was most pronounced on forecasts of those series where uncertainty was high, and historical relationships were changing. Possibly, as Klein and Linneman[6] note, judgmental scenario writing is best able to anticipate those 'historyless' events that are so pervasive in today's business environment.

THE SCOPE OF SCENARIOS

Scenarios have been constructed to study futures of varying levels of aggregation. At one extreme lies the 'worldviews' popularized by Herman Kahn. Such forecasts are all-encompassing. Their goal is nothing less than to identify a set of plausible global futures and their consequences to man. Such efforts almost inevitably rely on scenario writing due to the large number of factors that must be considered.

Business persons, with an eye towards corporate planning, are usually attracted to more focused scenarios. These scenarios tend to focus more on those aspects of the environment that directly affect their products and markets. While this is a more feasible task, it carries the increasing danger that as the scope of the scenario narrows, the accuracy of the scenarios will be affected by an event that was not considered. There appears to be a tradeoff between the feasibility of considering a large number of factors, and the validity of considering only a few.

A large number of industry-level scenario studies have been published in the business literature. For example, Wilson[16-18] discusses scenario generation at General Electric, and its relation to marketing strategy. Zentner[19] lists some other applications. All told, the applications of scenario analysis far outnumber the investigations of the approach itself.

The greatest potential for the use of scenario analysis in business forecasting probably lies within this more narrow focus. Many industries, products and markets are primarily affected by only a handful of factors, that are fairly easy to identify, but notoriously difficult to predict. Scenario analysis should perform well in such instances.

THE CONTENT OF SCENARIOS

There is some confusion in the literature as to what types of information scenarios should contain. Most authors equate scenarios with environmental forecasts, against which plans are laid. That is, the scenarios identify plausible future environments that the firm might face. The firm then draws plans in light of these forecasts. In this sense, scenario analysis and planning are concerned with two distinct activities.

Other authors bundle into the scenarios themselves plans and the outcome of the plans.[20] That is, the scenarios contain not only environmental forecasts, but how well a given plan will fare in it. In this case, scenario analysis is complicated by the inclusion of additional uncertainties. Not only must potential future environments be identified, but the performance of plans must be estimated.

The content of scenarios should be determined by where the uncertainty lies. In some instances, it is the future course of the market itself that presents questions. In others, it is the market's response to strategic maneuvres. In each case the content of the scenarios would be different.

However, it is essential to keep the number of factors that are considered to a minimum. If too many factors are considered, scenario analysis becomes unwieldy, and an exercise in speculation. Scenario analysis seems best suited for those situations where a few crucial factors can be identified, but not easily predicted.

TIME HORIZON

Scenario analysis has been used primarily in long-term forecasting. The characteristics of the approach—providing more than one forecast, each in the form of a purposely vague narrative—are best suited for more distant, less certain forecasting applications. However, there is no empirical evidence that scenarios are inappropriate over shorter time horizons.

Linneman and Klein[4] found that most firms that used scenario analysis employed a 5-year horizon. Planners at Xerox Corp. have stated that they extend their scenarios 15 years ahead.[21] Zentner,[22] of Shell Oil, notes that they generate scenarios with at least 15-year horizons, and frequently longer. He also notes that the content of their scenarios become progressively more vague as the time horizon lengthens.

It appears that the ideal time horizon of scenario analysis is specific to the industry, product or market under consideration. A number of authors have observed that long-range and short-term forecasts are not absolute terms. Linneman and Kennell[23] suggest that the 'acid test' for deciding on a time horizon is 'How far in the future are you committing resources?' Similarly, Armstrong[2] defines a long-range forecast as 'the length of time over which large changes in the environment can be expected to occur' (p. 5).

THE NUMBER OF SCENARIOS TO GENERATE

There seems to be a consensus in the literature that three scenarios are best. Some schemes propose only two, and some propose more than three, but the general feeling is that two tend to be classified as 'good-and-bad', while more than three become unmanageable in the hands of users, resulting in their attending to only a subset anyway.

Wilson[17] offers one of the only caveats regarding the use of three scenarios. He suggests that in some instance this number will result in users focusing mostly on the scenario that seems to represent the 'middle ground'. This is particularly true when the future path of a quantifiable trend is under study. A graphical display of three scenarios would be categorized by the user as 'high', 'low' and 'middle ground', with the middle projection being selected as the safest bet. He prescribes that in such cases the scenarios should be distinctly 'themed' to make them appear equally likely.

Only two schemes actually propose generating only two scenarios. Beck[24] contends that at Shell U.K. 'the fewer the better' (p. 18). He raises the same issue as above: that planners tend to dwell on the middle scenario when three are offered. Schnaars[15] also found two scenarios to be preferable for a projection of automobile sales series.

Another dissenting viewpoint is offered by Mason,[25] and extended by Mitroff and Emshoff.[26] They propose a novel approach to scenario analysis based on dialectical methods that derives only two scenarios, a 'best-guess' forecast and its 'deadliest enemy'. If nothing else, this approach forces a firm to confront the 'worst' scenario, and plan in light of it.

Industry seems to agree with the consensus. Linneman and Klein[4] found that more companies used three scenarios than any other number.

ARRAYING SCENARIOS

Scenarios are inevitably arrayed over some back-ground theme. This gives the forecaster some criterion for selecting scenarios, and conveys to the user that each is part of a coherent set. Four background themes are commonly found in scenario studies.

Favorability to the Sponsor

The most widely used procedure is to array scenarios according to their favorability to the sponsor. This usually entails selecting a scenario that represents an 'optimistic' prediction, and another that represents a 'pessimistic' prediction. These then serve as alternatives for what Kahn calls a 'surprise-free' or 'baseline' scenario.

It should be noted that a 'surprise-free' scenario is different from a 'most likely' scenario. The former is a forecast based on the assumption of no unexpected changes, which may or may not be the most likely.

The central issue regarding this procedure for arraying scenarios is the same one that was mentioned in the previous section. Will planners attend to the 'surprise-free' at the expense of the alternatives? If so, then the central objective of scenario analysis, to get planners to jointly consider a set of possibilities, is destroyed.

Probability of Occurrence

This scheme arrays scenarios according to their likelihood of occurrence. Usually, this means that one of the scenarios is labeled as 'most likely'. The implication is that one scenario is more likely to occur, but that other outcomes are also possible. Vanston,[27] for example, uses a 'most likely' scenario.

Quantitative methods of generating scenarios, such as cross-impact analysis, take this a step further. They actually attach probabilities to the scenarios they derive. The scenarios are then ranked by how likely they are to occur.[28]

Some judgmental schemes also assign probabilities to scenarios. For example, Edesess and Hambrecht[29] and deKluyer[30] adopt this procedure.

Many authors take issue with the practice of providing a 'most likely' scenario. Kahn, Brown and Martel,[31] Congressional Research Service,[32] and Zentner[22] all feel that no 'most likely' or 'most probable' scenario should be offered. They contend that in such instances planners will again focus on only the most likely scenario, again defeating the objective of scenario analysis.

Another criticism, aimed particularly at the quantitative methods, is that in most business applications it is probably folly to attempt to assign probabilities to scenarios. Such estimates can be nothing short of misleading. The precision they imply is not warranted by either (1) the data that were used to derive them, or (2) the phenomenon they purport to predict. Scenarios are possibilities, not probabilities.

Finally, there is some persuasive empirical evidence that judgmental probability estimates are subject to a host of biases.[33] It is probably best not to assign probabilities to scenarios.

Single, Dominant Issue

In some applications there is a single dominant factor whose outcome is central to the item being forecast. Frequently, this dominant factor is the economy, or government policy. In such instances, scenarios can be arrayed over plausible outcomes for this dominant factor. For example, Dickson, Ryan and Smulyan[34] offer three scenarios for the future role of hydrogen as an energy source. Government funding is the crucial unknown. Each of their scenarios provides market estimates for differing levels of government interest.

Themes

In most business applications there is more than a single unknown. There are many issues which compete, combine and interact with one another to characterize the future. Arraying scenarios according to this scheme tries to capture this. For example, Vanston et al.[27] offer three scenarios labeled 'economic expansion', 'environmental concern' and 'technological domination'. Each of these scenarios emphasizes a different aspect of the future environment. It also focuses attention on some of the disparate possibilities that have so frequently laid waste to even the best-drawn plans.

MacNulty,[35] Chapman[36] and Linneman and Kennell[23] have all employed this scheme to array their scenarios.

METHOD OF CONSTRUCTING SCENARIOS

Most of the current methods of generating scenarios that are available today have their roots in the Rand Corporation of the 1950s. At that time, both Herman Kahn and Olaf

Helmer worked on defence-related projects at Rand. Kahn pioneered scenario writing and Helmer developed the Delphi technique. Kahn's approach stressed the judgmental aspects of forecasting. He believed that the most important part was 'simply to think about the problem' and engage in 'systematic conjecture' (p. 5).[8] In contrast, Helmer focused on methodology. His Delphi technique attracted a great deal of attention, and spawned the currently popular Cross-impact Analysis. Both Delphi and Cross-impact are attempts to structure and formalize judgmental forecasting.

This division is still evident today. Cross-impact analysis, which now exists in many versions, is still essentially concerned with methodological issues, while most other scenario generating procedures try to provide guidelines for those who wish to write scenarios.

Some Highly Qualitative Procedures

Kahn rejected the notion of quantitative model-building, in favor of a more qualitative approach. His criticism was that quantitative models focus only on those aspects of a problem that are easily quantified, and, therefore, represent only a partial formulation of the forecasting problem. He felt that when all of the clever mathematical manipulations were stripped away, model building 'comes down to a simplistic intuition or an expression of bias rather than a careful synthesis and balancing of the analysis with more subtle qualitative considerations' (p. 99).[37]

Kahn's approach is deceptively simple. It identifies the basic trends underlying a forecasting problem, projects these trends to construct a 'surprise-free' scenario, then alters some of these projections to create alternate futures—a stage he calls 'Canonical Variations'.[37]

Some scenarists are even stronger advocates of qualitative analysis. Godet[38] offers 'Exploratory Prospective Analysis', as an alternatve to more structured forecasting methods. He lambasts quantitative methods, and adds to Kahn's criticism the problems of inaccurate data and unstable relationships encountered by these models. His approach stresses a 'holistic' and integrative analysis.

Durand[39] offers another highly qualitative approach. It too stresses intuitive analysis.

The primary problem with these procedures is that they rely so heavily on intuitive and subjective analysis that they are difficult to implement. There is really no procedure to follow. What they propose is abstract and difficult to apply in practice. It would be very hard for a planner to sit down and adopt their advice. In many respects these authors are more lucid in their criticism of quantitative methods than they are in explaining their alternative approaches.

Some Practical Procedures

Another set of qualitative procedures offers a more practical means of generating scenarios in a business environment. Essentially, these recipes provide a set of sequential steps that can be followed to construct scenarios. Table 1 compares a sampling of these procedures.

These procedures are similar in many respects. They all begin by identifying those factors that are expected to affect the forecasting situation at hand. They then postulate a set of plausible future values for each of these factors. Then, from the large number

Table 1. A comparison of selected scenario generating procedures

	Becker (1983)	deKluyer (1980)	Linneman and Klein (1977)	McNulty (1977)	Vanston et al. (1977)	Wilson (1978)	Zentner (1975)
Number of scenarios	3	3	3 or 4	3 or 4	3–6	3 or 4	3
Length of scenarios	–	–	1 or 2 paragraphs	–	7–10 pages	–	<50 pages
Base scenario	Most likely	Most likely	None	Surprise-free	Most likely	Surprise-free	None
Alternative scenarios	Opt./pess.	Opt./pess.	Themed	Themed	Themed	Opt./pess.	Themed
Are probabilities assigned?	No	Yes	No	–	No	No	No
Does it use Cross-impact Analysis?	No	No	No	Yes	No	Yes	No
How is the number of factors reduced?	Considers only key factors	Considers only key factors	Considers only key factors	It is not	Considers many factors	Scoring by probability and importance	–
How are the scenarios selected?	Selects plausible combinations of key factors	Judgmental translation into opt./pess. and most likely	Selects plausible combinations of key factors	Judgmental integration of trends and intuition	To conform to the themes	Scenario writing and Cross-impact Analysis	–

of possible combinations of the values of these factors, they select a few plausible scenarios.

It is on this last point that the procedures diverge. Each employs a different strategy for reducing the large number of possible scenarios to the few that are selected. Essentially, these strategies follow one of two paths. The first considers only a few key factors to start with. This greatly reduces the number of possible scenarios to select from. The other considers a larger number of factors but either constrains the possible values of these factors by setting the theme of the scenarios beforehand, or mentally integrating this larger number of factors into a consistent set of scenarios. Some examples should make this difference clearer.

Vanston et al.,[27] for example, rely on a deductive approach. This scheme first selects the dominant background themes for each of the scenarios (e.g. economic expansion, environmental concern, technological domination), and then forecasts each of the key factors in light of each of these themes. That is, the procedure is inherently deductive, the tone of the scenarios is set by their theme and the forecasts are made to conform to this tone.

Conversely, the Linneman and Kennell[23] and Becker[7] procedures are inductive. They focus on only a few important 'impacting' factors, and postulate possible future values for each of them. Linneman and Kennell then tally every possible combination of these values (e.g. low inflation, high unemployment, low consumer confidence), and select a set of three or four distinct, but plausible, scenarios from the total concatenation of variables. Becker follows a similar strategy.

MacNulty[35] and deKluyer[30] use a more intuitive approach to integrate the factors into scenarios. Their procedures rely on a judgmental integration that is less mechanical, but also less descriptive.

Finally, McNamara,[40] Cazes[41] and Gershuny[42] offer additional procedures for constructing scenarios.

The advantage of the deductive approach is that the factors can be combined into a set of consistent scenarios that capture the general theme of the future environment. The danger is that some unexpected combination of factors will be overlooked. The inductive approach allows all combinations to be considered, but since only a few factors are considered, an important one might be omitted. In short, the former approach risks the elimination of a key scenario, the later the omission of a key variable.

One possible solution would be to try both approaches. It would probably be a better strategy to employ the results of a number of simple methods, such as these, rather than spend a great deal of time on a single, complex method. Armstrong[2] has argued persuasively for a greater use of 'eclectic' research in forecasting.

Cross-impact Analysis

Cross-impact Analysis emerged from early work on the Delphi Technique. Delphi was developed shortly after the end of World War II, but was first introduced in the published literature by Dalkey and Helmer.[43] Since then it has attracted a great deal of attention. Among other things, it has (1) become an accepted method of forecasting, (2) been soundly criticized by Sackman,[44] (3) been used to generate alternate scenarios,[45] and (4) spawned the development of Cross-impact Analysis.

According to most accounts, Cross-impact was first used to generate scenarios at Kaiser Aluminum in 1966. Gordon and Hayward[46] provide the first published account of the technique. Since then a plethora of articles in the futures research literature have offered refinements, alternatives and, also, criticisms of this method.

The basic philosophy of Cross-impact Analysis is that no development occurs in isolation. Rather, it is rendered more or less likely by the occurrence of other events. Cross-impact attempts to capture these 'cross-impacts' from the judgmental estimates of experts.

There is no one method of Cross-impact Analysis. Instead, there are many techniques which pursue this same basic philosophy. Essentially, all rely on experts to provide some estimate of how likely it is that an event will occur by some given time period. They then ask how likely it is that the event will occur given the occurrence of some other event. These data (either for a single expert or an average or consensus of experts) are then input into a computer simulation or mathematical program. The result is either a single 'most likely' scenario, or multiple scenarios ranked by probability.

A great deal of effort has been expended over the years in deciding how to stir the pot. For example, Enzer[47] argues that an 'odds-ratio' should be used to transform an expert's estimates into cross-impact probabilities, instead of the 'quadratic' function suggested by Gordon and Hayward. Turoff[48] argues that a 'log-odds ratio' is even better. Dupperin and Godet[28] disagree with all of these simulation approaches and propose SMIC-74, an approach based on mathematical programming that, believe it or not, can actually provide probability estimates for every possible scenario. Even Helmer has recognized that there are problems with existing models, and offers some additional mathematical refinements.[49]

These are all superfluous issues. The key problem with Cross-impact is that judgmental estimates are surely not amenable to any such mathematical machinations. As Kelly[50] notes, 'to suggest that any method exists which might extract such blood from such stones is wishful thinking' (p. 342). McLean[51] adds, 'in putting the emphasis on computation rather than conceptualization it tended to conceal the contradictions inherent in the approach' (p. 349).

Finally, Klein and Linneman[6] note that fancy methods have not been widely adopted. This should not be interpreted as a lack of innovativeness on the part of planners. Rather it is a commendation of their common sense.

In sum, the underlying idea of Cross-impact Analysis is a reasonable one. It recognizes that many events are interdependent. But researchers in this field have gone awry. They have focused too intently on the methodology of Cross-impact Analysis, at the expense of practical issues. Those interested in using scenario analysis as a practical business forecasting tool would be best advised to continue to avoid cross-impact procedures, and instead, adopt some of the helpful guidelines offered in the previous section.

HOW TO DEVELOP AND USE SCENARIOS

The literature on scenario analysis suggests some guidelines that can aid in the development and use of scenarios. Generally, these guidelines speak to two issues: (1) how to construct scenarios and (2) in what situations scenario analysis should be selected over other forecasting approaches. Some of these guidelines are presented below.

Herman Kahn was probably not far off the mark when he noted that the most important part of scenario analysis is simply to think about the problem. There appears to be no advantage to complex mathematical methods of constructing scenarios. Although we live in a world surfeit with automated processes, there is really no mechanical method of generating scenarios. To believe that there is, is to deceive yourself.

In particular, it is important to think about the assumptions that underlie the scenarios. Obtaining accurate assumptions is far more important than selecting the 'best' method of constructing them. A forecast based on untenable assumptions is more likely to go awry than one that used the wrong model-form.

While there may be no mechanical method of generating scenarios, there are some guidelines to follow. These guidelines answer some of the key questions regarding the construction of scenarios.

The most difficult issue in scenario analysis is how to reduce a large number of potential future outcomes to a few plausible scenarios. The number of possible scenarios grows quickly as the number of factors increases. Two methods have been proposed to handle this problem. Each approaches the problem in a different way, and is tailored to serve a different application.

In some business applications, it is possible to identify a few key factors that will affect the future outcome of a product or market. If the number of factors is small (e.g. less than five), and only a small number of possible future values offered for each (e.g. two or three), then one way to develop scenarios is to examine every possible concatenation of these possible future values, and select a few plausible scenarios from this set. The scenarios can be selected to represent either optimistic and pessimistic outcomes, or some dominant 'theme' of the future environment (e.g. robust economic expansion, severe competition, renewed inflation). Essentially, this approach is inductive, it 'builds up' from the factors to the scenarios.

When many factors are considered an alternative method is suggested. Rather than examining every possible combination, an onerous task when there are many factors, this procedure first sets the tone of the scenarios. That is, the first step is to decide whether the scenarios will represent an optimistic and pessimistic view of the future, or characterize some dominant 'themes'. Once the tone of the scenario is set, future values of the factors are postulated that conform to this tone. This approach is deductive; it proceeds from the scenarios to the factors that describe them. It is especially useful when many factors are considered.

In either case, avoid assigning probabilities to the derived scenarios. Such probabilities are misleading. They convey a sense of precision that is not there.

Besides the goal of scenario analysis is to generate a set of equally likely outcomes against which plans can be drawn, not a 'most likely' scenario that may be attended to at the expense of the other, less likely outcomes.

Instead of assigning probabilities, array scenarios using either the 'optimistic/pessimistic' format (with or without a 'surprise-free'), or 'theme' them according to some possible dominant aspects of the future environment. Either of these procedures is superior to arraying the scenarios according to their likelihood of occurrence.

In most applications, two to four scenarios should suffice. A greater number tends to be confusing (and unworkable), and less than two (one) is a point-estimate forecast.

It is difficult to state whether two, three or four is best. It probably depends on the specific application and the goals of the analysis. Most authors argue strongly that 'three scenarios are best', and point up a host of deficiencies with other numbers (e.g. two will be classified as 'good' and 'bad'). Others contend that there are problems with three scenarios (the one in the middle will be selected as the most likely and the others will be ignored), and suggest that two (of four) is the best number. Whatever the case, either two, three or four scenarios can be strongly supported in business applications.

Scenarios should be limited to environmental forecasts. They should not include plans, or the response of the market place to plans, It is a difficult enough task to estimate the future environment, without attempting to bundle into the scenarios additional uncertainties. To do so, is to render scenario analysis an exercise in sheer speculation.

Scenarios should also be targeted to applications of a narrow scope. It is important in scenario analysis to limit the number of factors that are considered. Ideally, scenario analysis should be applied to industries, products and markets that are primarily affected by a small number of factors that are fairly easy to identify, but very difficult to predict. These situations are more amenable to scenario analysis than those that are much wider in scope (e.g. world-views), are affected by many more factors, and are hence more speculative.

Scenario analysis seems best suited for longer time horizons. Over longer time horizons, the accuracy of most forecasts deteriorates appreciably. This highlights the more contextual format of scenarios, as well as the fact that more than a single forecast is offered. This purposeful impreciseness is more attuned to the vagaries of longer time horizons.

Long term is a relative notion. It is not possible to state precisely at what point scenario analysis should be preferred to other forecasting methods. A rough rule of thumb might be to gauge how long it takes for changes in historical trends and relationships to occur in your industry. In applications such as stock prices this time period might be measured in years. Whatever the case, scenario analysis seems to offer the greatest advantage over quantitative methods when the assumptions of stability that underlie these models cannot be supported.

Scenario analysis offers the greatest advantage over other methods when uncertainty is high, and historical relationships are shaky. In such instances, traditional forecasting models, such as time-series and econometric models, will perform poorly since they focus solely on historical data.

Similarly, scenario analysis is ideally suited for those situations where the future is likely to be affected by events that have no historical precedent. Scenarios can include anticipations, whereas quantitative methods rely solely on historical patterns and relationships.

In short, scenario analysis seems to be more attuned to the current business environment. Many of the events that will undoubtedly affect business in the coming years are not discernible solely from the manipulation of historical data. This has been shown consistently over the past decade by the poor performance of quantitative forecasting models. Scenario analysis holds that a careful consideration of future possibilities is more valuable than even the most elegant of computations that will later turn out to be mistaken.

REFERENCES

(1) Spyros Makridakis *et al.*, The accuracy of extrapolation (time-series) methods, *Journal of Forecasting*, **1**, 111–153, April–June (1982).
(2) J. Scott Armstrong. *Long-Range Forecasting: From Crystal Ball to Computer*, John Wiley, New York (1978).
(3) Herman Kahn, *On Thermonuclear War*, Oxford University Press London (1960).
(4) Robert E. Linneman and Harold E. Klein, The use of multiple scenarios by U.S. industrial companies, *Long Range Planning*, **12**, 83–90, February (1979).
(5) Herman Kahn, *The Japanese Challenge*, Thomas Y. Crowell, New York (1979).
(6) Harold E. Klein and Robert E. Linneman, The use of scenarios in corporate planning, *Long Range Planning*, **14**, 69–77, October (1981).
(7) Harold S. Becker, Scenarios: a tool of growing importance to policy analysts in government and industry, *Technological Forecasting and Social Change*, **23**, 95–120, March (1983).
(8) Herman Kahn and A. J. Weiner, *The Year 2000*, Macmillan, London (1967).
(9) Rodney L. Carlson and M. Michael Umble, Statistical demand functions for automobiles and their use for forecasting in an energy crisis, *Journal of Business*, **53**, 193–204, April (1980).
(10) William Ascher, *Forecasting: An Appraisal For Policy-Makers and Planners*, Johns Hopkins University Press, Baltimore (1978).
(11) Steven Schnaars and Conrad Berenson, Growth market forecasting revisited: A look back at a look forward, *Calif. Mgmt. Review*, **28**, Summer (1986), 71–88.
(12) Tarja Meristo, The multiple scenario approach—an aid to strategic planning as part of the information base, unpublished paper presented at International Symposium on Forecasting, Philadelphia, PA, 7 June (1983).
(13) John McHale and M. McHale, An assessment of futures studies worldwide. *Futures*, **8**, 135–145 (1976).
(14) Robert E. Linneman and Harold E. Klein, The use of mutiple scenarios by U.S. industrial companies: a comparison study, 1977–1981, *Long Range Planning*, **16**, 94–101, December (1983).
(15) Steven P. Schnaars, A comparison of scenario writing and simple econometric models, unpublished paper presented at International Symposium on Forecasting, Philadelphia, PA, 7 June (1983).
(16) Ian H. Wilson, Futures forecasting for strategic planning at General Electric, *Long Range Planning*, June (1973), pp. 39–42.
(17) Ian H. Wilson, Scenarios. In *Handbook of Futures Research*, pp. 22–47, Jib Fowles (Ed.), Greenwood Press, Westport, CT (1978).
(18) Ian H. Wilson, W. P. George and P. J. Solomon, Strategic planning for marketers, *Business Horizons*, **21**, 65–73 (1978).
(19) Rene D. Zentner, Scenarios, past, present and future, *Long Range Planning*, **15**, 12–20, June (1982).
(20) Russel L. Ackoff, *A Concept of Corporate Planning*, Wiley-Interscience, New York (1970).
(21) Piercing future fog in the executive suite, *Business Week*, 28 April (1975), pp. 46–52.
(22) Rene D. Zentner, Scenarios in forecasting, *Chemical and Engineering News*, 6 October (1975), pp. 22–34.
(23) Robert E. Linneman and John D. Kennell, Shirt-sleeves approach to long-range plans, *Harvard Business Review*, **55**, 141–150, March–April (1977).
(24) P. W. Beck, Corporate planning for an uncertain future. *Long Range Planning*, **15**, 12–21, August (1982).
(25) Richard O. Mason, A dialectical approach to strategic planning, *Management Science*, **15**, B-403–414, April (1969).
(26) Ian I. Mitroff and James R. Emshoff, On strategic assumption-making: a dialectical approach to policy and planning, *Academy of Management Review* 4, 1–12, January (1979).
(27) John H. Vanston Jr., W. P. Frisbie, S. C. Lopreato and D. L. Poston, Alternate scenario planning, *Technological Forecasting and Social Change*, **10**, 159–180 (1977).
(28) J. C. Dupperin and M. Godet, SMIC—a method for constructing and ranking scenarios, *Futures*, **7**, 302–312, August (1975).

(29) Micael Edesess and George A. Hambrecht, Scenario forecasting: necessity, not choice, *Journal of Portfolio Management*, **6**, 10–15, Spring (1980).

(30) Cornelis A. de Kluyer, Bottom-up sales forecasting through scenario analysis, *Industrial Marketing Management*, **9**, 167–170 (1980).

(31) Herman Kahn, W. Brown and L. Martel, *The New 200 Years: A Scenario for America and the World*, William Brown, New York (1976).

(32) Congressional Research Service, Library of Congress, *Long Range Planning*, Serial BB, U.S. Government Printing Office, May (1976).

(33) Daniel Kahneman, Paul Slovic and Amos Tversky, *Judgment Under Uncertainty: Heuristics and Biases*, Cambridge University Press, Cambridge (1982).

(34) E. M. Dickson, J. W. Ryan and M. H. Smulyan, *The Hydrogen Energy Economy*, Praeger, New York (1977).

(35) Christine A. Ralph MacNulty, Scenario development for cororate development, *Futures*, **9**, 128–138, April (1977).

(36) Peter F. Chapman, A method for exploring the future, *Long Range Planning*, **9**, 2–11, February (1976).

(37) Herman Kahn, The alternative world future's approach. In *New Approaches to International Relations*, M. A. Kaplan (Ed.), St. Martin's Press, New York (1968).

(38) Michel Godet, Reducing the blunders in forecasting, *Futures*, **15**, 181–192, June (1983).

(39) Jaques Durand, A new method for constructing scenarios, *Futures*, **4**, 325–330, December (1972).

(40) James F. McNamara, Trend impact analysis and scenario writing strategies for the specification of decision alternatives in educational planning, *Journal of Educational Administration*, **14**, 143–161, October (1976).

(41) Bernard Cazes, The future of work: an outline for a method of scenario construction, *Futures*, **8**, 405–410, October (1976).

(42) J. Gershuny, The choice of scenarios, *Futures*, **8**, 496–508, December (1976).

(43) Norman C. Dalkey and Olaf Helmer, An experimental application of the Delphi method to the use of experts, *Management Science*, **9**, 458–467 (1963).

(44) Harold Sackman, *Delphi Critique*, D. C. Heath, Lexington, MA (1975).

(45) J. C. Derian and F. Morize, Delphi in the assessment of research and development projects, *Futures*, **5**, 469–483 (1973).

(46) T. J. Gordon and H. Hayward, Initial experiments with the Cross Impact Matrix method of forecasting, *Futures*, **1**, 100–116, December (1968).

(47) Selwyn Enzer, Delphi and Cross-impact techniques: an effective combination for systematic futures analysis, *Futures*, **3**, 48–61, March (1971).

(48) Murray Turoff, An alternative approach to Cross-impact Analysis, *Technological Forecasting and Social Change*, **3**, 309–339 (1972).

(49) Olaf Helmer, Reassessment of Cross-impact Analysis, *Futures*, **13**, 389–400, October (1981).

(50) P. Kelly, Further comments on Cross-impact Analysis, *Futures*, **8**, 341–345, August (1976).

(51) Mick McLean, Does Cross-impact Analysis have a future? *Futures*, **8**, 345–349, August (1976).

_____ Part IV

Corporate Modelling

Chapter 11

A Conceptual Framework for Corporate Modeling and the Results of a Survey of Current Practice

Thomas H. Naylor

Duke University and Social Systems, Inc.

This paper attempts to ascertain the current state of the art of corporate simulation models by summarizing the results of a survey of 346 corporations in North America and Europe. It considers who is using corporate models, why, how, and which resources are required for implementation. A conceptual framework for corporate modeling is also given.

WHY CORPORATE PLANNING MODELS?

Through direct personal contact we have identified nearly two thousand firms in the United States, Canada, and Europe that are either using, developing, or experimenting with some form of corporate planning models. Corporate planning models represent an attempt to describe the complex inter-relationships among a corporation's financial, marketing, and production activities in terms of a set of mathematical and logical relationships which have been programmed into computer.

In 1969 George Gershefski was able to identify only 63 firms from a sample of 1900 firms in the United States which were actually using corporate planning models.[1,2] More recently Peter H. Grinyer and J. Wooller[3,4] have reported on a survey of 65 firms in the United Kingdom which are using corporate planning models.

In September of 1974, Social Systems, Inc. conducted a survey of 1881 corporations which were thought to be either using, developing, or planning to develop a corporate planning model. Of the 346 corporations which responded to the survey, 73% were either using or developing such a model. Another 15% were planning to develop a corporate planning model, and only 12% had no plans whatsoever to develop a planning model.

Reprinted by permission from *Operational Research Quarterly*, Volume 27, No. 3, pp. 671–682, Copyright ©1976, Operational Research Society Ltd.

The reasons for using corporate planning models include: (1) economic uncertainty, (2) shortages of energy and basic raw materials, (3) a levelling off of productivity, (4) international competition, (5) tight money and inflation, (6) political upheavals, (7) environmental problems, and (8) new business opportunities. That is, top management has become increasingly aware that the old ways of 'muddling through' are not adequate to meet the complex problems facing corporations in the future. The need for a more systematic approach for evaluating the consequences of alternative managerial policies and socioeconomic and political events on the future of the corporation has become self-evident. A change in pricing or advertising policies affects production operations, cash flow, and the profit-and-loss statement. Difficulty in borrowing additional funds to finance inventories leads to reverberations not only in the balance sheet but also in marketing strategies and production plans. The problem is that everything is related to everything else. *Ad hoc* plans which focus on only one functional area of the business are likely to be myopic and ineffective.

In order to survive during these turbulent days, corporate plans must be both comprehensive and systematic.

Corporate planning models are an attractive, viable alternative to informal, *ad hoc* planning procedures. The uses of corporate planning models vary from company to company depending on managerial objectives. The Memorex Corporation used a financial planning model to negotiate a more favourable credit with a bank. A Swedish shipyard employs a corporate financial model to determine which currencies to use to buy raw materials when building ships and which currencies to use when the ships are sold. Merger and acquisition decisions are evaluated with the Dresser Industries model. The Treasurer of United Air Lines generates alternative financial scenarios with across-the-board fare increases, additions and deletions of different types of flight equipment, and increases in the price of jet fuel. On the other hand, American Airlines uses a corporate marketing model to forecast the profitability of different cities in its route structure. Firms like Monsanto, Tenneco, and Royster use corporate planning models to forecast cash requirements.

WHO IS USING CORPORATE MODELS?

In our survey we asked those firms which are using corporate simulation models to indicate the actual users of the model. The results are tabulated in Table 1. The table shows the percentage of firms in our sample for which a particular person is receiving and using information produced by the corporate model.

These results are indeed encouraging for they indicate that in approximately half of the corporations which are using corporate simulation models, the right people are

Table 1. People receiving and using output from the model

User	Percentage
Vice president of finance	55
President	46
Controller	46
Executive vice president	32
Treasurer	30

Table 2. Sales of firms using corporate models

Sales	Percentage
Under $50 million	7
$50 million–$100 million	3
$100 million–$250 million	8
$250 million–$500 million	16
$500 million–$1 billion	21
Over $1 billion	38
No response	7
Total	100

receiving and actually using the output generated by the models. There is abundant evidence available to support the hypothesis that it is crucial to the success of any corporate modeling project to have the active participation of top management in both the problem definition phase of the project and the implementation stage. The fact that the president and senior financial executive of half of the firms using corporate models are among the users of these models bodes well for the future of corporate modeling.

Next we examine the relative size of the firms in our sample which are using corporate simulation models. Total sales are used as a measure of the size of these corporations (Table 2).

Although over half of the firms in our sample of corporate model users have sales in excess of $500 million, it is interesting to note that 10% of the users of corporate models have sales which are less than $100 million. With the advent of timesharing computer languages, corporate modeling is now economically feasible for firms with sales of less than $10 million.

WHY ARE THEY USED?

Cash flow analysis, financial forecasting, balance sheet projections, financial analysis, *pro forma* financial reports, and profit planning are the most popular applications of corporate simulation models (Table 3).

Table 3. Applications of corporate models

Applications	Percentage of users
Cash flow analysis	65
Financial forecasting	65
Balance sheet projections	64
Financial analysis	60
Pro forma financial reports	55
Profit planning	53
Long-term forecasts	50
Budgeting	47
Sales forecasts	41
Investment analysis	35

Table 4. How corporate models are used

Use	Percentage
Evaluation of policy alternatives	79
Financial projections	75
Long-term planning	73
Decision making	58
Short-term planning	56
Preparation of reports	47
Corporate goal setting	46
Analysis	39
Confirmation of another analysis	35

HOW ARE THEY USED?

Table 4 indicates that corporate simulation models are used most often (1) to evaluate alternative policies, (2) to provide financial projections, (3) to facilitate long-term planning, (4) to make decisions, and (5) to facilitate short-term planning.

RESOURCE REQUIREMENTS

Most (67%) of the existing corporate models were developed in-house without any outside assistance from consultants, 24% were developed in-house with outside consulting, and 8% were purchased from outside.

Eighteen man-months was the average amount of effort required to develop models in-house without outside assistance. The average cost of these models was $82 752.

For those models which were developed in-house with the help of outside consultants, the average elapsed time required to complete the model was ten months. The average cost for those models was $29 225.

In terms of computer hardware, 42% of the models are run on in-house computing equipment, 37% are run on an outside timesharing bureau, and 19% are run both in-house and on a timesharing bureau. Of the firms using corporate models in our sample, 62% run their models in conversational mode while 56% utilize the batch mode of computation. In our sample of firms using corporate models, 43% run these models on IBM computers, 5% on UNIVAC, 4% on Honeywell, 3% on Xerox, 2% on Burroughs, 1% on Digital Equipment Corporation and 1% on NCR.

FORTRAN is by far the most widely used computer language for programming corporate simulation models. Fifty percent of the existing models were programmed in FORTRAN, 8% in COBOL, 5% in PL/1, 4% in APL, 2% in Assembler, and 1% in DYNAMO. Another 26% of the models were programmed in one of over forty planning and budgeting languages which are available to facilitate the development and programming of corporate planning models. These include languages like PSG, SIMPLAN, and BUDPLAN. These languages tend to be much more user (management) oriented than scientific languages such as FORTRAN, APL, and PL/1. Although firms with sales less than $100 million typically would not employ scientific programmers, it is possible to teach financial analysts a language like SIMPLAN[5] in a matter of a few hours. With the availability of planning languages on timesharing

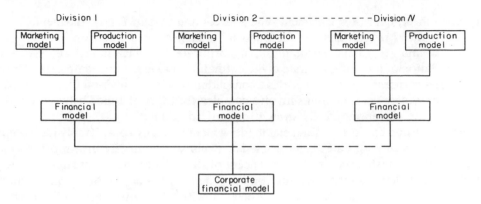

Figure 1. A conceptual framework for corporate models

bureaus, much smaller firms now find it economically feasible to develop and use corporate models.

Although econometric modeling techniques are not used very extensively even by the largest corporations in the United States, Canada, and Europe, we found that 57% of the firms using corporate models subscribed to some national econometric forecasting service.

CORPORATE MODELING TERMINOLOGY

A Taxonomy for Corporate Models

In describing corporate planning models, we find it useful to make use of the conceptual framework outlined in Figure 1. We shall assume that a typical corporation consists of multiple divisions. In some companies like General Electric, divisions are called Strategic Business Units. In other companies they are called Groups or Businesses.

We further assume that the corporation is completely decentralized. That is, each division has its own separate financial, marketing, and production activities. Although there is a centralized corporate financial function for the corporation as a whole, there are no centralized marketing or production activities for the firm.

Each division can be represented by a division model which consists of a front-end division financial model which is driven by a division marketing model and a division production model. For example, a corporation like Babcock and Wilcox has fourteen divisions. There will then be fourteen separate division models each consisting of a separate financial, marketing, and production model. When the entire set of division models is consolidated, the result is a total corporate financial model.

The conceptual framework described in Figure 1 is widely used among corporations who have developed some form of corporate planning model, including Santa Fe, Monsanto, Dresser Industries, Honeywell, and United Air Lines.

Financial models. The front-end of every corporate planning model is an overall corporate financial model, the outputs of which consist of an income statement, balance sheet, cash flow statement, and sources and uses of funds statement, i.e. the usual financial reports used by the financial management of the firm.

For a multi-divisional corporation, a corporate financial model represents the consolidation of all of the separate division financial models. For example, the Dresser Industries corporate financial model is a consolidation of seven division financial models. Frequently these consolidations involve complex transfers of funds between divisions and are, therefore, not merely straightforward additions.

Each division has its own financial model which is usually considerably less complex than the overall corporate financial model. It consists primarily of a profit-and-loss statement. In most corporations the concept of the balance sheet is meaningless at the division level. Revenue and sales forecasts are generated by the division marketing model. Operational and production costs associated with alternative levels of output are generated by the division production model.

The corporate financial model can be used to check the economic feasibility of alternative financial plans for the different divisions of the firm and also to evaluate the financial impact of alternative cash management, depreciation, capital investment, and merger-acquisition policies.

Both division and corporate financial models are relatively straightforward to develop. They are essentially definitional in concept and are based entirely on the firm's given accounting relationships.

Marketing models. Each of the division models in Figure 1 has its own marketing model which are used to explain or predict sales and market share by product or major project group. We shall consider two different types of marketing models—short-term forecasting models and econometric policy analysis models. Short-term forecasting models are naive, mechanistic models, devoid of any explanatory power. They cannot be used to do 'what if' analysis. On the other hand, econometric models are rich in explanatory power and may be used to link sales to the national economy and to conduct marketing policy simulation experiments. With econometric marketing models, it is possible to simulate the effects on sales and market share of alternative advertising, pricing, and promotional policies.

Marketing models provide the sales forecasts which are required to drive both financial and production models. That is, sales forecasts generated by marketing models are external to both financial and production models. Table 5 indicates the extent to which forecasting models have been utilized in the corporate models in our sample.

Table 5. Forecasting techniques used in corporate models

Forecasting technique	Percentage
Growth rate	50
Linear time trend	40
Moving average	22
Exponential smoothing	20
Non-linear time trends	15
Adaptive forecasting	9
Box-Jenkins	4

Production models. Each division model in Figure 1 also contains a production model. For given levels of output, production models generate operating costs and costs of goods sold. Our approach to production models is essentially an activity analysis approach in which the cost of operating at different levels of output is built up in terms of the resource requirements for each production process. Some firms such as Exxon, CIBA-GEIGY, Schlitz and Anheuser-Busch have used mathematical programming to determine the minimum cost production schedule for each level of output. This is one area of corporate modeling in which there is a definite need for more theoretical development as well as empirical experience.

Sales forecasts generated by marketing models provide input into production models. On the other hand, production models yield cost of goods sold and other production information required by financial models.

Corporate models. Of those firms which indicated they are using a corporate simulation model, 39% claimed to have modelled the 'total company'. We suspect that this figure overstates the case and may reflect differences in interpretation of what constitutes the 'total company'. In actual practice, relatively few firms have managed to integrate the financial, marketing, and production activities of the firm into truly integrated corporate simulation models. Three notable exceptions to this rule are CIBA-GEIGY, IU International, and Anheuser-Busch. Each of these firms has successfully achieved the development and implementation of a total corporate simulation model. The CIBA-GEIGY model is probably the most sophisticated corporate simulation model in existence today. It is used extensively by corporate and division management to evaluate long-range plans.

Most (76%) of the corporate planning models in use today are 'what if' models, i.e. models which simulate the effects of alternative managerial policies and assumptions about the firm's external environment. Only 4% of the models in our sample were optimization models in which the goal was to maximize or minimize a single objective function such as profit or cost, respectively. However, 14% of the models use both approaches. The remainder of the firms in our sample either did not respond to the question or use some other approach.

Model Specification

Once we have defined the input and output variables for our model, we must then specify a set of mathematical and logical relationships linking the input variables to the output variables. The average number of equations in the models in our sample was 545. The range varied from 20 to several thousand equations, most of which are definitional equations which take the form of accounting identities. The average number of such equations was 445. The average number of behavioural (empirical) equations was only 86. Behavioural equations take the form of theories or hypotheses about the behaviour of certain economic phenomena. They must be tested empirically and validated before they are incorporated into the model.

Definitional. Definitional relationships are exactly what the term implies—mathematical or accounting definitions. Definitional relationships are encountered most often in the formulation of corporate financial models. They are typically defined by the firm's accountants and financial analysts. The following is an example of a definitional equation.

$$CASH = CASH(-1) + CAR + NDEBT - NASSET - PAP - LPAY \qquad (1)$$

Equation (1) is a typical cash equation in a corporate financial model. It states that beginning cash (CASH) is equal to previous period cash ($CASH(-1)$) plus collection of receivables (CAR) plus borrowing ($NDEBT$) minus the purchase of assets ($NASSET$) minus the payment of accounts payable (PAP) minus loan repayments ($LPAY$).

Equation (2) provides us with a second example of a definitional equation.

$$INV = INV(-1) + MAT + DL - CGS \qquad (2)$$

It may be interpreted as follows. Beginning inventory (INV) is equal to previous period inventory ($INV(-1)$) plus new material purchases (MAT) plus direct labour costs (DL) minus the cost of goods sold (CGS).

Some definitional equations are determined by government regulations such as tax laws, investment credit allowances, and depreciation rates.

Behavioural. Behavioural relationships are hypotheses which are subject to empirical testing and validation. They are theories which reflect management's understanding of certain internal and external relationships affecting the firm.

Perhaps the best known behavioural model is called by economists 'law of demand'.

$$Q = a - bP \qquad (3)$$

Equation (3) implies that higher prices (P) will be associated with reduced consumption of the commodity or product (Q) in question (Figure 2). The law of demand can be tested empirically by collecting some data on P and Q, estimating the parameters a and b, and determining whether or not there is a significant negative relationship between P and Q. (This is an oversimplification for there are certain well known econometric problems in dealing with such a simplistic model.)

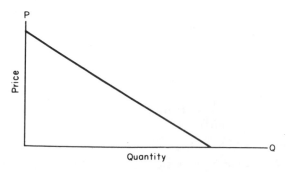

Figure 2. The law of demand

Equation (4) represents a more realistic example of a behavioural equation.

$$SALES = a + bP + cADV + dGNP + eRD + fP_c + u \tag{4}$$

This equation hypothesizes a linear relationship between the quantity sold of a given product and price (P), advertising expenditures (ADV), Gross National Product (GNP), research and development expenditures (RD), the price of the firm's leading competitor (P_c), and a random error term (u). If we have time series or cross sectional data on $SALES$, P, ADV, GNP, RD, and P_c, we can estimate the values of the parameters a, b, c, d, e, and f. We can test the statistical significance of the parameter estimates and evaluate the overall explanatory power of the model. Finally, we can simulate the effects on sales of alternative pricing, advertising, and research and development strategies. We can also experiment with alternative assumptions about the national economy as measured by GNP.

THE POLITICS OF CORPORATE MODEL BUILDING

Crucial to the successful implementation of any corporate simulation model is the political support of top management. Although suitable models and computer software are necessary for the success of corporate modeling, they are by no means sufficient. If the president of the company or at least the vice-president of finance is not fully committed to the use of a corporate model, then the results are not likely to be taken seriously and the model will have only limited use.

To get some feeling for the political environment in the firms where corporate modeling is being used, we asked a series of questions concerning the interest of management in the corporate modeling activities of their firm. The findings displayed in Table 6 seem to imply that the corporate models included in our survey enjoy a relatively high degree of political support from management. In 60% of the firms which are using corporate models top management is 'somewhat interested' in corporate modeling while another 30% are 'very interested'. On the other hand, the degree of interest in corporate modeling expressed by planning and finance departments is even higher.

BENEFITS OF CORPORATE SIMULATION MODELS

The primary benefits to be derived from the use of corporate simulation models stem from the ability to use these models to conduct 'what if' experiments. That is, alternative

Table 6. Attitudes of management towards corporate modeling

	Very interested (%)	Somewhat interested (%)	Indifferent (%)	Not at all interested (%)	No response (%)
Top management	30	60	8	1	1
Planning	67	22	4	1	6
Finance	54	37	5	3	1
Marketing	23	39	24	8	6

Table 7. Benefits of corporate models

Benefits	Percentage
Able to explore more alternatives	78
Better quality decision making	72
More effective planning	65
Better understanding of the business	50
Faster decision making	48
More timely information	44
More accurate forecasts	38
Cost savings	28
No benefits	4

Table 8. Limitations of corporate models

Shortcomings	Percentage
Is not flexible enough	25
Poorly documented	23
Requires too much input data	23
Output format is inflexible	11
Took too long to develop	11
Running cost is too high	9
Development cost was too high	8
Model users cannot understand model	8
No shortcomings	9

scenarios can be generated reflecting a wide variety of different managerial policies and assumptions about the external environment in which the firm will operate. Scenarios can be produced almost as fast as the human mind can conceive of alternative policies and/or assumptions about economic, political, and social conditions confronting the firm.

Once one has developed an adequate database, formulated a set of mathematical and logical relationships describing the firm's functional activities, and expressed the relationships in the form of a computer program, then one automatically has the ability to answer two other equally important questions. We call these the 'what is' and 'what has been' questions. That is, if one has gone to the trouble to construct a corporate simulation model, then a natural by-product of such an undertaking is the capability to access the firm's database and ask questions about the current status of sales, cost of goods sold, cash, profitability, etc. In other words, a corporate simulation model can be used as the front-end of a management information system.

But not only can we answer the 'what is' types of questions, we can also answer the 'what has been' types of questions. Again, using the corporate model as the front-end of a total management information system, we can interrogate the database and produce instantaneous historical reports. We can also conduct experiments with the historical data to ascertain what might have been. In other words, we may want to evaluate the previous consequences of alternative strategies which have been used in the past as a means of providing guidance in developing long-range plans for the future.

According to our survey, the major benefits which present users of corporate models have derived include: (1) ability to explore more alternatives, (2) better quality decision making, (3) more effective planning, (4) better understanding of the business, and (5) faster decision making.

LIMITATIONS OF CORPORATE MODELS

Opinions about the limitations of corporate models do not appear to be as intense or as well defined as opinions about the benefits of these models. The three shortcomings mentioned most often were: (1) lack of flexibility, (2) poor documentation, and (3) excessive input data requirements.

SUMMARY

In this paper we have examined the nature of the increase in the use of corporate planning models which has taken place since 1969. Employing a conceptual framework for corporate modeling and the results of a recent survey, we have attempted to shed some light on who is using corporate planning models, why they are used, how they are used, and the resources required to implement them.

REFERENCES

[1]GEORGE W. GERSHEFSKI (1969) Corporate models—the state of the art. *Mgrl Plan.*
[2]GEORGE W. GERSHEFSKI (1970) Corporate models—the state of the art. *Mgmt Sci.* **16**.
[3]PETER H. GRINYER and D. C. BATT (1974) Some tentative findings on corporate financial simulation models. *Opl Res. Q.*, **25**. 149–167.
[4]PETER H. GRINYER and J. WOOLLER (1975) *Corporate Modelling Today*. Institute of Chartered Accountants, London.
[5]SIMPLAN: *A Planning and Modeling System* (1975) Social Systems, Chapel Hill, NC.
[6]THOMAS H. NAYLOR and TERRY G. SEAKS (1976) *Corporate Planning Models*. Addison-Wesley, Reading, MA.

Chapter 12

A Corporate System Model of a Sports Club: Using Simulation as an Aid to Policy Making in a Crisis

Roger I. Hall and William B. Menzies
University of Manitoba and City of Winnipeg

The sports club, described in this study, was losing members and in dire financial straits. It became obvious from the optimistic forecasts and fragmented historical records that the membership system was poorly understood by the club's decision making groups and committees. A corporate system model of the club was developed from interviews with the club executive and influential club members. In this way an understanding was gained of the fundamental system of relations determining the viability of the club. Various suggestions for remedial action were tried out on a simulation version of the model and the results communicated to the board of directors. The study serves to illustrate the use of computer simulation modeling, not as an optimising or forecasting tool, but as an aid to policy making in a crisis. It became part of the organizational behavior process for coping with an extreme situation that, in this case, had a happy ending. The study attempts to relate the scientific process of synthesizing a formal model with the psychological and socio-political processes of decision making in a complex system during a crisis.

INTRODUCTION

Sports clubs, like many other types of organizations, can find themselves in a downward spiral of events that is difficult to reverse. The voluntary members who direct the club

This paper received honorable mention in the 1981 annual International Prize Competition sponsored by the College on Organization of The Institute of Management Sciences for the most original new contribution to the field of Organizational Analysis and Design.

may have little understanding of the nature of the problem and command few resources to unravel the often complex system of cause-and-effect contributing to the evolving crisis. This study describes the desperate situation facing a long-established Curling club in a western Canadian city, and the use of a corporate system simulation modeling approach to assist in the organizational and political process of searching for a survival policy.

The sport of Curling—the 'roaring game' as it is sometimes called—was imported from Scotland. The game is in some respects similar to lawn bowls but played on ice. It is as much an institution as a sport in Canada! Curling clubs, many with Scottish sounding names, such as the Heather, Caledonian, Thistle and Highlander, compete annually for the honour of representing their country in the international championship. One such club, the Great Glen Curling Club,[1], has a history going back to the year 1880 and includes, among its honours, spawning a famous rink (a curling team) that twice won the World Championship. However, the Great Glen Curling Club has been experiencing a steady decline in membership over the past several years. Combined with loose control over financial matters in the past, this trend nearly resulted in the collapse of the club. The club was approaching its centennial year and the need was expressed to see its future secured and its existence perpetuated.

The club's responses to the problem of financial viability have always assumed a steady, if not a growing membership base and a relatively price inelastic membership fee schedule. The budgeting process for each season's operations has consistently used an overly-optimistic forecast of membership level. Because the membership level has a major effect on all the aspects of the operation of the club, an understanding of the determinants of membership would seem to be essential to ensure satisfactory performance. Yet, the optimistic forecasts and fragmented historical membership records seemed to indicate that the membership system was poorly understood.

System Dynamics,[3,4] offers a tool for modeling, not only the membership system, but also the complete operation of the club as a corporate system[6]. A System Dynamics model differs from most other corporate models in that it generates its own history from relationships built into it, rather than merely computing the financial results to be expected from a given sales forecast using company financial ratios based upon past performance (see Schrieber[20] for examples of corporate simulation models).

Axelrod[1] has observed that whereas a policy maker may not have a clear map of his policy terrain, he has no difficulty in accepting the causal links making up a more comprehensive map. As he states it:

> Even sophisticated decision makers operating in the field of their competence have a very strong tendency to conceptualize causation in a way that prevents them from spontaneously recognizing feedback in their policy environments.
> People have no trouble accepting the separate beliefs that make up a feedback cycle when each link is given explicit attention . . . But when they spontaneously describe their environment, they do not include even implicit feedback cycles. Thus the explanation seems to be in the way people conceptualize causation: they seem to see it as flowing outwards, and not turning back to affect some other concept variable that is regarded as causally prior (p. 238).

As an example, Roberts[18] was able to show that experts in Urban Transportation were unable to see the recursive relations in an Urban Transport system. However, a

_____

1. A disguised name.

directed diagraph model put together from their collective wisdom exhibited several feedback loops and unexpected dynamics.

System Dynamics provides an aid to sensitizing policy makers to the feedback cycles and their implications by constructing influence diagrams using the directed diagraph method[3,7]. This is perhaps the major strength of the technique. Although it does not supply optimal solutions to problems, System Dynamics can provide the necessary understanding of the complex operations of an organization that helps policy makers find, at least, good solutions. It focuses on the processes causing the deterioration of the performance of the system which serves to stimulate the search for more creative decisions—to thinking about the broad issues and looking for sensible policies for stability and survival with a more comprehensive map—when the pressures of events tends to have the opposite effect with an entrenchment of views and a narrowing of perspective[7,21,22].

System Dynamics encourages the modeller to lay out his assumptions in a systematic way for others to challenge. This places the methodology in the 'refutationist' tradition of Science[2]. This tradition has been described by Popper[15] as:

> Once put forward, none of our 'anticipants' are dogmatically upheld. Our method of research is not to defend them, in order to prove how right we were. On the contrary, we try to overthrow them. Using all the weapons of our logical mathematical and technical armory we try to prove that our anticipations were false–in order to put forward, in their stead, new unjustified and unjustifiable anticipations, new 'rash and premature prejudices' (p. 279).

The successive stages of refinement of the model, involving participants in the organization criticizing the model formulation, greatly reduces the chance of leaving out important cause-effect relations. As Miller and Friesen[11] put it (p. 1017): 'Specification error is less likely to occur in this kind of research than in almost any other.'

The model, to be described, was built on the best advice that could be obtained from the people who actually ran the club. It cannot be validated in any rigorous sense because of a lack of membership data and resources, and in any case, time was of the essence. When historical time series data are available to compare actual and simulated results, a mismatch between these does not necessarily invalidate the model. For instance, small errors in parameter estimation, transient disturbances caused by initialization procedures (see, for example,[10] pp. 296–299) and special exogenous events (such as the spurious effect on club membership of a local rink winning the World Championship) can conspire to cause large period-by-period absolute errors. Despite this, the patterns of actual and simulated behavior might be startlingly similar lending credence to the model. Coyle[3] argues for a 'defensible' (well argued) model, and Forrester and Senge[5] discuss a large number of subjective tests concerning model structure and behavior more appropriate to building confidence in a System Dynamics model. There are, then, philosophical considerations dictating the validation methods required for a model to be used, on the one hand, for the more traditional Management Science purposes of prediction and optimization, and on the other hand, for the purpose of applying Science to Management for a journey of discovery into the policy areas of an organization.

There is some question as to the benefit of a more rigorous validation attempt in this instance, since nothing may be gained in terms of understanding how the system works. Rather, the intention at the time was to take the fragmented cause-maps of the club's various officials—upon which they base their individual decisions anyway—and weave these into a whole map of the club's policy domain. The assumptions implicit in these cause-maps were examined for plausibility, and vaguely defined or missing parts supplied by further inquiry among the participants (see Coyle,[3] pp. 69–70, for a test of completeness and closure of a system model). As mentioned above, the process can be likened to a journey of discovery by charting the here-to-fore poorly understood or largely unrecognized parts of the policy environment of the organization. If the resultant map is found to be a satisfactory representation of reality by the original participants for the purpose in hand, then it is, from the organization's point of view, *valid*. Furthermore, if it results in insights and understanding that permits more complexity to be understood by the participants and, hence, introduced into their policy determinations, where crude but forceful arguments based on simplistic assumptions prevailed before, then, at the very least, it is a *useful* model. The model, therefore, is presented here, not as an optimizing or accurately predicting device, but as a tool for *organizational intervention, learning* and *change* in a time of crisis.

THE CORPORATE SYSTEM MODEL

The essential features of the club corporate system can be described in terms of (1) the club membership, (2) the various revenues flowing from membership, (3) ice rental income, (4) bar and food revenues, and (5) quality of management of the club facilities. Together, these affect the profit of the club, the fee structure and quality of service that, in turn, influence the level of membership. Influence diagramming techniques,[3,7] were used to develop a diagram of causality for the club corporate system.

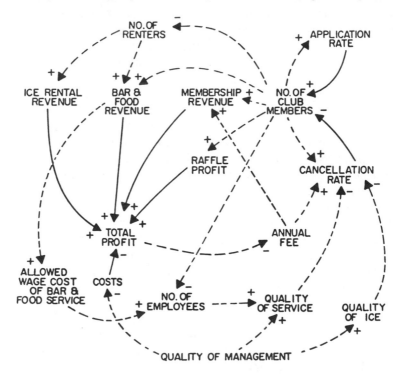

Figure 1. Simplified corporate system model of a curling club

The Club Membership

The Great Glen Club membership consists of four major types. The first is Mixed curling which became quite popular in recent years and now exhibits a fairly stable membership level. A second group is the Clubhouse members. These members pay a house membership fee which allows the use of all clubhouse facilities. These members do not curl; rather, many of them use the club for business entertainment due to its downtown location. Thirdly, the major group of members is the Active Curler group. These members include once-a-week curlers, and intermediate curlers (aged 24 and under). This type of membership has traditionally been the mainstay of the club but has shown a decline in recent years. Finally, a Business Girl league was initiated recently whose membership is expected to grow in the next few years. These curlers consist of working women who cannot curl during the morning and afternoon draw times of regular women's leagues.

Each type of membership has an identical cause-effect structure but different parameters influencing its individual level and hence each is modelled separately. Limits to the capacity of the club for the various membership categories and minimum numbers of loyal members, who would not leave whatever the fee or service level, are incorporated in the model too. However, for the sake of simplicity in explaining the model, the membership system is depicted in aggregated form (made possible by the identical causal structures of the different membership categories) in the influence diagram of Figure 1.

The current membership level, it can be seen from Figure 1, influences both the application rate and the cancellation rate. That is, a certain number of members recruit new members each year, and a certain fraction of current members cancel their memberships each year, so that the more members there are, the higher both the application rate and the cancellation rate. Growth or decline in membership, therefore, depends on the relative difference between these rates. The membership sector is central to the complete model. It is the origin of the major revenues for the club.

The Membership Revenue

The model incorporates a fee setting sector that automatically raises membership fees when a loss is reported. From the influence diagram (Figure 1) it can be seen that, as the number of members increases, so the membership revenue also increases. Since expenses are largely fixed, the resulting increase in profit assures that no increase in the annual membership fee will be needed. The member cancellation rate does not rise and the total number of members increases or does not decrease so quickly as a result. Conversely, if membership drops, revenues and profits also drop, and a membership fee increase is enacted to prevent the club making a loss. The fee increase causes some members to leave and the cycle repeats itself.

The club annual raffle is now a permanent part of club operations. Members sell tickets in this lottery and, because expenses are minimal, a large profit is realized. So, as shown in Figure 1, when the numbers of members increases, the raffle profits and, hence, total profits increase. This also assures that no increase in the membership fee will be needed and, hence, no detrimental change in membership will occur. The opposite takes place when membership decreases.

The Ice Rental Revenue

If the number of curling members decreases for any reason, the amount of ice available for rental increases. As more ice is rented to other organizations, such as office clubs, additional rental revenue is earned and total profits are positively affected. This assures no increase in the membership fee and no change in the member cancellation rate. However, the demand for rental ice is relatively fixed, and the effect of this on revenues and profits of the club is limited. These relations are also shown in Figure 1.

The Bar and Food Revenue

The bar and food expenditure of each member is represented in the system model as a normal distribution with a mean and standard deviation estimated from club accounts. There are three feedback loops concerning the bar and food services in Figure 1. In the first loop, as the number of members and/or renters increases, the bar and food revenues increase. The increased bar and food profit improves total profit performance, which provides for no fee increase, and membership cancellation rate is unaffected.

In the second loop, as the number of members and/or renters increases, the bar and food revenue increases. The additional bar and food business causes additional service personnel to be hired, which results in an improvement in the variety and quality of service and a decrease in the member cancellation rate. The club becomes more attractive to members. In the third loop, as the number of members decreases, the number of employees per member increases. The resulting improvement in quality of service causes fewer people to cancel their memberships and, as a result, the overall membership level improves.

Quality of Management

The quality of management of the club is modelled as a factor that can change certain operating ratios and organizing parameters. For instance, costs will be held in line, employees will be selected and motivated to give a better service to club members and the quality of curling rink ice will be improved. These in turn will affect the quality of the club, as perceived by members, with subsequent effects on membership cancellations. The quality of management is an exogenous factor that can be changed to demonstrate its effect on the operations of the club. An improvement in the quality of management is introduced in the second year of the simulation of the club's operations to model the effects of a new club management.

All the above mentioned influences will be acting simultaneously and continuously, so that it is not intuitively obvious how the system will behave. A computer simulation version of the model was built to explore its dynamic behavior.

EXPERIMENTS WITH THE MODEL

The corporate system model was programmed in the Dynamo simulation language.[16,17] Dynamo has been specifically designed for this kind of application and offers some significant advantages over other high level languages (see, for example, 6, p. 186).

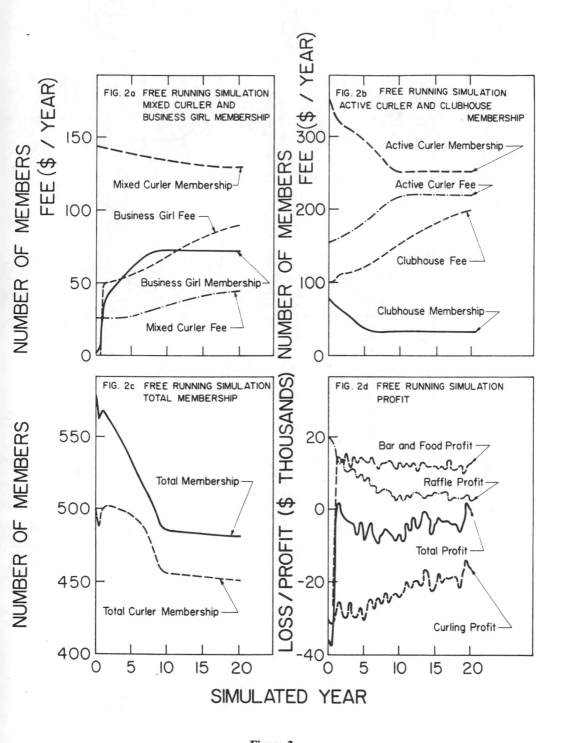

Figure 2.

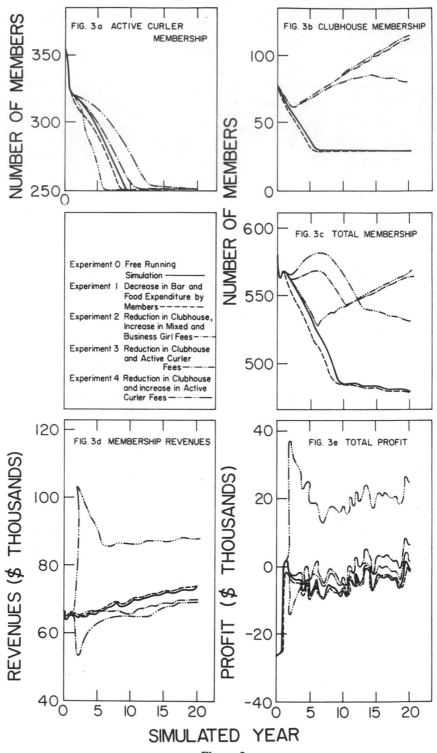

FIG. 3a ACTIVE CURLER MEMBERSHIP

FIG. 3b CLUBHOUSE MEMBERSHIP

FIG. 3c TOTAL MEMBERSHIP

FIG. 3d MEMBERSHIP REVENUES

FIG. 3e TOTAL PROFIT

Experiment 0 Free Running Simulation ———
Experiment 1 Decrease in Bar and Food Expenditure by Members – – – – –
Experiment 2 Reduction in Clubhouse, Increase in Mixed and Business Girl Fees –·–·–
Experiment 3 Reduction in Clubhouse and Active Curler Fees –··–··–
Experiment 4 Reduction in Clubhouse and increase in Active Curler Fees –···–···–

NUMBER OF MEMBERS

NUMBER OF MEMBERS

REVENUES ($ THOUSANDS)

PROFIT ($ THOUSANDS)

SIMULATED YEAR

Figure 3.

The procedures detailed by Forrester[4] and Coyle[3] were followed in transforming the influence diagram into a Dynamo computer simulation program representing the operations of the club. First, the behavior of the model, which incorporated performance improvements stemming from the new club management, was simulated for a twenty year period. Second, the response of the system to a contemplated uncontrollable external shock was tested. Lastly, three experiments with various suggested changes in membership fees were carried out.

The Free-running Experiment

Figure 2 exhibits the time-series plots of the major variables of the system. The first plot (Figure 2a) shows the growth of the Business Girl membership to its upper limit fairly rapidly. At the same time, the Mixed curler membership exhibits a marginally decreasing level of curlers. These results are what one would expect; Business Girl curling has become very popular in recent years, and Mixed curling membership has levelled out.

The second plot (Figure 2b) of the Clubhouse membership and the Active curler membership tells a different story, however. Each membership level exhibits a rapid deterioration to its lower limit of core members. This downward trend in members reverberates throughout the whole club and eventually results in a decline in the total membership (Figure 2c).

The system works in the following manner. Because the Active curlers and Clubhouse members form a large proportion of total membership, the downward trend in the levels of these two groups causes a general decline in total membership and membership revenue. The decrease in membership also causes a decrease in the utilization of the bar and food service, and the total bar and food profit falls. In addition, the decreasing membership results in a decreasing sale of raffle tickets, and the raffle profit declines. Because the demand for rental ice is relatively fixed in the city, the club realizes only a marginal increase in ice rental revenue from outside organizations. The net effect is that the club must use a decreasing revenue to cover a constant or only slowly decreasing level of operating costs. To cover the deficit, the management increases the membership fees (Figures 2a and 2b). Although this increases membership revenue and total revenue, it causes additional members to cancel their memberships. A further decrease in membership level results in the cycle repeating itself until the minimum core membership level is reached.

Eventually, membership fees are raised to a level where a profit can be realized. The cost of such a process, however, is an exclusive club; only a relatively small number of members remain who are wealthy enough to pay a large membership fee to ensure the operation of the club. It suggests that the improvements already enacted by the new management, within the assumptions of the model, alone are not going to turn the club around. These results provide the bench mark against which to compare other experiments with the model.

Experiment 1—A Decrease in Bar and Food Expenditure per Member

The results of this and subsequent experiments are shown in the comparative time plots of Figure 3, to facilitate comparison with the Free-running simulation.

The first experiment illustrates the effect of an uncontrollable external shock to the system. It simulates a decrease in the average bar and food expenditure per member for one season. These figures represent the impact of a threatened strike of Liquor Commission workers, that would effectively cut off the supply of alcoholic beverages, on the operation of the club. The initial impact is the reduction of the bar and food profit during the first year. This creates a slightly larger deficit for the first year than was evident during the free-running simulation (Figure 3e). The larger loss causes a larger increase in fees, thereby resulting in additional members cancelling their memberships. The increased cancellation rate accelerates the membership decline, such that the minimum Active curler and Clubhouse memberships are attained one year earlier than under the free-running model (Figures 3a and 3b). It requires about five years for the total profit to recover to its former level (Figure 3e). Unfortunately for the club, the anticipated strike took place, adding a further burden to the club's problems. The experiment, however, illustrates the importance of profitable food and bar operations to the club's viability.

Experiment 2—A Reduction in Fees for Clubhouse Members and an Increase for Mixed and Business Girl Members

The club's problems, as we have seen, stem from a decline in Active curlers and Clubhouse members. The increases in Mixed curlers and Business Girl curlers are not sufficient to offset this decline. Since the Clubhouse members do not use the expensive-to-maintain sheets of ice used for the game of Curling, it would seem reasonable to reduce their fees. To compensate, the fees of the popular categories of Mixed curlers and Business Girls could be raised.

Hence, the second experiment simulated a $50 reduction in the Clubhouse member fee, a $10 increase in the Mixed curler fee, and a $25 increase in the Business Girl fee for year 2. It should be noted that these changes are in addition to those automatically implemented by the built-in fee setting sector in the model which tries to correct deficits.

The most dramatic effect of this experiment is turnaround in Clubhouse membership (Figure 3b). Although the Clubhouse member fee reduction causes a lower total membership revenue (Figure 3d), over the long term this is more than offset by growth in bar, food and raffle profits. The resulting improved profit situation (Figure 3e) actually reduces the rate of escalation of fees. This results in a reduction of the Active curler cancellation rate and a slower decline in this category of membership (Figure 3a).

This appears to be a strategy the club might follow. A reduction in the Clubhouse membership fee could regain a number of valuable Clubhouse members. An increase in the Mixed curler and Business Girl fees should take advantage of the higher demand evident for these categories. In addition, such a decision would partially cover the lost membership revenue due to the reduction in the Clubhouse member fee. Only the Active curler membership decline remains a problem (Figure 3a).

Experiment 3—A Reduction in Fees for Clubhouse and Active Curling Members

The third experiment similarly simulated a $50 reduction in the Clubhouse member fee. A $30 reduction in the Active curler fee was added to see if it would reverse the Active curler membership decline. As before, these changes are in addition to those implemented by the fee setting sector in the model.

Although the Clubhouse membership decline was reversed by this fee schedule, it did not grow as rapidly as was evidenced in the second experiment. This is because the Active curler fee reduction only slowed (not reversed) the decline of the Active curler who comprise the majority of members. As a result, membership revenue is reduced quite substantially, when compared to the free-running model (Figure 3d). Although bar and food profit performance and raffle profit performance compare favourably to those of the free-running model, total profit performance is worse (Figure 3e). Thus, it appears excessively costly to maintain the Active curler membership through fee reduction to be subsidised by the other club members.

Experiment 4—Reduction in Fees for Clubhouse and Increase for Active Curling Members

A number of board members of the Great Glen felt that the Active curler fee should be increased dramatically to ensure the successful operation of the club. This experiment simulated the effect of a $50 reduction in the Clubhouse members fee and a $130 increase in the Active curler fee for year 2, over and above normal increases.

The results are quite dramatic. Clubhouse membership exhibited a growth pattern identical to that illustrated in the second experiment (Figure 3b). Active curler membership, however, declines very rapidly until the minimum number of core members is attained (Figure 3a). Because the Active curler fee is so high, membership revenue and, hence, total profits soar (Figure 3e). The result is an exclusive club. The only difference between this experiment and the one determined by the free-running model, is that the exclusive club is achieved at a faster rate and by intent. In addition, the Active curlers subsidise the Clubhouse membership in such a situation. Clearly, the objective of operating a curling club for Active curlers is not met by this policy.

IMPLICATIONS OF THE RESULTS

Searching for a Policy

At the time of the study, the club was caught in a downward membership spiral. As has been demonstrated, a decline in membership reduces three major sources of revenue: bar and food profits, raffle profits, and membership revenue. The ice rental market was not large enough to cover the revenue losses from membership reductions. Traditionally, the management of the club has responded by increasing membership fees. Unfortunately, this has had a further debilitating effect on membership.

The experiments with the model strongly suggest that the normal process of increasing fees to cover deficits is leading, at the best to an exclusive club, or at the worst to the collapse of the club (Experiments 1 and 4). On the other hand, reducing membership fees indicates a beneficial effect on Clubhouse membership. It does nothing, however, other than slow the inevitable decline of Active curlers (Experiments 2 and 3). Increases in food and bar profits can counter the need to increase fees and, conversely, decreases can accelerate fee increases and membership decline (Experiment 1).

Clearly, manipulating membership fees alone is not going to reverse the downward spiral of events. Something more positive needs to be done to attack the cancellation rate of members. The members' perceptions of the quality of the club's services vis-à-vis fees needs to be changed in some way. Promoting the food and bar services offers a means of boosting profits and holding down fee increases.

CONCLUSIONS

The Role of System Simulation in a Crisis

The results of the simulation experiments should be viewed in the context of the controversies that raged between various factions (the old and the new guard) about the future orientation of the club, the lack of data about membership upon which to make a sensible analysis and the pressure of events (the liquor strike and mounting deficit). At one stage, closing the club was seriously considered.

Clubs, like other organizations, develop over time an internal culture that provides, to some extent, the guiding set of principles on which decisions are based. The phenomenon has been described by Roberts[19] as:

> The current structure of an organization, its incentive system, and the beliefs and values of its personnel will all reflect its responses to past problems. Hence, an organization's immediate response to current problems, as well as its subsequent reactions if those initial efforts should prove unsuccessful, will tend to reflect its past history and development p. 418).

Similarly, Miller and Friesen[12] have described the effects of continuity and momentum on organizational adaption as:

> In fact the conscious elements of the old strategy and structure are those most likely to be viewed as the causes of past and future success and will be extended . . . The less explicit elements are not included in the manager's model of reality and therefore are not tracked even though they may be flagging a crucial need for reorientation (p. 604).

As has been mentioned, the traditional response of the executive of the club to a deficit was to raise fees—something that had worked well in the past when the sport of Curling was more popular. This very human process for selecting policies stands in stark contrast to the 'refutationist' tradition of science mentioned previously. It seems that organizational members never challenge their beliefs, or policies based on these beliefs, until forced to by such events as a crisis that threatens the survival of the organization. It has been suggested that a potentially important role for simulation studies of organizations might be to startle the management into examining their beliefs and policies before the onset of a real crisis from which the organization may not recover[8].

Turner[23] has noted the stages in the development of an organizational crisis from an incubation period where symptoms of the impending disaster pass unnoticed to the salvage operation to rescue the organization. The organization usually undergoes some sort of cultural revolution where there is an internal upheaval, a new top team takes over, and the organization heads off in a new direction. During the time of the study, the club went through just such an upheaval.

Weick[24] has suggested that the selection and retention processes of organizational adaptation are driven by the need to reduce equivocality and not necessarily to optimize *per se*. In a crisis situation, the procedures for reducing equivocality tend to become political—the dominant group prescribes a policy most in line with its interests.[9,13]

The lack of attention to both complexity and novel alternatives in the deliberations of an organization during a threat have been noted by Staw, Sanderlands and Dutton[21]:

> . . . search for information may change as a threat develops, from an initial flurry when a threat is recognized, to a low point as channels become overloaded, and on to a second peak as decisions are confirmed or implemented. However, throughout these changes in information search, the number of genuinely new or novel alternatives considered by the organization may still be relatively low. Even when search is increased, information received is likely to be similar to that of the past, due to heavy reliance on standard operating procedures, previous ways of understanding, or communication that is low in complexity . . . (p. 513).

Alternatively, crude and emotive arguments based on simplistic assumptions hold sway and complexity and uncertainty are assumed away.[22] The chance of selecting an inappropriate policy is obviously increased by such primitive group processes. As Pettigrew[14] puts it:

> For organizations as for groups and individuals, extreme situations provide the opportunity for learning which will only be taken up if the participants have the capacity to unravel what has been experienced from what has been learnt, and the motivation to do the after-the-fact reflection and analysis which will entangle the noise of the experience from the message of learning (p. 7).

System modeling can be invaluable in a crisis situation (particularly when survival is at stake) by reducing the equivocality surrounding the problem (an essential step in coping) yet aiding in the construction of a rich map of the policy terrain with which to search for a safe passage. It becomes a part of the organizational process for learning to cope with an uncertain and threatening situation. Using a system model in this way as an organizational intervention tool would seem to provide a fruitful field for future action research and a potentially important extension of Management Science in Organizational Behavior issues.

Epilogue—What Happened

The system modeling approach was used to help clarify the issues and unravel the noise of the experience from its message for members of the organization. A presentation of the model and its simulation results was made to members of the Board of Directors during the period of the crisis. They were then in a better position to understand in which direction the organization was drifting unassisted and why. If the members wanted an exclusive club as a *fait accompli*, then nothing needed to be changed. But if this was not acceptable to the majority (which it was not, as it transpired), then some positive action would be required to redirect it. The members, however, had to determine this value-laden issue for themselves by the due process within the rules governing the club— the model merely facilitated the process.

The newly elected executive of the club attacked the cancellation rate problem through the use of special membership newsletters, social evenings and other devices aimed at altering members' image of their club and perceptions of the services available relative to fees charged. An active recruitment of new members was also undertaken. The Clubhouse membership fee was lowered but all other fees remained unchanged. New clubhouse and ice managers with reputations for excellence were hired to improve the quality image of the club's services. The restaurant and bar were actively promoted for members dining downtown when attending evening entertainments and social engagements.

Table 1. Club Membership Figures

Category of Membership	1st Year Following the Crisis	2nd Year Following the Crisis	Change
Active Curlers	356	349	−7
Mixed Curlers	144	136	−8
Business Girl	72	72	0
Clubhouse	80	118	+38
Total	652	675	+23

Table 2. Report Net Income of the Club

	The Crisis Year	One Year Later	Two Years Later
Reported Net Income (Loss)	$(25 000)	$1200	$19 200

Selected membership and financial summaries for the years following the crisis are shown in Tables 1 and 2. It can be seen that the total membership has improved, although loss of Active curlers is still a problem. The financial situation on the other hand shows a dramatic improvement.

As a final note, the original detailed report of this study is now required reading for all new members of the Board of Directors of the club—an indication of its perceived importance in helping the club survive.[2]

[2]The preparation of the study for publication was supported by a research grant from the Social Sciences and Humanities Research Council of Canada.

REFERENCES

1. AXELROD, ROBERT, *Structure of Decision*, Princeton Univ. Press, Princeton, N.J., 1976.
2. BELL, J. A. AND SENGE, PETER M., 'Methods for Enhancing Refutability in System Dynamics Modelling' in A. A. Legasto, Jr., J. W. Forrester and J. M. Lyneis (eds.), *TIMS Studies in the Management Sciences: System Dynamics*, Vol. 14, North-Holland, New York, 1980, pp. 67–73.
3. COYLE, R. G., *Management System Dynamics*, Wiley, London, 1977.
4. FORRESTER, JAY W., *Principles of Systems*, Wright-Allen Press, Cambridge, Mass., 1968.
5. ____ AND SENGE, PETER M., 'Tests for Building Confidence in System Dynamics Models' in A. A. Legasto, Jr., J. W. Forrester and J. M. Lyneis (eds.), *TIMS Studies in the Management Sciences: System Dynamics*, Vol. 14, North-Holland, New York, 1980, pp. 209–228.
6. HALL, ROGER I., 'A System Pathology of an Organization: The Rise and Fall of the Old Saturday Evening Post,' *Admin. Sci. Quart.*, Vol. 21 (1976), pp. 185–211.
7. ____, 'Simple Techniques for Constructing Explanatory Models of Complex Systems for Policy Analysis,' *Dynamica*, Vol. 4 (1978), pp. 101–114.
8. ____, 'Simulating a Crisis,' in Highland, Spiegel and Shannon (eds.), *1979 Winter Simulation Conference*, IEEE, New York, 1979, pp. 195–203.
9. ____, 'Decision Making in a Complex Organization' in England, G. W., A. Neghandi and B. Wilpert (eds.), *The Functioning of Complex Organizations*, Oelgeschlager, Gunn and Hain, Cambridge, Mass., 1981, Ch. 5, pp. 111–144.
10. MEIER, R. C., NEWELL, W. T. AND PAZER, H. L., *Simulation in Business and Economics*, Prentice-Hall, Englewood Cliffs, N.J., 1969.

11. MILLER, DANNY AND FRIESEN, PETER H., 'The Longitudinal Analysis of Organizations: A Methodological Perspective,' *Management Science*, Vol. 28 (1981), pp. 1013–1034.
12. ____ AND ____, 'Momentum and Revolution in Organizational Adaption,' *Acad. Management J.*, Vol. 23 (1980), pp. 591–614.
13. PETTIGREW, ANDREW M., *The Politics of Organizational Decision Making*, Tavistock Press, London, 1973.
14. ____, 'Learning from Extreme Situations,' International Institute for Advanced Studies in Management, Brussels, Working Paper 74–33, 1974.
15. POPPER, K. R., *The Logic of Scientific Discovery*, Basic Books, New York, 1959.
16. PUGH, ALEXANDER L. III. *Dynamo II User's Manual*, M.I.T. Press, Cambridge, Mass., 1970.
17. RATNATUNGA, A. K. AND STEWART, C. J., *Dysmap User's Manual*, University of Bradford, Bradford, 1977.
18. ROBERTS, FRED S., 'Strategy for the Energy Crisis: the case for commuter transport policy,' in Axelrod *op. cit.*, pp. 142–179.
19. ROBERTS, MARC J., 'An Evolutionary and Institutional View of the Behavior of Public and Private Companies,' *Amer. Econom. Rev.*, Vol. 62 (1975), pp. 415–426.
20. SCHRIEBER, A. N., *Corporate Simulation Models*, Univ. of Washington, Seattle, Wash., 1970.
21. STAW, BARRY M., SANDELANDS, LANCE E., AND DUTTON, JANE E., 'Threat-Rigidity Effects in Organizational Behavior: a multilevel analysis,' *Admin. Sci. Quart.*, Vol. 26 (1981), pp. 501–524.
22. STEINBRUNNER, J. D., *The Cybernetic Theory of Decision*, Princeton Univ. Press, Princeton, N.J., 1974.
23. TURNER, BARRY A., 'The Organizational and Interorganizational Development of Disasters,' *Admin. Sci. Quart.*, Vol. 21 (1976), pp. 378–397.
24. WEICK, KARL E., *The Social Psychology of Organizing*, Addison-Wesley, Reading, Mass., 1969.

Chapter 13

Strategy Support Models

John D. W. Morecroft

*Sloan School of Management, Massachusetts Institute of Technology,
Cambridge, Massachusetts, USA*

SUMMARY

A major challenge in strategy development is to deduce the consequences of the interacting programmes underlying strategy. The paper argues that behavioural simulation models can help meet this challenge by acting out the consequences of strategy proposals in their full organizational setting. However, the real key to effective strategy support is not simply having a model, but using it in a structured dialogue with executives. To illustrate the idea, the paper presents a system dynamics simulation model used to aid executives of an advanced office equipment firm in setting their marketing strategy. The paper describes the process by which the model was created and brought to the attention of executives. Several examples are provided of the dialectical use of the model, showing how differences in management intuition and model-generated opinion led to improved insight into the consequences of strategy.

INTRODUCTION

The Concept of Support

Over the past decade considerable attention has been given to advanced computational aids used in support, rather than replacement, of managerial judgement. Here, computational aid includes not only rapidly advancing computer hardware but also the algorithms and numerical methods that have become feasible with the existence of the hardware. Underlying the concept of management support is the recognition that the human mind is itself a very powerful, flexible, and agile problem-solving and decision-making 'machine' and should remain an integral part of the decision-making process. The key to support is to identify the activities in which our built-in, flesh-and-blood

---

Reprinted from *Strategic Management Journal*, Volume 5, pp. 215–229 (1984). © 1984 John Wiley & Sons Ltd.

computers are weakest and remedy the weakness with our new, chip-and-board computers.

The field of management information systems has clearly identified one weakness of our flesh-and-blood computers—their ability to collect and process information. Decision support systems (Keen and Scott-Morton, 1978) come to the rescue by massaging business information, making it more compact, easy to access and absorb so that managers can be better informed and therefore, presumably, better able to make decisions.

This paper extends the notion of support to strategy support, in which a man/machine combination is used to provide more effective assessment of strategic proposals.[1] But what kind of support can be usefully brought to bear on highly unstructured strategy questions? Here we suggest that management intuition and experience must serve as the primary architects of strategy, to bring form and substance to otherwise unstructured issues. The initiative for defining alternative markets to be served, resources to be deployed, organizational responsibilities, and allocation of budgets must lie with senior management. Strategy support can be provided by a tool that provides sharper insights into the *consequences* of pursuing strategy proposals once formulated.

Figure 1 illustrates the analogy between decision and strategy support. The figure shows both the human and machine components of decision making and strategy development. The decision-making process is depicted as being strongly supported by natural human ability to formulate, articulate, and communicate a decision. However, it is much less strongly supported by the ability of the human mind to collect and process information (Simon, 1971). A decision-support system provides reinforcement by storing relevant information, reworking and condensing it, indexing it and providing easy access. By analogy, the strategy development process is depicted as being supported by natural managerial ability to formulate strategy, to set a course for the corporation, and create the administrative structure necessary to implement strategy. But it is much less strongly supported by the ability of the human mind to deduce the consequences of the strategy (Cyert, Simon and Trow, 1956). A strategy support tool should reveal flaws and inconsistencies in proposals that might not otherwise come to light until the proposals are implemented and under way.

Strategy Support, the Dialectic Method and the Role of Models

A common approach to the evaluation of strategy in business and government institutions is argument and debate. From this method we can learn much about the way a strategy support tool should interact with executives. If the consequences of a given proposal are difficult to assess, it is certain there will be widely differing opinions on the outcome. Debating these opinions in a meeting will force people to scrutinize and justify their reasoning and will provide clearer insight into the viability of the proposal. This process may be usefully summarized as the dialectic method, defined in *Webster's Twentieth Century Dictionary* as

The art or practice of examining opinions or ideas logically, often by the method of question and answer, so as to determine their validity.

---

1. The term strategy support was coined by my colleague Dr. Alan K. Graham of the M.I.T. System Dynamics Group.

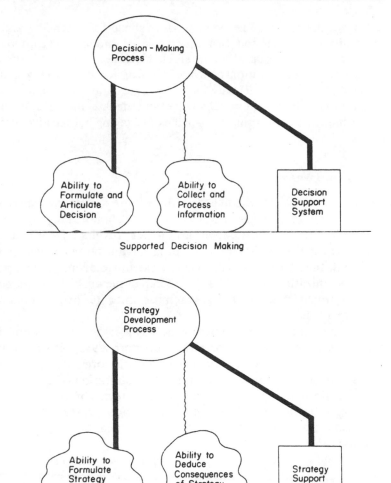

Figure 1. The analogy between decision support and strategy support

Successful formalizations of the approach have been described by Mason (1969) and Mitroff and Emshoff (1979) for corporate planning, and by Schon (1983) for urban planning.[2]

A most natural extension of the dialectic method is the introduction of a formal model into the discussion with which to temper the prevailing opinions. In the standard dialectic method, debate and discussion draw on opinion from the 'mental models' of a management team. A formal model merely adds another viewpoint, which, though perhaps more carefully formulated, is nevertheless an opinion.

_____

2. Some recent theoretical advances in the formal analysis of the logic of policy are described by Mitroff, Mason and Barabba (1982).

To be effective, the model must be seen as a vehicle for extending argument and debate—quite different from the customary role of models. The model must be brought down from the pedestal of the infallible black box (where it is often ignored) to occupy a more modest position as a complement to the thinking and deducing powers of management. The model must be seen as a generator of opinions, not answers. Executives must be encouraged to challenge and debate model conclusions, and members of the modelling team must be capable of engaging in executive, non-technical argument.

The Use of System Dynamics

The remainder of this paper will illustrate the use of system dynamics simulation modelling (Forrester, 1961; Lyneis, 1980) as a strategy support tool. System dynamics is an appropriate tool for a number of reasons. First, it provides effective graphic display methods for illustrating the policy structure of an organization. A management team can easily relate to these graphics. They can see the range of interlinked policies that constitute their organization. They can see the complex network of communication and control through which strategic initiatives must filter to bring about change in organizational performance.

A system dynamics model is descriptive of the way a company functions; it does not contain idealized decision-making processes (Morecroft, 1983). It shows the division of responsibilities, the goal and reward structure of the organization, as well as the inconsistencies of policy that are a part of any real organization (Hall, 1976). It reveals the limitations on information flow that can produce distorted or even conflicting images of performance at different parts of the organization. Together, these descriptive features of the model lend a realism necessary to good communication as the model comes to be used in a discussion.

The simulation analysis methods of system dynamics are very effective in argument and debate. Simulation can be used to create clear strategy scenarios to challenge the collective intuition of a management team. Simulation runs create time charts of important business variables that bring to life the consequences of policy change and bring discipline to the subsequent discussion (Probert, 1982).

CREATING A STRATEGY SUPPORT MODEL—AN EXAMPLE

A strategy support model is intended to influence executive opinion in a company. To do this it must be aimed at a problem that engages the executives' attention, it must have political support within the organization, and its structure and insights must be widely communicated (Roberts, 1977).

In this section we will use a case study to illustrate how a strategy support model is created. The example is based on the analysis of marketing strategy for a supplier of advanced office equipment.[3] To retain anonymity the company is referred to as Datacom Corporation.

---

3. For a more detailed account of the case study and subsequent policy analysis, see Morecroft (1982).

Starting the Project

At the start of the modelling project a small project team was assembled that included a senior and a junior manager, an M.I.T. consultant, and several staff analysts. The managers involved in the project both had some prior exposure to system dynamics modelling.

Preliminary discussions between the managers and consultant revealed that Datacom was faced with an important strategic problem, common in high-technology industries, of managing a market conversion from a base of old-technology equipment to a new generation of more advanced equipment. This issue certainly had executive attention. The company had experienced loss of market share during the early stages of the transition. There was uncertainty over how rapidly the conversion should take place and over the combination of sales efforts and price incentives that would be most effective at bringing about the conversion. The modelling project was, therefore, addressed to this problem.

The next step was to sketch a conceptual model showing key elements of the existing decision-making structure of the market and the sales organization. In the market, we wanted to understand what induces customers to switch from old- to new-technology equipment and how they make the choice between equipment offered by Datacom and the competition. In the sales organization, we wanted to look at factors affecting selling effort and its allocation to different activities in the market. At an early stage we ruled out the need to consider factors such as product development, production, and delivery. The new-technology equipment was already developed, and there was adequate capacity to meet projected market needs.

Round-table meetings were held by the project team and subject area experts. On the table we had our sketch of the decision-making processes in the market and sales organization. We discussed how these processes worked and how they are linked, using the descriptive knowledge of company participants and the structuring principles of system dynamics.

The diagram served as the focal point for meetings. It was very useful as a communication tool to management and staff, pointing out internal linkages between company programmes and procedures, and external linkages to the market. There were frequent revisions to the diagram as our understanding of the system improved. The diagram also served to generate a feeling of involvement and commitment in the project by the numerous people who contributed to its construction, thereby aiding the communication process. Finally, the diagram served as a valuable interface between the formal mathematical model ultimately developed, and the mental models of the various project participants.

Policy Structure of the Market

Figure 2 shows the conceptual model of the market that was arrived at in meetings with the project team and subject area experts from the sales force and marketing staff. Notice first the heavy black lines showing the installed base of systems. The installed base is divided into three categories shown as system levels. At the top of Figure 2 there are old systems, all of which have been sold by Datacom and reflect the company's strong initial market position. As time goes by, old systems are upgraded until, eventually,

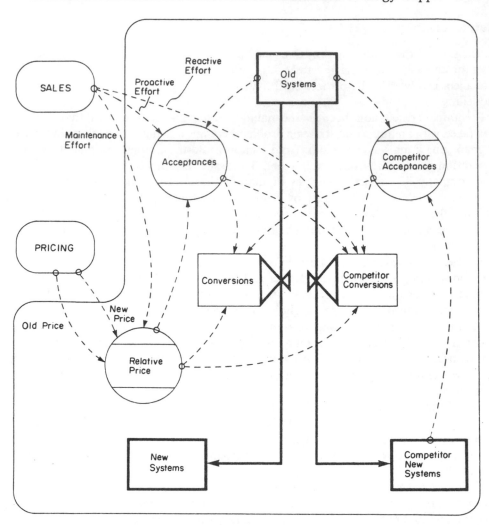

Figure 2. Policy structure of the market

all have been converted either to new Datacom or new competitor systems. Ownership of the installed base is, therefore, gradually redistributed between Datacom and the competition. Notice that in this particular market (uncharacteristic of many high-technology markets) the size of the total installed base is fixed. All business customers who need the equipment offered by Datacom already have it, at least in its old-technology form. Thus, the only way to sell new equipment is to exchange it for old. Finally, the reader should also note that Datacom leases much of its equipment to the market. Sales revenues are, therefore, generated both by the base of installed systems (old and new) and by the conversion from old to new systems.

The remainder of Figure 2 shows how a customer decided to convert. By talking with members of the sales force, we learned that the first step is simply one of making the customer aware of the new technology. Customers must be contacted, talked to, and convinced that the switch to new technology is worth while. In Figure 2 this process is called acceptance. The number of acceptances depends primarily on proactive sales effort, where the sales force takes the initiative in contacting the customer. Acceptances depend also on price. If old prices are low in relation to new-equipment prices, acceptance will be less likely. Acceptances further depend on the number of old systems that remain to be converted. As the base of old systems is depleted, there are fewer and fewer customers to contact, until only the diehards are left.

Customers convert to new systems only after they have accepted the usefulness of new technology. Figure 2, therefore, shows conversions dependent on acceptances. Interestingly, Datacom conversions depend not only on acceptances generated by Datacom sales effort, but also to some degree on acceptances generated by competitor sales effort. Customers who are aware of the new-technology option may choose to obtain their equipment from any of the system vendors in the market. Some cross-talk between competitor sales effort and Datacom, and vice versa conversions is, therefore, a natural and very important feature of the market. The degree of cross-talk depends on the relative price of Datacom and competitor systems. If Datacom prices rise in relation to competitor prices, the company wins fewer conversions, and a correspondingly greater number go to the competition.

Discussions with the sales force indicated that relative price should be viewed as a rather subtle decision-making process in its own right. Price perception in the office-equipment market is quite complex. There are lease and purchase options to consider. There are price/performance characteristics to judge. There are new, old, and competitive prices to consider. The customer does not make price judgements in a highly objective way but is swayed by general sales effort (labelled maintenance effort in Figure 2), by price reputation, and by other subjective factors. Figure 2 captures these intangibles in price perception by showing that old and new prices first pass through a decision-making process labelled relative price before they affect acceptance or conversion.

Competition is treated in a simplified way that focuses on the growth capability of competitive firms as a whole. Competitor acceptances depend, in the aggregate, on the installed base of competitor systems. In general, the more installed systems there are, the greater the revenue base and the greater the competition's ability to support marketing effort. Competitor conversions depend on competitor *and* Datacom acceptances modified by relative price and Datacom's reactive sales effort. If competitor prices are relatively low, competitor share of conversions will be high. Such price advantages can be counteracted to some extent by Datacom's reactive sales effort. Datacom knows about competitor attempts to win customers and can respond by putting in sales time to lure customers away from the competition.

Policy Structure of the Sales Organization

The conceptual model of the sales organization focuses on policies that can affect sales capability and its allocation among three principal market activities: proactive sales effort, reactive sales effort, and market maintenance. Figure 3 shows the structure that emerged from round-table discussions between the project team and subject area experts from the sales force and the market planning area.

The size of the sales force is a key determinant of overall sales capability. The sales force, which is shown by heavy black lines at the top of the figure, is increased through hiring and decreased through quits. Hiring adjusts the sales force to an authorized level,

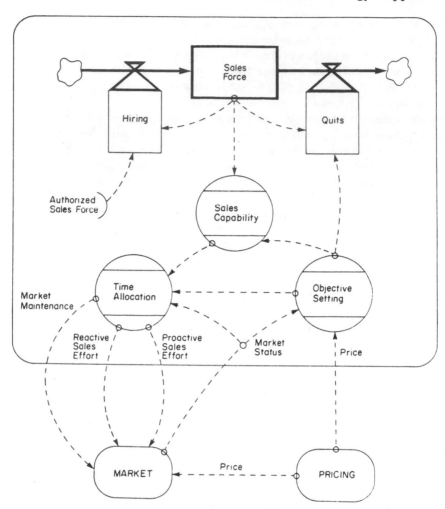

Figure 3. Policy structure of the sales organization

which can be varied experimentally in the formal model. Sales capability is also affected by overtime and by the motivation of the sales force, which in turn depend on sales objectives. By raising objectives, overtime and sales capability may be increased. But sustained periods of high overtime or poor performance that result from overly ambitious sales objectives can lower motivation and ultimately lower the capability of the sales organization. Our conceptual model shows this fluid, variable nature of the output of the sales force.

Sales capability is a measure of the total effective effort that the sales organization can bring to bear on the market. This total effort is allocated among different marketing activities according to the time-allocation policy of the individual salesmen. Discussion with salesmen revealed that there is a natural hierarchy in the allocation of time. The highest priority goes to reactive sales efforts, the process of responding to competitor attempts to win Datacom customers. The rest of the time is split between proactive sales effort, the process of converting existing old-technology customers, and general market maintenance. Second highest priority goes to proactive effort, unless the product sales objective has been completely satisfied.

This allocation of time is probably not optimal in an economic sense, but it is a very natural and powerful hierarchy from the salesman's viewpoint within the sales incentive system. Reactive sales effort gets high priority because a competitive loss is a direct threat to revenue and a very visible form of loss. By contrast, proactive effort, which is highly effective at bringing about conversion, gets lower priority, because a reduction in proactive effort will result in a loss of opportunity, not a highly visible competitive loss. Market maintenance, the process of keeping in touch with the entire customer base, naturally receives lowest priority, since it produces the least tangible pay-off in terms of revenue or sales.

The final policy shown in Figure 3 is the setting of objectives. The sales organization is motivated through objectives for revenue and for product sales. In reality, these objectives are quite difficult to set. There are many customers, a variety of products and different types of price contracts. Consequently, objectives tend to depend strongly on historical performance. The current year's objectives are set by looking at last year's objectives and negotiating a 'stretch' or challenge that is intended to sustain high productivity. Setting objectives by negotiation around an historical standard is a natural and effective way to deal with the complexity that underlies sales performance.

USE OF THE STRATEGY SUPPORT MODEL

Once a formal simulation model has been created, it is then the responsibility of the project team to ensure that model-generated opinion gains the attention of the executives involved in formulating and implementing strategy.

In the Datacom case the senior manager in the project team was aware of the issues being debated in the market conversion strategy and of the key executives who should be influenced. He played a very important liaison role, arranging meetings, sounding out executive response and generally creating an environment where model-based opinion would be taken seriously. The liaison role must be filled by a person who has political insight, the respect of colleagues and higher-level executives, and a high level of comfort with modelling methods.

The project team should arrange meetings in which the model is used for debate and argument, in order to challenge the preconceptions of management. This dialectic use of the model is at the heart of strategy support, but does not happen automatically. It is essential that model runs be organized around clear scenarios, that executives be encouraged to challenge and debate model conclusions, and that members of the project team be capable of engaging in executive, non-technical argument. With these conditions satisfied, it is possible for both executives and modellers to clarify their understanding of the consequences of strategy.

Steps in the Dialectic

Figure 4 illustrates the use of a model as practised at Datacom for six high-level meetings. The first step is to select a proposal that is already under active discussion in the company. The former model is then run and analysed to render an opinion on the consequences

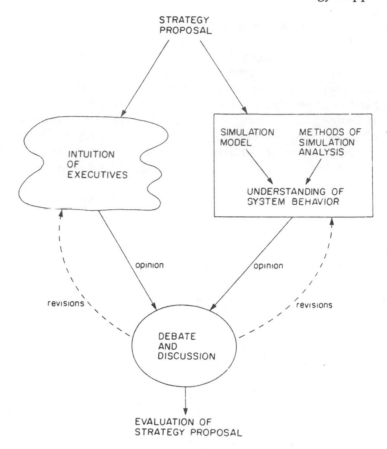

Figure 4. Using a system dynamics model to evaluate strategy proposals

of the proposal. This kind of analysis should not be done at the meeting, but rather beforehand, when there is adequate time to diagnose and understand the simulation runs. It is essential to develop a clear intuitive explanation for simulation runs, and this always takes time.

In the next step managerial opinion and model opinion are brought together in debate and discussion. Meetings can last as long as 2 or 3 hours. Modellers should be expected to provide a clear explanation of why the model behaves as it does and why it differs from executive expectation (if it does). Executives should feel free to point out when their intuitive opinion on the proposal differs from model-generated opinion. The explanation of differences will lead to revisions and clarifications in both executive intuition and the formal model that will ultimately improve the evaluation of the strategy proposal. The central role of the model, then, is to clarify the consequences of the proposal and to anticipate surprises. As Mass (1981) has pointed out:

> Some of the most important insights into real system behavior can arise from model results that at first appear to be at odds with knowledge of the real system, but which in fact suggest important new interpretations of perceived facts.

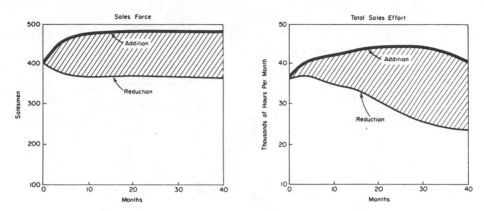

Figure 5. Force size and sales effort

THE PROCESS IN ACTION—INSIGHTS FROM THE MODEL

The conceptual model described above was translated into a formal simulation model using the DYNAMO simulation language. It took 4 months to assemble and test a first model worthy of executive attention. The model was then used for about 8 months, first to examine the effectiveness of force additions in the market conversion strategy, then later to explore pricing policy. It is interesting to note that, during the 8 months of model use, time spent on the project was about equally divided between model development and the elucidation and communication of results.

To illustrate the use of the model, we will concentrate on the evaluation of the proposal to change sales force size. We compare two alternatives: a 20 per cent force addition versus a 10 per cent force reduction. What would the market and financial consequences be of pursuing the conversion strategy under these alternative scenarios? The formal model was run for 40 months, and it showed a number of controversial outcomes that became a focus of discussion in meetings with executives. We will review some of these outcomes to show how they contributed to understanding and consensus on the proposal. (Note that numerical values in the simulation runs have been modified for the sake of confidentiality. For the same reason, no financial results are shown, although the model did include a full set of accounting equations.)

Sales Force Reductions Lower Sales Productivity

The left half of Figure 5 shows the alternative sales force scenarios. The right half of Figure 5 shows the corresponding behaviour of total sales effort, which is measured in thousands of hours per month and includes the effect of both overtime and sales force motivation. A comparison of the two simulation runs clearly shows that total sales effort is not perfectly correlated with the number of salesmen. During the first 6 months of the reduction scenario, sales force falls, but total sales effort actually increases slightly and only then begins to fall. After month six in the same scenario, sales force remains constant, but total sales effort continues to fall. Comparison of the shaded areas in the two runs shows that the force reduction causes a loss of sales effort that is much

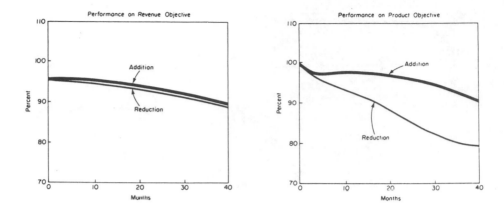

Figure 6. Performance against product and revenue objectives

greater than can be accounted for by the smaller number of salesmen. In other words, force reductions cause the productivity of individual salesmen to fall, whereas additions sustain high sales productivity. This result ran counter to the opinion of some members of management and, therefore, demanded further explanation.

The model suggested that the behaviour of sales productivity could be explained in terms of sales force motivation, which was in turn related to the performance of the sales force against sales objectives. To illustrate this point we examined a simulation run of performance against product and revenue objectives, as shown in Figure 6. Under both scenarios performance against revenue falls as the size of the revenue-generating base is eroded by competition. Erosion makes it progressively more difficult to repeat the revenue performance achieved in the past, thereby creating the potential for demotivation and lowered productivity. Force reductions exacerbate the motivation problems. Not only is it difficult to attain revenue objective but also product objective. Poor performance on both measures leads to a decline in motivation, a decline in sales effort, and a further deterioration in performance. By contrast, force additions relieve the danger of becoming trapped in this downward spiral by making it easier to attain the product objective.[4]

Sales Force Additions Encourage the Growth of Competition

This result was particularly surprising to management, who had intuitively expected that sales force additions would act as a brake on competitive growth. Figure 7 shows the

4. The lesson from the simulation runs has one subtle twist. It says, *given* that objectives are set on past performance, and *given* that the revenue-generating base is being eroded, force reductions will precipitate spiral decline in performance and motivation. However, changes in the objective-setting procedure introduced simultaneously with force reductions may overcome the difficulty, but that is another issue and was not an explicit part of the force reduction plans.

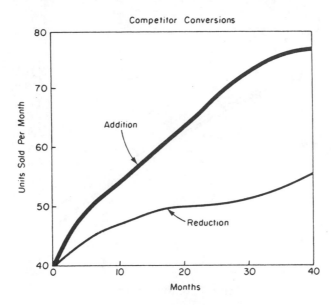

Figure 7. Competitor conversions

number of competitor conversions (by all competitor companies), starting at 40 systems per month. Under the force additions scenario conversions nearly doubled by the end of the run. Under the reductions scenario competitor growth is much more gradual, showing an increase of less than 40 per cent by the end of the run.

The reason that sales force additions lead to an increase in competitor conversions is a consequence of the structure of the market. Force additions increase proactive sales effort, which has the initial impact of informing customers of the existence and advantages of new-technology equipment. These customers can choose to convert to Datacom *or* competitor equipment. By supplying more product information to the market, the additional sales force gives a boost to the sales of competition (except in the extreme and unlikely situation that every customer is loyal to the company that informed him of the new equipment).

The behaviour has a simple and compelling explanation based on the decision-making structure of the market. Once the explanation has been given, it seems almost trivially obvious. Yet in the real strategy-evaluation process, it was surprising at first. The explanation provided sharper insight into the role of the sales force in market conversion.

Sales Force Additions Depress Market Share

Market-share behaviour was another surprising result that ran counter to initial management intuition. Figure 8 shows Datacom's market share under the two sales force scenarios. Share starts about 90 per cent and in both cases declines to below 70 per cent by the end of the simulation run. With force additions, market share actually declines more quickly, because additions *accelerate* the conversion process. Customers convert sooner to new-technology equipment, and inevitably some of them go to the competition.

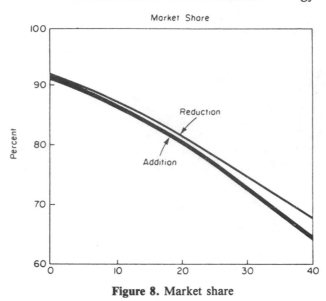

Figure 8. Market share

Intuition suggests there should be a market advantage from additional sales effort. The advantage, however, is one of completing the conversion process rapidly and, thereby, gaining a larger share of the new-technology base. Total market share (share of old *and* new systems) hides the advantage because it obscures the larger share of the *new* base resulting from force additions. Only when the conversion process is complete under both scenarios will market share properly reflect the advantage of the additions scenario. But the conversion takes more than 3 years! The simulation brings this fact to life, and dispels the expectation that force additions and market share are closely correlated.[5]

ASSESSING THE IMPACT OF THE MODEL

The impact of a strategy support model is often intangible. It is an insight generator and, therefore, differs from many common business models such as financial-planning and econometric models. The model does not get implemented in the sense that it is run weekly or monthly to produce a particular report or to execute a particular decision. By its very nature a strategy support model is involved in the amorphous to-and-fro of managerial and political debate. If it generates an insight, the insight can often quickly be absorbed into managerial thinking (mental models are, after all, much more agile than any formal simulation model, which is, by comparison, a rather cumbersome piece of intellectual infrastructure). The insight becomes part of intuition, particularly if it was backed with clear simulation analysis. Sometimes the model will form the basis for a specific recommendation but, usually, it will not contain the detail needed to state precisely how the recommendation should be translated into operating procedures. Like any strategic recommendation, it will need to pass through the usual

5. It should be added that neither scenario shows very attractive market-share behaviour. Further simulation experiments show that combination policies involving price initiatives, force additions, and more flexible objective setting can restrict market-share erosion to less than 10 per cent.

communication and administrative channels to be fleshed out and receive operational identity.[6]

In the market-strategy case it was clear that the model had an impact on management opinion in a number of areas. For example, the insight that force reductions can precipitate a spiral of declining productivity and motivation eroded executive enthusiasm for such a measure. In fact, a moderate increase in sales force was approved. The insight that force additions depress market share served to sharpen understanding into the short- and long-run trade-offs involved in accelerating the market conversion. This new understanding brought into question the desirability of rapid conversion as a goal in its own right, and led to further work on combination changes in force size and product price.

There are other, less direct indications of the impact of a strategy support model. Since the model becomes an integral part of the strategic dialogue in the company, it is, like any other member of the management team, judged useful if it continues to hold the interest and attention of management. Admittedly this is not a very tangible or scientific measure of impact, but it is a valid political measure of impact. The market-strategy model received ample attention from senior management. It was used in numerous high-level meetings, spanning 6 months, and its range of strategic enquiry was gradually expanded to include pricing and objective setting.

CONCLUSION

Strategy development remains an intuitive, intangible activity that is still a long way from yielding to formal analysis. Executives must be the primary architects of strategy. Where formal analysis can play a role is in strategy support—providing support in deducing the consequences of particular strategic proposals. It is in deducing consequences that the human mind is often inaccurate and misleading, even when starting from a clear understanding of the organizational elements of the strategy.

We have suggested that a valuable tool for strategy support is a formal simulation model that can act out the consequences of a new strategy in its full organizational setting. The formal model should contain the policies and communication and control structure of the organization through which strategy will be implemented.

However, the real key to effective strategy support is not simply *having* a formal model, but using it in dialogue and discussion with the managers responsible for the strategy. The formal model is used in interactive support or challenge of managerial intuition. In this dialectic role, the model is removed from the pedestal of the infallible black box to occupy a more modest (and appropriate) position as a complement to the powers of deductive thinking of a management team. The formal model should be used to set up scenarios. Managers should be challenged to think through the consequences of the scenarios for themselves. Their intuitive deductions and the formal deductions of the model can then be played off one against the other in discussion. Any differences in deduced outcome should be seized upon as opportunities for improving insight or correcting the formal model.

6. Lyneis (1981) has made the point that system dynamics models used for strategy purposes should be constructed at a level of detail that enables them to interact with the detailed planning procedures of an organization. In that way they become more tangibly integrated into company operations and are in a sense implemented. Although there is satisfaction in such tangible outcomes, the formal model loses its agility and becomes less effective as a basis for argument.

ACKNOWLEDGEMENTS

The author thanks David F. Andersen, Alan K. Graham and Nathaniel J. Mass for helpful comments received on an earlier draft of this paper, and Andrew M. Plummer for valuable editorial assistance. He also thanks James P. Cleary and William D. Kastning of the sponsoring company both for their comments on the paper and their enthusiastic support of the modelling project. Funds for the preparation of the paper were provided by the System Dynamics Corporate Research Program of the Sloan School of Management, M.I.T.

REFERENCES

Cyert, R. M., H. A. Simon and D. B. Trow. 'Observations of a business decision', *Journal of Business*, **29**, 1956, pp. 237–248.

Forrester, Jay W. *Industrial Dynamics*, The MIT Press, Cambridge, 1961.

Hall, R. I. 'A system pathology of an organization: the rise and fall of the old Saturday Evening Post', *Administrative Science Quarterly*, **21** (2), June 1976, pp. 185–211.

Keen, P. G. W. and M. S. Scott-Morton. *Decision Support Systems*, Addison-Wesley, Reading, Massachusetts, 1978.

Lyneis, J. M. *Corporate Planning and Policy Design—A System Dynamics Approach*, The MIT Press, Cambridge, 1980.

Lyneis, J. M. 'Increasing the effectiveness of corporate policy models', *Proceedings of the 1981 System Dynamics Research Conference*, Rensselaerville, NY, 14–17 October 1981, pp. 204–213.

Mason, R. O. 'A dialectical approach to strategic planning', *Management Science*, **15** (8), 1969, pp. B403–B414.

Mass, N. J. 'Diagnosing surprise model behavior: a tool for evolving behavioral and policy insight', *Proceedings of the 1981 System Dynamics Research Conference*, Rensselaerville, NY, 14–17 October 1981, pp. 254–272. Also available as *M.I.T. System Dynamics Group Working Paper D-3323*, M.I.T. Sloan School of Management, Cambridge, MA 02139, 1981.

Mitroff, I. I. and J. R. Emshoff. 'On strategic assumption-making: a dialectical approach to policy and planning', *Academy of Management Review*, **4**, 1979, pp. 1–12.

Mitroff, I. I., R. O. Mason and V. P. Barabba. 'Policy as argument—a logic for ill-structured decision problems', *Management Science*, **28** (12), December 1982, pp. 1391–1404.

Morecroft, J. D. W. 'System dynamics: portraying bounded rationality', *Omega*, **11** (2), March 1983, pp. 131–142.

Morecroft, J. D. W. 'Aspects of marketing strategy in the office equipment market', *System Dynamics Group Working Paper D-3352*, Sloan School of Management, M.I.T., Cambridge, MA 02139, August 1982.

Probert, D. E. 'System dynamics modeling within the British telecommunications business', *Dynamica*, **8** (Part II), Winter 1982, pp. 69–81.

Roberts, E. B. 'Strategies for effective implementation of complex corporate models', *Interfaces*, **8** (1), November 1977.

Schon, D. A. 'Conversational planning', forthcoming in Bennis, W. G., K. D. Benne and R. Chin (eds), *The Planning of Change*, Holt, Reinhart and Winston, New York, 1983

Simon, H. A. 'Designing organizations for an information rich world', in Greenburger, M. (ed.) *Computer Communications and Public Interest*, The Johns Hopkins Press, Baltimore, 1971, pp. 38–52.

_____ Part V

Performance Measurement, Gap Analysis and Selection

Chapter 14

Capital Investment Appraisal

R. G. Dyson and R. H. Berry
University of Warwick, England

Capital investment appraisal is defined as the financial evaluation of decisions involving capital investments. The paper introduces and discusses a number of financial appraisal methods, including discounting methods which are designed to take account of the time value of money. Various approaches to handling the uncertainty of future cash flows are presented, including risk analysis and the capital asset pricing model. Finally the sources of interdependencies between capital projects and methods of resolving the resultant complications are discussed.

INTRODUCTION

This paper deals with the financial appraisal of capital investment decisions. The methods and measures involved in current best practice are discussed as are the ideas, methods and measures which seem likely to underpin best practice in the next decade. Best practice here refers to the advice of specialists in many management disciplines. The gap between best practice and actual practice as discovered by the various studies of business behaviour will also be commented on and some explanations for the gap offered. These explanations have implications for attempts to put best practice into action.

Financial appraisal is often presented as an adequate basis for deciding whether or not to undertake a capital investment, and for some levels and classes of expenditure this may be so. However, for others, and in particular for major strategic decisions involving capital investments, financial appraisal by no means forms a complete framework for analysis. It clearly fails to deal with non financial issues such as the extent to which a project contributes to the social objectives of the workforce and the local and national communities. Furthermore, some economic factors such as improvements in the firm's competitive position may be difficult to quantify in strictly financial terms, so that measures such as market share and size of product range becomes relevant to the decision making process.[1] As a consequence of all this, the fact that an investment project is financially acceptable does not necessarily mean that the project should be undertaken.

It is of course possible to argue that the techniques of cost–benefit analysis can be brought to bear on the social aspects of an investment, and that conceptually at least, factors such as market share can be translated into cash flow figures. However, there are consequences of putting these responses into action which should not be overlooked: the cost–benefit approach involves implicit value judgements which might be better kept explicit, and translation of non-financial measures into cash flows may involve a loss in quality of estimate.[2]

There is another sense in which financial appraisal is not the whole of the story. Before any appraisal, project ideas must have been generated and forecasts produced. After any appraisal a decision must be made, and if that decision is to undertake the project, the project must be implemented, and a series of post completion audits carried out. In this sense appraisal is a part of a larger capital budgeting exercise, and although the non appraisal aspects of capital budgeting are not dealt with in this paper, this does not imply that they are unimportant.

AN OVERVIEW OF CAPITAL INVESTMENT APPRAISAL

A capital investment typically involves a current cash outflow which is relatively certain in amount and a series of rather less certain cash inflows spread over several years. This is not to say that uncertain future cash outflows cannot occur. Indeed, the need to be aware of potential problems with standard appraisal approaches when faced with uncertain future outflows will be emphasised later. However, many real life investments (and most textbook examples) have an initial outflow of cash followed by a series of anticipated inflows.

The end product of a financial appraisal is a meaningful summary measure of this stream of financial costs and benefits. There are two obvious problems involved in developing a summary measure. The first arises from the fact that the cash flows occur at different points in time. Cash available in the current period can often be lent at a positive real rate of interest. Therefore a cash amount available now is worth more than a similar amount available at some point in the future. A summary measure of a series of cash flows must cope with this time dimension, either by discounting, or some other procedure. This paper discusses summary measures based on discounting, truncation of the cash flow stream, and the simple response of ignoring the problem.

A second problem involved in developing a summary measure stems from the uncertainty inherent in future cash flows. Two basic responses to this problem are discussed in the paper. Firstly it is possible to generate probability density functions for the summary measures, and secondly it is possible to represent each uncertain cash flow by a typical figure and then calculate a summary measure based on these typical figures. The first approach is generally known as risk analysis. However, there are many versions of the second approach, some based on managers' perceptions of risk and others on shareholders' perceptions.

There are two less obvious problems involved in financial appraisal; what are financial benefits and what problems are involved in measuring them? So far in this paper, financial costs and benefits have been identified with cash flow rather than profit concepts based on accounting, and this will continue to be the case. (Only during the discussion of the accounting rate of return summary measure is there any consideration of accounting profit.) Two simple arguments can be marshalled in support of cash flow. Firstly cash and not accounting profit pays bills, interest and dividends. Secondly accounting profit is designed to provide a measure of performance over an arbitrary slice of the life of a firm or project. In investment appraisal the concern is with the entire economic life of the project. There is no need to worry about apportioning costs to arbitrary accounting periods. The differences between profit and cash flow for investment appraisal purposes will be discussed later in the paper.

It is certainly the case that managers often express concern about the consequences of accepting a project for the appearance of profit and loss accounts. The potential impact on share price seems to be the focus of their concern. However, evidence[3] supports the view that it is cash flow to which stock markets respond, not accounting profits.

The second subsidiary problem relates to the difficulty of identifying a project's cash flows. Because of interdependencies that can arise between the project being evaluated, other proposed projects and the existing activities of the organisation, it can be difficult to identify the cash flow consequences attributable to a specific project. A variety of sources of interdependencies and their resolution will be discussed in the paper.

SUMMARY MEASURES AND DECISION RULES

A number of measures are available for summarising into a single value the stream of cash flows associated with a capital investment. These include the payback period, the accounting rate of return, the net present value and the internal rate of return.

In what follows C_0 will represent the cash flow at the beginning of the life of the capital project (usually a negative initial investment), and C_i the cash flow in each following year i. It is assumed that C_i occurs at the end of year i. The cash stream representing the project is thus:

$$C_0, C_1, \ldots, C_i, \ldots, C_n,$$

where n is the life of the project in years. The cash flows from C_1 to C_n are usually assumed to be positive at the planning stage (as distinct from the outcome) but this may not be generally true and C_n in particular may be negative if the end of the project involves a tax payment or some kind of cleaning up operation (e.g. levelling and restoring the site after mining).

Payback Period

The simplest summary measure in common use is the payback period. This is the number of years before the project's initial investment is paid back by the project's later cash flows. For the cash stream shown below, the payback period is three years. This is calculated by cumulating project cash flows, after the initial investment, until the cumulative exceeds the initial investment.

YEAR	0	1	2	3	4	5	6	7
CASH FLOW	(10 000)	985	3739	8840	9682	17 096	7485	(622)
CUMULATIVE CASH FLOW		985	4724	13 564				

Note () indicates a cash outflow.

A decision rule would involve comparing the calculated payback period with some predetermined target period. A calculated figure less than target indicates that the project should be accepted.

There are a number of obvious inadequacies with the payback period. Firstly it does not use all the available information, ignoring as it does the cash flows outside the payback period. (The discounted payback rule is a variant designed to remedy this shortcoming.) Finally there is no indication of how to set the target payback period.

Despite these factors, the payback period has its defenders, and surveys indicate that it is in common use in combination with other summary measures.[4,5] This may be because it is a crude measure of liquidity, and hence useful to firms unwilling to use outside sources of finance. It may also be a reflection of management's perception of the quality of available cash flow data or of the costs of data collection. Finally there is always the possibility that it is a simple approach to dealing with uncertainty by managers who see cash flows arising further in the future as having greater risk.

Accounting Rate of Return (ARR)

This summary measure, alone among those considered in this paper, is based on accounting profit rather than cash flow. There are innumerable variants of the measure differing only in the way in which the accounting numbers involved are defined. Essentially the measure is a ratio. The numerator is the average profits of the project after depreciation and taxes, while the denominator is the average book value of the investment. The profit figures, and book value of investment corresponding to the cash flow figures used earlier in this section, might be as follows. (Remember there are many possible variants.)

YEAR	0	1	2	3	4	5	6	7
PROFIT		2825	5539	9140	9082	10 596	485	(2112)
ASSET	6000	5000	4000	3000	2000	1000	0	0

The project ceases operation after six years (although there are tax consequences in year 7). Average profit over the six years is £6278; average asset value is £3000. Therefore accounting rate of return is 209%!

A decision rule would be based on some predetermined target value. Calculated ARR greater than target value would indicate that the project should be accepted.

Once again this summary measure suffers from a number of problems; arbitrary target value and arbitrary definition of accounting numbers being the major ones. More and more finance texts, and more and more firms are tending to ignore this measure.[6]

Net Present Value

The fact that £1 received next year is worth less than £1 received now has already been pointed out. If money can be lent at 10%, £1 today will be worth £1.10 next year, assuming no inflation. The link between value today (present value) and value next year (future value) is:

$$\text{PRESENT VALUE } (1+r) = \text{FUTURE VALUE}$$

where r is the interest rate, an opportunity cost of holding cash. The link between value today and value in N years' time is equally simple:

$$\text{PRESENT VALUE } (1+r)^N = \text{FUTURE VALUE}.$$

Discounting makes use of this simple relationship to express future cash flows as present values.

$$\text{PRESENT VALUE} = \frac{\text{FUTURE VALUE}}{(1+r)^N}.$$

This approach allows cash flows arising at different times to be compared.

Net Present Value (NPV) is a cash flow based summary measure produced by a discounting exercise. All the cash flows generated during the project's economic life are discounted back to their present values. These present values are then aggregated. The initial investment is included in the aggregation and is of course already in present value terms. The general formula for the Net Present Value is:

$$NPV = C_0 + \frac{C_1}{1+r} + \frac{C_2}{(1+r)^2} + \ldots + \frac{C_n}{(1+r)^n}.$$

If the interest rate is 10% then the NPV of the cash flow data used earlier in this paper is:

$$NPV = -10\,000 + \frac{985}{(1.1)} + \frac{3739}{(1.1)^2} + \frac{8840}{(1.1)^3} + \frac{9682}{(1.1)^4} + \frac{17\,096}{(1.1)^5} + \frac{7585}{(1.1)^6} - \frac{622}{(1.1)^7} = 21\,761$$

A decision rule for NPV would be to accept any project with a positive NPV and reject all others. A positive NPV means that the project is yielding higher returns than can be obtained by simply lending at the rate of return r. This interpretation suggests that r is a minimum acceptable rate of return.

A rate of return r is usually known as the discount rate in NPV calculations and its determination is not straightforward. In fact r is usually taken to have three components, a real rate of interest, a component equal to the expected level of inflation and a component to allow for the riskiness of the project. A typical value for r in percentage terms might thus be made up as follows:

$$r\% = \text{real rate of interest} + \text{inflation rate} + \text{risk premium}$$
$$= 1 + 5 + 3$$
$$= 9\% \text{ say.}$$

The problems posed by inflation and risk in capital investment appraisal, particularly the problem posed by risk, will be considered in later sections. NPV is much favoured by the finance textbooks. It is cash flow based, takes all cash flows into account, and takes into account the time value of money. Furthermore, with an appropriate discount rate, it has an interpretation in terms of impact of share price. According to recent surveys the use of this and other discounting methods is increasing.[5]

Net Terminal Value

A similar measure to NPV which uses the same discount rate but assesses the value of the project at its termination is the net terminal value (NTV). Using the previous notation we have:

$$NTV = C_0(1+r)^n + C(1+r)^{n-1} + \ldots + C_i(1+r)^{n-i} + \ldots + C_n,$$

and hence $NTV = NPV\ (1+r)^n$.

NTV is thus the surplus available at the end of the project after repaying the investment and assuming that money borrowed or surpluses invested during the life of the project both attract an interest rate of r. A decision rule to accept any project with a positive NTV would lead to the same decision as the NPV decision rule.

Internal Rate of Return

The internal rate of return (IRR) is a discounted cash flow method like NPV and is defined as the rate of return that yields a zero NPV. Hence it is the value of r such that:

$$C_0 + \frac{C_1}{1+r} + \ldots + \frac{C_i}{(1+r)^i} + \ldots + \frac{C_n}{(1+r)^n} = 0$$

The above equation can be solved by an iterative procedure. The attraction of IRR is that it yields a rate of return measure which can be interpreted as the highest rate of interest at which the company could afford to finance the project. Hence a decision rule for IRR would involve a target rate of interest to be exceeded by the IRR if the project is to be accepted.

IRR and NPV will generally yield similar results in determining the acceptability of a project. (Assuming NPV is a smoothly declining function of the discount rate). However, the methods can rank projects differently so that if not all acceptable projects can be undertaken, for example because they are mutually exclusive, the methods can yield a different selection. There is also the problem that a project can have multiple rates of return. For the cash stream evaluated in the NPV section, the corresponding IRR is 48.8%.

Textbook wisdom compares IRR unfavourably with NPV, because it can fail to give rankings consistent with NPV. However it remains popular with practitioners. This may be because it reflects corporate objectives such as growth, or because it is a familiar measure which managers feel they understand.[7]

Fixed Interest Equivalent Rate of Return (FIE)

The popularity of IRR has led to several reformulations designed to remove perceived problems with the measure while retaining its essential characteristics. FIE is one example. In the calculation of IRR it is assumed that any surplus funds generated by the project can be reinvested at a rate of return equal to the IRR. For a project yielding a high return this may be an optimistic assumption, and as a result the IRR may be an unrealistically high measure. A more realistic assumption would be to assume that surplus funds can be reinvested, and capital raised at the discount rate used in an NPV calculation.

An alternative interest rate measure can be obtained using these assumptions by computing the net terminal value of the project and calculating the interest rate required to yield a similar terminal value if the funds were invested in a fixed interest investment. Using the same example, and a 10% discount rate, we have:

YEAR	0	1	2	3	4	5	6	7
CASH FLOW (£)	(10 000)	985	3739	8840	9682	17 096	7485	(622)

$$\begin{aligned} \text{NET TERMINAL VALUE} = & -10\,000(1.1)^7 + 985(1.1)^6 + 3739(1.1)^5 \\ & + 8840(1.1)^4 + 9682(1.1)^3 + 17\,096(1.1)^2 \\ & + 7485(1.1) - 622 \\ = & \ 42\,407 \end{aligned}$$

Net terminal of an equivalent fixed interest investment at $r\%$

$$\begin{aligned} &= \text{TV (investment)} - \text{TV (cost of investment)} \\ &= 10\,000(1+r)^7 + 622 - 10\,000(1.1)^7 - 622 \end{aligned}$$

(This assumes the investment to be 10 000 initially and 622 at the end of year 7.)

The rate of interest required for the two terminal values to be equal is obtained by solving:

$$10\,000(1+r)^7 - 10\,000(1.1)^7 = 42\,407$$
$$\text{i.e. } (1+r) = 1.299$$

and $r = FIE = 29.9\%$.
(This compares with IRR = 48.8%.)

FIE is thus a rate of return measure taking account of the time value of money. In general it will give a lower rate of return than IRR for acceptable projects. Its computation can be done simply and precisely and it has a straightforward interpretation.

FIE is a similar measure to IRR* as defined by Weston and Brigham[8] in that it is terminal value based. It has been presented here to stress its interpretative value.

RISK IN CAPITAL INVESTMENT APPRAISAL

The approach to financial appraisal introduced in the previous section implicitly assumed that the future cash flows are known with certainty. This is generally an invalid assumption. Future revenues depend on uncertain demand conditions in markets for final products and future costs depend on uncertain activity levels and factor market conditions. A number of approaches to handling this uncertainty exist. They differ in technique but also in whose perception of risk, shareholder or manager is involved. This paper discusses several approaches, taking care to identify the interest group involved in each case. Since risk may mean different things to managers and shareholders, the implication is that multiple appraisals may have to be carried out for a project and a trade off between conflicting interests established.

Risk Analysis: A Management Viewpoint

Risk analysis has a long history, being first proposed by Hertz[9] in this context. It explicitly recognises uncertainty by assigning probability distributions to factors affecting the various components that are aggregated to make up project cash flow. So for example sales revenue in a given year might be represented by the equation,

$$\text{SALES REVENUE} = \text{SALES} \times \text{PRICE}$$

and both sales and price would be assigned probability distributions. This would of course result in sales revenue having a probability distribution. The same approach would be applied to the various cost elements, tax flows and changes in working capital generated by a project. Hence cash flow in each time period appears with a probability distribution.

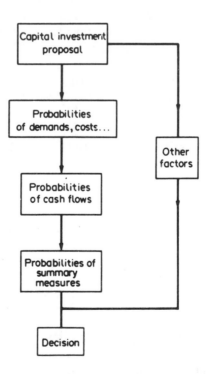

Figure 1. The risk analysis process

These cash flow distributions are then combined to give a probability distribution for any summary measure of interest, e.g. NPV or IRR.

A flow diagram of the risk analysis process appears in Figure 1.

The probabilities of cash flows and summary measures are produced by simulation. This involves selecting a single value from the distribution of each component of the cash stream using random numbers and combining these values through the appropriate computation to produce a value for NPV or whatever summary measures are of interest. This procedure is then repeated many times until distributions for each relevant measure are built up. This procedure is illustrated in Figure 2.

The result of the simulation exercise is that management has available a distribution for each summary measure of interest. These are pictures of project risk as well as expected performance. Management can use them in decision making perhaps by calculating probabilities of failing to meet set targets.

The risk analysis process presents few computational problems assuming computing facilities are available. It does, however, present measurement problems. A requirement of the process is an ability to build up a probability distribution of the components of the cash stream. This is likely to involve experts in interrogating management to determine first, the plausible range of the value of a component and second, a picture of the relative chances of different values occurring. This procedure may be difficult and hence when distributions are obtained their validity is still open to doubt. A further complication arises from the existence of dependencies between components and between time periods. For example, price and demand components will be related with higher prices tending

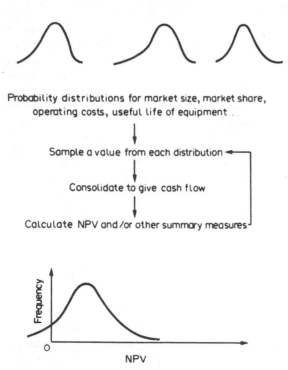

Probability distributions for market size, market share, operating costs, useful life of equipment...

↓

Sample a value from each distribution ←

↓

Consolidate to give cash flow

↓

Calculate NPV and/or other summary measures

Frequency

O

NPV

Figure 2. Simulation for capital investment appraisal

to lead to lower demand. Ideally such relationships should be taken account of in the computer simulation, but the specification of conditional probability distributions considerably complicates the process. Hertz and Thomas[10] discuss all these issues. As far as dependency is concerned, they consider that suitable approaches are not yet well developed. Hull[11] also addresses the dependency problem.

The advantage of the approach is that the fullest possible picture of the uncertainty is developed and used in the analysis. The management can assess the financial benefits and risks of the project and apply their judgement, values, and knowledge of non-financial aspects to determine the acceptability of a project.

Risk Adjusted Rates and Certainty Equivalents: Management Viewpoint

In risk analysis, the management attitude to risk enters the analysis after distributions of summary measures have been obtained. This means of course that any discounting involved in the calculation of the distributions should use a risk free discount rate. There is an alternative approach; in fact a linked pair of alternative approaches. One possibility is to represent an uncertain future cash flow by its expected value and discount it at a rate which reflects the riskiness of the cash flow and management's attitude to risk. This approach is called risk adjusted discounting. The present value of an uncertain future cash flow, occurring one period hence, is given by:

$$PV = \frac{EV(X)}{1+k}$$

where EV is the expected value operation and k is the risk adjusted discount rate.

A second possibility is to find a certain cash amount which management views as no more and no less acceptable than the uncertain cash flow X. This new cash amount is called a certainty equivalent. A more precise treatment in the context of a utility function is given shortly. The present value of an uncertain cash flow X occurring one period hence, is then given by:

$$PV = \frac{CE(X)}{1+i}$$

where CE is the certainty equivalent operator and i is the risk free rate.

It is often useful in theoretical discussions to recognise that:

$$PV = \frac{EV(X)}{1+k} = \frac{CE(X)}{1+i} = \frac{EV(X) - RP}{1+i}$$

where RP is a risk premium which changes EV into CE. These approaches are similar to risk analysis in so far as a thorough analysis of the uncertainty of the components of the cash stream is required. These components are then combined to give a cash flow distribution for each future time period. The present value of an uncertain future cash flow is then obtained by applying the risk adjusted discount rate to the expected value of the future cash flow or by discounting the certainty equivalent at the risk free rate.

The process will yield an NPV for a project which in general will be lower than the expected value of the NPV obtained via risk analysis, assuming the management is risk aversive.

The process can be illustrated analytically by assuming that a future cash flow is normally distributed with known parameters, and assuming a particular utility function for management. Suppose that the uncertain cash flow is $x \approx N(\mu, \sigma^2)$ and that the utility function for a cash amount x can be represented by:

$$U(x) = 1 - \exp(-ax)$$

This form of utility function exhibits constant risk aversion. To determine the appropriate risk adjusted discount rate it is necessary to use the notion of a certainty equivalent (CE) to an uncertain cash amount. The CE is defined as being the certain cash amount that would be equally as acceptable as the uncertain cash amount, given management's attitude to risk. In other words the certain cash amount has utility equal to the expected utility of the uncertain cash amount.

If x is the uncertain cash amount then given the assumptions on the distribution of x and the utility function, it follows that:

Expected utility of $x = EV\{U(x)\}$

$$= \int \{1 - \exp(-ax)\}. \frac{1}{\sigma\sqrt{2\pi}} \exp \frac{\{-(x-\mu)^2\}dx}{2\sigma^2}$$

$$= 1 - \exp(-a\mu + \tfrac{1}{2}a^2\sigma^2)$$

where EV stands for expected value.

By definition

$$U\{CE(x)\} = EV\{U(x)\}$$

$$\text{hence } CE(x) = U^{-1}EV\{U(x)\}$$

If $U(x) = 1 - \exp(-ax)$, then $U^{-1}(y) = -\frac{1}{a}\log(1-y)$, for any y.

Hence $CE(x) = -\frac{1}{a}\log\{1 - (1 - \exp(-a\mu + \tfrac{1}{2}a^2\eta^2))\}$

$$= \mu - \tfrac{1}{2}a\sigma^2$$

If the cash flow x occurs one year ahead, then as had been said, either CE(x) can be discounted at a risk free rate i, or μ can be discounted at the risk adjusted rate r.

$$\text{i.e.} \frac{CE(x)}{1+i} = \frac{\mu}{1+r}$$

$$\text{hence } 1+r = \frac{\mu(1+i)}{CE(x)} = \frac{\mu(1+i)}{\mu - \tfrac{1}{2}a\sigma^2}$$

so that for positive a, implying risk aversion, for this cash flow r will exceed the risk free rate i. However, if the cash flow is an uncertain cash flow, r will be less than the risk free rate.

Example

Let $\mu = £2000$, $\sigma^2 = 800$, $i = 10\%$ and $a = 0.2$.

$$1 + r = \frac{\mu(1+i)}{\mu - \frac{1}{2}a\sigma^2} = \frac{2000 \times 1.1}{2000 - \frac{1}{2} \times 0.2 \times 800} = 1.146.$$

Hence the risk adjusted discount rate $r = 14.6\%$.

This approach to accommodating risk presents a number of practical difficulties. As in risk analysis, it requires the formulation of probability density functions, but additionally it requires the formulation of a utility function. The latter raises a number of questions, such as whose utility function, how can a utility function be formulated, should the cash be taken as incremental to the wealth of the company, how should cash outflows be treated? Hertz and Thomas[10] describe methods of formulating utility functions for individuals and groups of individuals, and the problem of validity has been addressed by Hershey, Kunreuther and Schoemaker.[12] Berry and Dyson[13,14] discuss the treatment of cash outflows, and consider the issue of incrementality as do Lioukas and Moore.[15]

Risk Adjusted Rates and Certainty Equivalents: Shareholders' Viewpoint

An alternative to managerial expected utility maximisation as an objective in capital budgeting is maximising the expected utility of the firm's current shareholders. It might appear that this is an impossible objective, since different shareholders are likely to have different utility functions. However, it can be shown that in complete, competitive and frictionless capital markets, maximising the price of current shares is equivalent to maximising current shareholders' expected utility.[16] The basic idea is that by maximising its contribution to shareholders' wealth the firm allows each shareholder to make his/her own utility maximising choice of consumption pattern.

If management is to act in the interests of its shareholders, then it must accept investments that increase share value and reject those that do not. What management would like to be able to do is to find a firm traded on the stock market which is an exact replica of the project it is considering. It can then compare the cost of undertaking the project with the value the stock market would place on the project if it were undertaken. An excess of market value over cost would indicate that the project should be accepted. If a replica cannot be found, then management must try and discover and apply the valuation mechanism which generates share prices.

One view of this mechanism which has achieved widespread popularity is the capital asset pricing model (CAPM).[17] This model identifies a risk adjusted discount rate which can be applied to project cash flows. The process of applying CAPM is described in the next section. Following that, alternative views of the market valuation mechanism are described. These include Time State Preference, Option Pricing Theory and Arbitrage

Pricing Theory. These models emphasise the calculation of prices for cash flows appearing at different points in time and in different states of nature. They therefore generalise more easily to the situation where cash flows at different points in time also have different degrees of risk and hence require different risk adjusted discount rates. CAPM is reintroduced as one method of calculating these time-state prices.

Capital Asset Pricing Model: A Practical Approach

In this section a practical approach to investment for share value maximisation based on CAPM will be developed. In addition the issue of how to finance an investment will be touched on.

Given that a set of expected cash flows has been developed, the requirement is for a risk adjusted discount rate to apply to them. Given that impact on share price is a consideration, the stock market is an obvious place to look for one. Whatever the nature of the investment project under consideration the aim is to find a stock market investment, a share, of comparable risk, and calculate the required rate of return on this.

CAPM defines the required rate of return as:

$$k_j = i + \beta_j [EV(\widetilde{R}_m) - i]$$

Here i is once again the risk free rate, $[EV(\widetilde{R}_m) - i]$ is the return the market portfolio (a value weighed portfolio of all shares) earns over and above the risk free rate, and β_j, or Beta, is a measure of the share's risk relative to that of the market. In other words, k is the risk free rate plus a risk premium. The risk adjustment is, however, unusual in that it is based on the covariance between the return on the share and the market portfolio. Covariance is the relevant risk measure because shareholders are seen as capable of holding diversified portfolios of shares. Therefore, relevant risk is non-diversifiable risk, the extent to which returns on a share move in line with the market portfolio.

As has been said, Beta is covariance based, showing the extent to which return on a share moves with the return on a well diversified portfolio. Beta is usually measured as the slope coefficient in a regression of return on a share against return on the 'All Share Index' (a very well diversified portfolio).[18] So, if the investment project under consideration involved a foundry operation say, the Beta of a share in an existing foundry operation could be used as a proxy for the project's risk. In fact it might be better to calculate Betas for several such firms and average them. An alternative to carrying out the Beta calculations is of course to use a 'Beta Book' such as the London Business School 'Risk Measurement Service'.[19]

Having calculated a project risk measure, the next step is to calculate a required rate of return using CAPM. The elements in the CAPM equation are relatively easily available: i can be found in a daily newspaper, as the rate on Treasury Bills, after personal tax (there is some controversy here);[20] β_j can be calculated as described; a long term average of $EV(\widetilde{R}_m) - i$ of about 8% after personal tax has been calculated by Dimson and Brealey.[21] If $\beta = 0.7$, $i = 6\%$ and $EV(\widetilde{R}_m) - i$ is 8%, then an investment in the stock market of comparable risk to the investment project under consideration offers an expected return of:

$$k = 0.06 + (0.7 \times 0.08)$$
$$= 0.116 = 11.6\%$$

This discount rate should be applied to cash flow data, such as that included in the discussion of NPV. The investment project under consideration must offer at least this rate of return if it is not to depress the company's share price.

There is one complicating factor still to be taken into account. Calculating project Beta by averaging firm Betas, has allowed financing mix to affect the calculation. Each firm's Beta will reflect the line of business the firm is in *and* the presence of any debt in the firm's capital structure. Thus firm Betas must be ungeared before they can be used as a proxy for project risk. This is easily done if the simplifying assumption of risk free debt is made (formulae which do not require this assumption are given in Buckley[22] and Schnabel).[23] Then the equation:

$$\beta \text{Business} = \beta \text{Equity} \frac{\text{Equity}}{\text{Equity} + \text{Debt}} + \beta \text{Debt} \frac{\text{Debt}}{\text{Debt} + \text{Equity}}$$

reduces to:

$$\beta \text{Business} = \beta \text{Equity} \frac{\text{Equity}}{\text{Equity} + \text{Debt}}$$

It must be remembered in both these equations that equity and debt are in market values. The simple equation form is based on the additivity of covariances. If the 0.7 Beta in the numerical example related to one firm, and that firm had 30% debt in its capital structure, then the business Beta or *all equity* Beta would be 0.49 and the corresponding required rate of return for the project, p, would be:

$$p = 0.06 + (0.49 \times 0.080)$$
$$= 0.099$$

The traditional finance argument for the use of debt is that interest payments are deductible for corporation tax purposes. It has been suggested that since a project will increase a firm's borrowing capacity, the project should be credited with the tax shield generated by the interest on new debt raised. However, modern finance and the 1984 budget indicate that the cheapness of debt relative to equity finance is a thing of the past.[24] Thus the project's weighted average cost of capital (the most commonly advocated mechanism for taking into account the cheapness of debt) would simply be:

$$\text{WACC} = k \left(\frac{\text{Equity}}{\text{Debt} + \text{Equity}} \right) + i \left(\frac{\text{Debt}}{\text{Debt} + \text{Equity}} \right)$$

$$= 0.116 \times 0.7 + 0.06 \times 0.3$$
$$= 0.099$$

This is simply the required rate of return on ungeared equity.

There is an alternative method for taking the tax shields on debt into account. This is Myers' Adjusted Present Value Method. This is advocated by Myers[25] on the grounds that it involves fewer unrealistic assumptions than the calculation of a weighted average cost of capital. Since it is a simple way of taking into account other 'special' cash flows, it deserves attention even in the absence of debt based tax shields.

Time State Preference

In the time state preference model (TSP) uncertainty about the future takes the form of not knowing which one of a set of mutually exclusive states of nature will occur.[26] An uncertain cash flow can then be viewed as a set of cash payoffs, each one associated with a particular state of nature. A simple, one period, two state example should make these ideas clear. Tomorrow the economy will be in one of two possible states, $1 =$ boom or $2 =$ slump. Boom has probability P(1) and slump probability P(2). An investment of £100 by a firm in plant and machinery now generates a cash flow of £200 tomorrow if a boom occurs, and a cash flow of £40 tomorrow if a slump occurs. These data are diagrammed below:

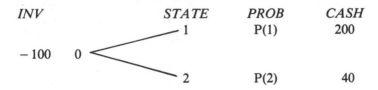

INV		STATE	PROB	CASH
		1	P(1)	200
− 100	0			
		2	P(2)	40

Cash flow uncertainty is then simply a reflection of uncertainty about which future state will occur.

Suppose that in the capital market it is possible to find a pair of pure securities, (a pure security is one which pays £1 in one state and £0 in all others), one of which, S(1), pays off in state 1, while the other, S(2), pays off in state 2. Let the pure security which pays off in state 1 have a current price V(1) and the one which pays off in state 2 a current price V(2). These prices are formed in the market. To mimic the future consequences of the investment opportunity it would be necessary to spend $200V(1) + 40V(2)$. Therefore if $200V(1) + 40V(2) > 100$ the firm has a positive NPV investment which should be taken on. The firm can purchase the future cash flows more cheaply than its shareholders can buy them in the market, and therefore should do so on their behalf.

Capital Asset Pricing Model

In the above description of the TSP framework no specific pricing mechanism has been introduced. V(1) and V(2) have been assumed to be known. The pricing mechanism most commonly assumed to operate in well developed capital markets is the capital asset pricing model (CAPM). In certainty equivalent form this is:

$$PV(\tilde{X}) = \frac{EV(\tilde{X}) - \lambda \, \text{cov}(\tilde{X}, \tilde{R}_m)}{1 + i}$$

where:

$\tilde{X}$ is the uncertain future cash flow.
$\tilde{R}_m$ is the uncertain future return on the market portfolio.
PV indicates present value.
EV indicates expectation.
cov indicates covariance.
i   is the risk free rate of interest.

The remaining element in the formula is λ, which is:

$$\lambda = \frac{EV(\tilde{R}_m) - i}{\sigma^2_m}$$

where:

σ^2_m is the variance of the market return.

The derivation of this equation from the risk adjusted discount rate form can be found in, among others, Haley and Schall.[26]
   The economics of this pricing model are quite straightforward. Present value is given by discounting, at the risk free rate, a certain cash amount equivalent to the uncertain cash flow. The only unusual feature is the nature of the adjustment factor which transforms the expected value $EV(\tilde{X})$ into a certainty equivalent. This is based on cash flow risk as measured by covariance. As has been said, shareholders are seen as capable of holding diversified portfolios of shares. Therefore relevant risk is non-diversifiable risk, the extent to which the cash flow moves in line with the market portfolio.
   Given forecasts about R_m, the return on the market, and i, the risk free rate, CAPM can be used to calculate time state prices V(1) and V(2) and hence can be used to value the firm's investment opportunity. The calculation of covariances is straightforward, as is shown in Exhibit 1, because of the simple cash flow pattern offered by a pure security.

EXHIBIT 1

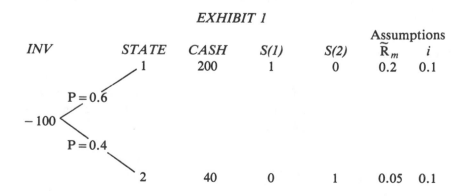

INV		STATE	CASH	S(1)	S(2)	Assumptions $\tilde{R}_m$	i
		1	200	1	0	0.2	0.1
-100	$P=0.6$						
	$P=0.4$						
		2	40	0	1	0.05	0.1

Preliminary calculations of market parameters gives:

$$\lambda = \frac{EV(\tilde{R}_m) - i}{\sigma^2_m} = \frac{0.14 - 0.1}{0.0054} = 7.4.$$

Let V(1) be the price of pure security S(2), then by CAPM

$$V(1) = \frac{0.6 - 7.4 \times 0.6 \times 0.06}{1.1} = 0.303$$

Let V(2) be the price of pure security S(2), then by CAPM

$$V(2) = \frac{0.4 - 7.4 \times 0.4 \times (-0.09)}{1.1} = 0.606$$

From TSP, NPV $= 200 \ V(1) + 40 \ V(2) - 100$

$$= (200 \times 0.303) + (40 \times 0.606) - 100$$
$$= -15.16$$

Hence the firm should not take on the investment.

Option Pricing Theory

While CAPM can be applied in this fashion, current financial theory offers alternatives to doing so. CAPM makes assumptions about the form of the distribution of returns, normality in particular, which seem less appropriate as the time horizon lengthens. An alternative model is based on option pricing theory. Banz and Miller have developed tables of state prices using this approach which can be used in a TSP evaluation.[27]

Arbitrage Pricing Theory

One further pricing model deserves mention in this brief overview of risk from the point of view of shareholders. This is the arbitrage pricing model, APT, developed by Ross.[28] The argument here is simple. In a world of well functioning capital markets two assets offering the same outcomes should trade at the same prices. Look again at the data used in the CAPM numerical example. The following diagram simply presents once again the assumptions about market returns and risk free rates, but this time as cash payoffs.

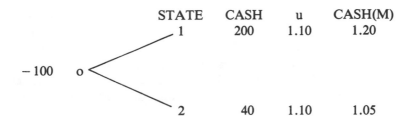

STATE	CASH	u	CASH(M)
1	200	1.10	1.20
2	40	1.10	1.05

-100 o

The diagram shows that £1 lent at the risk free rate will generate £1.10 one period from now and an investment of £1.00 in the market portfolio will generate, one period from now, £1.20 if state 1 occurs and £1.05 if state 2 occurs. To apply ATP to the capital budgeting problem it is necessary to identify a portfolio of lending and investment in the market portfolio that mimics the project's cash flow. This can be done by solving a pair of simultaneous equations.[29]

$$200 = 1.10x + 1.20y$$
$$40 = 1.10x + 1.05y$$

The LHS of the equations are simply project cash flows and the RHS of the equations are the cash flows from the lending and portfolio investment decisions. The values $x = -981.82$; $y = 1066.67$ solve the equations. These imply that an investment of £1066.67 in the market portfolio, and *borrowing* of £981.82 will mimic the project's uncertain future cash flow. The investment in the market portfolio and the borrowing imply a current cash outflow of $(£981.83 - £1066.67) = -£84.84$. To acquire the future cash flow by undertaking the project would involve a current cash outflow of £100. This is £15.16 more than is required to acquire a similar future cash flow in the capital market. (NB: Compare this amount with the project NPV as calculated using CAPM). Therefore the project should not be undertaken.

This section has identified three models which can be used to price future uncertain cash flows. (TSP is essentially a framework into which specific pricing models can be slotted.) CAPM is the most widely recommended in finance texts while OPT and ATP are relative newcomers. The shift from the statistical computations of CAPM to the more general, economic style of argument implicit in ATP is symptomatic of what is happening in financial theory at the present time.

The simple examples used in this section have made use of discrete distributions and single period cash flows. These restrictions were introduced for convenience only. CAPM, OPT and APT can all cope with their relaxation.

A Synthesis of Shareholder and Managerial Viewpoints

The managerial attempts to cope with risks that have been examined have been based around variance of project cash flow. An alternative view would be that it is a project's contribution to variance of firm's cash flow that is important. But even so, concern is with a total risk measure. However, for a shareholder, relevant risk is based on covariance with the market portfolio.

These are different concepts of risk rather than different ways of looking at the same thing. Therefore, as was said earlier, two separate evaluations may be appropriate.

There is another possible source of confusion stemming from these two viewpoints. The NPV figure, which is generated using a capital market based valuation mechanism, can be interpreted as a market value. This is not the case if valuation is based on a managerial utility function. Nor is it the case that the expected value of a distribution of NPVs generated by a risk analysis can be interpreted as a market value. Different concepts underpin the NPV title in these situations and this can be a source of confusion.

CASH FLOW DATA

Much has been made so far of the fact that it is cash flow rather than accounting profit which is relevant to the investment appraisal process. A distribution of cash flow in each period is a prerequisite for all the performance measures so far discussed. Except in the simplest cases, these cash flows are probably best produced by a stochastic simulation model of the kind referred to earlier. This section makes no attempt to construct such a model. What it does do, however, is identify the elements of cash flow for capital budgeting purposes. These can be split into four groups: the accounting cash flows such as turnover and costs of goods sold (which would normally include depreciation); changes in current assets and liabilities; cash flows on acquisition and disposal of assets; and tax based cash flows. See Table 1. Since depreciation is a non-cash expense it is added back in the cash flow calculation.

Table 1 can be used as a checklist when deciding which items are relevant to a cash flow calculation (however, there may be additional opportunity cost elements to consider if a project makes use of scarce existing resources). The data in Table 1 should be familiar by now, since they have been used in many of the numerical examples presented so far. The table is based on a series of assumptions. These are:

(a)   The project begins on 31st December 1986. That is to say expenditure is incurred and plant comes into use on that date.
(b)   The company considering the project has an accounting year end on March 31st and pays tax 9 months after that.

(Assumptions (a), (b) generate the one year lag in tax payments evident in Table 1. Other lag structures are possible under UK tax law.)

(c)   There is no system of stock relief.
(d)   Capital allowances can be claimed on a 25% reducing balance basis.
(e)   Corporate tax rate of 35%.

The above assumptions correspond to the steady state system implied by the 1984 budget.)

Table 1.

	1	2	3	4	5	6	7
Turnover		16 500	30 300	46 600	51 200	56 400	26 500	
Cost of goods sold		(12 200)	(21 900)	(33 000)	(35 700)	(38 600)	(17 900)	
(Expenses)		(2000)	(2100)	(2200)	(2300)	(2400)	(2500)	
Deprec.,		1000	1000	1000	1000	1000	1000	
(Tax)			(1155)	(2555)	(4340)	(4970)	(5740)	(2485)
(Inv.,)	(6000)							
Tax benefit of alls.,		525	394	295	222	166	125	373
Scrap							600	
(Tax)								(210)
(Stock)	(4500)	(3000)	(2000)			(6000)	3500	
(Debtors)		(1400)	(1100)	(1300)	(400)	(500)	2500	2200
Creditors	500	300	300				(600)	(500)
Total	(10 000)	985	3739	8840	9682	17 096	7485	(622)

(f)   The project is discontinued on sale of machine and a tax allowance against profit is given on the loss. (It is unclear from the budget speech how end of project life issues will be dealt with, but this will have been resolved in the 1984 Finance Act.)

It is in calculating cash flows that a manager/analyst needs to combine the skills of economist and accountant. An economist will identify relevant cash flows, e.g. tax. An accountant will have the knowledge of relevant tax legislation which allows the calculation to be made. The area of tax as can be seen from the cash flow patterns will remain a significant factor in investment appraisal even after the 1984 budget.

The cash flows shown in Table 1 are in nominal terms. That is to say, they are in inflated prices. In producing cash flow estimates it is sometimes assumed that all cash flow terms will inflate at the same rate. This is unlikely to be true. Capital allowances, for example, are based on a percentage of historic equipment cost. They will not inflate at all. However, even ignoring this particular item, a common inflation rate for different cost elements should generally be seen as a dubious assumption.

INTERDEPENDENCIES

Capital investment appraisal often assumes that a project can be evaluated in isolation from the other activities of the organisation, although it is recognised that the appropriate cash stream for the project is the marginal change in the overall cash stream of the organisation, due to adding the project to the existing activities. In practice isolating the project cash stream may be complicated, due to a variety of reasons, and in general interdependencies will arise between the project, existing activities and other proposed projects and competitors. The causes of interdependency can be due to logistics, capital rationing, manpower rationing, the tax system, correlations between cash flows, competitive reaction and utility. The latter cause was referred to in the section on risk adjusted discount rates.

Logistics

Logistics comes into play when the capital investment is associated with introducing new capacity into a production/distribution system. For example, if a new production facility were added to an existing system the pattern of supplying the various markets will be perturbed. The resultant change in product flow will need to be evaluated, perhaps using a model of the system, in order to determine the cash stream corresponding to the new facility.

Capital and Manpower Rationing

Capital and manpower rationing can both constrain the number of projects undertaken. The implications for project selection are that simple accept/reject decisions cannot be made on individual project proposals as the total number of projects accepted might require capital or manpower in excess of the amounts available. If this is the case then formal constraints must be added to the appraisal process and as a result a model including the resource pattern of the ongoing activities and all proposed projects may be required. The use of linear programming for capital rationing was proposed by Weingartner[30] and an early application in a practical situation is due to Chambers.[31] These models are typically multi-time period models with constraints applying in each year. A linear programming approach assumes the divisibility of a project and if this is unrealistic then an integer programming formulation may be necessary. A solution to a linear or integer programming model would give the set of projects which maximises the NPV or NTV subject to the various constraints imposed. An alternative to a (mathematical) programming approach would be to use a financial simulation model which evaluates the financial consequences of accepting any particular selection of projects.

It is often argued that capital rationing constraints are illusory in the sense that capital for good projects is always available through the financial markets. Certainly there is usually no reason why capital constraints should be hard in the sense that they cannot be violated under any circumstances. Mathematical programming models need not be rejected under this assumption, however, and indeed can be an effective tool for exploring the consequences of different levels of availability of capital. This can be particularly useful if additional capital can be obtained at a premium rate of interest.

Manpower constraints can become necessary, due to the limited availability of management and other skills. These are also unlikely to lead to hard constraints and can be accommodated in the same way as capital constraints. If necessary both kinds of constraints could be modelled simultaneously.

The existence of capital or manpower constraints implies that projects can no longer be assessed in isolation. If uncertainty is to be admitted into the assessment, then a risk analysis approach is still feasible as a financial simulation model can be designed to allow a risk analysis. The incorporation of uncertainty into a mathematical programming model leads to the field of stochastic programming, in which the models are generally difficult to solve.

Taxation Induced Interdependencies

The UK corporate tax system is currently in transition in so far as the system of capital allowances and corporate tax rates is being changed. Prior to April 1984 a capital investment in plant or machinery attracted up to 100% initial allowance which meant that the entire investment could be offset against profits. Lower allowances were available for other investments such as buildings and offices. As a result of the capital allowances, companies were required to pay corporation tax only on the profits that exceeded the capital allowances due. Berry and Dyson[32] showed that this allowance system itself caused interdependencies between ongoing activities and proposed projects, even in the absence of capital rationing constraints. This process is illustrated in the following example. As a result of the erosion of the 100% initial allowance the

Table 2. Cash Streams £000s

	Year 1	Year 2	Year 3
Ongoing profits	(100)	20	20
Project A	(100)	200	110
Project B	(140)		190

interdependencies due to the tax system will be less strong, but nevertheless will still exist.

Consider a firm with profits from ongoing activities and with two projects being considered for adoption with the cash streams shown in Table 2.

If the projects are evaluated independently then for Project A, assuming a 10% discount rate, and ignoring taxation:

$$\text{NPV (A)} = -100 + \frac{200}{1+0.1} + \frac{100}{(1+0.1)^2}$$

$$= 172.7$$

$$\text{and NPV(B)} = 17.0$$

Each project, when evaluated independently, has a positive NPV and is therefore acceptable under the usual decision rule.

A project should ideally be evaluated in terms of the marginal benefit contributed by the project and this should include the taxation effects. Assuming a 100% initial allowance, and a 52% corporate tax rate, we can evaluate the NPV of the firm's ongoing activities, and the change in NPV due to each project. The analysis is as follows:

Ongoing activities:

	Year 1	Year 2	Year 3
Firm ongoing activities	20	20	20
Tax at 52%	10.4	10.4	10.4
Net profit	9.6	9.6	9.6

$$\text{NPV (ongoing)} = 9.6 + \frac{9.6}{1.1} + \frac{9.6}{(1.1)^2} = 28.26$$

Ongoing plus project A:

	Year 1	Year 2	Year 3
Ongoing profits	20	20	20
Project A	(100)	200	110
Capital allowance used	20	80	—
Taxable profit	—	140	130
Tax at 52%	—	72.8	67.6
Net cash flow	(80)	147.2	62.4

In the above computations the taxable profits have been calculated after taking account of the capital allowance as follows. The investment of 100 secures a capital allowance of 100, assuming 100% initial allowance. As profits available in year 1 are 20, these can be offset by an equal capital allowance so that no tax is payable in year 1. The remaining capital allowance, 80, not used in year 1 is carried forward to year 2. The taxable profit in year 2 is then the amount by which total profits exceed the allowance carried forward, i.e. $220-80=140$. The net cash flows are calculated by subtracting the tax payments from the total income.

$$\text{NPV (ongoing}+A)= -80+\frac{147.2}{1.1}+\frac{62.4}{(1.1)^2}=105.39$$

The net benefit from project A is thus:

$$\text{NPV (ongoing}+A)-\text{NPV (ongoing)}=77.13$$

Thus allowing for tax, project A is still worth while.

Ongoing plus project B:

	Year 1	Year 2	Year 3
Ongoing profits	20	20	20
Project B	(140)	—	190
Capital allowance used	20	20	100
Taxable profit	—	—	110
Tax at 52%	—	—	57.2
Net cash flow	(120)	20	158.8

NPV (ongoing $+B$) $=24.46$.

The net benefit from project B is thus:

$$\text{NPV (ongoing}+B)-\text{NPV (ongoing)}=24.46-28.26$$
$$=(3.8)$$

Project B makes a negative contribution.

The above evaluation of project B ignored the possibility of project B being undertaken along with project A. It is possible, therefore, to obtain another evaluation of project B—its marginal contribution to the firm plus project A.

	Year 1	Year 2	Year 3
Ongoing profits	20	20	20
Project A	(100)	200	110
Project B	(140)	—	190
Capital allowance used	20	220	—
Taxable profit	—	—	320
Tax at 52%	—	—	166.4
Net cash flow	(220)	220	153.6

NPV (ongoing $+A+B$) $=106.94$

Under this assumption the net benefit of project B becomes:

$$\text{NPV (ongoing}+A+B)-\text{NPV (ongoing}+A)=1.55$$

Project B thus makes a positive contribution and is worth undertaking provided project A is undertaken.

The above analysis demonstrates the interdependency of proposed projects amongst themselves and with ongoing activities, and demonstrates that individual project evaluation is not possible under a tax system incorporating capital allowances (and other features of the UK tax system), in which profits from one project can be offset against investments in another.

The example assumed the pre-April 1984 tax system. From 1984 onwards the capital allowance for plant and machinery is being reduced progressively to a 25% reducing balance, i.e. an initial allowance of 25% of the investment with further allowances of 25% of the balance in subsequent years. Although this change requires a different analysis, the retention of a capital allowance system ensures that the interdependencies remain. Berry and Dyson[32] show how various aspects of the UK tax system can be incorporated into a mathematical programming model for project selection. The tax rules could also be incorporated into a financial simulation model. (It is worth noting that capital allowances taken in subsequent years are not increased in line with inflation so that the benefit is diminished in inflationary times.)

Correlations

Assuming that future cash flows are uncertain, a further source of interdependency can be due to correlations between a project's cash flows and other uncertainties. In the section on the CAPM the importance of the correlation of a project with the market portfolio was stressed. The assumption there is that a diversified shareholder is concerned to reduce his risk and an important aspect of the evaluation of a project is the risk pattern of the project, compared to that of the capital market.

Correlations can also be important if a project appraisal is being carried out taking account of the management preferences and attitude to risk. The concern now is with the correlation of a project's cash stream with the cash streams from ongoing activities and from other proposed projects. It is the existence of such correlations which might cause a project to sell ice-cream to be viewed particularly attractively by the manager of a fish and chip shop thinking of diversification as it would reduce the total risk of the operation. These correlations can be incorporated into a financial simulation model for corporate risk analysis, and Berry and Dyson[14] discuss the modification of risk adjusted discount rates to allow for statistical dependencies. The identification of these dependencies and the measurement of the correlations is by no means straightforward.

Competitive Reaction

A capital investment proposal can often involve an attempted expansion of market share and such a proposal can lead to a strong competitive reaction. This interdependency with competitors can be a major source of uncertainty affecting market size, market share, price and revenue. Risk analysis does not, of course, exclude the competitive dimension, but contemporary business policy teaching and research places competitiveness as the primary issue for many organisations (see Porter).[33]

Adopting this stance, the risk analysis process can be elaborated as shown in Figure 3.

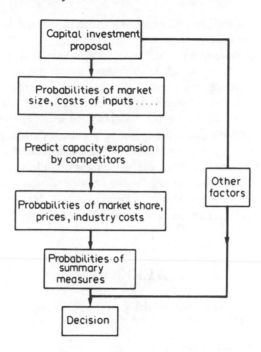

Figure 3. The competitive risk analysis process

As in risk analysis the probabilities of the summary measures are produced by a simulation process, but the simulation of the competitive element becomes an explicit component.

Competitive reaction also affects the calculation of risk adjusted discount rates. If the management viewpoint is taken, the effect of competition will be reflected in the level of uncertainty of the cash stream and hence in the risk premium. If the shareholder's viewpoint is taken, in a competitive market the additional uncertainty should be reflected in the β value and also in the mean level of the return on the project. Again this will lead to a change in the risk premium. Broyles and Franks[20] discuss the modification of the risk premium depending on whether the capital investment involves a replacement of capacity, an increase in capacity or whether it is a new market.

CONCLUSION

This paper has provided an overview of financial investment appraisal. A variety of approaches which can contribute to the process have been discussed, and the sources of difference between them emphasised. One question remains to be answered: how best to put the component parts of an appraisal together in practice?

This paper takes the view that there is no single procedure which is correct at all times. Current orthodoxy in finance couples a stochastic simulation to generate cash flow distributions with risk adjusted discount rates based on CAPM. However, for many projects this may be like taking a sledge-hammer to crack a nut. For others it may ignore important strategic and social issues, as among other things it assumes that the interest of shareholders is pre-eminent.

In essence this paper recommends a flexible approach in which multiple summary measures are generated and in which both financial and non-financial issues appear.

To this extent the recommendations of the paper mirror current practice far more than many, how to do it, tracts. However, this is not simply an easy path to acceptance by management. It is more a reflection of a belief that a gap between the recommendations of experts and management practice should prompt a search for reasons why, rather than a simple statement that management is wrong again!

Theory should certainly inform practice. This paper includes comment on tax induced links between projects, and discounting future cash outflows, among other things, of which practitioners of investment appraisal should be aware. However, it is not impossible that the environment in which they work requires a response other than slavish conformity to theory.

REFERENCES

[1] I. G. Ansoff (1965) *Corporate Strategy*, McGraw-Hill, USA.

[2] G. J. A. Stern (1976) SOSIPing, or sophistical obfuscation of self-interest and prejudice. *Opl. Res. Q.* **27**, 915–930.

[3] S. Sunder (1973) Relationship between accounting changes and stock prices: problems of measurement and some empirical evidence. In *Empirical Research in Accounting: Selected Studies*, 1–45.

[4] H. M. Weingartner (1969) Some new views on the payback period and capital budgeting decisions. *Mgmt. Sci.* **15**, 594–607.

[5] R. H. Pike (1983) A review of recent trends in formal capital budgeting processes. *Accounting and Business Research.* **13**, 201–208.

[6] R. Brealey and S. Myers (1981) *Principles of Corporate Finance*, McGraw-Hill, USA.

[7] R. Dorfman (1981) The meaning of internal rates of return. *Journal of Finance*, **36**, 1011–102.

[8] J. F. Weston and E. F. Brigham (1981) *Managerial Finance*, The Dryden Press, Hinsdale, Illinois.

[9] D. B. Hertz (1964) Risk analysis in capital investment. *Harvard Business Review* **42**, 95–106.

[10] D. B. Hertz and H. Thomas (1983) *Risk Analysis and its Applications*, Wiley.

[11] J. C. Hull (1980) *The Evaluation of Risk in Business Investment*, Pergamon.

[12] J. C. Hershey, H. C. Kunreuther and P. H. H. Schoemaker (1982) Sources of bias in assessment procedures for utility functions. *Mgmt. Sci.* **28**, 936–954.

[13] R. H. Berry and R. G. Dyson (1980) On the negative risk premium for risk adjusted discount rates. *Journal of Business Finance and Accounting* **7**, 427–436.

[14] R. H. Berry and R. G. Dyson (1984) On the negative risk premium for risk adjusted discount rates: reply and extension. *Journal of Business Finance and Accounting*, forthcoming.

[15] S. K. Lioukas and P. M. Moore (1983) Incremental evaluation of risky choices. *J. Opl. Res. Soc.* **34**, 413–418.

[16] J. E. Copeland and J. F. Weston (1983) *Financial Theory and Corporate Policy*, Addison-Wesley.

[17] J. Mossin (1966) Equilibrium in a Capital Asset Market. *Econometrica* **34**, 768–783.

[18] M. Theobald (1980) An analysis of the market model and beta factors using UK equity share data. *Journal of Business Finance and Accounting* **7**, 49–64.

[19] E. Dimson and P. Marsh (eds) *Risk Measurement Service*, London Business School, quarterly.

[20] J. E. Broyles and J. F. Franks (1973) Capital project appraisal: a modern approach. *Managerial Finance* **2**, 85–96.

[21] E. Dimson and R. A. Brealey (1978) The risk premium on UK equities. *The Investment Analyst* **38**, 14–18.

[22] A. Buckley (1981) Beta geared and ungeared. *Accounting and Business Research* **42**, 121–126.
[23] J. A. Schnabel (1983) Beta geared and ungeared: an extension. *Accounting and Business Research* **50**, 128–130.
[24] J. R. Franks and J. E. Broyles (1979) *Modern Managerial Finance*, Wiley.
[25] S. C. Myers (1974) Interactions of corporate financing and investment decisions—implications for capital budgeting, *Journal of Finance* **29**, 1–25.
[26] C. W. Haley and L. D. Schall (1979) *The Theory of Financial Decisions*, McGraw Hill.
[27] R. W. Banz and M. H. Miller (1978) Prices for state-contingent claims: some estimates and applications. *Journal of Business* **51**, 653–672.
[28] S. A. Ross (1979) A simple approach to the valuation of risky streams. *Journal of Business* **52**, 254–286.
[29] A. K. Gehr (1981) Risk adjusted capital budgeting using arbitrage. *Financial Management* **10**, 14–19.
[30] H. M. Weingartner (1963) *Mathematical Programming and the Analysis of Capital Budgeting Problems*, Prentice Hall, Englewood Cliffs, NJ.
[31] D. J. Chambers (1967) Programming the allocation of funds subject to restrictions on reported results. *Opl. Res. Q.* **18**, 407–432.
[32] R. H. Berry and R. G. Dyson (1979) A mathematical programming approach to taxation induced interdependencies in investment appraisal. *Journal of Business Finance and Accounting* **6**, 425–442.
[33] M. E. Porter (1980) *Competitive Strategy*, The Free Press.

Chapter 15

The Capital-Investment Appraisal of New Technology: Problems, Misconceptions and Research Directions

R. W. Ashford, R. G. Dyson and S. D. Hodges
School of Industrial and Business Studies, University of Warwick

The application of traditional techniques of capital-investment appraisal to new technology has been criticized for its bias towards short-term gains and the consequent favour of the *status quo*. This paper considers four classes of criticisms. They relate to the use of payback and discounted cash-flow methods, the assumptions made about the future, benefits of new technology which are ignored, and issues related to management control. The paper rehearses the criticisms and discusses their validity. The overall conclusion is that the biases in capital-investment appraisal are avoidable. The criticisms are not valid with regard to the overall approach of capital-investment appraisal, and the apparent bias is due to misapplication of the techniques.

INTRODUCTION

The purpose of this paper is to consider the claim that the introduction of new technology is inhibited by traditional methods of capital-investment appraisal.

Industrial activity has always been subject to change. At various times, changes of different types and effectiveness have predominated. Over the past 10 years there have been fairly radical changes caused by what is loosely called 'new technology', and these may be regarded as an industrial revolution. This revolution is still taking place, and there is little doubt that some areas will experience yet greater change in the next 10 years. These changes have included developments in computer technology, robotics and automation, biotechnology, and materials science.

By new technology we mean recent technological developments in areas such as these. They often require investments of a different nature from those made in the past.

Reprinted by permission from the *Journal of the Operational Research Society*, Volume 39, No. 7, pp. 637–642, Copyright ©1988, Operational Research Society Ltd.

Investment items tend to be much larger, the uncertainties associated with them apparently much greater and their organizational impact more widespread. Moreover, they tend to have a much greater strategic importance than investments in well-established plant, processes and products.

Criticism has been directed at the way in which investments in new technology are appraised. By appraisal we mean the prior financial analysis which seeks to evaluate the pecuniary benefits and disbenefits of the investment. It has been suggested[1-3] that there is a bias against new technology and that the practice of appraising investment on a short-term financial basis may not be appropriate.[4] Specifically, it has been alleged that the traditional appraisal methods of payback, discounted net present value (NPV) and internal rate of return (IRR) undervalue the long-term benefits; that traditional financial appraisals assume a far too static view of future industrial activity, under-rating the effects and pace of technological change; that there are many benefits from investments in new technology which are difficult to quantify and are often ignored in the appraisal process; and lastly, it is claimed that the systems of management control often employed by large organizations compound the bias against those investments which, although expensive, reap rewards vital for long-term viability. The first issue is a criticism of financial technique; the next two are criticisms of the way in which business operations are modelled; and the last is an issue of organizational control and behaviour.

We address each of these four areas of criticism in turn. Broadly we suggest that financial appraisals, like other exercises in quantitative management, depend upon the proper application of a quantitative model to commercial decision-making. We show that the criticisms directed at traditional appraisal methods may to some extent be based on misconceptions of the financial models and the ways in which they are best used. Suggestions are made for the better application of these models and the use of techniques which reduce or eliminate the bias against new technology.

Traditional investment-appraisal methods are considered first. Assumptions about the future are then discussed before the more important benefits of new technology that traditional financial appraisals are claimed to ignore. Finally we discuss pertinent issues of management control, before concluding with the view that the criticisms are valid only in so far as the financial instruments are misunderstood or misapplied.

TRADITIONAL APPRAISAL METHODS

Senker[2] attacks the use of both payback methods, whether discounted or not, and discounted cash-flow (DCF) techniques of NPV and IRR.

The objection to payback methods is that they ignore all cash flows after the desired payback period, which may be as short as 2 or 3 years. Thus they take no account of the long-term advantages that many large investments in new process technology bring, so the use of payback criteria is worthy of comment.[5] Payback can be insensitive to considerable variation among projects (in terms of cash flows).[6] Payback methods are simple rules of thumb. Their attraction is their simplicity, and robustness for making judgements on possibly optimistic costings and uneasily quantified business risks. However, they do ignore medium- and long-term cash flows, and it is perhaps surprising that they seem to be regarded as serious tools of financial analysis. The criticisms of payback methods are therefore valid, but these are criticisms that generally predate the advent of new technology, and examples of their being used as the sole appraisal technique are, in practice, rare. The argument usually given for their use is that they are a simple approach to safeguarding against undue risk, as projects with a short payback are likely to be less risky. Too much stress on their use can thus indeed operate against proposals for new technology.

A similar objection is raised to the use of NPV and IRR. The claim is that discounting future cash benefits under-emphasizes the future benefits of new technology. This problem may be exacerbated by the application of risk premia to the discount rate. New technology is assumed to be riskier than that which has been well established, in that the usual market risks are compounded by uncertainties in installation, throughput, performance and the like. These may be appreciable—especially when combined with those of developing and exploring new markets. Hence high discount rates are employed which severely diminish the impact of future cash benefits on the appraisal.

The argument that discounting places too little weight on the future rests purely on the magnitude of the discount factors used. It is not uncommon for companies' discount rates to be considerably higher than the figure a financial economist would estimate for the opportunity cost of capital. The risk premium may overstate the market's view of the uncertainties of investing in new technology, and fail to recognize the way in which flexible systems can reduce risk through their ability to manufacture a range of products. The discount rate may also be inflated to compensate for non-profit-making projects, such as canteen facilities. Further, it is not unknown for companies to project cash flows in real rather than inflated terms, and then to discount them at a nominal inflated interest rate instead of a real one. The combination of these effects is an exaggerated discount rate which biases the appraisal against long-term rewards. The error is thus not in the notion of discounting, but in the determination of the appropriate discount rate and in the consistent use of real cash flows with a real discount rate, or nominal cash flows with a nominal discount rate.

Whilst recognizing the difficulty in discount-rate determination, there can be little reason for systematic error as there is a considerable literature on estimating required rates of return.[7,8] The correct procedure from the shareholders' viewpoint is to take the risk-free rate, i.e. that on short-term government bonds, plus some risk premium to cover the uncertainties inherent in the projects of which the investments are a part. The rationale behind the risk premium lies in the market's valuation of the firm: for a given expected return, investors prefer investments of lowest risk, and for investments of a given riskiness, investors prefer those with the highest expected return. The risk premium normally used arises from the established capital-asset pricing model (CAPM), and although it is an approximation, it works well in most practical situations (see Haley and Schall,[9] p. 169). For example, it has been used in appraising advanced automation.[10] Company managers' interests may well conflict with those of their shareholders, and if the managers' interests are to be reflected in appraisals, a premium appropriate to the total risk would be employed. As this is always greater than the risk relative to the market as a whole, the calculated risk premium will also be greater. Again, the criticism that the rate is too high is not a criticism of the investment-appraisal method, but rather of its application.

ASSUMPTIONS ABOUT THE FUTURE

In carrying out a traditional investment appraisal it is often assumed that, without a particular investment project, the company can operate as before, that industry costs remain the same, and that the demand for goods and services stays unchanged. This combination of no investment and an unchanged environment is sometimes called the base case. Appraisals of new investments are made relative to this base case, and only investments showing a clear benefit beyond the base case can be justified.

The potential weaknesses of this approach are fairly obvious: the base-case analysis can easily overstate the true position. The environment within which the company operates is dynamic, with markets, inputs, technology and competitors changing, and this is particularly true in markets with a potential for technological innovation. In these circumstances, a company opting for no investment or innovation will find that its products are displaced by advanced products from its competitors, or its prices are undercut by more cost-effective processes. The true base-case analysis should thus show a deterioration in the company's position so that investments compared to this should appear more favourable. This weakness can thus lead to bias against new technology, but again this is due to incorrect application of appraisal methods rather than any weaknesses in the methods *per se*. The correct approach would require forecasts or scenarios of the environment which should be incorporated into both the base-case analysis and the appraisal of new technology. There is thus a key and often neglected role for model-based forecasting within the investment-appraisal process.

Recent financial textbooks[11,12] now stress the importance of a careful definition of the base case, sensitivity analysis and scenario analysis, and analysis of comparative advantage and competitive reactions. Simmonds[13] provides some useful insights. However, quantification of competitive actions and reactions is a difficult and under-researched area. Costing of some form is thus necessary but difficult, and should be carried out, perhaps on a scenario basis, using cash-flow simulations.[10,14,15]

BENEFITS IGNORED

New technology often brings operational changes which, it is claimed,[16] are both beneficial and frequently ignored in the appraisal process. Some changes are undeniably more beneficial, and the most prominent of these are flexibility,[17,18] reduced inventories and work-in-progress,[2,19] improved quality control[20] and reduced lead-times.[21] Moreover, these benefits may themselves be related: for example, improved quality control may reduce work-in-progress and hence lead-times; flexibility reduces inventory levels. Examples of new technologies which bring these benefits are CAD/CAM systems, numerically controlled machine tools, flexible manufacturing systems and computerized MRP and inventory systems. The financial implications of each of these operational benefits can, in principle, be evaluated.

The abandonment option can be used to value flexibility within the familiar operational-research device of decision trees. Essentially, uses of a new technological investment that are alternative to its principal use should be regarded as options, which can be valued. In the case of the abandonment option, this means reusing the asset for another purpose if the project of which it is a part fails. The decision-tree approach to validate this kind of flexibility in capital budgeting is described in most modern texts on corporate financial management (see Brealey and Dimson,[7] Chap. 23). In addition, the application of the recent sophisticated techniques of option-pricing theory is beginning to be applied to this kind of problem.[22,23] The option-pricing approach depends on being able to identify a key economic variable (or variables) to characterize relevant future uncertainty. It is necessary to estimate the stochastic process of the variable(s). The immediate benefits of reduced stock levels and work-in-progress can be valued as their primary cost is that of committed capital. Other costs, such as those of storage, wastage and deterioration, can also be estimated. Improvements to quality control are harder to quantify, but immediate costs, such as those of remedying sub-standard work before sale and rectifying faulty products after sale, are more easily identified. Defect costs are starting to be quantified in the US, and a link may be inferred between defect rates and production costs.[24] Surprisingly, both vary together—costs falling as the defect rate falls. The most difficult costs to quantify are market effects due to a reputation for product reliability,[10] and those of customer goodwill. These are often issues of management policy as well as market reaction. The same problem besets the valuation of customer responsiveness, where the issue is more largely one of goodwill. We cannot suggest easy solutions to these problems, but we do suggest that they be identified as part of the appraisal process, perhaps as separate measures.

There are other major changes wrought by new technology, which may or may not be beneficial, but which are also commonly ignored in investment appraisal. Arguably the most important of these are interaction effects, both financial, physical and organizational.

The financial interaction which seems to have been most studied concerns capital budgeting under capital rationing or under tax rationing. Where a number of projects are competing for scarce funds (in one or more periods), it is well established that the best subset of projects to undertake can be selected by solving a mathematical-programming problem. In the case where funds will only be scarce in the current time-period, projects can be weighted according to their profitability indices (the ratio of present value to initial outlay). It seems unlikely that if cash is constrained in one period, it will be unconstrained in all future periods. To cope with this situation, a programming approach is needed which must also incorporate perceived opportunities for profitable investments in the future.[25] Similar, but usually more complex mathematical-programming methods can also be used to optimize with respect to tax positions which depend on the investments undertaken.[26,27] There is a certain amount of disagreement about how serious these types of rationing are. Some authors have suggested that capital markets are close to perfect and the supply of capital is very elastic. Rationing may be deliberately imposed as a rough but effective way of dealing with cash-flow forecasts from managers that tend to have an optimistic bias.

If purely financial interactions may not be very important, physical ones certainly are. These arise in a large variety of ways. Investment in a new product will often affect the life cycle of other substitute products made (or proposed) by the firm. Investment in new equipment will affect the utilization of other existing equipment. For example, the utility of CAD systems is greatly enhanced by links to CAM facilities, but this is often ignored.[28] The choice of new activities is also likely to be constrained by the availability of factory space, key management or labour, and possibly also capital equipment.

A particularly instructive example of an interaction caused by fluctuations in the level of output is given in Brealey and Myers[11] (Chap. 14). Existing machines with high running costs may be replaced with new ones which are cheap to operate but which involve high capital-costs. With a constant level of demand, one would normally expect a single type of machine to be used exclusively. However, with fluctuating demand, it is optimal to meet the base load with new machines, and to retain some of the old machines to meet peak demands. The interactions created by changing product mixes may be much more complex than this, and future interactions may be quite impossible to forecast. Given the degree of analytical intractability which clearly exists, what can and should companies do? The best prescription seems to lie in attempting to localize the extent of the interactions. Manufacturing cells are defined in such a way as to minimize their interactions with other manufacturing cells. Decisions about any given cell are taken in such a way that the interaction effects within the cell are properly recognized, albeit in a relatively informal manner.

Technical and management skills are the most prominent source of organizational interactions. The cost of acquiring new skills is almost always underestimated,[2,29] and is a likely consequence of inadequate effort at the planning and preparation stage. Japanese companies, in stark contrast to some of their British counterparts, experience fewer problems here but invest heavily in planning and training.[30]

To summarize, it may be extremely difficult to analyse all the financial consequences of investment in new technology. In the view of the ACARD[4] report (p. 19), 'it is difficult to assess precisely the financial benefits of new technologies before prototype installations have proved the new processes and techniques'. However, specific areas in which new technology yields benefits have been identified, and some of these are amenable to quantitative treatment. Research on financial appraisal has been conducted in specific technological areas—for example, flexible manufacturing cells,[31] multi-arm robotic assembly[32] and NC machine tools.[33] Where benefits cannot be quantified at all, these should not be omitted from the appraisal but formally stated as potential benefits.

MANAGEMENT CONTROL

The system of financial control exercised by many organizations is a disincentive to the rational appraisal of large investments whose lifetime is in excess of the time spent by managers in their posts. Managers are less likely to approve those projects which yield rewards for which someone else will take the credit than those which generate the bulk of their profits whilst they are still in the same post. The practice of establishing small profit centres and appraising them on a short-term basis encourages projects yielding quick returns at the expense of those that may be more beneficial in the long run.[2,34] The competition within companies thereby created by managers of such profit centres is often detrimental to the overall performances of the firm.[35] Moreover, the local orientation of such profit centres discourages recognitions of benefits which accrue to another profit centre—for example, quality of manufacture resulting from CAD. This is therefore another source of benefits of new technology that may potentially be ignored. Although these effects may be disastrous to the overall performance of the organization, they are a reasonable human reaction to bad systems of financial control, and investment-appraisal methods designed for such profit-centred organizations may often inhibit the introduction of new technology. These problems of local orientation may be approached by striving for a balance between centralized control and local autonomy, or by a realistic system of transfer pricing. Essentially, goods and services provided by one profit centre for use by another should be priced at a level to give maximum overall profit for the firm. This is somewhere between the marginal cost and the market rate. The problem of commitment to long-term projects emphasizes the need to use many performance measures, which should be more in accord with the long-term goals of the firm.[24]

It is also the case that those proposing investments and making the initial financial appraisal often lack the information required to account properly for its benefits and disbenefits within the context of the firm.[29] This is usually because the proponents are often the more technologically aware junior members of staff in whom companies would not have sufficient confidence to allow access to information outside their particular area. The process of innovation is often driven from the bottom up as well as from the top down.

CONCLUSIONS

In this paper we have considered the principal components of the alleged bias of traditional investment-appraisal methods against new technology. We conclude that bias in the appraisal process may exist, but that any such bias is not inherent but is due to the way in which the techniques are applied.

Payback methods are inadequate appraisal techniques and should never be used alone. NPV and IRR are appropriate ways of valuing future cash-flows. Any bias in their application will be due to a systematic use of too high a discount rate, but this can be avoided by correct analysis. Assumptions about the future can lead to bias if an over-optimistic picture of the no-investment position is taken, but again this is an avoidable pitfall. As for the benefits ignored, many of these can be quantified and brought formally into the analysis. Where benefits cannot be quantified, they should nevertheless be stated so that they can be given proper consideration when a final judgement is made. The bias due to the use of short-term financial criteria can be removed by the use of measures reflecting the longer-term benefits of present investments.

In principle, then, the biases of capital-investment appraisals are avoidable, but one difficulty remains. New technology invariably leads to greater complexity, and any unwillingness to face this complexity in the capital-investment process is likely to lead to bias against change.

REFERENCES

1. G. E. PINCHES (1982) Myopia, capital budgeting and decision making. *Financial Mgmt* Autumn, 6–9.
2. P. SENKER (1984) Implications of CAD/CAM for management. *Omega* 12, 225–231.
3. B. W. SMALL (1983) Paying for the technology—making the intangibles tangible. Proceedings of the 2nd European Conference on Assembly Automation, Birmingham.
4. ADVISORY COUNCIL FOR APPLIED RESEARCH AND DEVELOPMENT (1983) New opportunities in manufacturing: the management of technology. HMSO, London.
5. A. E. OWEN (1982) Automated assembly can equate with short payback periods. Proceedings of the 3rd International Conference on Assembly Automation.

6. H. OGDEN (1980) Justifying assembly automation economic methods. Proceedings of the 2nd International Conference on Assembly Automation, IFS, Bedford.
7. E. DIMSON AND R. A. BREALEY (1978) The risk premium on UK equities. *Invest. Analyst* **52**, 14–18.
8. R. G. IBBOTSON AND R. A. SINQUEFIELD (1982) Stocks, bonds bills and inflation: the past and the future. Financial Analysts Research Foundation, Charlottesville, Va, USA.
9. C. W. HALEY AND L. D. SCHALL (1979) *The Theory of Financial Decision*, 2nd edn. McGraw-Hill, London.
10. N. KULATILAKA (1984) Financial, economic and strategic issues concerning the decision to invest in advanced automation. *Int. J. Prod. Res.* **22**, 949–968.
11. R. A. BREALEY AND S. MYERS (1984) *Principles of Corporate Finance*, 2nd edn. McGraw-Hill, New York.
12. C. J. HIGSON (1986) *Business Finance*. Butterworth, London.
13. K. SIMMONDS (1982) Strategic management accounting for pricing. *Account. Bus. Res.* **12**, 206–214.
14. R. H. BERRY AND R. G. DYSON (1980) On the negative risk premium for risk adjusted discount rates. *JBFA* **7**, 427–436.
15. R. H. BERRY AND R. G. DYSON (1983) On the negative risk premium for risk adjusted discount rates: a reply. *JBFA* **10**, 157–159.
16. R. KAPLINSKY (1982) *Computer Aided Design*. Pinter, London.
17. B. GOLD (1982) CAM sets new rules for production. *Harvard Bus. Rev.* Nov./Dec., 88–94.
18. J. R. WILLIAMS (1983) Schumpeterian economies of scope. GSIA Working Paper, Carnegie-Mellon University.
19. R. JONES (1983) How to clear the justification hurdle. *The FMS Mag.* Jan., 119–121.
20. H. A. TOMBARI (1978) Factors to be considered when evaluating the purchase and use of numerically controlled machine tools. *Prod. Invent. Mgmt* **19**, 52–62.
21. C. A. VOSS (1984) The management of new manufacturing technology: eight propositions and illustrations for CAD/CAM and FMS. AGSM Working paper series, University of South Wales.
22. S. MYERS AND S. MAJD (1983) Calculating abandonment value using option pricing theory. MIT Sloan School Working Paper, No. 1462–83.
23. R. S. KAPLAN (1983) Measuring manufacturing performance: a new challenge for managerial accounting research. *Account. Rev.* **58**, 686–705.
25. D. J. ASHTON AND D. R. ATKINS (1979) Rules of thumb and the impact of debt in capital budgeting models. *J. Opl. Res. Soc.* **30**, 55–62.
26. R. H. BERRY AND R. G. DYSON (1979) A mathematical programming approach to taxation induced interdependencies in investment appraisal. *JBFA* **6**, 425–441.
27. R. W. ASHFORD, R. H. BERRY AND R. G. DYSON (1986) Taxation induced interactions in capital budgeting. IMRAD Working Paper No. 8, University of Warwick.
28. E. ARNOLD AND P. SENKER (1982) Designing for the future: the implications of CAD interactive graphics for employment and skills in the British engineering industry. EITB Occasional Paper, No. 9.
29. B. GOLD (1980) On the adaptation of technological innovations in industry: superficial models and complex decision processes. *Omega* **8**, 505–516.
30. G. F. BALL (1980) Report on vocational education and training for employment in engineering in Japan. British Council/EITB.
31. D. R. HUGHES, B. R. KILMARTING AND R. LEONARD (1983) Selection and financial appraisal of flexible manufacturing cells. Proceedings of the 2nd European Conference on Assembly Automation, Birmingham.
32. A. H. REDFORD, E. K. LO AND P. KILLEEN (1983) Cost analysis for multi-arm robotic assembly. *Assembly Automat.* Nov., 202–208.
33. J. FINNIE AND J. SIZER (1984) Simplichange: guidance notes for the financial evaluation of numerically controlled machine. London: ICMA with Machine Tool Industry Research Association.
34. I. C. MAGAZINER AND T. M. HOUT (1980) Japanese industrial policy. Policy Studies Institute.
35. E. SCIBERRAS (1982) Technical innovation and international competitiveness in the television industry. *Omega* **19**, 585–596.

_____ Chapter 16

Robustness and Optimality as Criteria
for Strategic Decisions

Jonathan Rosenhead, Martin Elton and Shiv K. Gupta
*London School of Economics, Institute for Operational Research
and University of Pennsylvania*

The use of 'optimality' as an operational research criterion is insufficiently discriminating. Ample evidence exists that for many problems simple optimization (particularly profit maximization) does not represent the aims of management. In this paper we discuss the nature of the problem situations for which alternative decision criteria are more appropriate. In particular the structure of strategic planning problems is analysed. The provisional commitment involved in a plan (in contrast to the irrevocable commitment of a decision) leads to the development of a particular criterion, *robustness*—a measure of the flexibility which an initial decision of a plan maintains for achieving near-optimal states in conditions of uncertainty. The robustness concept is developed through the case study of a sequential factory location problem.

INTRODUCTION

The operational research profession shows a persistent devotion to 'optimal' solutions to management problems. By definition these solutions should be the best available . . . and yet they often prove to be unacceptable to managers. This is a paradox worthy of resolution.

There are, of course, numerous proposed explanations. But it seems to us that many cases of the non-implementation of recommendations (and of the implementation of inappropriate recommendations) are due to failures in one of the most fundamental O.R. activities—the specification of objectives and of criteria.

In current O.R. usage, the concept of optimality has become largely restricted to profit maximization or cost minimization, or at least to finding the extreme values of some single objective function which can be treated exactly as if it were profit or cost.

Reprinted by permission from *Operational Research Quarterly*, Volume 23, No. 4, pp. 413–431, Copyright ©1972, Operational Research Society Ltd.

This approach excludes from consideration or distorts genuinely multiple objective situations, in which the different objectives are not commensurable. A further exclusion or distortion has been applied to problems in which a salient feature is that the outcomes of actions are not known with certainty—here the concentration has been on probabilistic expectation as the measure of optimality. As we discuss below, these simplifications are not appropriate for many classes of problems, and especially for planning problems.

The rationale for this restricted focus in model building has been the search for an optimality which is *objective*, in the sense that any manager or O.R. practitioner would agree on the same solution. This requires there to be only one, universally recognized criterion for any situation. If one is seen to choose among criteria, the essential subjectivity of any decision about preferred or best actions or outcomes is revealed. We would not regard this as a disadvantage—such choices *are* subjective, and do not cease to be so because we impose a uniform format on the formal decision process.

THE CONCEPT OF OPTIMALITY

The classical theory of economics was built upon the 'rational man' and his equally elusive counterpart, the profit-maximizing firm. For many years now this theory has been under challenge from prominent economists. Simon[1] and others point out that the managers of a large corporation rarely own more than a small proportion of the company's equity, and control over them by even the largest of institutional shareholders is exercised very loosely. According to Galbraith[2] the effective policy of the large corporation is to earn profits which are large enough to satisfy the shareholders and to insulate the corporation from undue pressure of the stock or money markets. Within this constraint, the managers pursue other objectives—frequently the maximization of sales revenue or of market share.[1] Baumol[3] and Williamson[4] suggest in explanation that managerial prestige and salaries are more closely tied to the scale of corporate operations than they are to profit. However, the attachment of O.R. practitioners to the (pseudo-) objective criterion of long-term profit maximization has been remarkably impervious to these arguments. Profit maximization and optimizations are still widely used as interchangeable terms.

In criticizing the current assumptions about what constitutes 'optimality', we do not mean that the profit-maximizing approach is always invalid. Profit maximization is appropriate in situations where the manager's motivation is based on a simple cash criterion—for example in tactical problems, particularly those concerned with operating systems for repetitive processes. However, in strategic decisions of the 'once-for-all' variety, which affect the long-term direction and viability of the organization, there are almost certain to be other relevant objectives besides simple profit maximization. This is especially true in the case of strategic (corporate) planning, which we will consider below at some length. But first we must discuss the way in which risk and uncertainty in single or multiple objective decision-making can affect the choice of decision criterion.

---

1. Baumol[3] gives simple illustrative examples of managerial problem situations in which profit-maximizing decisions will not necessarily maximize sales revenue, and vice versa.

RISK, UNCERTAINTY, MULTIPLE OBJECTIVES AND DECISION CRITERIA

Decision situations have been conventionally divided (see Luce and Raiffa[5]) into three categories—certainty, risk and uncertainty. In a *certainty* situation (one where no element of chance intervenes between decision and outcome) with only a single objective, there is no choice about criterion: we apply *simple optimization*, and prefer the decision which gives an outcome scoring highest on the objective function. The complexity of certainty problems (for example, linear programming or simple job-shop scheduling) arises principally because of the large number of possible outcomes which may need to be identified and compared.

If there are multiple objectives in a certainty situation, we are presented with a choice of criteria. The problem can be reduced to a single objective situation by transforming the different objective measures onto a common scale of value. Cost–benefit analysis is an example of such an approach—but the apparent achievement of objectivity through use of simple optimization is offset by the frequent subjectivity of the trade-offs. Alternatively, the criterion of *satisficing* can be used—defined variously by March and Simon,[6] and Simon[7] as finding any decision whose outcome achieves minimally satisfactory levels on all objective measures, or as finding which of such satisfactory decisions rates highest on just one of the objective measures. (The behaviour of large corporations, as described by Galbraith,[2] is an example of the second type of satisficing.) This criterion can be interpreted as equivalent to simple optimization under constraints, but there is a difference of emphasis. As Simon[7] says 'If you allow me to determine the constraints, I don't care who selects the optimization criterion'.[1]

A third, neglected decision criterion for multiple objective, certainty situations is that of *lexicographic ordering*. In this the decision is taken in terms of a prime objective; only in the event of a tie will the decision be taken in terms of a secondary objective, and so on.

In *risk* situations (where the link between decisions and outcomes is probabilistic) the range of criteria is extended. Conventionally the expected value of a single objective is taken as the measure over which to optimize. This measure has the disadvantage of ignoring much information contained in the probability distribution of the objective function. Sensitivity analysis is often used to explore the scale of possible variations. Methods which take more formal account of risk (see Byrne[9]) include *risk discounting* and *certainty equivalents*. For the former, the expected profit is reduced by an amount proportional to the spread of the distribution of profit; for the latter, risk-indifference curves are plotted for the standard deviation of profit against the expected value of profit. Each of these criteria results in a measure which is a conceptual extension of expected profit. Alternative criteria (whose appropriateness will depend on the probability distribution of profit—for example, the minimization of the probability of loss, or of a profit below some specified level. For multiple objective risk situations all the criteria developed for comparable certainty situations can be employed, provided that measures related to expected profit are used for each objective.

There is also a range of criteria, from which choice is necessarily subjective, for *uncertainty* situations—those in which it is impossible to attribute probabilities to the

---

1. The distinction between satisficing and optimizing approaches, and its relevance to public as opposed to private decision-making, is discussed by Eilon.[8]

possible outcomes of any decision. This can occur when the outcome of a decision may depend on a simultaneous or subsequent decision of a competitor whose objectives conflict with one's own, or on future external events of a non-repeatable variety, for which the estimation of probabilities is a dubious exercise. It may be possible to convert an uncertainty problem into a risk problem, for example by the subjective estimation of probabilities, and used appropriately this can be a valuable simplification. However, some aspects of the future are genuinely unknowable, even in the probability sense. To insert notional probabilities may make the decision-maker more comfortable, but that is not necessarily the objective in tackling a decision problem.

One possible criterion for uncertainty situations is the *minimax* criterion, under which the decision-alternative to choose is that for which the lowest level of benefit (taken across all possible competitive decisions or external events) is as high as possible. Use of the minimax criterion necessarily results in conservative decisions, based as it is on an anticipation that the worst might well happen. In a competitive situation this may be appropriate—if your competitor's interests conflict with yours, and he pursues them rationally, he will choose policies which will reduce your gains to a minimum. Another possible criterion is that of *minimax regret*. Here the first step is to compute the 'regret' associated with each combination of decision and external circumstance, regret being the difference between the resulting benefit to the decision-maker, and the benefit from the decision he would have taken had he known which particular external circumstance would occur. The minimax criterion is then applied to the regret values, so as to choose the decision with the least maximum regret. A decision using this criterion will be less conservative, since it gives weight to missed opportunities.

Other criteria for single-objective uncertainty situations (see Byrne[9]) include *Laplace*—assign equal probabilities to all possible outcomes of a decision; *maximax*—choose that decision whose maximum pay-off is the highest; and *Hurwicz*—a compromise between minimax and maximax, with weighting at the discretion of the decision-maker.[1] These criteria could be applied to multiple objective uncertainty situations if a trade-off between objective is effected. Alternatively Hausner[11] and Thrall[12] show how lexicographic ordering of multi-dimensional utilities can be used in conjunction with the minimax criterion.

Roy[13] has discussed particular features of multiple objective decision-making, in particular the problems which arise when only a partial ordering of preferences among the *n*-tuple outcomes is available. He develops the concept of an 'outranking' relationship which is weaker (and therefore richer in its use of information) than simple dominance. This permits the identification of a 'kernel' of alternative decisions of which no one can be clearly preferred. Attention is concentrated on these decisions, and further information sought to reduce the uncertainty and incomparability.

1. A striking illustration of the possibly divergent effects on decision-making of using these different criteria is provided by Milnor.[10] If:

$$\begin{bmatrix} 2 & 2 & 0 & 1 \\ 1 & 1 & 1 & 1 \\ 0 & 4 & 0 & 0 \\ 1 & 3 & 0 & 0 \end{bmatrix}$$

is the pay-off matrix of a game against nature, then the indicated strategy for the row-player will be row 1 if he adopts the Laplace criterion; row 2 if he uses minimax; row 3 if he uses the Hurwicz criterion (with $\alpha > \frac{1}{4}$); and row 4 if he uses minimax regret.

These numerous examples of available decision criteria should illustrate our claim that the choice of simple optimization as a standard criterion, and the consequent attempt to force decision situations into its mould cannot remove subjectivity in decision-making—it can conceal it. The more vigorously the subjective elements are restrained, the more likely it is that the manager will feel that the O.R. analysis and recommendations are inappropriate or irrelevant to the problem he faces.

Another element in problem formulation is the time dimension. Time frequently enters as a variable in O.R. models, but its effects on decision criteria has been almost exclusively through the concept of time discounting of future benefits. The measures of profit or of other objectives in certainty, risk or even uncertainty situations can be adjusted for the time effect before applying one of the criteria discussed in the previous section. The role of time in the structure of the decision process itself has not been embodied in modifications of existing criteria. This is of particular importance for long-range planning problems, where both the time dimension and the prevailing uncertainty are of the essence.

We believe that the absence of criteria which take account of the basic structure of planning problems has been a major hindrance to the development and application of the O.R. approach in this area. In following sections we propose and explore two complementary criteria—robustness and stability—which allow for the implicit uncertainty and sequential nature of planning problems.

ROBUSTNESS

Plans must be distinguished from decisions. A plan contains a set of prospective decisions to be implemented at different future dates. A decision is a commitment of resources which is not reversible except by a further decision (and resources). At any point in the life of a plan, some of the prospective decisions will have been implemented, while others will have yet to be put into effect and so may more easily be changed. It is this possibility of revision of later decisions which is the distinctive characteristic of planning situations. (Howard[14] has proposed *proximal decision analysis* as a method for handling the effect of uncertainty in large decision problems. In this approach the optimal setting of decision variables is seen as being conditioned by the current state of knowledge about the uncontrollable environmental state variables. The effect on 'value' due to changes in the state of knowledge and to the resulting compensatory changes in the decision variables is analysed. However, the aim is still seen as the achievement of optimal, uni-dimensional value.)

Whether in industry or the public domain, a plan is needed to give cohesion to a host of tactical decisions; it is necessary so that decisions when taken are compatible with or lead towards states which are considered desirable for the company, agency or community. Planning has been defined (Ackoff[15]) as the design of a desired future and of effective ways of bringing it about. Yet as a plan is implemented new information will become available, attitudes to what is desirable or feasible may change, and the planning horizon will recede into the future.

Little of what is known about the system being planned for is known with certainty. Much of what is not known cannot be expressed in terms of probabilities—the future behaviour of other companies, agencies or governments and changes of public attitudes and priorities. The situation is one of uncertainty. As these uncontrollable and often unpredictable external events unfold, more information becomes available on the desirable future state and how to achieve it. In the light of this information it is natural and appropriate to reconsider and perhaps modify the as yet unimplemented stages of the plan. But if the possibility of making revisions has played no role in the specification of the earlier, implemented decisions, there may no longer be adequate residual flexibility. All decisions limit the future by committing the present. A plan whose initial decisions limit the future as little as possible has an evolutionary advantage in an uncertain world.

Consider a planning problem in which one decision must be chosen from a set $\mathbf{D}\{\equiv(d_i)\}$ of short-term decisions; and in which one of a set $\mathbf{S}$ of alternative plans (or solutions) will be realized in the long run. Any initial decision d_i will restrict the attainable plans to a subset $\mathbf{S}_i$ of $\mathbf{S}$.

Suppose that some subset $\hat{\mathbf{S}}$ of $\mathbf{S}$ is currently considered 'good' or acceptable according to some combination of satisficing criteria. A subset $\hat{\mathbf{S}}_i$ of $\hat{\mathbf{S}}$ will be attainable after an initial decision d_i. Then the *robustness* of d_i (see Gupta and Rosenhead,[16] and Friend and Jessop[17]) is defined as:

$$r_i = n(\hat{\mathbf{S}}_i)/n(\hat{\mathbf{S}}),$$

where $n(\mathbf{S})$ is the number of elements in set $\mathbf{S}$.

Robustness, a measure of the useful flexibility maintained by a decision, has characteristics which make it a suitable criterion for sequential decision-making under conditions of uncertainty. It handles the uncertainty of the environment, not by imposing a probabilistic structure, but by stressing the importance of flexibility. It makes explicit the distinction between committed decisions and planned solutions. It reflects the sequential nature of decision-making, by placing less emphasis on The Plan, but more on the continuous process of planning.

The initial committed decision of a plan, whether derived using robustness or a more conventional criterion of optimality, is specified against a framework of other decisions to be taken or implemented subsequently. But part of the uncertainty of the future is uncertainty about our own future actions. For reasons either external or internal to the planning organization, the decision-sequence may be truncated after the initial implemented decision so that subsequent stages of the plan are not activated. We say that the initial decision (or decisions) is *stable* if the system as modified by these decisions has a long-run performance which is satisfactory (relative to the alternatives) should no further stages of the decision-sequence be implemented.

Both robustness and stability are criteria for the choice of initial decision from the set $\mathbf{D}$, rather than for the selection of a solution from the set $\mathbf{S}$. This is, we suggest, the appropriate emphasis in planning. Before making a number of more detailed comments on the robustness–stability approach, we shall show how it was applied in a particular case.

A PLANT LOCATION PROBLEM[1]

Let us consider the not altogether hypothetical case of the YZ Manufacturing Corporation. The YZ Manufacturing Corporations had a number of factories scattered across the

1. An earlier analysis of this problem will be found in reference 16.

United States. In recent years sales of its consumable products had been booming, and considerable extra production capacity would soon be needed. The question which the YZ management posed to its O.R. consultants was, 'How many factories should be built in the next ten years, and where?'

In initial discussions with management, many factors were excluded from consideration. For example, it was concluded that location had no effect either on the cost of constructing the plant or on the annual running cost. The cost of land could also be excluded, for although land prices do vary from location to location, the differences are insignificant compared with the other variable costs. It could also be assumed that adequate labour, skilled and unskilled, was available at every location under consideration.

A restriction on the solution to the problem was that YZ Manufacturing had already commissioned detailed engineering designs for factories of a fixed capacity of half a million units per annum. These designs had the facility that two plants of half a million units capacity each could be constructed on a single site to produce a double-size factory, but this was the only possible variation in plant capacity. Such engineering studies were so costly that management were not prepared to re-open the debate on factory size. Finally, management presented the O.R. team with a set of 21 particular locations from which factory sites were to be selected. There was also the possibility of expanding the capacity of two of the existing factories.

How should an O.R. team tackle this problem? The first reaction might be that the problem was straightforward. All that was required was to forecast future sales, and so work out the number of half-million capacity plant units which would be needed. The only cost variable of significance was the cost of transportation from the factories to the customers. Transport costs from plants of known location and capacity to customers with known locations and demands can be minimized using the transportation method of linear programming. So provided one had forecasts of the geographical distribution of demand, all that was needed was to try each possible combination of locations for the right number of new plant units with the existing factories, use the transportation method to find the minimum cost solution for that configuration and then choose the configuration for which this minimum cost was lowest. There would then remain only the problem of deciding in which order construction of factories at the different indicated locations should take place—a question of second-order importance and no difficulty.

If this was the first reaction, some second thoughts should complicate the simple picture. If one new plant unit was required, there would be just 23 plant configurations to consider. If as many as 5 new plant units were to be called for, the number of possible factory configurations would be 70 339—prohibitive in cost and time.

Another difficulty was in agreeing a forecast. There was already in progress an acrimonious dispute between the marketing department and the firm's internal O.R. department about the trend of future sales—the marketing department's forecast for 10 years ahead being the greater by 50 per cent. Indeed, the team discovered that projecting historical sales data (which were available in suitable form for only the last 8 years) it was quite possible to obtain radically divergent forecasts, since either arithmetic or geometric growth could be assumed. Uncertainty is intrinsic to long-term sales forecasts in this sort of market; the two divergent internal forecasts each represented entirely possible anticipations of the future—one optimistic, one conservative. Yet the difference is between one new plant and five new plants in the next ten years.

Let us consider first the most complex case of five new factories. To be sure of finding the true 'optimum' set of five locations which will minimize transportation costs it would be necessary to work out the transportation cost for each of the more than 70 000 sets of five locations. In practice one might use intuition plus trial and error, or a more formal computational procedure, to seek out the best sets in a more economical manner; the best set which was found could then be accepted as being near enough to the true optimum for all practical purposes.

But any such procedure is tantamount to treating the location problem as just *one* decision which must be taken now. In fact it could be shown that under the optimistic forecast the first of the five new factories is needed in year 6 while the last need not go into production until year 10. Allowing for the delays which can affect any complex construction project, a decision on the first location is indeed needed as soon as possible. But even if we select an 'optimum' decision-set of five locations, four of the locations will remain just *planned* decisions, in the sense we have discussed. They will not become actual (irreversible) decisions for a varying number of years; they will therefore be subject to revision as new information becomes available on, for example, the geographic distribution of sales demand.

Another factor is that no one plan may be clearly superior, even for the predicted conditions. For the YZ Manufacturing problem, a total of 297 decision-sets (each consisting of five additional locations) was investigated by a trial and error procedure. As shown in Table 1, the best of these sets yielded an annual transport cost of $8.88 million but there were 31 sets with costs below $9.28 million and 78 sets with costs below $9.70 million. These differences of 10 per cent or less are not significant in the context of the imprecise data on which the computations are based—data about costs of transportations, national sales projections and forecasts of how these sales will be divided between different sales areas. Objectively it is very hard to prefer any of these decision-sets to any of the others. This situation is not atypical of location problems and a variety of other sequential decision problems.

Table 1. Annual transport costs (in $m) arising from different decision-sets

Decison-set	New factories	Transport cost	Decision set	New factories	Transport cost
1	A, B, M, N, S	8.88	17	B, D, J, L, N	9.14
2	B, G, M, N, S	8.92	18	B, M, N, R, Z	9.16
3	A, B, M, N, T	8.96	19	B, J, L, N, R	9.16
4	B, G, M, N, T	8.98	20	B, H, M, N, T	9.18
5	A, B, M, N, Z	8.99	21	A, B, I, L, N	9.20
6	B, D, M, N, S	8.99	22	B, G, L, M, N	9.21
7	A, B, L, N, R	9.01	23	B, G, I, L, N	9.21
8	B, G, M, N, Z	9.02	24	B, H, M, N, Z	9.22
9	B, M, N, R, S	9.03	25	A, B, L, M, N	9.22
10	A, B, D, L, N	9.05	26	B, M, N, S, U	9.23
11	B, G, L, N, R	9.07	27	B, H, L, N, R	9.24
12	B, D, G, L, N	9.09	28	B, D, H, L, N	9.26
13	B, D, M, N, Z	9.09	29	D, M, N, S, U	9.27
14	B, D, M, N, T	9.11	30	A, B, N, R, Z	9.27
15	B, M, N, R, T	9.12	31	A, B, H, M, S	9.28
16	B, H, M, N, S	9.13			

An escape from this impasse could be attempted by attaching subjective probabilities to each of a number of different forecasts of the future state of the environment (here, the pattern of future demand). We have already indicated our reservations about this procedure. Another objection is that when expected costs are computed differences will blur, and the expected costs of the alternative decision-sets will if anything become closer to each other than were the previous costs based on just one forecast of the future. The justification for selecting one set in preference to the others now rests on scientific-sounding probabilities but the situation is really unchanged.

We may apply robustness-analysis to this problem, taking the decision-sets in Table 1 as our set $\hat{S}$ of good solutions, so that $n(\hat{S}) = 31$. If the initial decision is for location A, only 9 of these solutions are attainable, so that $n(\hat{S}_A) = 9$, and the robustness of location A is $r_A = 9/31 = 0.29$. The robustness of each possible decision is shown in Table 2. Locations B and N each have a robustness of 0.97, so that one or other of these two would appear to be the indicated initial decision.

In this particular case, an initial decision for, say, location N does not exclude the (apparently) best decision-set, number 1. But the reverse need not hold. Use of the conventional optimality criterion would lead to decision-set 1; and then the choice of the order in which to construct the factories would be made by means, for example, of a discounted cash flow study of the 120 possible sequences of A, B, M, N and S. It is quite possible that N would not have been the first in 'optimal' sequence which maximized the discounted cash flow. In this case for a (probably) marginal advantage in discounted future profits, based on unreliable projections, a considerable degree of flexibility would have been abandoned.

The analysis so far has ignored a distorting factor. Suppose that in a certain region (call it α) four alternative sites are available—let us call them $\alpha 1$, $\alpha 2$, $\alpha 3$ and $\alpha 4$. The sites are quite close to each other, and therefore the performance of any decision-set incorporating location $\alpha 1$ will be not much different from the performances of the three decision-sets formed by substituting $\alpha 2$, $\alpha 3$ and $\alpha 4$ for $\alpha 1$,

Table 2. Robustness of initial decisions

Location	No. of occurrences	Robustness
B	30	0.97
N	30	0.97
M	20	0.65
L	12	0.39
A	9	0.29
D	8	0.26
R	8	0.26
S	8	0.26
G	7	0.23
H	6	0.19
Z	6	0.19
T	5	0.16
I	2	0.06
J	2	0.06
U	2	0.06
		5.00

Table 3. Transport costs if one new factory is built

New factory locations	Annual cost ($m)
L	9.28
S	9.48
T	9.62
N	9.66
Z	9.69
M	9.73
B	10.30

It follows that if, as here, decision alternatives are approximate substitutes for each other, they must feature with approximately equal frequency in the 'good' plans. This inevitably dilutes the robustness-score of any single one of the alternatives. Even if *one* location in region α features in every good plan, no single location will have a robustness-score much in excess of 0.25. So by offering too many alternatives in region α the balance will have been weighted not in favour of the region, but against.

Our example is in its essence not hypothetical. Examination of Table 1 shows that in the YZ Manufacturing case, one (and only one) of locations L, S, T and Z features in each of the 31 'good' plans. Arising out of the geography and population distribution of the United States these four locations, although up to several hundred miles apart, are approximate substitutes for each other in a region which it is expensive to supply from elsewhere. So to the robust initial locations B and N, each with a robustness of 0.97, we must add a notional location (call it α) somewhere in the L-S-T-Z region, with a robustness of 1.00.

In this case robustness has narrowed down the choice of initial decision to one of three locations, but does not distinguish meaningfully between them. One factor which can be taken into account is the short-run cost incurred by each of these decisions. Another, related factor is the cost-level associated with each decision if only one factory is constructed before the planning horizon is reached—this may well be the situation if the conservative demand forecast proves to be accurate. However, an interruption of the decision sequence can arise from other causes—financial strain, or a change in management policy. We therefore pose the problems more generally, in terms of *stability*-analysis. How would the system fare if, in the long run, no location decisions after the first were implemented? To answer this question, we compute transport costs for the system as augmented by each possible new location in turn—for a national demand in year 10 of a magnitude which requires only one new factory. These costs are shown in Table 3.

Of course the planned development may be aborted after more than one new factory has been built. Table 4 shows the annual cost[1] of the best pairs of new factories, if national demand in year 10 requires only two. (Three and four factory cases can be analysed similarly.)

Consideration of Tables 3 and 4 shows the greater stability of an initial factory in the α-region. In fact if L is the α-factory, the gain over its nearest rival is nearly $400 000

---

1. The variation in the general cost levels between the different tables is the product of several interacting factors—the scale of demand, the dependence of mean distance travelled on the number of factories, and the extent of surplus capacity.

Table 4. Transport costs if two new factories
are built

New factory locations	Annual cost ($m)
L, N	8.73
H, L	8.75
N, S	9.01
H, S	9.04
A, L	9.06
N, T	9.08
G, L	9.08
H, T	9.11
N, Z	9.15
H, Z	9.17
B, L	9.27
M, N	9.28

per annum if only one factory is constructed. The two-factory case is more complicated. While the best decision-pair incorporates both L and N, once the distorting effect of the α-region is removed it can be seen that 5 of the 6 best two-factory solutions incorporate L, but only 2 incorporate N.

On grounds of robustness and stability, criteria which make allowance for two types of uncertainty, the indicated single initial decision is L. Yet there are other tests which an initial decision might need to pass to prove itself an acceptable location. One might be its short-term profitability, before all stages of the plan have been completed. Other criteria will no doubt be appropriate in particular situations to meet particular types of uncertainty.

SOME COMMENTS ON ROBUSTNESS

Robustness as a game against Nature

Application of the robustness criterion can be regarded as solving a game against Nature. Consider a game in which (in our earlier notation) the decision-maker has as possible strategies the elements of **D**, while Nature's possible strategies correspond to the elements $\{s_j\}$ of **S**. The pay-off to the decision-maker is 1 if the initial d_i, is included in s_j, and 0 otherwise. The Laplace criterion—maximize the expected pay-off under the assumption that each state of Nature is equally likely—is then equivalent to the maximizing of robustness.

This interpretation is advanced, not because we regard robustness analysis as essentially a special case of game theory, but because it can provide a convenient and familiar framework for discussing some features of robustness.

In this formulation, the problem of the distortion of robustness scores when several of the alternative initial decisions are equivalent (as happened in the case study reported in Section 5) can be seen in a new light. If an extra row is added to the game by including in **D** a decision d_i' which is in every way identical to d_i, then there is a consequent large increase in the number of columns. For every element of **S** which contains d_i, a new element with d_i' substituted for d_i must be added. If the old element featured in the set **Ŝ** of good solutions, so will the new element. So the addition of a redundant alternative initial strategy for the decision-maker results in the addition of many irrelevant strategies for Nature. Under the Laplace criterion it is known that the inclusion of irrelevant strategies for Nature can distort the solution. The distortion of robustness scores through the inclusion of redundant alternative decisions is equivalent to this.

It would be comparatively easy to avoid this trap in small-scale problems, or where the decisions are simple alternatives. When the equivalent game matrix is large, or when the substitutability of decisions is less clear cut, the combinatorial problems in screening out all redundant alternatives can be formidable. However, a good knowledge of the structure of the system under study coupled with systematic inspection of the constitution of the membership of $\hat{S}$ should reveal any major effects.

Efficient Use of Information

In the definition of robustness, no information about the members of the set S is used, other than whether each is a member of the set $\hat{S}$. In a case such as that of the YZ Manufacturing Company, we have information on the 'value' $V(s_j)$ (for our example, the negative of cost) of each solution s_j. We believe that the suggestion that it would be wasteful not to use this information by giving a higher rating to those solutions with higher values is dubious.

The justification for the robustness approach is that the situation is one of uncertainty, so that the 'values' $V(s_j)$ are hedged about with doubt. The only assumption implicit in robustness analysis is that solutions which appear 'good' in terms of the predicted values $V(s_j)$ are more likely to be good under the conditions which are eventually realized.

In the YZ example the value differences between different good solutions were relatively small, so that little information was sacrificed. If variations of value within $\hat{S}$ are regarded as too high for the loss of information to be negligible, one possibility is to raise the satisficing level; alternatively, a modified robustness index:

$$r_i = \sum_{s_j \in \hat{S}i} V(s_j) \Big/ \sum_{s_j \in S} V(s_j)$$

could be used. This would be equivalent to allowing the pay-offs in the associated game to take values other than 0 and 1.

Choice of Satisficing Level

In practice a decision will be needed as to an appropriate satisficing level to determine the members of $\hat{S}$. In some situations a level representing an agreed threshold for acceptable solutions may be discoverable. In other cases it will be worth undertaking sensitivity analysis on the effect on the ordering of robustness scores as the satisficing level is varied. This was carried out in the YZ Manufacturing case, and the results showed there was little sensitivity. This is not unexpected. If a lower satisficing level gives corresponding sets $\hat{S}'$ and $\hat{S}_i'$, then $\hat{S}$ is a subset of $\hat{S}'$, and $\hat{S}_i$ is a subset of $\hat{S}_i'$. Writing (for short):

$$n = n(\hat{S}), \quad n_i = n(\hat{S}_i)$$

and:

$$n' = n(\hat{S}') = n + n^*, \; n_i' = n(\hat{S}_i) = n_i + n^*_i$$

we find that:

$$r_i - r_i' = (n_i n^* - n^*_i n)/n(n + n^*)$$

Now $r_i = n_i/n$; we may write $n^*_i/n^* = kr_i$. Then $r_i - r_i' = r_i(1 - k)n^*/n'$. So the difference in robustness is proportional to the product of terms representing the local difference in robustness and the ratio of new to total number of good solutions. It follows that robustness scores can be expected to exhibit insensitivity to changes in satisficing level.

Planning Horizon

In robustness analysis, solutions (or plans) are classified as good (i.e. placed in $\hat{S}$) according to their performance at (or up to) a planning horizon. The choice of planning horizon is necessarily a compromise between increasing complexity and uncertainty on the one hand, and inadequate cohesion and lack of preparedness on the other. The effect of different choices of planning horizon on robustness can be explored by sensitivity analysis. Thus in the case of YZ Manufacturing, robustness could be computed over a four (rather than five) factory horizon. Again, a good deal of continuity can be expected. If great sensitivity were uncovered, it would be *prima facie* evidence that the planning horizon had been placed too close.

However, the precise specification of the planning horizon is a secondary concern. The process of adaptive planning, which is the only context in which robustness can be employed, involves a regular re-appraisal of the plan as new information becomes available, with the planning horizon further advanced into the future.

The Cost of Robustness

Flexibility is normally achieved only at a cost. The robust initial decision will not necessarily be an element of the plan with highest 'value'. It may be necessary to weigh the apparent loss of value involved in adopting a robust decision, against the apparent loss of flexibility in adopting the 'optimal' decision. The balance will tend to favour robustness in conditions of high uncertainty.

The search for robustness may be misrepresented as a recipe for inaction. This need not be so: while inactivity keeps many options open, it forecloses on others. Inaction will be robust only if it leads with higher frequency to possible good solutions. What is true is that robustness analysis will favour the rejection of unnecessary or premature commitment to decisions. In cases where there is a pressure for commitment (see Friend and Jessop[17]) extraneous to the problem under consideration, it may be necessary to over-ride a robust inactivity.

Balancing the Short and Long Term

Robustness, by emphasizing flexibility, favours longer-term interests. To ensure that due weight is attached to short-term benefits, it would be possible to compute robustness based on the present discounted value of each member of **S**. This approach, while more sophisticated, could easily undervalue the long-term effects—and it is in the long term that uncertainty is greatest. One would have more confidence in this approach if the subset **Ŝ** of good solutions proved relatively insensitive to changes in discount rate, but it would then be unlikely to give results very different from these of simple robustness analysis.

An alternative way of handling the time dimension would be to set satisficing levels for all time periods up to the planning horizon. The subset **Ŝ** would then consist only of solutions which were satisfactory at each point on the time path.

Robustness and Multiple Objectives

Robustness can be extended to cover multiple objective situations, in which good solutions may be defined as those which satisficed on each scale of benefit. It has been pointed out to us that in certain areas (such as urban planning) the scales of benefit may be associated with particular pressure groups, interests or organizations.[1] The robustness approach would then result in a compromise seeking strategy. This does not seem intuitively unreasonable, but it does imply a particular decision-making style, which may on occasions conflict with conventional management practice.

RESEARCH DIRECTIONS

In this paper we have suggested that the concept of 'optimality' has been too narrowly limited to profit maximization and equivalent or related criteria. For any category of decision problem there is a range of possible decision criteria, and no one of them is universally appropriate. The choice between them in a particular case should depend on both subjective and objective factors.

A class of problems for which (profit-maximizing) optimality is particularly inappropriate is that of strategic planning, a special case of decision-making under uncertainty. A plan consists of a number of currently preferred future decisions, and only one decision or group of decisions which must be irrevocably implemented at this stage. The subsequent preferred decisions which constitute the plan can each be reviewed in the light of up-to-date information when their commitment times arrive. In this situation an appropriate criterion for the initial decision is one based on the degree of useful flexibility for future decisions which will be maintained.

Robustness is such a criterion of flexibility in achieving near-optimal solutions in conditions of uncertainty. Its advantages are discussed, as well as the factors which currently qualify its use. A related criterion, *stability*, has been suggested as a measure of the performance of different initial decisions should the full plan not be activated.

The range of conditions under which robustness and stability may be appropriate criteria illustrates the need to specify the nature of the prevailing uncertainty. One major distinction is between uncertainty as to system performance for a given 'state of the environment' (set of values of the uncontrollable exogenous variables), and uncertainty as to which of a number of discrete states of the environment will occur. In the YZ

---

1. Mayberry[18] develops a game theoretic approach to a related problem, where various interest groups have different, incommensurable pay-off functions. The different pay-off functions are defined as Nature's strategies, and Nature's minimax regret strategy is adopted as the compromise pay-off function to be maximized.

Manufacturing example, the uncertainty was handled as if it was of the former type. The approach used is appropriate also for cases of uncertainty as to the future state of the environment, provided that the particular state of the environment which is analysed is representative of the possible future states, and that the performance indices of the system vary smoothly with changes in state of the environment. When this continuity assumption cannot be made, no valid conclusions as to the useful flexibility left by a decision can be drawn by considering only one state of the environment.

When there is uncertainty as to which state of the environment will occur there is often also uncertainty as to system performance within any one state of the environment. How to handle the two types of uncertainty simultaneously is the subject of continuing research. Some possible alternative approaches may be indicated here, by means of a simple example.

Consider a two-stage decision problem, in which any pair of decisions from among A, B, C, D and E constitutes a possible plan. There are two possible discrete states of the environment, I and II. Under I, the 'good' plans are AB, AC, AD and AE; under II they are AD and BD. Which initial decision is more robust, A or D?

(i) If the probabilities associated with I and II are $\frac{1}{3}$ and $\frac{2}{3}$ (so that the uncertainty as to states of the environment is transformed into risk), we may compute an expected robustness of $(\frac{1}{3})(1)+(\frac{2}{3})(\frac{1}{2})=\frac{8}{12}$ for A. Similarly, the expected robustness for D is $\frac{9}{12}$. So D is the more robust.

(ii) If no probabilities are attributable to I and II, but there is no uncertainty *within* either of these states, then we may choose any initial decision which features in at least one good plan in each state. So A, B and D are equally acceptable, provided that for the second-stage decision we will have knowledge of which state of the environment will prevail.

(iii) If uncertainty as to the state of the environment will still be present for the second-stage decision, the two stages can be regarded as one. We may choose any decision *pair* which features in each state. This restricts us to AD. So either A or D is equally acceptable as an initial decision. The choice between them can incorporate secondary criteria.

(iv) It may well be that no good plan is common to the different states of the environment, or that uncertainty within states of the environment is a significant factor. We may then regard the situation as a game against Nature, with robustness scores as the pay-offs. Consider the same example, but with AD excluded from the list of good plans for state I. Table 5(a) shows the game matrix, in which strategies B, C and E are dominated. The 2×2 game which results (Table 5(b)) has an optimal minimax strategy for the decision-maker in which A is chosen with probability $\frac{2}{3}$ and D with probability $\frac{1}{3}$.

Table 5. Game matrix

	Nature				Nature	
	I	II			I	II
A	1	½		A	1	½
B	½	½		D	0	1
C	⅓	0				
D	0	1		(b)		
E	⅓	0				

(a)

Robustness and stability are two criteria which are appropriate in particular circumstances. Optimality is a criterion which will continue to have wide and useful application. Our argument is that criteria must be matched to circumstances; that more criteria are available than are often considered; and that new criteria can be developed when the need exists. If the criteria are related to the real requirements of the problem situation, their novelty need not be a bar to their understanding and acceptance by management.

ACKNOWLEDGEMENTS

We wish to thank both John Friend and Roger Pye for stimulating discussions and for very useful formulations, several of which are embedded in this paper.

REFERENCES

[1] H. A. Simon (1959) Theories of decision-making in economics and behavioural science. *Am. econ. R.* **49**, 253.

[2] J. K. Galbraith (1967) *The New Industrial State*. Hamilton, London.

[3] W. J. Baumol (1963) *Economic Theory and Operations Analysis*. Prentice-Hall, Englewood Cliffs, New Jersey.

[4] O. E. Williamson (1963) *The Economics of Discretionary Behaviour: Managerial Objectives in a Theory of the Firm*. Prentice-Hall, Englewood Cliffs, New Jersey.

[5] R. D. Luce and H. Raiffa (1954) *Games and Decision: Introduction and Critical Survey*. Wiley, New York.

[6] J. G. March and H. A. Simon (1958) *Organizations*. Wiley, New York.

[7] H. A. Simon (1964) On the concept of organisational goal. *Admin. Sci. Q.* **9**, 1.

[8] S. Eilon (1972) Goals and constraints in decision-making. *Opl Res. Q.* **23**, 3.

[9] E. T. Byrne (1969) Models of the firm under risk and uncertainty. In *Microeconomics and Decision Models of the Firm* (T. H. Naylor and J. M. Vernon, Ed.). Harcourt, Brace and World, New York.

[10] J. Milnor (1954) Games against Nature. In *Decision Processes* (R. M. Thrall, C. H. Coombs and R. L. Davies, Ed.). Wiley, New York.

[11] M. Hausner (1954) Multidimensional utilities. In *Decision Processes* (R. M. Thrall, C. H. Coombs and R. L. Davies, Ed.). Wiley, New York.

[12] R. M. Thrall (1954) Applications of multidimensional utility theory. In *Decision Processes* (R. M. Thrall, C. H. Coombs and R. L. Davies, Ed.). Wiley, New York.

[13] B. Roy (1970) *Problems and Methods with Multiple Objective Functions* (mimeographed). S.E.M.A., Paris.

[14] R. Howard (1971) Proximal decision analysis. *Mgmt Sci.* **17**, 507.

[15] R. L. Ackoff (1970) *A Concept of Corporate Planning*. Wiley, New York.

[16] S. K. Gupta and J. V. Rosenhead (1968) Robustness in sequential investment decisions. *Mgmt Sci.* **15**, B18.

[17] J. K. Friend and W. N. Jessop (1969) *Local Government and Strategic Choice*. Tavistock, London.

[18] J P. Mayberry (1964) Alternative payoff-function in statistical decision theory. In *The Proc. Third Int. Conf. on Operational Research* (G. Kreweras and G. Morlat, Ed.). English Universities Press, London.

Chapter 17

A Land Use Evaluation
Technique for Decision Makers

Michael C. Poulton

*Department of Urban and Rural Planning, Technical University of
Nova Scotia, Halifax, Nova Scotia B3J 2X4, Canada*

INTRODUCTION

None of the most widely known evaluation techniques used in planning were specifically designed to help decision makers[1] make the best possible judgements. The purpose of this paper is to offer a framework for such a technique. It is called the Evaluation Matrix for Decision Makers (EMDM).

To explain why this new approach is valuable it is first necessary to examine the existing array of methods. They evolved in response to demands that were often sudden and intense and they frequently reflect the idiosyncrasies of their inventors. As a result, when they are looked at in the light of requirements for a methodology designed to serve participants in the political decision-making process that surrounds land use planning, it is seen that few are consistently effective.

A CLARIFICATION OF EVALUATION TECHNIQUES

The extensive application of *formal* evaluation strategies in the land use planning process is a relatively recent phenomenon. This is not to say that no evaluations of planning proposals were ever carried out until a few years ago. They were, but they consisted primarily of reliance on guidelines to set standards and reviews by interested parties to resolve conflicts.

In the 1960s the situation changed. The use of cost-benefit analysis in transportation planning was firmly established after its application in the Chicago Area Transportation Study (State of Illinois, 1962). The successful use of the Planning Balance Sheet (PBS), a form of social cost-benefit analysis, by Nathaniel Lichfield in Swanley (1966),

Reprinted by permission from *Regional Studies*, Volume 16, No. 2, pp. 85–96, Copyright © 1982, Cambridge University Press.

Cambridge (1966) and Stevenage (1969) was very influential, as was Morris Hill's critique of this approach (Hill, 1968) and advocacy of an alternative—the Goals Achievement Matrix (GAM).

Hill was profoundly influenced by what McLaughlin, 1969, called the systems approach to planning. The idea that land use planning could and should be treated as a means of directing urban or regional change toward socially desirable objectives overwhelmed earlier concepts and encouraged widespread acceptance of the GAM and similar evaluation formulations.

Towards the end of the 1960s a more intense concern in the United States with long term damage to the physical environment resulted in the setting up of the National Environmental Protection Agency (NEPA) and the insistence that major development proposals be analysed through the use of Environmental Impact Statements. At the same time, similar concerns encouraged Ian McHarg and others to develop the technique he called Landscape Suitability Analysis (McHarg, 1969).

Evaluation methods that are variants of cost-benefit analysis or objective achievement analysis swept the field to such an extent that at least one author (Kettle, 1972) suggested that *all* evaluation methods were either based on welfare economics or based on measuring progress toward objectives. This assertion is not correct because there are techniques, such as land suitability analysis which is based on notions concerned with the 'inherent' value of landscape, that would not be included within either group. But, while Kettle's dichotomy is false it does point to a more fundamental one that is true. Evaluation techniques presently in use can be divided into those developed from *exogenous value axioms* and those relying on *endogenous value assertions*.

Evaluation Methods Based on Theories of Values

Methods based on *theories of values* have in common the fact that the evaluation techniques themselves incorporate the rules for making value judgements.

The most widely used technique of this type is *Cost-Benefit Analysis*. There is an extensive literature on the method dealing with both theory (Mishan, 1972; Layard, 1972; Dasgupta and Pearce, 1972) and practice (Harberger, 1971 and subsequent; OECD, 1972 and subsequent). It has been used most widely in transportation planning and economic development planning.

The theoretical foundations of cost-benefit analysis derive from welfare economics, a branch of economic thought that has had a very powerful influence on the practice of evaluation. The principal thesis derived from welfare economics and applied in cost-benefit analysis is that it is the felt, real benefits or costs to individuals that count and these alone. If these can be identified, quantified and summed it is possible to determine whether a project yields a net benefit or not. The method is individualistic in that it presumes a person is the best judge of what he or she wants and it looks to individual behaviour to reveal the value placed on acquiring benefits and avoiding costs. The values asserted in cost-benefit analysis have been widely accepted but practical applications of the method have been heavily criticized, primarily over inaccurate quantification of the costs and benefits pertaining to the proposal in question.

The *Planning Balance Sheet* is the invention of Lichfield. He emphasizes that the PBS is an extension of cost-benefit analysis particularly suited to the assessment of land use and transportation plans. The method is largely a presentational device for identifying and describing particular costs and benefits and assigning them to the groups of people affected.

Originally the 'balance sheet' attempted to identify the parties involved in transferring a specific harmful or beneficial effect as producers and consumers in a manner analogous to the recording of commercial transactions. This approach has largely been abandoned in favour of identifying the various sectors in the community who are affected adversely or beneficially and describing 'sectoral' or 'instrumental' objectives for sub-groups of 'consumers' and 'producers'. For example, some consumers in the Ipswich Study (Lichfield and Chapman, 1970) are 'industrialists and workers' and their instrumental objectives are taken to be 'occupational quality' and 'expansion space'. In the 'balance sheet' individual costs and benefits are described as precisely as possible, as a result some are expressed in money terms, others in physical units and still others, intangibles, are expressed using a simple preference scale.

Although Lichfield *et al.*, 1975, p. 60, argue strongly that the PBS conforms to the precepts of cost-benefit analysis, this is only true at the most general level. The balance sheet does not try to measure the net present value of a proposal. Rather it defines groups, makes presumptions about their likes and dislikes and attempts to quantify the degree to which people are made better or worse off in a variety of different respects.

Environmental *impact studies* along with economic impact studies, and to a lesser extent, social impact studies have long been carried out to supply basic quantitative evidence on the expected effects of proposals.

However, the predominant demand for impact studies in recent years has come not from the need to assemble information for comprehensive evaluation but rather from the hope that quantitative information will settle disagreement about the extent of specific harms or benefits. As a result, despite being designed only to elicit quantitative descriptions of impacts, the studies are frequently used as evaluation techniques in their own right. The impact statements required by NEPA for example, were to highlight irreversible effects and their significance and propose potential means of mitigation (Dishroom, 1975; Burchell and Listokin, 1975). These requirements at first provoked an *ad hoc* approach to the assertion and application of values in impact statements, but of late have stimulated serious attempts to develop and justify procedures that would extend impact statements into evaluation studies (Lichfield and Marinov, 1977).

There are several techniques that evaluate from an avowedly limited point of view. Instead of dealing with the first step of the evaluation problem as do impact statements, they take a specific aspect of the problem and deal with it from a particular point of view.

One such technique is *Threshold Analysis* (Kozlowski and Hughes, 1972). This technique defines the areas most suitable for development on the basis of development costs. The method concentrates on the avoidance of large costs incurred in going beyond capacity thresholds. Typically thresholds are encountered when development reaches a scale where major new infrastructure investments are required.

Land Suitability Analysis produces an index which shows the compatibility of a particular type of development with a particular location and parcel of land. The index is derived on the basis of the characteristics of the parcel and the disruptive or sympathetic potential of the type of development proposed. The land attributes are usually physical and biological but may just as easily be social or cultural.

In its original form the technique relied upon shaded map overlays to indicate degree of suitability in various respects (McHarg, 1969), but the whole process can be adapted to use numerical codes (Sinton, 1977; Hopkins, 1977).

Evaluation Methods Based on Theories of Process

The second type of evaluation approach does not incorporate a theory of value, rather it relies on a *theory of government* to justify the *process* whereby social values are discovered and legitimized. Methods that follow this line evaluate against a set of objectives.

The most well known comprehensive method to use endogenously generated values, the *Goals Achievement Matrix* (GAM), is a tableau that records the contribution made by a plan in pursuit of a series of objectives valued by the affected community. On one axis population sub-groups are listed and on the other are objectives, which specify ways toward more general goals. The extent to which each alternative plan produces progress for each sub-group and each objective specified on the margins is estimated and the value indicated in the appropriate cell. Quantification is pursued as far as possible in obtaining values, and money units are preferred because they allow the most extensive value comparisons. Criticism of the GAM has centred on two features of the method. These are: (1) the way in which goals are decided and valued; and (2) the validity of the process whereby values from the matrix are aggregated to give summary comparisons of alternate plans (Lichfield *et al.*, 1975, Chapter 6; Kettle and Whitbread, 1973).

Cost-Effectiveness Analysis is the name given to techniques that relate outputs of a plan or project to inputs when these are measured on different scales. Frequently, the inputs can be measured as money costs while the outputs must be measured by some form of simple or compound performance indices. The term is also applied in a narrower sense to refer only to mathematical programming techniques which, although used (Brown *et al.*, 1972), have mathematical constraints that mitigate against their widespread acceptance in planning.

Conceptually the techniques that allow for the endogenous definition of values are more straightforward than those which rely on exogenously determined value systems. This is because values may be culled as necessary without disturbing the format of the analysis, but the problem of setting values is only displaced, it is not disposed of.

CRITICISMS OF EVALUATION METHODS

Each of the methods described above can be criticized for reasons that are peculiar to the method in question. But there are more general criticisms that relate to most or all of the techniques mentioned. These concern either limitations of the evaluation exercise whatever approach is adopted or a mismatch of methods and user wants. The latter group can be tackled by rethinking the evaluation framework adopted while the former prove intractable because they generally relate to inaccessible information. The former limit the potential value of a particular methodology and are of three types as follows: (1) disagreement over the logically correct procedures to adopt; (2) inaccuracy and incompleteness of data; and (3) the moral justification for one means of value determination over another when both are consistent with the axioms of the methodology in use.

Cost-benefit studies have been particularly prone to the first type of criticism, probably because the underlying theory is much more clearly defined and connected to basic value axioms than it is with other methods. An example is the World Bank's practice of using world market prices as shadow prices for tradeable goods in cost-benefit studies of development projects. This approach is not consistent with the principle that input values should be based on opportunity costs and is therefore an incorrect procedure for a cost-benefit study (Sen, 1972).

All studies must work with incomplete information and so are always vulnerable to criticisms of the second type. Time and budget restrictions limit the amount of data that can be assembled and analysed, much would-be pertinent information relates to future conditions that are uncertain, and project impacts are often so diffuse that they are swamped by other influences. Some studies may also be criticized for the way in which the information they have used was obtained and interpreted. For example, the money value of time savings frequently crops up as the most important benefit mentioned in the assessment of transport plans. But both the experiments used to establish values for time savings and the interpretations placed on these values have been censured (Heggie, 1969).

Issues of the third type can be illustrated by the question of how much to invest in reducing mortal hazards. This is difficult to judge because the value to put on saving life, or more precisely increasing life expectancy, is a moral question and one to which empirical evidence from past behaviour gives very little indication of a consistent value preferred by society.

While the internal problems arising from information gaps and disagreements about values can only be dissipated to a limited extent, it ought to be possible to do much to erase the external problems connected with the matching of methodology and user wants. Here the difficulties relate to: (1) inconsistency between the methods and aims of the evaluation process and the methods and aims of the decision-making process; and (2) inadequate development of methods that are consistent with the decision-making process.

There are many examples of the former type of problem. Cost-benefit analysis as used in planning has become less and less acceptable as the sole procedure for evaluation, and cost-benefit studies in transport and water resource analysis are now generally buttressed by extensive environmental impact analyses (Advisory Committee on Trunk Road Assessment, 1977; Fairchild, 1973). Evaluation on the basis of accepted objectives for decision-making, an essential feature of the GAM and similar approaches, is hard to do because firm commitment to explicit objectives in advance of concrete decisions is not required and may be infeasible in the political decision-making process (see, for example, Poulton, 1979). The latter failure can stem from inadequate execution of an acceptable approach or from the use of methods that are useful as far as they go but lack sufficient depth or breadth. Impact studies used as evaluation exercises often exhibit both problems. The problems of inconsistent logic and insufficient application to the needs of the decision-making process are tractable, but dealing with them can involve trade-offs. In particular, the sacrifice of rigour in the logical design of the methodology may be required in order to be pragmatic in supplying useful information to decision makers. The performance of the PBS and the GAM is very instructive in this regard.

Hill, 1966, takes Lichfield and the PBS to task for not conforming to a rational view of planning yet Litchfield, 1975, claims that, in practice, GAM and PBS do not differ greatly. This, if true, represents a remarkable convergence because the two methods are based on entirely different principles and reflect entirely different views of the planning and decision-making process. The reason that it is possible is that neither technique adheres rigorously to its purported basis. Hill, 1966, cannot convincingly legitimize either the selection and valuing of objectives and sectors or the weighting and aggregation procedures he proposes. Lichfield, 1969, 1970, does not stick at all closely to the principles of cost-benefit analysis. Both methods summarize evaluative information disaggregating by sector and describing, through the objectives mentioned, the source of benefits accruing to different groups of people.

The two methods have contradictory purposes and the authors are uncertain about their contribution to evaluation and decision-making. This is most clearly shown by Lichfield where he says on the one hand that the purpose of the PBS is *to point out the welfare implications* of alternative decisions (Lichfield *et al.*, 1975, p. 95) and on the other that it is explicitly a decision-making tool designed to give decision takers the disinterested information they need to make rational judgements. The former it may be, the latter it assuredly is not—because it is limited to a utilitarian view of welfare that does not accommodate alternative ethical positions. The GAM is expressly a 'rational' means of evaluation, but only so long as the objectives used have an understood and *agreed upon* value as a basis for decision-making. If they are ambivalent or unstable the argument supporting the method loses much of its force.

Both methods are tugged one way by methodological requirements and another by the effort to supply practical information. To eliminate the resulting distortions it would be necessary to change them so that they either deliberately present the outcome of a principled point of view, or are stripped of their theoretical baggage altogether so as to present evaluative information in a format designed solely to assist decision makers to reach judgements. But if the latter option is chosen it makes more sense to go back to first principles and develop an evaluation framework from an understanding of what users want rather than attempt to rejig methods designed with other purposes in mind.

REQUIREMENTS FOR EVALUATION PROCEDURES

The purpose of evaluation is to convey information for decision-making. Both Hill, 1966, and Lichfield, 1975, accept this statement of intent and indeed it is unexceptional. They treat it as one of many considerations in designing the GAM and PBS. We will make it the *sole* motive in the design of an evaluation process.

As such, it suggests a role for the evaluator that is analogous to that of a judge in summing up a trial. The judge concentrates the attention of the jury on the key points of the evidence and arguments and on the alternative decisions that can be made. The judge does not make the decision but he sifts, critiques and summarizes the evidence and alerts the jury to the consequences of possible decisions. To help the jury come to a decision he makes value judgements on what evidence is important and why. He make take a value stance and explore its consequences but he neither loses sight of the decision takers nor the process by which judgement is made.

The evaluator, like the judge, should be 'objective' in the sense that he should present a disinterested, fair and reasoned weighing of the evidence.

This statement of role and purpose is very general but it provides a foundation on which to build an evaluation framework that is quite specific. If an evaluation is going to be succinct and informative without being restrictive or biased it must be assembled on the basis of requirements that ensure these qualities are protected. The requirements together with the statement of purpose will then control the form of the evaluation.

Requirements may relate to content or format. Seven follow—they mould an evaluation designed for decision makers.

Requirement 1: The evaluation should aim to be of the greatest possible decision-making value within the budget and time constraints placed upon its production.

This means that effort should be allocated in proportion to the marginal decision-making value of the resources employed. In practice, this translates into a work strategy that focuses on resolvable conflicts and clarification of the key issues in the decision to be made. It follows that effort should *not* be allocated on the basis of how far different, recognized costs and benefits or valued impacts can be quantified.

This latter position, accepted by Lichfield *et al.*, 1975, p. 90, and Hill, 1973, p. 53, only makes sense in a situation where there is no foreknowledge about which information is likely to be significant in forming decisions and which is not. This is rarely, if ever, the case. Claims and stances on the issue by organized interest groups often provide an immediate pointer showing where factual information and careful investigation can profitably be employed. Indeed, the Cambridge study done by Lichfield, 1966b, and reworked by Hill, 1966, was just such a situation.

Requirement 2: The evaluation should use a format that presents information in a manner that is succinct and easily assimilable.

A literary presentation is sequential and does not exploit the two-dimensional capability of visual formats. A *matrix* or a diagrammatic format does use this potential and these are therefore likely to be less restrictive and more compact than a sequential format. The careful use of colour codes or shade density can add a 'third dimension' to a matrix and produce patterns that are very effective in revealing the thrust of a proposal. Part of the appeal of the GAM is that it appears compact and cohesive while the PBS as, for example, typified in Table A of the Swanley Study (Lichfield, 1966a), is an inefficient and confusing format. Land Suitability Analysis uses a means of diagrammatic display, map overlays or computer generated maps, that is immediate and direct and successfully conveys a lot of information very succinctly.

Requirement 3: The methodology should be intelligible to the layman.

The derivation of final results should avoid overt or covert arguments (mathematical or otherwise) that are abstruse, must be taken on trust, can only be validated between experts. The reason for this is that the evaluation will only be readily absorbed into the decision-making process if users can understand and respect the conclusions proffered. If users must take results on trust, especially when experts disagree on them, they will be reluctant to accept those that undercut their preferred position.

Cost-benefit analysis is frequently beset by a ground-swell of opposition based on the suspicion that it distorts results while the PBS is not, even though it is based on cost-benefit analysis. It is not esoteric and this helps to account for its appeal.

Requirement 4: The method used should be compatible with the decision-making process.

This means that the basis for decisions and the way they are arrived at must be correctly perceived and complied with. In planning, the decision-making process is public and political. The decision takers will be recipients of advice and persuasion from a variety of interests. They also take decisions as a group and their effective decisions are limited to concrete items—passing laws, making agreements, budgeting projects. As a group or as individuals they may adopt positions, but these have no effective force until embodied in legislated commitments. Failure to appreciate the significance of this last point undermines the importance of the weighted, validated objectives in the GAM.

Requirement 5: The analysis should be able to identify and address all objectives that are either directly or indirectly important to actors in the decision-making process.

It should not rely on a community consensus to specify values, means or objectives. Such a consensus implies a purely technical decision-making situation not a conflict resolving one. It is the latteer that is typical in planning.

Curiously the PBS appears to recognize this more clearly than the GAM. Lichfield's method identifies the desires of different sectors of the population explicitly but emphasizes the welfare of affected groups rather than the interests of those with a concern in the decisions to be made. The GAM goes no further than assessing how much progress toward community objectives is of value to individual, homogeneous sectors.

Requirement 6: All groups with a significant interest in the decision to be made should be recognized in the evaluation.

The groups or sectors may be identified by any common feature. The ones most likely to be included are socio-economic status, residence location and business interests. But the sectoring process should not automatically exclude such groups as the civic administrative bureaucracy (which will have to manage the results of decisions made) or any other group with a commonality of interest. Nor should it exclude groups of people who individually have a slight interest but collectively have a substantial one.

A restriction of the PBS is that it groups individuals on the basis of activities—residents, travellers, industrialists, and so on. This is suitable for stating transactions in the balance sheet but is not necessarily the most useful way of subdividing the population as far as decision-makers are concerned. Indeed, it is recognized as an awkward constraint by the author of the method because it hampers the ability of the PBS to reveal equity concerns (Lichfield *et al.*, 1975 p. 93).

Requirement 7: The evaluation should not be so designed that plausibly influential values are automatically excluded from consideration.

Concepts of fairness and deservingness, or beliefs about the way people ought to behave, as well as immediate self-interest affect people's attitudes. Conservationist stances, for instance, reflect a willingness to forego immediate tangible, personal benefits so that environmental qualities can be preserved and benefits for future generations safeguarded.

Values that do not conform to the precepts of the evaluative system adopted are easily overlooked. This is most evident in the utilitarian framework of cost-benefit analysis. The methodologies that use endogenous value-setting techniques would appear to avoid this problem but this is not necessarily so. The GAM relies on the assertion of objectives by the community or its representatives and assesses performance on the basis of the value of direct, sectoral benefits obtained through the pursuit of these objectives. Benefits or costs to individuals that are not reflected in the community objectives are therefore not captured by the Matrix.

It is instructive to see which requirements are satisfied by the methods mentioned in Table 1. Table 2 is a checklist that rates their performance. From this table it is evident that even the methods which profess to be comprehensive do not perform well.

The PBS and GAM are the top scorers in meeting the seven requirements of a decision oriented evaluation method. A new methodology designed strictly on the basis of these requirements should be superior to both of them. We shall describe such a methodology in the next section, call it the Evaluation Matrix for Decision Makers (EMDM), and show it in use.

Table 1. A classification of evaluation techniques

| Type | Completeness | | |
	Comprehensive	Limited depth	Limited breadth
Exogenous value axioms	Cost-benefit analysis PBS	Impact analysis (implicit value assertions)	Planning standards Threshold analysis Cost-revenue analysis Energy analysis Land suitability analysis
Endogenous value assertions	GAM	Impact analysis (no implicit value assertions)	Cost-effectiveness analysis

EVALUATION MATRIX FOR DECISION MAKERS

The EMDM consist of four separate but linked matrices. The column headings are alternative design options. The row headings are, in the first and second matrices values and objectives of importance because they are either widely held or of major importance to a number of individuals. The third matrix deals with direct public sector ramifications. Budget effects and administrative requirements are invariably of immediate importance to decision takers and it is important that decision makers review the evidence relating to the immediate implementing problems along with the expected results of the options in relation to aims and personal benefits. In the fourth matrix the row headings are sectors with a significant interest in the decisions to be made or a significant influence within the decision-making process.

Table 2. Degree to which methodologies meet requirements

| | Methodologies | | | | | | | | | | |
| | Based on exogenous value axioms | | | | | | | | Based on endogenous value assertions | | |
Requirements	Cost-benefit analysis	PBS	Impact analysis	Planning standards	Cost-revenue analysis	Energy analysis	Threshold analysis	Land suitability analysis	GAM	Impact analysis	Cost-effective-analysis
1. Maximizes decision-making value of inputs	**	**	*						**	*	
2. Matrix or diagrammatic format		*	**	*		*	**	***	***		
3. Intelligible to layman	*	**	**	**	**	**	*	**	**	**	**
4. Compatible with decision-making	**	**	**	*	***	*	*	*	***	**	**
5. Recognizes all significant objectives	*	*	*						**	*	
6. Recognizes all significant interest groups	*	**							***		
7. Open to all influential values	*	*							**	*	

Degree to which methodologies meet requirements: low*, medium**, high***.

Each cell of the matrix contains the result of the analysis for the relevant row-column headings along with the principles on which it is based and the argument for the value indicated. The cells are shaded or carry other indicators that record the apparent importance of the factor analysed there. This draws attention immediately to the key items in the evaluation.

There is no explicit attempt to convey interrelationships other than by user recognitition of overlaps. However, there is also no restriction on overlapping categories and so the principal factors of interest to any individual may be scrutinized and considered collectively in any way the person concerned thinks fit.

No attempt is made to provide single figure ratings for the alternatives. This is self defeating and distracting because first, the process of adjudication must be subjective and second, it directs attention away from the EMDM summary. However, there should be a commentary that accompanies the matrix in which general conclusions are presented and justified according to different points of view.

A CASE STUDY OF THE EMDM IN USE—
THE EXAMPLE OF HARBOUR PARK

The Harbour Park issue is typical of many planning conflicts in that it involves mutually exclusive land use options supported by active partisan interests and the ultimate decision takers are elected municipal politicians. As an illustrative case, it has the advantages that the issues and groups are clear cut and the alternatives proposed and stances adopted in response to them are well documented.

The City Council of Vancouver must decide what development to allow on a 14 acre (5.7 hectares) site called Harbour Park. The site is located adjacent to a very large and attractive park, on the waterfront, close to the central business district and affords spectacular views of the sea and mountains (Figure 1). The form that development should take has been a matter of controversy since 1963 when the site was first zoned for commercial development.[2]

Between 1963 and 1973 several developers put forward proposals incorporating hotels, apartment towers, offices and retail space. Opposition to this style of development was vociferous enough to compel the City to acquire the site. In 1974, Council did this and determined to limit development to that needed to recoup the $4.5 million paid for it. However, opposition to development continued and in April 1977 Council decided to thoroughly review the whole issue. The review generated a set of objectives for use of the site which were adopted by the Council as a whole in November 1977. They are summarized in Table 3.

Throughout, the imprint of the strongest pressure groups is clear. The Engineering Department as transportation developer was able to get its specific development proposals accepted in the guise of objectives. The 'green space' lobby was able to remove all direct encouragement to commercial development but was not able to get it disbarred. The 'pro-development' council minority was able to concede changes without agreeing to any words that would specifically rule out revenue raising development. The upshot is a set of objectives that provide a good reflection of the political state of play but are virtually useless as a firm guide for design or evaluation.

Unfortunately, the quest for acceptable objectives diverted attention and contributed

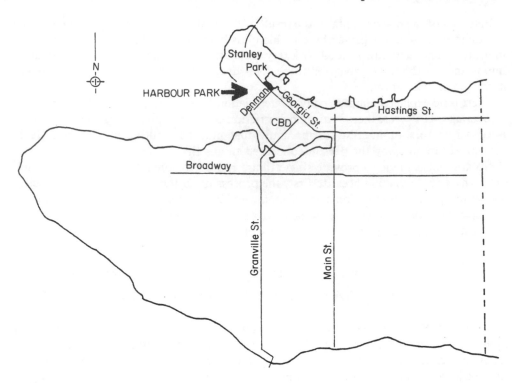

Figure 1. Location of Harbour park

to the information vacuum in which the conflict was allowed to proceed. Despite the fact that the two key areas of disagreement, the *actual* amenity value of the site and the scale of development required for the City to recover its spending, were well known, no serious analysis of either was undertaken until late in 1977 when a brief cost-revenue study of three types of development was commissioned (Urbanics, 1977). This report was delivered after Council had approved objectives for the site and showed that a development containing two tower blocks of apartments could fully recover the City's spending on the site. No quantitative analysis of the amenity issues was undertaken until early 1978 (Poulton and Eyre, 1978).

Table 3. Objectives for Harbour Park adopted by Vancouver City Council on 14 December 1977

1. The Harbour Park Site should be retained primarily for public use and enjoyment.
2. There should be some marina and marine-orientated use.
3. Any development should respect and maintain to the greatest possible extent the views of the water from Georgia Street.
4. Additional City capital expenditure should be recoverable from the development package.
5. A pedestrian waterfront walkway should be provided.
6. Provision should be made for a waterfront transit connection to the Park.
7. There should be provision for a 12 feet (4 metre) widening strip to facilitate future transit improvements.

Resolution—Council accepts the proposition that the approximately $4.5 million intended to be recovered from site is not now recoverable and therefore, this sum be permanently allocated to the site from revenue reserve. (*Source:* Vancouver City Planning Department memorandum of 22 March 1978.)

These two reports provided much of the quantitative information used in the EMDM. Data on traffic speeds and flows was obtained from the City Engineering Department. The Poulton and Eyre study also summarized the information contained in the Urbanics Report, 1977, and in relevant internal memoranda prepared by the City of Vancouver Planning and Engineering Departments. As a result, a complete and detailed statement of the sources and data used in the EMDM (Table 4) can be found in Chapters 4, 5 and 6 of that study. Here the results are simply stated with explanations and comments.

The main conclusions drawn from the EMDM are:

1. The City would definitely *gain* from development of the Marina in Harbour Park with rental revenue exceeding annualized costs by $30 000 per annum in each scheme.
2. The City's design 'concept' for a retail commercial development would *cost* the City $12 000 a year. In contrast, a larger and more attractive, but still unobtrusive, commercial development with shops and offices would yield $146 000 per annum to the city. Addition of luxury apartment towers would yield $3000 per apartment per year—150 apartments would cover all site acquisition and development costs.
3. The park experience provided by Harbour Park is *not of great value* and will cost about $240 000 annually to provide. Harbour Park is a small appendix to Stanley Park and is severely compromised by the six lanes of traffic on the adjacent arterial, Georgia Street.
4. No scheme other than the large scale hotel complex is expected to add more than one year's normal growth to the traffic on Georgia Street.
5. Present residents in the area of the West End adjacent to Harbour Park will be adversely affected in some ways. Construction will create some discomforts, and activity at the Park will put more pressure on local on-street parking space. Each development alternative will improve foreground views for local residents. Building one or two apartment towers will block more distant views to a *slight extent* (at the same time it will, of course, *create* new dwellings with views).
6. A large scale hotel complex on the site would create significant disbenefits to local residents and intensify traffic problems. Support for such development is not evident in the objectives, fiscal or otherwise, and its implications run counter to many of them.

CONCLUSIONS

The EMDM lacks the apparent rigour of the PBS or GAM but satisfies the concerns of parties to the decision-making process better than either. Their rigour is more apparent than real and is often more of a straitjacket than a support.

The EMDM's virtues are: (1) It is intelligible. All quantitative values are explained and related to the item of concern through the commentary—confusing symbols and indices are avoided. (2) Quantification and research are concentrated on the matrix elements that are most significant in making the final decision and the degree to which this is done is indicated for each item. In the Harbour Park example it is not fruitful to pursue quantification beyond the most general level in assessing the performance of a hotel/apartment complex because this type of development is virtually ruled out as a politically feasible option. On the other hand, the revenue benefits from an apartment development on a small part of the site are substantial and it is important to pinpoint

Table 4. Evaluation matrix for decision makers: Harbour Park

Item	Commentary	Alternatives				
		Park only	Large scale development	Planning development concept	Break-even development	Development to recover site costs
Values	General values exerting influence on final decision					
Fairness	1 Concern with unusual confiscation of property rights	—	—	—	Same	—
Equity	1 Transfer of benefits from few people to many or vice-versa	Many→few (park acquisition)	Size zoning changed Few→many (revenues to city)	many→few (park acquisition)		
Objectives	Synthesized by City Planning Dept., reflect all major concerns					
Public Use	4 % area in public use	*100%*	20%	75%	75%	75%
Yacht marina	4 number of berths provided	*350*	?	350	350	350
View at ground level	4 % frontage blocked at ground level	*0*	80%	0	40%	40%
Transport improvement	3 Flow capacity and quality increase in excess of generated demand	+	−	+	+	+
No hotels, offices apartments	Anti-development position expressed as a constraint	Yes	No	Yes	Yes	Yes
Fiscal Objectives	Revenue to the City					
Break-even on commercial operations	*Revenue from operation of marina and developments* 5 covers costs (min. position)	$30 000 p.a. surplus on Marina	*Large surplus*	$18 000 p.a. surplus, $2000 loss on comm. dev.	$176 000 p.a. surplus	$94 000 p.a. deficit
All costs covered	5 All operating and site preparation costs covered; substantial contribution to site acquisition costs	$252 000 p.a. deficit on operations and site preparation costs	*Large surplus*	$264 000 p.a. deficit	$94 000 p.a. deficit	2 towers of apartments yield $450 000 rent to city: $365 000 p.a. surplus
Affected Parties:	Includes all groups on behalf of which strong pleas have been made					
Site users						
Park users	2 Park is small and disturbed by traffic, excellent substitutes are available	*Slight benefit*		*Slight benefit*	*Same*	*Same*
Boat owners	3 Rent and services increased, net effect beneficial to some	Slight benefit		Slight benefit	Same	Same
Apartment owners	2 Buyers obtain net benefits that exceed those from other options		Benefit— possibly large			Benefit— uncertain size
Users of commercial developments	Hotel and retail customers, office and shop renters		Benefit— possibly large from use of view location	Benefit— slight views not greatly exploited	Same	Same

Affected Parties:
Non-users

	Description					
Local residents	Largely consist of the adjacent community and passing road traffic. [4] Threatened with extra noise, pressure on street parking space, loss of views	*Noise/parking* 0 *View loss* 0 *Foreground* + *Distance* 0	*Noise/parking* – – *View loss* 40% Blocked for 97 apts *Foreground* – – *Distance* – – View transfers to new properties + +	*Noise/parking* 0 *View loss* 0 *Foreground* + *Background* 0	Same	*Noise/parking* – *View loss* 5% Blocked for 97 apartments *Foreground* + *Distance* – *View transfers to new apartments* + +
Property owners	[3] Property values affected by development and uncertainty	Values +	Values + +	Values +	Same	Same
Local businesses	[3] Competition and generation of customers	Comp. 0 Custom 0	Comp. + Custom + +	Comp. + Custom + +	Same	Comp. 0 Custom +
Car users	[4] Traffic conditions, route attractiveness	Safety + Time + view +	Safety 0 Time – (substantial new traffic) view +	Safety + Time + (traffic generation less than one-year's normal growth) View –	Same	Same
Pedestrians	[3] New underpass mandatory saves time, increases safety	Safety + Time + View +	Safety + + Time + + View + +	Safety + Time + View +	Same	Same
Transit users	New transit priority facilities mandatory	Time + View +	Time – – View –	Time + View +	Same	Same

Notes:

All items derived from results contained in *Harbour Park: A Social Cost-Benefit Analysis*, M. C. Poulton (Ed.), 1978.

Code numbers attached to items indicate degree of quantification used. This is based on decision-making value of quantities sought and degree of difficulty encountered in obtaining them. The scale is as follows:

Concern is named	1
Direction of change indicated	2
Ordinal scale used	3
Physical quantities used	4
Money values used	5

General values were not explicitly acknowledged as issued in this problem, but two, **fairness** to existing residents with first come view rights, and **equity** in terms of use of city revenues were subsumed in several objectives.

The factor importance scale is based on priority as indicated by decision-makers' actions and has two levels—high (indicated by italic) and low (by roman).

the degree of visual disamenity created by the two towers needed, so that the harm done is neither exaggerated nor dismissed. (3) Key matrix elements are highlighted rather than abstracted as in Lichfield's 'Table B' (see, for example, Lichfield, 1969). This leaves them in context and 'weights' them by drawing decision makers' attention to them.

In a recent book reviewing and questioning current evaluation methodologies, McAllister, 1980, p. 277, appeals for an evaluation approach that enables public officials and individuals to reach personal judgements on the basis of the best obtainable information. Transforming personal judgements into group decisions he notes, is a political problem that should remain within the realm of accepted political procedures. It follows that the evaluative information assembled should be in tune with the political decision-making process. McAllister does not find any methodology designed to do this and instead suggests the use of *ad hoc* compendia of existing techniques. The EMDM fills this vacant role.

In a paper presented at a recent conference, Rees, 1979, called for improved mechanisms to appraise decision makers of the diversity of public opinion and preferences bearing on specific development proposals. The EMDM fills this role too.

A critic might protest that the virtues of the EMDM are obtained by tolerating an essentially eclectic methodology. Such a complaint forgets that the procedure is guided and that the eclecticism serves a specific purpose, and that purpose is ultimately the measure by which a practical evaluative method must be judged—how much does it help decision makers to act wisely in accordance with their own values.

NOTES

1. The term 'decision makers' is used to refer to all those with an interest, active or passive, in a particular decision. Decision takers are those charged with reaching decisions and making specific commitments.
2. For more background information see Collier R. W. (1975) *Contemporary Cathedrals: Large Scale Developments in Canadian Cities*. Harvest House, Montreal.

REFERENCES

Advisory Committee on Trunk Road Assessment (1977) *Report of Advisory Committee on Trunk Road Assessment: The Leitch Report*. HMSO, London.

Burchell R. W. and Listokin D. (1975) *The Environmental Impact Handbook*. Center for Urban Policy Research, Rutgers—The State University.

Brown, H. J. *et al.* (1972) Empirical models of urban land use: suggestions on research objectives and organization, Exploratory Report 6: 38–52, National Bureau of Economic Research, Washington.

Dasgupta A. K. and Pearce D. W. (1972) *Cost-Benefit Analysis: Theory and Practice*. Macmillan, London.

Dishroom H. (1975) A guide to preparing environmental assessment for community development. National model cities community development directors association, Washington.

Fairchild W. D. (1973) Principles and standards: two objectives, four accounts, *Water Spectrum*, **5**, 22–7.

Harberger A. C. *et al.* (Eds.) (1971 and following) *Benefit Cost Analysis: An Aldine Annual*. Aldine-Atherton, Chicago.

Heggie I. G. (1969) Are gravity models a valid technique for planning regional transport facilities? *Operational Res. Quart.* **20**, 93–110.

Hill M. (1966) A method for evaluating alternative plans: the goals achievement matrix applied to transportation plans, Ph.D. Dissertation, University of Pennsylvania, Philadelphia.

Hill M. (1968) A Goals-achievement matrix for evaluating alternative plans, *J. Am. Inst. Plann.* **34**, 19–29.

Hill M. (1973) Planning for multiple objectives, Monograph Series No. 5, Regional Science Research Institute, Philadelphia.

Hopkins L. D. (1977) Methods for generating land suitability maps: a comparative evaluation, *J. Am. Inst. Plann.* **43**, 386–400.

Kettle P. (1972) A comparison of the planning balance sheet and goals-achievement matrix methods of evaluation, Working Paper No. 7, School of Environmental Studies, University College, London.

Kettle P. and Whitbread P. (1973) An ordinal method of evaluation: a comment, *Urban Studies*, **10**, 93–9.

Kozlowski J. and Hughes J. T. (1972) *Threshold Analysis: A Quantitative Planning Method.* Architectural Press, London.

Layard R. (Ed.) (1972) *Cost Benefit Analysis.* Penguin Books, Harmondsworth.

Lichfield N. (1966a) Cost benefit analysis in town planning—a case study: Swanley, *Urban Studies*, **3**, 215–49.

Lichfield N. (1966b) Cost-benefit analysis in town planning: a case study of Cambridge, Cambridge and Isle of Ely County Council, Cambridge.

Lichfield N. and Associates (1969) Stevenage: cost/benefit analysis of alternative public/private transport modal split, 2 volumes, Stevenage Development Corporation, Stevenage.

Lichfield N. and Chapman H. (1970) Cost-benefit analysis in urban expansion—a case study: Ipswich, *Urban Studies*, **7**, 153–88.

Lichfield N., Kettle P. and Whitbread M. (1975) *Evaluation in the Planning Process.* Pergamon Press, Oxford.

Lichfield N. and Marinov U. (1977) Land-use planning and environmental protection: convergence or divergence, *Environ. Plann. A* **9**, 985–1002.

McAllister D. M. (1980) *Evaluation in Environmental Planning: Assessing Environmental, Social, Economic and Political Trade-offs.* M.I.T. Press, Cambridge, Mass.

McHarg I. (1969) *Design with Nature.* Nature History Press, New York.

McLoughlin J. B. (1969) *Urban and Regional Planning: A Systems Approach.* Faber and Faber, London.

Mishan E. J. (1972) *Elements of Cost-Benefit Analysis.* George Allen and Unwin, Hemel Hempstead.

Organization for Economic Cooperation and Development (OECD) (1972 and following), Series on cost-benefit analysis, Development Centre Studies, Paris.

Poulton M. C. (1979) Planning, policy evaluation and the uselessness of objectives, Proceedings: PTRC Summer Annual Meeting, 1979, pp. 67–78, PTRC Education and Research Service Ltd., London.

Poulton M. C. and Eyre P. (Eds.) (1978) Harbour Park: evaluation of alternatives and commentary on the planning process, School of Community and Regional Planning, University of British Columbia, Vancouver.

Rees W. (1979) Environmental impact assessment: the problem of evaluation, Proceedings: Second Environmental Impact Assessment Conference, pp. 83–98, Centre for Continuing Education, University of British Columbia, Vancouver.

Sen A. K. (1972) Control areas and accounting prices: an approach to economic evaluation, *Econ. J.* **82**, 486–501.

Sinton D. F. (1977) The user's guide to IMGRID—an information manipulation system for grid cell data structures, Department of Landscape Architecture, Harvard University, Cambridge, Mass.

State of Illinois (1962) Chicago area transportation study, Final Report, Volume 3, Bureau of Public Roads, Washington.

Urbanics Consultants Ltd. (1977) Harbour Park: development alternatives, City of Vancouver, Vancouver, BC.

Chapter 18

Applications of the Analytic Hierarchy Process to Long Range Planning Processes

James R. Emshoff and Thomas L. Saaty

Campbell Soup Company, NJ, USA, University of Pittsburgh, PA 15260, USA

This paper considers the long range planning process from the point of view both of projecting forward likely or desired changes from the curent position to define a possible future state, and of identifying desirable future states and working backwards from those to consider ways in which they could be reached. This process is repeated until consistency between the forward and backward looking processes is achieved. A theory of analytic hierarchies is used to give a formal structure of the process. An application to an actual corporate plan is briefly discussed.

INTRODUCTION

Long range planning processes can be formulated as a two-point boundary problem. One of the boundaries is fixed at the present state from which a process projects forward into the future. The other boundary is fixed at a future state (and time) and by working backwards, one attempts to overcome those obstacles which prevent the forward process from moving towards the desired state. This process is iterated until consistency between the forward and backward process is reached. A theory of analytical hierarchies is used to give a formal structure of the process.

We first give a theoretical discussion of how this method works and then present a detailed case study in Section 4. The application is to an organization planning problem and illustrates how we involved line staff personnel in solving the problem.

We use the theory of ratio scales, priorities and hierarchies in our approach to planning. Expositions of the theory and some of its applications have appeared in the literature, and hence we have set aside only a small part of the paper to show how it works [12].

Reprinted by permission from *European Journal of Operational Research,* Volume 10, pp. 131–143, Copyright © 1982, North-Holland.

The ideas relating to planning within an interactive forward-backward framework as used here are new. In passing, we mention that this procedure has already been applied to the following areas of planning: The Future of Higher Education in the U.S. [13], The Conflict in Northern Ireland [8,9], Corporate Planning [4], and Planning for the Navy. See also [10] and [11]. We begin a brief analysis of traditional long-range planning.

The Analytic Hierarchy Process used here was developed by Saaty in 1971. It is described in detail in [15] and [16], [17] contains applications.

REMARKS ON PLANNING

Planning is an ongoing decision process whose purposes are:

(1) to specify the ideals, objectives and goals an organization desires in the future;

(2) to define the programs that must be undertaken to achieve these ends; and

(3) to procure the resources, create the organization, and control the results of planning implementation.

An implicit assumption underlying an organization's long range planning process is that actions based only on what is best for present day considerations (i.e. tactical decisions) will not be sufficient for getting the organization to where it ought to be in the future. Were this assumption not so, the future could 'take care of itself when we get there'. However, the process by which an organization determines its strategic decisions is more complicated than that for day-to-day tactical decisions. Among the issues are:

(1) *Performance Criteria:* To determine ends, long-range strategies must address a wider set of values than do short range ones.

(2) *Feedback:* Strategies in long-range planning are difficult to evaluate because of lack of feedback.

(3) *Controllability:* An organization is better able to control short-range than long-range decisions. However, it has greater *potential* influence over long-range outcomes.

To achieve a measure of success, it is essential that there be *coordinated* participation in the planning process by managers and staff throughout the organization. Furthermore, the planning must be a *continuous* process that is *integrated* systematically with day-to-day tactical decisions. See [1] and [5].

These are essential attributes in the *theory* of strategic planning. To complete the picture, one must consider the practice of planning. Our experience with planning suggests that the gap between planning theory and practice is large. See also Caldwell [2], Lucado [6], Steiner and Schollhammer [18].

We believe that this gap is related to *what* is not done rather than to the way activities are carried out. For example, one of the most commonly reported omissions in planning is managerial participation. Mace [7] identified this in an early assessment of the role of the president in corporate planning:

Probably the single most important problem in corporate planning derives from the belief of some chief operating executives that corporate planning is not a function with which they should be directly concerned. They regard planning as something to be delegated, which subordinates can do without responsible participation by chief executives. They think the end result of effective planning is the compilation of a 'plans' book. Such volumes get distributed to key executives, who scan the contents briefly, file them away, breathe a sigh of relief, and observe 'thank goodness that is done—now let's get to work' (p. 50).

Planning often becomes merely a process for specifying annual budgets, an activity for preparing scenarios of organizational futures, a means of forecasting changes in the external environment, or a merger/aquisition function. Clearly, all of these activities are part of long-range planning; however, specialization in one of the areas is inadequate to reflect the full domain of planning.

One major reason why it is difficult to initiate integrated planning is that there are many relevant factors that must be simultaneously coordinated. Once the process begins, adaptive learning procedures can be designed to improve the quality of planning. If the initial design does not include all factors, success is as likely as running an automobile without a fuel pump; work to improve the other components will not correct basic design deficiencies.

FOUR ESSENTIAL REQUIREMENTS IN PLANNING

What is needed to insure that a planning process maintains its systemic properties? We believe that the process has the following four explicit characteristics:

(1) *Basic Orientation:* a succinct statement of the core systems process that represents the heart of long-range planning.

(2) *Organization Principle:* a vehicle for organizing current information about the variables that affect planning decisions by the organization.

(3) *Prioritization Procedure:* a vehicle for incorporating managerial attitudes and beliefs that will emphasize various components of the planning system.

(4) *Adaptive Process:* a method by which staff inputs can focus on planning issues where detailed analysis can improve the quality of strategic decisions.

We now consider each of them in turn.

Basic Orientation

Planning consists of two basic interacting phases. The first phase involves an assessment and optimum utilization of present capabilities. It is called the *Projected Planning Process,* which is a one point boundary problem whose boundary is fixed at the present state. It is what we also call the *forward process,* a primarily *descriptive* approach concerned with the following kind of question: given the present actors and their policies, what will (is believed or likely to) be the future resulting from their actions? Assessment of the impact of the present is usually made in terms of projection scenarios which span the future. The result is a composite scenario which is an integrated assessment of the individual projections.

That aspect of planning which is concerned with working backwards from a desired or idealized future and developing plans to bring such a future about is what we call *Planning For A Desired Future* or the *backward process*. It is a *normative* approach concerned with the question: given a desired future, what *should* our policies be to attain that future? This again is a one point boundary problem fixed at the future.

It is clear that the backward process is limited by constraints on the policies to be developed and possible conflicts with existing policies. One is not at complete liberty to select policies to meet that future even if these were workable. This is due to the substantial constraints imposed by the present habits, commitments and policies. Conversely, projecting a likely future from present policies comes in conflict with the valued or desired future. When put together, the forward and backward processes demonstrate that one is not free to pursue planning from the present without understanding and evaluating where one wants to go, nor where one wants to go without examining one's present potentials and capabilities. If our existing policies fall short of what is needed to attain that future, then, just as strongly, futures which result from present policies may fall short of the desired future which we value. Making these two processes compatible is one of the major challenges facing planners. It is an even-handed pragmatic process which is an enrichment of the conservative tendencies of the forward process and a 'pragmatization' of a fantasy-prone backward process. It seems that the study of planning is not a simple benevolent art freely concerned with the improvement of living. Rather, it makes a psychological contribution to the fulfillment of our values and desires for the future as strongly and intrinsically as it does to our satisfaction in the successes of our present actions.

The two-point boundary problem—present to future and future to present—is concerned with the following management process: given the present set of policies and given a desired future, modify the existing policies and design new compatible policies to attain that future. Then modify the desired future for greater compatibility with the effectiveness of new policies. Iterate the process until a good feasible solution (if there is one for the constraints represented in the hierarchy) arises.

The starting point is to project the likely future from present actions, adopt a desired future, design new policies, adjoin them to the set of existing policies, project a new future and compare the two futures for their main attributes: *the projected and the desired*. The desired future may need modification to reduce the disparity between the two futures. The process is diagrammed in Figure 1.

We note that planning has also been regarded in terms of a risk averse utility function subject to a set of constraints described by the present state (one-point boundary). In this approach, one seeks to minimize the potential costs of unexpected outcomes. One can also attempt to diminish the probability of the occurrence of an undesirable outcome by introducing additional constraints. Another approach to planning is to fix the boundary point in a future state and maximize a utility function representing desired ideals. The solution procedure is then to educate and sometimes even willfully force people to violate what are assumed to be self-imposed or artificial constraints.

We believe that the structure of the planning process needs integration. Clearly there is overlap between most approaches to planning. However, our experience has taught us that the two-point boundary approach is a rich framework for identifying projected

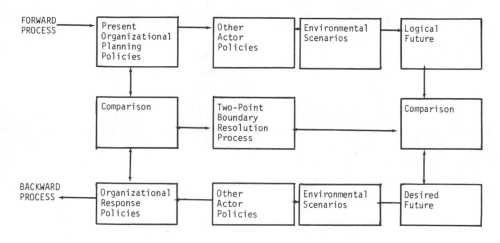

Figure 1. A schematic representation of the basic planning orientation

and desired outcomes and utilizing their strengths within the framework of analytical hierarchies to improve the outcome of a plan. It also encourages interaction and consensus, a crucial part of planning which induces participant commitment. Furthermore, it enables one to make tradeoffs in resource allocation by looking for balanced marginal benefits. Finally, it is ideally suited for reversing a plan due to the flexibility of both the hierarchical framework and the prioritization process and their robustness and the facility with which they can be used in studying planning as an ongoing process.

Organizing Principle

Formulation of a planning process as a two-point boundary problem enables us to structure explicitly the decision framework to be formulated. From decision theory, three basic variables are involved:

(1) *Planning policies* available to the organization,
(2) *Outcomes* the organization may realize in the future, and
(3) *Efficiencies* which show the probabilistic relationship between planning policies and outcomes.

These variables are common to all decision processes, but the relationship among them is different for the forward and backward planning processes. For the forward process the policies are *defined,* the efficiencies *estimated,* and the probable outcomes *deduced.* For the backward process, the outcomes are *valued,* the efficiencies *influenced* and the policies *developed.* This difference is fundamentally due to the way the problem is structured in each case. The organizing principle in both processes is *hierarchical,* but the dominance relationships are reversed. One of the purposes of this paper is to show that the use of hierarchies as an organizing principle for the two-point boundary planning problem enables rich solutions to be developed.

The hierarchy of the forward or projected process may be characterized in the sequence:

This process can be divided further by segmenting the efficiencies level into its two basic components: events caused by the purposeful behavior of other actors, and events caused by non-purposeful behavior (e.g. the weather). Purposeful behavior is itself a hierarchy, diagrammatically composed of:

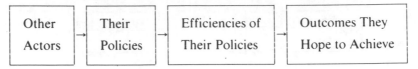

Emery and Trist [3] use the term *Transactional Environment* to describe other actors whose behavior directly affects organizational efficiencies. Such actors include suppliers, investors, customers, etc. This analysis can, in turn, be expanded by adding another level to analyze the elements that contribute to the efficiency of the behavior of members of the transactional environment. Purposeful behavior of such actors has an indirect effect on the original organization; Emery and Trist use the term *Contextual Environment* to describe such effects. A diagram of the hierarchy of the forward process with transactional environmental effects is shown in Figure 2.

EFFICIENCIES

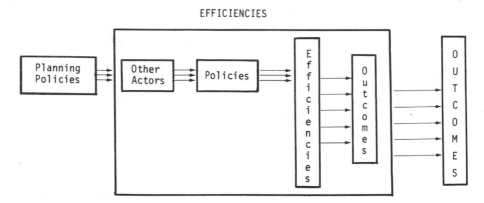

Figure 2. Hierarchy including transactional environment

Note that the natural branching of the hierarchy for the Forward process generates a large number of possible outcomes from a small number of initial policies. Sometimes the elements (state variables) of the different outcomes are compatible and can thus be combined into a single composite outcome. For example, the pure outcomes of generating energy from nuclear power, fossil fuels, and solar energy may be combined into a composite outcome. However, outcomes may have incompatibilities which cannot be combined. For example, different plant-site locations cannot be combined. Only one of the sites may be chosen.

The hierarchy characterized by the backward or desired process may be represented as in the following diagram:

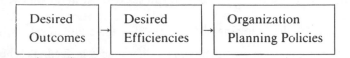

The backward process begins where the forward process ends. The organization first examines the range of projected outcomes and determines those outcomes which it prefers from those which it does not. Then it works back to the efficiencies to identify the changes that are critical to the achievement of a desired outcome. It identifies policies to influence other actors to achieve this outcome. The hierarchy for the desired process may be represented as follows:

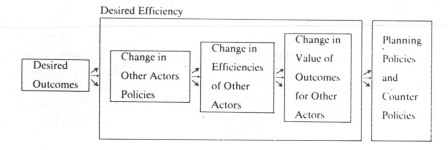

Prioritization Procedure

One would like to avoid a potential explosion of alternatives which arise from the hierarchies created for the forward and backward phases of the twopoint boundary problem.

A hierarchical system consists of several levels, each level containing one or more members or elements with a single element in the dominant top level. Let us begin by examining the nature of the problem as created by the hierarchical representation. Suppose that either the forward or backward phase has been structured into hierarchy levels with each level corresponding to a decision component such as the actors, their objectives, possible outcomes, etc. We need to address three important questions:

(1) how does one assess the importance of the elements at each level of the hierarchy, and
(2) how is the relative priority of the levels in the hierarchy determined, and
(3) of what use is such knowledge?

It turns out that a method of ratio scaling can be used to determine the importance of elements in a level with respect to each element in the adjacent upper level and the information thus generated can be integrated across the levels of the hierarchy. Prioritization uses pairwise comparisons of elements to create a matrix of assessment; the priorities are established by finding the largest eigenvalue and its corresponding eigenvector for this matrix [12]. It turns out that the largest eigenvalue λ_{max} (for a positive reciprocal matrix $\lambda_{max} \geqslant n$ always) may be used to measure consistency by forming the consistency index $(\lambda_{max} - n)/(n - 1)$ and comparing it with the average value of such an index for a large sample of randomly generated reciprocal matrices.

We now turn to the question of what numerical scale to use in the pairwise comparison matrices.

Our choice hinges on the following observation. The scale should satisfy the following:

(1) It should be possible to represent people's differences in feelings when they make comparisons. It should represent as much as possible all distinct shades of feeling that people have.

(2) If we denote the scale values by $x_1, x_2,...,x_r$, then it would be desirable that $x_{i+1} - x_i = 1$, $i = 1,...,r - 1$. We need uniformity between differences to make sure that the scale covers all judgments and that unity should be the difference between adjacent gradations of judgement.

Since we require that the subject must be aware of all gradations at the same time, and we agree with the psychological experiments which show that an individual cannot simultaneously compare more than seven objects (plus or minus two) without being confused, we are led to choose $r = 7 \pm 2$. Using a unit difference between successive scale values is all that we allow, and using the fact that $x_1 = 1$ for the identity comparison, it follows that the scale values will range from one to nine. The scale and the verbal conversion of comparative differences among two objects is shown in Table 1.

To illustrate the procedure for defining priorities, consider the following estimation problem. An experiment was conducted in search of relationship between

Table 1

Intensity of Importance	Definition	Explanation
1[a]	Equal importance	Two activities contribute equally to the objective.
3	Weak importance of one over another	Experience and judgment slightly favor one activity over another.
5	Essential or strong importance	Experience and judgment strongly favor one activity over another.
7	Demonstrated importance	An activity is strongly favored over another and its dominance is demonstrated in practice.
9	Absolute importance	The evidence favoring one activity over another is of the highest possible order of affirmation.
2, 4, 6, 8	Intermediate values between the two adjacent judgments	When compromise is needed.
Reciprocals of above non-zero numbers	If activity i has one of the above non-zero numbers assigned to it when compared with activity j, then j has the reciprocal value when compared with i.	

[a] On occasion in 2 by 2 problems, we have used $1 + \epsilon$, $0 < \epsilon \leqslant \frac{1}{2}$ to indicate very slight dominance between two nearly equal activities.

the illumination received by four identical objects (placed on a line at known distances from a light source) and the distance from the source. The comparison of illumination intensity was performed visually and independently by two sets of people. The objects were placed at the following distances measured in yards from the light sources: 9, 15, 21 and 28. In normalized form, these distances are: 0.123, 0.205, 0.288, 0.384.

Two observers (one of whom was a young child) independently constructed matrices of pairwise comparisons of the brightness of the objects labeled in increasing order according to their nearness to the source. They are:

Relative visual brightness
(First trial)

	C_1	C_2	C_3	C_4
C_1	1	5	6	7
C_2	$\frac{1}{5}$	1	4	6
C_3	$\frac{1}{6}$	$\frac{1}{4}$	1	4
C_4	$\frac{1}{7}$	$\frac{1}{6}$	$\frac{1}{4}$	1

Relative visual brightness
(Second trial)

	C_1	C_2	C_3	C_4
C_1	1	4	6	7
C_2	$\frac{1}{4}$	1	3	4
C_3	$\frac{1}{6}$	$\frac{1}{3}$	1	2
C_4	$\frac{1}{7}$	$\frac{1}{4}$	$\frac{1}{2}$	1

From the eigenvalue theory, the solutions to these matrices are as follows:

Relative brightness eigenvector
(First trial)
$C_1 = 0.62$
$C_2 = 0.24$
$C_3 = 0.10$
$C_4 = 0.05$
$\lambda = 4.39$

Relative brightness eigenvector
(Second trial)
0.62
0.22
0.10
0.06
$\lambda = 4.10$

To demonstrate that this approach leads to valid results in practice, we calculated the true relative brightness using the inverse-square law of optics. The results of this are as follows:
Normalized reciprocal distance square

$C_1 = 0.61$
$C_2 = 0.22$
$C_3 = 0.11$
$C_4 = 0.06$

Note the closeness of the human judgment to the true value. Several similar experiments have been conducted to validate the measurement procedure. The comparison scale was compared with numerous other scales and found to be the best (included in the book by Saaty [15]). See also [14].

What is noteworthy from this sensory experiment is the observation or hypothesis that the observed intensity of illumination varies (approximately) inversely with the square of the distance. Thus, judgment has been able to capture a law of nature.

Adaptive Process

The hierarchy method enables us to assess explicitly the impact of complex issues involved in the development of long range strategies. One of the most powerful characteristics of the method is the richness of the insight it gives from relatively little investment of time. An intensive session of several days' duration can provide answers to planning problems that had concerned managers for years but which could not be articulated otherwise.

Because the assessment process forces participation, managers become committed to the outcome; this is manifestly different from a planning process in which the planning staff takes the initiative and in which the managers are brought in to review and approve their work. We have frequently observed that the strength of managerial commitments to the results of planning are in direct proportion to their active participation.

Another important feature of the hierarchy method is that it leads to a continuous revision and improvement of people's plans and beliefs about outcomes. Furthermore, the priorities that have been defined by managers at a particular point in time provide an explicit focus for staff activities between planning sessions. The values assigned to specific elements and the assumptions which underlie the assignments are open to detailed evaluation by the staff. They can see the importance of the information they provide and its place in the overall structure.

The key point is that the hierarchy method provides a common language between managers and staff. Staff presentations can be made to managers before starting a later round of review sessions. To the extent the information persuades managers, they will change priority assessments in the hierarchy.

AN APPLICATION

The hierarchy method was recently applied to planning for a major corporation which produces and markets a number of consumer goods, with one major project dominating its sales and profits. For many years the company had been organized around four strong functional vice-presidents: production, marketing, administration, and new business development. Each of these vice-presidents had complete autonomy for his particular area, and there was little cooperative interaction among them.

The president wanted to increase the corporate rate of growth. He realized that the company's resources had to be coordinated to develop activities beyond the traditional dependence on one dominant product. To do this, the company reorganized. The four functional areas were split up and nine new vice-presidencies were established. Each vice-president had decentralized operating responsibility for his area. A corporate planning committee was formed consisting of the president and the nine vice-presidents. This committee was to focus on establishing corporate growth objectives and was to develop explicit strategies for achieving the objectives.

Although the reorganization helped promote corporate planning by removing some obstacles, the committee mechanism proved inadequate to insure a coordinated corporate planning process for the company. The corporate planning committee initiated a series of reviews of the divisional plans to familiarize all the vice-presidents with the planning issues addressed by other divisional areas and to provide a perspective from which the vice-presidents could together define planning issues. It had precisely the opposite effect. Members of the corporate planning committee began to spend more and more time on the details of each other's plans.

As this process was going on, the corporate planning staff, consisting of economists and O.R. people, found themselves with little meaningful work to occupy their time. Therefore, they began to develop economic forecasting models which they felt should be of some benefit to the corporate planning process. However, the staff was operating with little or no managerial direction from the committee.

Thus, the initial attempts at organizational change were unsuccessful. The company was no closer to having a corporate planning process than it had had with the previous structure; furthermore, the day-to-day operating efficiency had been substantially reduced.

The Test

A representative set of managers who were active participants in the corporate planning committee and corporate planning staff met in an intensive two-day planning session using the hierarchy method to see if it could produce agreement among the group on key corporate planning issues. The responsibility for running the actual session was given to outside consultants who coordinated the schedule of discussion and decision-making as the meeting progressed. However, the decisions were made entirely by the company representatives who participated.

The consultants proposed a basic hierarchical structure for both the forward and backward planning processes (see Figures 3 and 4).

The structures of the forward and backward planning hierarchies were arrived at as follows: In the forward process we asked: 'Who are the actors who influence the projected future of the company?' On occasion there are other levels between the first and the second. Following the actors we have a level of the objectives of each of the actors. We then identified a set of exploratory scenarios that would result if each actor were to pursue his own objectives unmindful of the others. It is from (the convex cone of) these scenarios that the logical or composite futures would be constructed. For detail of how to do this see [15].

The priority numbers in the boxes are the eigenvector components obtained by prioritizing in a single pairwise comparison matrix the relative importance of the actors with respect to their influence in shaping the future of the company. At the next level the objectives of the actors (not all shown in the diagram) were prioritized in separate matrices according to their importance to that actor. The eigenvector results for each actor are then multiplied by the priority of the actor. Objectives of low priority are left out and only the important ones (10% or more in this case) are included and shown in the diagram. Finally the four exploratory scenarios are prioritized in six separate matrices, one for each surviving objective according to the greater likelihood that they would be a consequence of that objective. Each of the six resulting eigenvectors is weighted by the priority of its corresponding objective and the results are added for each scenario. We have not gone into the detail of how to construct the composite future in which the different characteristics of the individual scenarios are emphasized according to their priorities by using a set of state variables describing the scenarios.

The backward process hierarchy is constructed as follows: A set of desired scenarios are identified and prioritized according to their desirability and feasibility. In the next level the problems and opportunities which are the key to these scenarios are developed. This is followed by a level of actors who control these problems and finally by a level of company policies which are perceived to affect the actors to solve the problems and attain the scenarios. The prioritization is as before except one must be careful to ask the questions in the proper direction as the forward process is descriptive (or predictive) while the backward process is perscriptive. In the forward process one examines the importance of the elements in a level as a consequence of each element in the next level above. In the backward process the question seeks to determine the relative importance of the elements in contributing to an element above.

As pointed out earlier, in other applications, the high priority policies of the backward process (as a means for optimizing the selection of best policies) can be added to the existing policies of the forward process and prioritization of the forward process is repeated at the level of policies (old and new) to test their effectiveness to steer the logical or composite future chosen (in the sense of satisfying) to the desired future. The desired future scenario can be synthesized from the exploratory scenarios of the backward process in a manner analogous to the construction of the composite scenario of the forward process briefly mentioned here. The backward process could be varied according to the relative emphases placed on its desired scenarios and to the different policies that could be creatively surmised and tested for high priority contributions. The combined forward–backward process is a useful tool for testing the effectiveness of new policies in producing desired outcomes.

Incidentally, the consistency of the set of judgments for an entire hierarchy may be computed (by multiplying each index by its corresponding priority and adding over all such products) and its acceptability is assessed by forming its ratio with a corresponding value with the same priorities but with the average indices for the matrices of corresponding sizes with randomly generated judgments. A value of around 10% or less is considered acceptable. The average consistency indices for randomly generated matrices of size n are as follows:

Size of matrix	1	2	3	4	5	6	7	8	9	10
Average consistency index	0	0	0.58	0.90	1.12	1.24	1.32	1.41	1.45	1.49

In the actual procedure of hierarchy assessment and prioritization, each level of a hierarchy was dealt with individually. At any particular level of the hierarchy, a set of elements relevant to the planning process at that particular level was presented to the company's management group. The elements were discussed for completeness and relevance. Once the final list was agreed upon, the process of prioritization was conducted. When the complete prioritization process was finished for a particular level, priorities were obtained by using an on-line computer terminal. With this information, decisions were made as to the relative importance of components at the next level of the hierarchy. The priorities of each element are indicated in the diagrams (Figures 3 and 4).

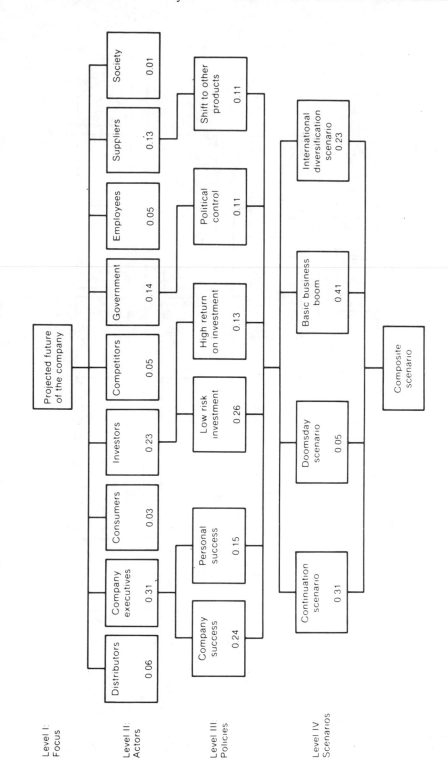

Figure 3. The forward planning process (Numbers represent the weight of importance of an element at a particular level of the analysis)

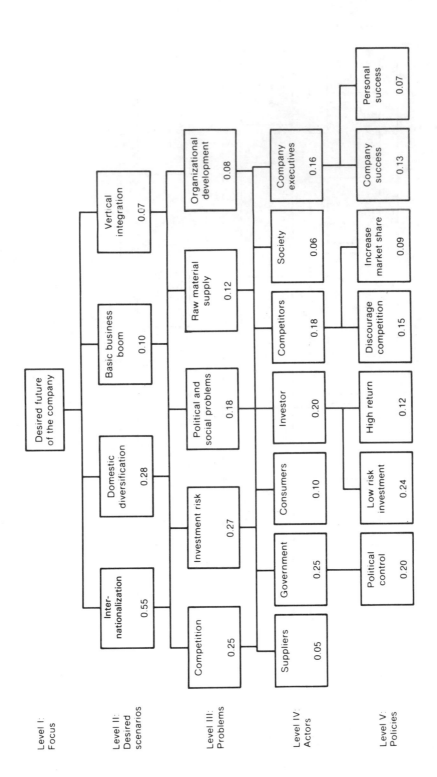

Figure 4. The backward planning process (Numbers represent the weight of importance of an element at a particular level of the analysis)

Forward process conclusions can be summarized as follows:

(1) The projected future suggests a successful concentration by the company on the development of the business area that has made it successful in the past. Some efforts for international diversification will take place, but these will be driven more by the failure of domestic markets to develop rapidly than by the attractiveness of internationalization. The projected future indicates a distinct possibility that the domestic market will not provide an acceptable growth rate, primarily because of either supplier or government actions.

(2) The actors most significant to the company's projected future are (in order of importance): the company's own vice-presidents, the major financial investors in the company, the government, and raw material suppliers. Product consumers were not considered to be particularly significant in the projected future, implying that purchasing habits would not change unless there were new actions by the company itself.

(3) The policy and objectives of the key company managers were oriented first toward company success and then personal success, implying that the development of existing functional areas has a high priority as long as that leads to acceptable growth for the company as a whole. Financial investors were thought to be motivated primarily by risk minimization and secondarily by maximization of investment return. The government desired political control, development, and revenue in that order. Suppliers were assumed to seek profit return and were not particularly loyal to the customers who purchased their products; hence, risks of supply availability existed.

In contrast to this, the major conclusions for the backward planning projection are as follows:

(1) International expansion is seen as a highly desired future.

(2) The major problems relevant to achieving the desired future are (a) competition in domestic and international markets, (b) risk involved in investing in new products and markets, and (c) political and social problems. For the desired future, the supply of raw material and organizational development are judged to be less significant than other problems.

(3) The most significant actors that would affect the outcome of the desired future are (in order of importance); the government, investors, competitors, and the company's management. It is significant that the government appeared to be the key actor in creating desired change. Also, the company's own management, which was the most influential actor in the forward process, is much less important here.

(4) Counter policies by company management were discussed briefly because of time limitations. However, the findings were that there is urgent need for (a) further knowledge, analysis and understanding of the behavior of key external stakeholders, (b) a method for evaluating risk and returns on alternative new growth strategies, and (c) developing methods for exerting greater influence over external factors that have a major impact on those future courses which the company might desire to pursue.

CONCLUSION

In general, space limitations do not permit us to discuss all of the requirements and iterative evaluations the company made using this methodology. There was implementation of the findings by redirecting corporate priorities and strategies. In particular, new strategy initiatives have been taken with the government, the major actor to influence in the backward process. The government has responded favorably to these initiatives.

A good illustration of the commitments of the participants to the process was an incident that occured at the end of one of our studies for a military group. After completing almost twenty hours of work using hierarchies, the military leader, an Admiral, met his wife and sat down to talk about a new boat they were thinking of buying. He laid the problem out through a hierarchial structure and jointly with his wife went through the prioritization process to assess purchase options. He bought the boat that was suggested by the hierarchy!

REFERENCES

[1] I. Ansoff, *Corporate Strategy* (McGraw-Hill, New York, 1975).
[2] G.T. Caldwell, Corporate planning in Canada: An overview, Conference Board of Canada (1975).
[3] F.E. Emery and E.L. Trist, *Towards a Social Ecology* (Plenum, New York, 1975).
[4] J.R. Emshoff and T.L. Saaty, Prioritized hierarchies as a vehicle for long range planning. Wharton Applied Research Center, University of Pennsylvania (1977).
[5] P. Lorange and R.F. Vancil, *Strategic Planning System* (Prentice-Hall, Englewood Cliffs, NJ, 1977).
[6] W.E. Lucado, Corporate planning – a current status report. *Managerial Planning* (Nov.–Dec., 1974).
[7] M.L. Mace, The president and corporate planning, *Harvard Business Rev.* (Jan.–Feb., 1965).
[8] T.L. Saaty and J. Alexander, The forward and backward processes of conflict analysis, *Behavioral Sci.* **22** (1977) 87–98.
[9] T.L. Saaty and J. Alexander, Stability analysis of the forward–backward process, *Behavioral Sci.* **22** (1977) 375–382.
[10] T.L. Saaty and J.P. Bennett, A theory of analytical hierarchies applied to political candidacy, *Behavioral Sci.* **22** (1977) 237–245.
[11] T.L. Saaty and J.P. Bennett, Terrorism: Patterns for negotiations; Three case studies through hierarchies and holarchies, Study for the Arms Control and Disarmament Agency (1977). Also: Facing Tomorrow's Terrorist Incident Today, U.S. Department of Justice, LEAA, Washington, DC 20531, pp. 28–31.
[12] T.L. Saaty, A scaling method for priorities in hierarchical structures, *J. Math. Psychology* **15** (1977) 234–281.
[13] T.L. Saaty, Higher education in the United States (1985–2000): Scenario construction using a hierarchical framework with eigenvetor weighting, *Socio-Economic Planning Sci.* **19** (1976) 251–263 with P.C. Rogers.
[14] T.L. Saaty, Theory of measurement of impacts and interactions in systems, *International Conference on Applied General Systems Research: Recent Developments and Trends*, Binghamton (1977); also in: R. Cavallo, Ed., *Systems Methodology in Social Science Research* (Kluwer-Nyhoff, The Hague, 1982).
[15] T.L. Saaty, *The Analytic Hierarchy Process* (McGraw-Hill, New York, 1980).
[16] T.L. Saaty, *Decision Making for Leaders* (Lifetime Learning Publications, a division of Wadsworth, Belmont, 1982).
[17] T.L. Saaty and L. Vargas, *The Logic of Priorities* (Kluwer-Nijhoff, The Hague, 1981).
[18] G.A. Steiner and H. Schollhammer, Pitfalls in multi-national long range planning, *Long Range Planning* (April, 1975).

PART VI

Conclusion

Chapter 19

Towards Effective Strategic Planning

Robert Dyson
Warwick University

EFFECTIVENESS

One definition of effectiveness is that it is the extent to which goals are achieved. With this definition strategic decision making would be effective if future organisational goals are achieved in the required time scale. There are, however, major weaknesses in this definition of effective strategic decision making as has been pointed out by Dyson and Foster (1980). The criticisms stem from the fact that strategic decision making takes place in a changing and uncertain environment, that setting goals is internal to strategic decision making rather than external, and that different groupings within an organisation may value goals differently.

With regard to uncertainty, in the period between commitment to a decision and realization of the outcome there may be significant changes in the environment beyond the control of the organisation. These may have been anticipated to some extent in the planning process but nevertheless the likelihood is that there may well be a significant gap emerging between the aspirations of the organisation as laid down in its goals and the actual achievement of the organisation. Although there may be some fault here with the planning process it would be difficult unambiguously to claim that the process had been ineffective in these circumstances. Indeed, the organisation's response to the circumstances may be as good as could have been expected.

The second weakness stems from the fact that goals have to be set as part of the planning process. If the planners and decision makers see themselves as being judged by the extent to which they meet the goals set, then there may well be a tendency to set modest goals which can be readily achievable. Again, this would hardly be a symptom of an effective planning system.

Finally, many organisations will have wide ranging goals and even in fairly steady circumstances it would be unlikely if all of these were achieved equally. Differences from different goals will, of course, be valued differently by groups or individuals within the organisation so that in this case, there would actually be different views on the effectiveness of the strategic decision making.

These difficulties with a goals/achievement view of effectiveness naturally lead on to wishing to define effectiveness for strategic decision making and planning in terms of the process itself. With this view, an effective strategic planning process is one that ensures the generation of a sufficient flow of worthwhile strategic options, which can assess uncertainty and evaluate the performance conditional on possible futures. It is this view of effectiveness that leads us, in Chapter 1, to identify elements of the strategic planning process essential for effective decision making. For strategic planning and decision making to be effective in an organisation, each of these elements needs to be in place and operating effectively. The book has focused on six of these elements as the ones where models and analytical techniques appear to have the greatest leverage. They are:

— objective setting and review
— strategic option formulation
— assessment of uncertainty
— corporate system model
— performance measurement
— gap analysis and selection

Additionally, models and techniques have a role to play in resource assessment but there is insufficient space in the book to go into detailed resource models such as manpower planning models. The remaining elements identified are either not part of the strategic planning process or are not amenable to models. The latter category would include feasibility checking, the feedback signal and securing resources. The final implementation process may well be amenable to models such as network analysis but is not part of the strategic planning process.

THE CONTRIBUTION OF ANALYTICAL TECHNIQUES TO STRATEGIC PLANNING

The readings in the book have introduced a range of techniques from SWOT analysis or the TOWS matrix through to the analytic hierarchy process. This chapter summarises the way that these techniques can strengthen and support the elements of the planning process but the individual reader may have formed a different view.

The *TOWS matrix* is a systematic method for matching environmental threats and opportunities with the organisation's weaknesses and strengths. This process is specifically aimed at generating strategic options, so that its primary purpose is to strengthen strategic option formulation. Although the method is future orientated it does not explicitly embody any mechanisms for handling the uncertainty of the future, neither does it attempt any holistic model of the organisation and does not contribute to gap analysis and selection. The process of carrying out a thorough internal and external appraisal, however, may well contribute to objective setting and review as the purpose of the organisation may well be called into question by the appraisal process. A reconsideration of objectives should also, of course, lead to a reconsideration of performance measures.

The basic message from the *experience curve* is that benefits can be obtained by increasing the volume of production. These benefits are primarily in the form of lower unit costs. The experience curve thus supports strategies aimed at increasing volume and market share and its primary impact on the planning process is to support strategic option formulation. The experience curve is also, clearly, a behavioural relationship which should be included in any corporate system model so that this element of the planning process is also supported. It does not explicitly help in the assessment of uncertainty or performance measurement, gap analysis and selection but affects the objective setting process in so far as knowledge of the experience curve may lead to high market shares and volumes being included in the goals of the organisation.

The *growth-share* matrix helps companies with a portfolio of businesses decide for each business whether to invest to increase market share, use a business as a source of finance for investment in other businesses, or whether to divest. It thus contributes to the strategic planning process by supporting strategic option formulation. By focusing on market share and industry growth and recognising these as indicators of profitability the technique also has a secondary impact on objective setting, performance measurement and selection. The technique makes no contribution to the assessment of uncertainty and although it could be argued that the growth-share matrix itself is a form of model of the organisation, it is not a model in the sense of system models discussed in other papers. The *industry attractiveness-business strength matrix* is a development of the growth-share matrix and has some features in common with the TOWS matrix. It can thus support the strategic planning process in a similar way to those techniques with its primary impact being to support strategic option formulation and secondary impacts on objective setting and review, performance measurement and selection.

The *PIMS model* helps in the development and appraisal of strategic plans and thus supports the strategic planning process in perhaps the broadest possible way. By identifying determinants of return on investment such as quality and market share, the PIMS model directly supports strategic option formulation. The PIMS model is itself a form of corporate system model which provides financial performance measurement, targets and a framework for gap analysis and selection. By identifying determinants of profitability the PIMS analysis may also support the objective setting and review process. Of the six essential elements considered here, the only one not supported by the PIMS model is the assessment of uncertainty.

The use of *cognitive mapping* in strategic planning is primarily aimed at objective setting through highlighting goals, and strategic option formulation. By identifying the supporting assumptions it may also incorporate uncertainty into the planning process. The cognitive map is also a formal model of the organisation in its environment. Although cognitive mapping does not exclude quantitive analysis it does not necessarily include it and therefore would support performance measurement, gap analysis and selection in only an indirect way.

Risk analysis is a technique for assessing uncertainty in a formal and explicit way. The technique also supports performance measurement as it allows the uncertainty to be reflected in the performance measures themselves. The technique is thus aimed primarily, if not exclusively, at the evaluation side of strategic planning and does not contribute to strategic option formulation or objective setting and review. It may enhance the corporate system model by adding a stochastic dimension.

As with risk analysis, *scenario development* also is aimed explicitly at representing and assessing uncertainty. However, the process is much more open ended and through its identification of key factors also contributes to strategic option formulation and objective setting. It does not, however, enhance the corporate system model nor support performance measurement, gap analysis and selection.

Corporate modelling and *system dynamics models* are modelling methods aimed explicitly at providing a formal corporate system model of the organisation. They also contribute to performance measurement and through performance measurement may stimulate the strategic option formulation process. They do not in themselves assess uncertainty but may contribute to the assessment when linked with risk analysis or scenarios. Neither do they explicitly help gap analysis and selection nor objective setting, as goals and targets will be set exogenously to the corporate model.

Capital investment appraisal provides a mechanism for financial performance measurement and by incorporating financial targets contributes explicitly to gap analysis and selection. Some versions of capital investment appraisal also include assessment of uncertainty and the technique contributes to objective setting through the setting of financial targets. *Robustness analysis* supports strategic planning in an almost identical way to capital investment appraisal except that the performance measures are non-financial and are measures of the robustness of a course of action to uncertainty.

In urban and regional planning interest groups and their objectives are at the fore of the planning process and the *evaluation matrix* explicitly recognises this. The matrix is primarily aimed at supporting the selection process but also requires explicit objectives and performance measures against them and therefore seemingly supports

Analytical Techniques	Objective Setting & Review	Strategic Option Formulation	Assessment of Uncertainty	Corporate System Model	Performance Measurement	Gap Analysis and Selection
1. TOWS Matrix	S	P			S	
2. Experience Curve	S	P		S	S	
3. Growth/Share Matrix	S	P			S	S
4. Industry Attrac/Bus. St. M	S	P			S	S
5. PIMS	S	P		S	S	S
6. Cognitive Mapping	P	P	S	S		
7. Risk Analysis			P	S	S	
8. Scenario Construction	S	S	P		S	
9. Corporate Modelling		S		P	S	
10. Systems Dynamic Models		S		P	S	
11. Capital Investment App.	S		S		P	P
12. Robustness Analysis	S		S		P	P
13. Evaluation Matrix	S				P	S
14. Analytic Hierarchy Process	S			S	P	P

P = primary impact
S = secondary impact

Figure 1. The impact of models and techniques on the strategic planning process

or triggers the objective setting and review process, performance measurement and gap analysis. The matrix does not, however, aid in the generation of strategic options nor does it help with the assessment of uncertainty or provide a corporate system modelling framework.

The *analytic hierarchy process* also mainly supports the evaluation and appraisal of plans and primarily supports performance measurement, and gap analysis and selection. In this case performance measures are priorities on the various strategic options. The process might support objective setting as it explicitly requires objectives and the hierarchical representation could be considered as a kind of corporate system model. The process, however, does not aid in strategic option formulation nor does it provide a mechanism for assessing uncertainty.

This discussion of the contribution of the analytical techniques to strategic planning can be summarised as in Figure 1. The matrix display not only indicates how the various techniques support different parts of the planning process but, by reading down the columns, also indicates for each of the six elements of the planning process which techniques can support or strengthen that particular element. This can be a valuable use of the matrix where it has been diagnosed that an element is either absent or weak.

REFERENCE

Dyson, R.G. and Foster, M.J. (1980). 'Effectiveness in strategic planning', *European Journal of Operational Research* **5** (3), 163–170.

Index